The Rise of AI in Academic Inquiry

James Hutson
Lindenwood University, USA

IGI Global
Publishing Tomorrow's Research Today

Published in the United States of America by
IGI Global
701 E. Chocolate Avenue
Hershey PA, USA 17033
Tel: 717-533-8845
Fax: 717-533-8661
E-mail: cust@igi-global.com
Web site: https://www.igi-global.com

Library of Congress Cataloging-in-Publication Data

CIP PENDING

ISBN13: 9798369369050
Isbn13Softcover: 9798369369067
EISBN13: 9798369369074

Vice President of Editorial: Melissa Wagner
Managing Editor of Acquisitions: Mikaela Felty
Managing Editor of Book Development: Jocelynn Hessler
Production Manager: Mike Brehm
Cover Design: Phillip Shickler

British Cataloguing in Publication Data
A Cataloguing in Publication record for this book is available from the British Library.

All work contributed to this book is new, previously-unpublished material.
The views expressed in this book are those of the authors, but not necessarily of the publisher.

Table of Contents

Preface

"The only kind of writing is rewriting" - Ernest Hemmingway

The rapid advancement of artificial intelligence (AI) technologies, particularly Large Language Models (LLMs), is fundamentally altering the landscape of academic research, reshaping how we discover, analyze, and disseminate knowledge. This preface introduces the seismic transformations brought about by these technologies, highlighting their potential to redefine traditional research methodologies and the way we educate the next generation of scholars.

LLMs are not just tools augmenting the research process; they are becoming central to it, offering capabilities that were once the relegated to speculative fiction. By parsing extensive datasets, identifying patterns, generating new hypotheses, and synthesizing complex findings, these tools enhance the efficiency, accuracy, and creativity of scholarly work. Yet, the rapid integration of such powerful tools into academia is not without its challenges. The integration of these technologies must involve critical assessment of ethical concerns including bias, accountability, and the authenticity of AI-generated content. This book considers these issues, advocating for robust AI literacy programs across disciplines to maintain the integrity of research outputs.

Moreover, this volume explores how the advent of AI tools is revolutionizing the sharing of scholarship and informing new teaching methodologies. As technology reshapes our research landscapes, it simultaneously redefines our educational approaches, creating a feedback loop where teaching informs technology use and technology reshapes teaching. Through detailed case studies across various disciplines—from the humanities to the sciences—the book illustrates practical applications and best practices, ensuring that readers can understand and leverage AI responsibly and effectively.

This book serves as a vital guide for graduate students who often must navigate the dual roles of researcher and educator in this swiftly evolving era. It examines how AI tools like Google Gemini and ChatGPT, along with databases such as PerplexityAI and Scite.ai, are revolutionizing traditional research and writing workflows.

Through a deconstruction of writing processes into modular, iterative steps, the book equips students with strategies that boost flexibility and efficiency in their scholarly activities. It introduces cutting-edge tools that support personalized exploration and creative brainstorming, fostering a tech-positive mindset among emerging scholars.

In light of rapid technological changes, the book underscores the necessity of developing critical and creative thinking skills that are both enduring and transferable, rather than focusing solely on the accumulation of factual knowledge. It advocates for a learning approach centered on metacognition and lifelong learning, particularly as new technologies continually reshape the landscape of academic and practical applications. This approach emphasizes the importance of deep understanding and robust problem-solving abilities across disciplines. Moreover, in an era where the initial creation of content can often be automated, the value of the first draft may diminish, especially at advanced levels of scholarship. Instead, as Ernest Hemingway famously remarked, "the only kind of writing is rewriting." This highlights the critical role of self-reflection and editorial revision in the writing process, suggesting that refining and improving an initial AI-generated draft is where significant intellectual effort should be directed, ensuring that scholars maintain a rigorous and reflective engagement with their work.

With the numerous challenges faced by the academy from questioning the role of higher education in society in general to the quickening pace of technological development, there is little doubt that we stand at the threshold of a new era in academic research, driven by the fusion of human intellect and computational power. As such, *The Algorithmic Researcher* offers vital insights into the potential of AI to transform academia. This book is designed not just to maneuver the current landscape but also to anticipate future developments, providing a comprehensive resource for scholars, educators, policymakers, and anyone involved in academic research or education. It encourages readers to embrace the interdisciplinary nature of modern scholarship, which cuts across traditional silos, reflecting the broad scope of my own research journey and inviting readers to explore further. In doing so, it calls not only for the adoption of new technologies but also for a commitment to the interdisciplinary collaboration that will be essential in the age of AI-enhanced academic inquiry.

RESEARCH AND SCHOLARSHIP EVOLVING

An overview of the evolution of research and scholarship in the age of AI reveals that the pace at which technology advances is outstripping the speed of both human researchers and the institutions that support them. While it is moving too fast to accurately predict the exact state of academic research will be by end of the decade, the trajectory suggests a landscape profoundly transformed by AI capabilities. This is because it is not just a tool but a fundamental force reshaping the methodology, scope, and very nature of academic inquiry. The rapid integration of AI technologies into research processes signals a shift that will likely alter every aspect of academia—from the expectations placed on new entrants into the field to the criteria for career advancement such as promotion in rank. Traditional benchmarks for evaluating academic contributions, such as the quantity and type of scholarship, are under review as the capability of AI to augment research output challenges longstanding norms.

In the broader landscape of education, the integration of AI is driving significant transformation across fields. The emergence of generative AI (GAI) technologies, notably exemplified by LLMs like ChatGPT-3, introduced in November of 2022, has elicited a range of responses from educational institutions worldwide. Initial reactions have varied greatly, with some, such as school districts in New York City, implementing bans on AI tools early in 2023. These cautious approaches stem from concerns about AI's impact on learning processes, mirroring historical apprehensions associated with disruptive technologies like Google (1998) and Wikipedia (2001). There was a prevailing belief that such technologies could undermine student ability to commit information to memory and diminish critical thinking skills, a concern highlighted in discussions by Petrilli (2008).

A comparable debate has emerged regarding the effects of generative AI on education, echoing a longstanding argument. This is not a novel concern. In Plato's dialogue *Phaedrus* (14, 274c-275b), he recounts how Socrates narrates an Egyptian myth about the invention of writing. As recounted by Socrates,

For this invention will produce forgetfulness in the minds of those who learn to use it, because they will not practice their memory. Their trust in writing, produced by external characters which are no part of themselves, will discourage the use of their own memory within them. You have invented an elixir not of memory, but of reminding; and you offer your pupils the appearance of wisdom, not true wisdom, for they will read many things without instruction and will therefore seem to know many things, when they are for the most part ignorant and hard to get along with, since they are not wise, but only appear wise.

The apprehension surrounding generative AI reflects a deep-seated worry that mirrors ancient concerns about the advent of writing. No less than Socrates articulated fears that writing could induce forgetfulness and a mere illusion of wisdom, as individuals might depend more on texts than on personal memory and understanding. Similar anxieties surfaced with the introduction of the chalkboard in 1801, which faced resistance from students and educators accustomed to memorization rather than note-taking (Krause, 2001). Historically, the shift away from rote memorization in education has been met with skepticism.

This ongoing debate about the impact of evolving technologies on traditional learning methods finds another parallel in the late 20th century with the introduction of calculators into mathematics education. Initially, in the 1970s, there was substantial concern that calculators might undermine students' ability to perform calculations manually, diminishing their capacity to estimate, learn from errors, and develop essential math skills (Werner, 1980). Despite these early reservations, by 1975 the National Advisory Committee on Mathematical Education (NACOME) and by 1980 the National Council of Teachers of Mathematics (NCTM) had endorsed the use of calculators across various educational levels, recognizing their potential to enhance the learning experience (Dreher, 2021). Connecticut's decision in 1986 to mandate calculators for state tests marked a significant milestone, reflecting a broader recognition that calculators could empower students to solve more complex problems (Romberg, 1992). This evolving acceptance of technology in educational settings mirrors the gradual but significant shift towards embracing AI in research and writing. Initially met with resistance, there is now a growing realization of the potential benefits of AI, particularly in how it can support rather than supplant the cognitive processes involved in writing.

At the same time, however, it is important to understand that while the acceptance of calculators in education may seem akin to the current integration of AI in writing, this comparison has its limitations. The implications and applications of GAI, particularly in research, are considerably more expansive than those of calculators. Comparisons to tools like ChatGPT should recognize that the role of the technology in research and scholarship is not just computational but deeply creative. These tools participate in complex language processing, content generation, and the development of ideas, paralleling the intellectual engagement found in literary composition (Phutane et al., 2023). Therefore, use in the research process is not merely a technological aid but a partner in the creative and intellectual processes, pointing to a profound shift from simple tool use to collaborative engagement in creative and scholarly activities.

But the impact is not just on research and writing as the dynamics between teachers and students are undergoing a transformation, moving away from traditional authoritative and evaluative relationships towards a more collaborative model. This shift is significantly influenced by the widespread adoption of GAI, which necessitates a redefinition of the role of professors to that of a facilitator and co-learner, helping students operate in a technology-saturated environment. In other words, we are witnessing the continued shift from the "Sage on the Stage" to the "Guide on the Side." As educational institutions progressively recognize the potential of these tools to revolutionize and personalize learning, there is an increasing emphasis on adapting teaching methodologies to accommodate these changes (Ruiz-Rojas et al., 2023). The evolution places a greater focus on developing skills such as critical thinking, problem-solving, and communication, as emphasized by Thornhill-Miller et al. (2023). Additionally, the growing reliance on AI technologies underscores the importance of skills traditionally cultivated within liberal arts curricula, such as critical thinking, creativity, and problem-solving, which are becoming increasingly vital as AI assumes routine tasks (Wilson, 2003; Autor & Dorn, 2013; Frey & Osborne, 2017). This transition signals a new era in education, research and writing, aligning with historical shifts seen in past industrial revolutions, and reimagining the collegiate experience as a continuous journey of acquiring essential skills and technological proficiency to remain relevant in a swiftly changing world (Weise, 2020; Detweiler, 2021).

The course of human civilization has consistently been shaped by significant periods of change that have redefined how we live and work. As the Fourth Industrial Revolution (Industry 4.0) unfolds, we witness transformations reminiscent of the Agricultural, Industrial, and Information revolutions, each bringing innovation and disruption that fundamentally altered societal structures. For example, the Agricultural Revolution around 10,000 BCE transitioned human societies from nomadic hunter-gatherers to settled agriculturalists, leading to the development of large permanent settlements and specialized roles within those communities (Kerridge, 2013). Similarly, the invention of writing in ancient Mesopotamia around 3400 BCE revolutionized communication, facilitating knowledge transfer across generations and significantly impacting societal advancement. The Industrial Revolution ushered in a shift to urban industrial centers from rural agrarian societies, demanding adaptability to new work environments like factories (Deane, 1979). Later, the Information Age transformed the global economy from industrial-based to knowledge-based, increasing the prevalence of digital professions and setting the stage for automation (Castells, 2010).

Now, driven by AI and the Internet of Things (IoT), Industry 4.0 merges digital, physical, and biological systems, heralding a novel chapter in human history that began in 2011 (Schwab, 2017). This new era emphasizes rethinking education, work, and societal roles within an interconnected world. The importance of the liberal arts is reinforced, highlighting critical thinking, creativity, and problem-solving as essential for considering the complicatedness of a technology-driven society (Hutson & Ceballos, 2023; Wilson, 2003). As we advance through this revolution, it becomes crucial to continuously adapt and learn, preparing for roles that may currently be unimaginable. Thus, Industry 4.0 is not merely a period of technological upheaval but a transformative phase that invites us to reconsider and reequip for a future where human creativity and technological innovations are intertwined, paving the way towards the Fifth Industrial Revolution (Industry 5.0).

THE CHALLENGES

The challenges we are now facing with the changing nature of research and scholarship are the result of rapid technological expansion. In fact, the advent of the Third Industrial Revolution, characterized by the rapid expansion of information technology, demonstrated humanity's capacity to adapt to swift changes in the work environment and communication methods. Although transformative, this revolution unfolded at a pace that appears gradual compared to today's rapid technological advances. The foundational technology of this era, the Internet, began in 1974 with the development of TCP/IP by Vint Cerf and Robert Kahn, which enabled the global interconnection of computers (Townes, 2012). In 1989, Tim Berners-Lee's conceptualization of the World Wide Web revolutionized how we access information, providing a graphical interface to operate in the Internet's vast resources (McPherson, 2009). This innovation set the stage for search engines, notably Google in 1998, to simplify online information retrieval (Kobayashi & Takeda, 2000). The early 2000s saw the emergence of social media platforms like Facebook (2004) and Twitter, which transformed social interactions and information sharing. Additionally, the 2007 release of the iPhone marked a significant milestone in the mobile revolution, offering unprecedented access to digital content and communication (Gikas & Grant, 2013).

The 2010s introduced the Internet of Things (IoT), ushering in an era where physical devices became interconnected and capable of exchanging data, leading to intelligent, responsive systems that are redefining human interaction with technology and the environment (Minoli, 2013). This integration, evident in the development of "smart cities," epitomizes the essence of the Third Industrial Revolution, bridging the physical and digital worlds and paving the way for the next technological leap: the rise of AI in education (Zanella et al., 2021).

Concurrently, a less visible but equally significant development was the rise of algorithmic culture, which refers to the pervasive influence of algorithms on our daily lives, work, and decision-making processes. Driven by advances in AI and machine learning (ML), this reliance on algorithms affects various sectors including business, education, and governance. Fry (2018) categorizes algorithms into four types: prioritization, classification, association, and filtering, and distinguishes between rule-based (RB) and ML paradigms. This framework helps in understanding their societal impacts. Rule-based algorithms operate on explicit instructions and provide transparency, whereas ML algorithms, which learn and adapt from data, handle complex tasks but often lack transparency, leading to perceptions of opacity.

The methodologies by which algorithms learn, as categorized by Morales and Escalante (2022) into supervised, unsupervised, and reinforcement learning, enrich our comprehension of their functions. Supervised learning trains an algorithm using labeled data, enabling it to predict outcomes on new, unlabeled data. Unsupervised learning identifies patterns within data without the need for labeled examples, while reinforcement learning employs a trial-and-error method, with the algorithm learning to optimize rewards through interactions with its environment. This nuanced understanding of algorithmic learning is particularly relevant when examining LLMs such as ChatGPT, Gemini or Claude. These sophisticated AI systems, which are part of the broader machine learning category, are typically trained on extensive text data, often utilizing both supervised and reinforcement learning techniques. For example, ChatGPT develops its capability to produce human-like text by training on a diverse set of language examples, which enables it to anticipate and generate coherent, contextually appropriate responses (Liu et al., 2023).

Algorithmic culture, driven by advancements in AI and machine learning, offers substantial opportunities and poses significant challenges, especially with LLMs. On one hand, algorithms can enhance decision-making efficiency and objectivity, as they are capable of processing large data sets and providing insights that are often beyond human analysis (Lepri et al., 2018). This capability can lead to equitable outcomes across various sectors, assuming the training data is free from biases (Kordzadeh & Ghasemaghaei, 2022). Moreover, algorithms have transformed access to information, with personalized recommendations facilitating discovery of content tailored to individual users (Gran, Booth, & Bucher, 2021). However, the downsides of algorithmic culture are also prominent. The opaque nature of many algorithms presents transparency challenges, complicating efforts to identify and correct biases (Saltelli et al., 2008). The risk of perpetuating existing biases and discrimination is a significant concern, particularly when algorithms are trained on flawed data (Angwin et al., 2016; Dwork & Roth, 2014). Additionally, an over-reliance on algorithms might undermine critical thinking and reduce human agency, as algorithms increasingly shape our values and decision-making in areas such as social media and online searches (Alvarado & Waern, 2018; Diakopoulos, 2019; Eslami et al., 2015; Feezell et al., 2021; Gillespie, 2014; Khan et al., 2020; Powers, 2017). Therefore, while LLMs and other algorithms offer transformative potential, they also require a thoughtful approach to manage their limitations and impacts on society.

These transformative changes and challenges within the arena of AI in academia are further exacerbated by a significant gap in AI literacy among academics and researchers. Many in the academic community lack a fundamental understanding of how these new AI tools function, the underlying data they are trained on, and their capabilities regarding data access and retrieval (Meyer et al., 2023). This deficiency in knowledge prevents the full benefits of AI from being realized and passed on to the next generation of researchers currently in graduate school. For example, without a clear understanding of the operational mechanics of these models, there is widespread misunderstanding about their capabilities and limitations. This includes why and how "hallucinations" occur—where AI models generate false or misleading information based on patterns recognized in their training data rather than factual accuracy.

A critical aspect of AI literacy is recognizing the role of LLMs in the content creation process. Similar to tools like talk-to-text or spellcheck, where the user must review and validate the final output, researchers must take responsibility for the content generated by AI. This responsibility underscores the necessity for thorough fact-checking and validation. Several legal cases illustrate this point, such as instances where lawyers used free tools like ChatGPT-3.5 to generate legal briefs without understanding that it did not pull from law databases, resulting in fabricated legal precedents (Maravilla & Scott, 2024). These individuals failed to fact-check and comprehend the workings of generative tools, emphasizing that the ultimate responsibility lies with the author. The tool is merely an aid, and its proper use depends on user understanding and diligence. This gap in understanding and effective use of AI tools leads to a disparity where some institutions and individuals advance rapidly, leveraging its potential, while others lag behind, hindered by misconceptions and inefficient use of technology.

Given these rapid changes in academia that will continue for the foreseeable future, the following considerations should be made with regards to areas of focus:

- **Technological Integration and Disruption:** AI technologies, including OpenAI's generative tools and Meta's research paper-writing AI, are set to revolutionize academic workflows and skill requirements, shifting the emphasis from technical skills to skills-based hiring, and expanding AI's role in various academic tasks.
- **Educational Paradigm Shift:** AI's integration aligns with the World Economic Forum's concept of Education 4.0, advocating for self-determined, lifelong learning and heutagogy, predicting that AI may replace human researchers in some roles, necessitating a comprehensive overhaul of educational curricula at all levels.
- **Redefining Expertise and Learning:** AI challenges the traditional role of subject-matter experts by elevating critical and creative thinking as the new "academic currency," potentially enhancing the relevance of some disciplines due to their focus on critical inquiry and creativity.
- **Interdisciplinarity and Individualized Learning Pathways:** Predicted dissolution of academic silos in favor of a skills-based, integrated educational model, with AI enabling personalized, competency-based education that moves away from traditional age-based grade progression.
- **Emotional and Cognitive Growth:** Emphasizes the importance of addressing both emotional intelligence and cognitive development in education, ad-

vocating for approaches that support the "whole person" and recognize the diverse needs and life stages of learners, particularly in higher education.

- **Preparing for a Superintelligent Future:** Reflects on the inevitability of superintelligence, highlighting the need to prepare educators and students for future challenges and opportunities, for when artificial general intelligence (AGI) arrives. AGI refers to a form of AI that either equals or exceeds human abilities across a broad spectrum of cognitive tasks, which contrasts with narrow AI, which is tailored to perform specific tasks.

Therefore, the integration of AI calls for a significant reevaluation of how curricula are structured and how teaching is approached, with the potential to democratize knowledge acquisition and deepen understanding of complex subjects. However, it also raises critical questions about the evolving role of educators and researchers, the importance of emotional and social development, and the potential emergence of new inequalities in access to technological resources.

LOOKING AHEAD

The rapid advancement of AI and its integration into educational curricula across diverse disciplines such as mathematics, history, and science foregrounds the potential automation of critical thinking processes. As observed by Pavlik (2023), text-based generative AI, with its sophisticated algorithms and extensive datasets, can automate the creation of new text, potentially circumventing the traditional, labor-intensive steps of information literacy. This development, while streamlining information synthesis, ignites concerns about the erosion of critical thinking and creativity. Turkle (2011) cautions that as algorithms increasingly influence choices and decisions, there is a risk of passivity and reduced critical engagement, which could stifle innovation and original thought.

As AI and LLMs continue to evolve, the educational landscape is set for profound transformation. Early iterations of LLMs, limited to training data up until 2021, exhibited notable limitations such as inaccurate citations, tendencies to produce erroneous or fabricated information (often termed 'hallucinating'), and a restricted understanding of context. These limitations raised concerns among educators and students about the reliability and applicability of these tools in academic settings. However, recent advancements in AI technology have markedly improved these aspects. The latest iteration, ChatGPT 4 turbo, represents a significant evolution. Unlike its predecessors, ChatGPT-4 Turbo can access live web data and incorporates training data up to April 2023, enhancing its relevance and accuracy. Its reduced tendency to 'hallucinate' and its improved ability to accurately cite and quote sources are critical for academic research, facilitating more reliable and efficient scholarly work.

Additionally, this model possesses multimodal capabilities that enable transitions from text to image and vice versa, expanding its utility in educational contexts. Its proficiency in generating data visualizations and connecting to academic databases to swiftly produce comprehensive literature reviews is particularly transformative for research-oriented tasks. The expanded context window of this model accommodates more nuanced and coherent interactions, supporting complex queries and discussions. Looking ahead, the continued evolution of these AI tools promises even greater capabilities, further merging digital technology with educational practice. While these advancements offer significant opportunities to enhance teaching and learning experiences, they also underscore the necessity for educators to guide students in effectively utilizing these tools. The emphasis must remain on cultivating critical thinking and creative problem-solving skills, ensuring that students not only become proficient in using AI technologies but also maintain their capacity for independent and innovative thought. This balanced approach is crucial for preparing students for a future where AI is an integral part of both educational and professional environments.

In light of these developments, the process of research, particularly within academic contexts, is undergoing a significant transformation. While AI technologies like ChatGPT offer unprecedented convenience in generating complex academic texts, they also highlight the ongoing need for in-depth training in research methodologies. The capability of AI tools to quickly produce coherent content from simple prompts has long been established; however, this does not diminish the importance for students to engage deeply with the craft of research. Understanding the methodologies, critically evaluating content, and iterating to develop sophisticated arguments and analyses remain essential skills. Despite the ease with which AI can produce research content, students often struggle to grasp the nuances of the generated material. The ability to discern the quality of research, evaluate the relevance and accuracy of evidence, and understand complex research frameworks remains essential not only for academic success but also for effective participation in professional and personal spheres.

Research training and AI literacy are essential for equipping working professionals and graduate students with critical skills necessary for handling the modern landscape of scholarship and information. This training not only teaches them how to construct logical arguments, use evidence effectively, and express ideas clearly and persuasively, but also helps researchers appreciate different research styles and methodologies, understand the expectations of scholarly audiences, and develop their unique scholarly voice using generative tools. Moreover, research methodology courses enhance analytical and critical thinking abilities, enabling the assessment of the quality of both traditional and AI-generated information and arguments—a skill that is becoming increasingly vital as AI-generated content becomes more prevalent.

As AI continues to infiltrate various aspects of academic life and professional work, the ability to interact with and critically evaluate AI-generated content becomes crucial. Training in AI literacy (to be discussed here) provides researchers with the tools to handle this evolving landscape, ensuring they can differentiate between AI-generated and human-produced research, understand the limitations of AI in capturing the nuances of human thought and expression, and contribute meaningfully to academic discussions and debates in an AI-integrated world.

Looking ahead, the future of human-AI collaboration in research promises a synergistic relationship where the unique strengths of both humans and AI are leveraged to enhance productivity and innovation. Scholars like Pan (2016) and Wu et al. (2021) have suggested that this partnership could lead to the creation of new knowledge and insights, surpassing what either could achieve alone. In this model, humans play a strategic role, providing oversight, critical evaluation, and infusing creativity and contextual understanding into AI-driven processes. This symbiosis is often compared to a co-pilot model, where AI assists in automating and enhancing tasks such as data analysis and literature reviews, while humans guide the overall direction and interpretive efforts of the research.

However, limitations of these tools, such as challenges in accurately citing sources or grasping nuanced human emotions, require a "human-in-the-loop" approach. The proposed model ensures the integrity of information and helps prevent the inadvertent perpetuation of biases or errors by AI systems. Aydın and Karaarslan (2022) highlight how AI can streamline processes like literature reviews, allowing human researchers to devote more time to deeper analytical work. The success of this partnership depends on a mutual understanding where AI systems align with human goals and values, and humans are well-versed in AI capabilities and constraints (Cai et al., 2019; Knop et al., 2022). Ultimately, this collaborative model underscores the indispensable role of human insight, context, and critical thinking, making it a cornerstone of future scholarly and creative endeavors.

ORGANIZATION OF THE BOOK

This book is organized into eight chapters that explore the integration of AI in academia and academic research, addressing its impact, ethical considerations, and future implications. A brief description of each of the chapters follows:

Chapter 1 explores the historical development of artificial intelligence within academic settings and provides an overview of generative AI tools. It also examines the impact of AI on academic identity, highlighting both the disenchantment and potential brought by these technologies.

Chapter 2 looks into the interdisciplinary applications of AI and its role throughout the research lifecycle. It focuses on how AI can aid in the ideation and topic selection process while promoting a culture of innovative research practices.

Chapter 3 discusses strategies for submitting research for initial interest and introduces AI agents that enhance research outreach. It includes a detailed look at the Six-Dimensional Emotional Model (6DE) and its application to generative AI research assistants.

Chapter 4 covers the use of AI tools for conducting preliminary research and enhancing literature reviews. It also explores how AI can adapt rhetoric for different audiences, ensuring comprehensive and contextually relevant communication.

Chapter 5 guides researchers through formulating hypotheses and designing methodologies with AI assistance. It includes case studies of AI in research design and provides insights into advanced AI tools for data collection, analysis, and visualization.

Chapter 6 focuses on the stages of writing and revising research drafts with the help of AI tools. It offers techniques for AI-assisted writing and strategies for incorporating feedback from reviewers effectively.

Chapter 7 addresses the ethical challenges of using AI in research, including rethinking plagiarism and understanding the author function in AI-assisted research. It also discusses ensuring the integrity of AI-generated research outputs.

Chapter 8 looks ahead to future directions for AI in academic research and discusses how to prepare the next generation of researchers. It emphasizes the importance of embracing AI technologies while maintaining ethical standards and critical thinking skills.

James Hutson
Lindenwood University, USA

REFERENCES

Alvarado, O., & Waern, A. (2018, April). Towards algorithmic experience: Initial efforts for social media contexts. In *Proceedings of the 2018 chi conference on human factors in computing systems* (pp. 1-12). DOI: 10.1145/3173574.3173860

Angwin, J., Larson, J., Mattu, S., & Kirchner, L. (2016). Machine bias. In *Ethics of data and analytics* (pp. 254–264). Auerbach Publications.

Autor, D., & Dorn, D. (2013). The growth of low-skill service jobs and the polarization of the US labor market. *The American Economic Review*, 103(5), 1553–1597. DOI: 10.1257/aer.103.5.1553

Aydın, Ö., & Karaarslan, E. (2022). OpenAI ChatGPT generated literature review: Digital twin in healthcare. *Available atSSRN* 4308687. DOI: 10.2139/ssrn.4308687

Cai, C. J., Winter, S., Steiner, D., Wilcox, L., & Terry, M. (2019). "Hello AI": uncovering the onboarding needs of medical practitioners for human-AI collaborative decision-making. *Proceedings of the ACM on Human-computer Interaction, 3*(CSCW), 1-24. DOI: 10.1145/3359206

Castells, M. (2010). The Information Age. *Media Studies. REAd (Porto Alegre)*, 2(7), 152.

Deane, P. M. (1979). *The first industrial revolution.* Cambridge University Press.

Detweiler, R. A. (2021). *The Evidence Liberal Arts Needs: Lives of Consequence, Inquiry, and Accomplishment.* MIT Press. DOI: 10.7551/mitpress/13954.001.0001

Diakopoulos, N. (2019). *Automating the news: How algorithms are rewriting the media.* Harvard University Press. DOI: 10.4159/9780674239302

Dreher, M. (2021). Turning principles of action into practice: Examining the National Council of Teachers of Mathematics' reform rhetoric. *Arguing with Numbers: The Intersections of Rhetoric and Mathematics*, 16, 252–280. DOI: 10.5325/j.ctv1mvw8dg.13

Dwork, C., & Roth, A. (2014). The algorithmic foundations of differential privacy. *Foundations and Trends® in Theoretical Computer Science, 9*(3–4), 211-407.

Eslami, M., Rickman, A., Vaccaro, K., Aleyasen, A., Vuong, A., Karahalios, K., & Sandvig, C. (2015, April). "I always assumed that I wasn't really that close to [her]" Reasoning about Invisible Algorithms in News Feeds. In *Proceedings of the 33rd annual ACM conference on human factors in computing systems* (pp. 153-162).

Feezell, J. T., Wagner, J. K., & Conroy, M. (2021). Exploring the effects of algorithm-driven news sources on political behavior and polarization. *Computers in Human Behavior*, 116, 106626. DOI: 10.1016/j.chb.2020.106626

Frey, C. B., & Osborne, M. A. (2017). The future of employment: How susceptible are jobs to computerisation? *Technological Forecasting and Social Change*, 114, 254–280. DOI: 10.1016/j.techfore.2016.08.019

Fry, H. (2018). *Hello World: Being Human in the Age of Algorithms*. W.W. Norton & Company.

Gikas, J., & Grant, M. M. (2013). Mobile computing devices in higher education: Student perspectives on learning with cellphones, smartphones & social media. *The Internet and Higher Education*, 19, 18–26. DOI: 10.1016/j.iheduc.2013.06.002

Gillespie, T. (2014). The relevance of algorithms. *Media technologies: Essays on communication, materiality, and society, 167*(2014), 167.

Gran, A. B., Booth, P., & Bucher, T. (2021). To be or not to be algorithm aware: A question of a new digital divide? *Information Communication and Society*, 24(12), 1779–1796. DOI: 10.1080/1369118X.2020.1736124

Hutson, J., & Ceballos, J. (2023). Rethinking education in the age of AI: The importance of developing durable skills in the Industry 4.0. *Journal of Information Economics*, 1(2), 26–35. DOI: 10.58567/jie01020002

Kerridge, E. (2013). *The agricultural revolution*. Routledge. DOI: 10.4324/9781315019888

Khan, W., Ghazanfar, M. A., Azam, M. A., Karami, A., Alyoubi, K. H., & Alfakeeh, A. S. (2020). Stock market prediction using machine learning classifiers and social media. *Journal of Ambient Intelligence and Humanized Computing*, 1–24.

Knop, M., Weber, S., Mueller, M., & Niehaves, B. (2022). Human factors and technological characteristics influencing the interaction of medical professionals with artificial intelligence–enabled clinical decision support systems: Literature review. *JMIR Human Factors*, 9(1), e28639. DOI: 10.2196/28639

Kobayashi, M., & Takeda, K. (2000). Information retrieval on the web. *ACM Computing Surveys*, 32(2), 144–173. DOI: 10.1145/358923.358934

Kordzadeh, N., & Ghasemaghaei, M. (2022). Algorithmic bias: Review, synthesis, and future research directions. *European Journal of Information Systems*, 31(3), 388–409. DOI: 10.1080/0960085X.2021.1927212

Krause, S. (2000). "Among the Greatest Benefactors of Mankind": What the Success of Chalkboards Tells Us about the Future of Computers in the Classroom. *The Journal of the Midwest Modern Language Association*, 33(2), 6–16. DOI: 10.2307/1315198

Lepri, B., Oliver, N., Letouzé, E., Pentland, A., & Vinck, P. (2018). Fair, transparent, and accountable algorithmic decision-making processes: The premise, the proposed solutions, and the open challenges. *Philosophy & Technology*, 31(4), 611–627. DOI: 10.1007/s13347-017-0279-x

Liu, Y., Han, T., Ma, S., Zhang, J., Yang, Y., Tian, J., He, H., Li, A., He, M., Liu, Z., Wu, Z., Zhao, L., Zhu, D., Li, X., Qiang, N., Shen, D., Liu, T., & Ge, B. (2023). Summary of chatgpt-related research and perspective towards the future of large language models. *Meta-Radiology*, 1(2), 100017. DOI: 10.1016/j.metrad.2023.100017

Maravilla, H., & Scott, C. (2024). A (I) ccess to Justice: How AI and Ethics Opinions Approving Limited Scope Representation Support Legal Market Consolidation. *Georgia State University Law Review*, 40(4), 957.

McPherson, S. S. (2009). *Tim Berners-Lee: Inventor of the World Wide Web*. Twenty-First Century Books.

Meyer, J. G., Urbanowicz, R. J., Martin, P. C., O'Connor, K., Li, R., Peng, P. C., Bright, T. J., Tatonetti, N., Won, K. J., Gonzalez-Hernandez, G., & Moore, J. H. (2023). ChatGPT and large language models in academia: Opportunities and challenges. *BioData Mining*, 16(1), 20. DOI: 10.1186/s13040-023-00339-9

Minoli, D. (2013). *Building the internet of things with IPv6 and MIPv6: The evolving world of M2M communications*. John Wiley & Sons. DOI: 10.1002/9781118647059

Morales, E. F., & Escalante, H. J. (2022). A brief introduction to supervised, unsupervised, and reinforcement learning. In *Biosignal processing and classification using computational learning and intelligence* (pp. 111–129). Academic Press. DOI: 10.1016/B978-0-12-820125-1.00017-8

Pan, Y. (2016). Heading toward artificial intelligence 2.0. *Engineering (Beijing)*, 2(4), 409–413. DOI: 10.1016/J.ENG.2016.04.018

Pavlik, J. V. (2023). Collaborating With ChatGPT: Considering the Implications of Generative Artificial Intelligence for Journalism and Media Education. *Journalism & Mass Communication Educator*.

Petrilli, M. J. (2008). Wikipedia or wickedpedia? Assessing the online encyclopedia's impact on K-12 education. *Education Next*, 8(2), 87–88.

Phutane, M., Jung, C., Chen, N., & Azenkot, S. (2023, October). Speaking with My Screen Reader: Using Audio Fictions to Explore Conversational Access to Interfaces. In *Proceedings of the 25th International ACM SIGACCESS Conference on Computers and Accessibility* (pp. 1-18). DOI: 10.1145/3597638.3608404

Powers, E. (2017). My news feed is filtered? Awareness of news personalization among college students. *Digital Journalism (Abingdon, England)*, 5(10), 1315–1335. DOI: 10.1080/21670811.2017.1286943

Romberg, T. A. (Ed.). (1992). *Mathematics assessment and evaluation: Imperatives for mathematics educators*. SUNY Press.

Ruiz-Rojas, L. I., Acosta-Vargas, P., De-Moreta-Llovet, J., & Gonzalez-Rodriguez, M. (2023). Empowering Education with Generative Artificial Intelligence Tools: Approach with an Instructional Design Matrix. *Sustainability (Basel)*, 15(15), 11524. DOI: 10.3390/su151511524

Saltelli, A., Ratto, M., Andres, T., Campolongo, F., Cariboni, J., Gatelli, D., & Tarantola, S. (2008). Introduction to sensitivity analysis. *Global sensitivity analysis. PRiMER: Peer-Reviewed Reports in Medical Education Research*, 1–51.

Schwab, K. (2017). *The Fourth Industrial Revolution*. Currency.

Thornhill-Miller, B., Camarda, A., Mercier, M., Burkhardt, J. M., Morisseau, T., Bourgeois-Bougrine, S., Vinchon, F., El Hayek, S., Augereau-Landais, M., Mourey, F., Feybesse, C., Sundquist, D., & Lubart, T. (2023). Creativity, Critical Thinking, Communication, and Collaboration: Assessment, Certification, and Promotion of 21st Century Skills for the Future of Work and Education. *Journal of Intelligence*, 11(3), 54. DOI: 10.3390/jintelligence11030054

Townes, M. (2012). The spread of TCP/IP: How the Internet became the Internet. *Millennium*, 41(1), 43–64. DOI: 10.1177/0305829812449195

Turkle, S. (2011). *Alone Together: Why We Expect More from Technology and Less from Each Other*. Basic Books.

Weise, M. R. (2020). *Long life learning: Preparing for jobs that don't even exist yet*. John Wiley & Sons.

Werner, M. (1980). The Hand-Held Calculator and Its Impact on Mathematics Curricula. *School Science and Mathematics*, 80(1), 29–36. DOI: 10.1111/j.1949-8594.1980.tb09556.x

Wilson, S. (2003). *Information arts: intersections of art, science, and technology*. MIT press.

Wu, Z., Ji, D., Yu, K., Zeng, X., Wu, D., & Shidujaman, M. (2021). AI creativity and the human-AI co-creation model. *Human-Computer Interaction. Theory, Methods and Tools: Thematic Area, HCI 2021, Held as Part of the 23rd HCI International Conference, HCII 2021, Virtual Event, July 24–29, 2021Proceedings*, 23(Part I), 171–190.

Zanella, A., Bui, N., Castellani, A., Vangelista, L., & Zorzi, M. (2014). Internet of things for smart cities. *IEEE Internet of Things Journal*, 1(1), 22–32. DOI: 10.1109/JIOT.2014.2306328

Acknowledgment

This book owes its existence and success to the profound appreciation and gratitude I hold for the myriad individuals and institutions whose contributions and unwavering support have been pivotal in bringing this work to fruition. It is with deep respect and acknowledgment that I begin by recognizing Dr. John Porter, whose innovative leadership in aligning the adoption of emergent technologies like artificial intelligence with educational initiatives has profoundly influenced the evolution of this tome. His vision and dedication to integrating AI in academic settings have provided an invaluable framework for the discussions presented in these pages.

Equally deserving of recognition is TJ Rains, whose dual role as CIO and a co-author on other projects has enriched this work immensely. His insights into the directions of AI within the industry have not only enhanced the content but have also been instrumental in shaping its practical applications in the academic sphere. His collaboration has been a cornerstone of the research and analysis that underpin the themes explored in this volume.

I am also immensely grateful to Dr. Kathi Vosevich, Dean of the College of Arts and Humanities, for her steadfast encouragement and support. Her belief in the potential of this research and her ongoing support have been fundamental in sculpting the contours of this volume. Dr. Vosevich's leadership and commitment to academic excellence have fostered an environment where innovative ideas can flourish, and for that, I am eternally thankful.

Further, the contributions of the research team, particularly Drs. Daniel Plate, Emily Barnes, and Erin Morris have been indispensable. Their efforts in breaking down academic silos and fostering collaboration across departments and institutions have significantly enriched this work. Their dedication to mapping out the future of research in an increasingly AI-integrated academic landscape has not only broadened the scope of this study but has also deepened its impact.

To all these individuals and the many unnamed who have contributed their time, expertise, and passion to this project, I extend my deepest gratitude. Your collective wisdom and encouragement have been the bedrock upon which this work stands, and it is with great pride that I share the results of our collaborative journey.

Introduction

The past few years have witnessed technological advances that have drastically accelerated the pace of change in academic research, far surpassing the rate of previous digital disruptions such as word processors, Google, Wikipedia, mobile and cloud computing, online learning, MOOCs, and learning management systems. Each of these technologies required a reevaluation of how research is taught, conducted, reviewed, and disseminated. Historically, academia had years, if not decades, to adapt to each new technological wave. However, the timeline has dramatically shortened with recent advancements.

Since the stable release of ChatGPT by OpenAI in November 2022, academic institutions and scholars have found themselves scrambling to keep up with the rapid evolution of generative artificial intelligence (GAI) tools. The academic community has oscillated between outright rejection and full adoption of these tools, indicating that we have surpassed the inflection point; there is no possibility of returning to a time before the advent of generative content creation capabilities.

This book arrives at a pivotal moment, offering a timely exploration of how Large Language Models (LLMs), combined with machine learning algorithms and scholarly databases, are transforming the academic landscape. These tools enable researchers to "converse" with extensive repositories of information, thereby discovering new insights and expediting research outcomes at an unprecedented pace. The accelerated research process and the vast availability of information necessitate a shift in the role of the human researcher from sole author to editor, evaluator, and, as Ethan Mollick describes, "Co-Intelligence."

This publication is not merely an academic exploration; it serves as a practical guide for the complex and often ambiguous waters of AI integration in research practices. The rapid adoption of AI technologies across various disciplines necessitates a reevaluation of research protocols and ethical frameworks. This book aims to address a significant gap in the current literature by providing insights into the capabilities and limitations of LLMs in academic research. Through detailed case studies, theoretical discussions, and practical guidelines, it equips scholars, educators, and policymakers with the knowledge to harness these tools effectively and responsibly. By integrating perspectives from diverse fields and incorporating a broad range of AI applications, the book underscores the central role that AI tools are already playing in the act of research and dissemination of scholarship.

Furthermore, this book serves as a crucial resource for a wide audience, ranging from seasoned academics to graduate students embarking on their research journeys. It addresses the foundational changes that AI is bringing to research methodologies, literature reviews, hypothesis generation, and data analysis. The book also explores how these tools are reshaping the educational landscape, altering how future researchers are trained. For educators, it outlines strategies for integrating AI into curricula and research programs, ensuring that students are both aware of and proficient in the latest technological tools. The discussion extends beyond the theoretical to address practical applications and the ethical implications of AI, making it an indispensable guide for approaching the future of academic research.

As we stand on the brink of what could be the most transformative period in the history of academic research, this book synthesizes years of interdisciplinary research spanning fields as diverse as neuroscience, business, robotics, artificial intelligence, extended reality (XR), game design, blockchain, finance, art history, education, and the performing arts. This broad spectrum underscores the book's approach to breaking down traditional academic silos, mirroring the overarching theme of my scholarship which seeks to foster interdisciplinarity and encourage a holistic view of knowledge. It serves as both a map and a compass, guiding readers through the exciting yet uncertain terrain that lies ahead. By advocating for a balanced approach to AI integration, it highlights the importance of AI literacy and invites readers to embrace the potential of new technologies and interdisciplinary approaches. This book is poised to become an essential reference for anyone involved in academic research or interested in the future of AI in education. It offers an in-depth look into the complexities of AI and provides a clear vision for its ethical and effective use in academia. This work reflects my personal journey to reevaluate the value and nature of scholarship and serves as a call to embrace not just the potential of this new technology, but of interdisciplinarity itself. I invite readers to explore the rest of my scholarship, which similarly cuts across and integrates multiple disciplinary boundaries.

Chapter 1
The Dawn of the Algorithmic Researcher

ABSTRACT

The first chapter traces the ascension of artificial intelligence (AI) within the academic sphere, highlighting pivotal developments that have shaped its role in research. First, an historical overview illustrates how AI evolved from simple computational tools to complex systems capable of performing tasks that traditionally required human intelligence. This section discusses key milestones in AI development and adoption across various disciplines, underscoring the transformative impact of these technologies on academic inquiry and methodology. Next, the technical and theoretical foundations of LLMs, such as GPT and GANs, shall be discussed. It explores their architecture, training processes, and the underlying algorithms that enable their ability to understand and generate human-like text, setting the stage for their application in academic research and beyond.

1.1 THE EVOLUTION OF ARTIFICIAL INTELLIGENCE IN ACADEMIA

We are currently experiencing the Fourth Industrial Revolution (Industry 4.0), a period defined by unparalleled technological advancement that is fundamentally altering every aspect of human life, including how we work, communicate, learn, and live (Schwab, 2017). This era necessitates a thorough examination of its impact, particularly in how research in higher education prepares its community—administrators, faculty, staff, and students—to adapt and flourish amidst these changes. The emergence of generative AI (GAI) and its impact on traditional educational frameworks underscore the necessity for academic institutions to critically assess and adapt their missions, curricula, teaching methodologies, and assessment strategies to accommodate the evolving demands of research and scholarship. This adaptation

DOI: 10.4018/979-8-3693-6905-0.ch001

will ensure that future scholars are well-equipped to thrive in a rapidly changing academic landscape. Historically significant shifts, similar to those seen during the Agricultural Revolution which stabilized societies, the Industrial Revolution which urbanized them, and the Information Age which digitized them, are occurring once again (Braidwood, 1960; Castells, 2010; De Vries, 1994). Industry 4.0, driven by advancements in AI and the Internet of Things (IoT), merges digital, physical, and biological systems, erasing the traditional boundaries between these realms. The rapid pace of change necessitates continuous upskilling and retooling, with existing roles being automated or modified, and new roles emerging, including in research. This ongoing transformation presents both challenges and opportunities, compelling researchers to swiftly and thoughtfully adapt to prepare not only today's graduate students but also lifelong learners for the emerging realities of a digitally interconnected world.

Human civilization has been profoundly shaped by innovation and transformation. Historically, each of the initial three "revolutions" introduced novel ways of working, living, and structuring society, alongside considerable disruption. The Agricultural Revolution around 10,000 BCE marked a shift from nomadic hunter-gatherer groups to settled agricultural communities. This transition enabled the establishment of large, permanent settlements through the development of agriculture and the domestication of animals, necessitating significant societal adjustments. People had to learn farming techniques, develop new tools, and adapt to a settled way of life, leading to specialization in roles such as farming, metalworking, pottery, and weaving. This specialization fostered the development of distinct skills and societal roles, with farmers mastering land management and crop cultivation, and artisans creating tools and goods (Kerridge, 2013).

The invention of writing by the Sumerians in Mesopotamia around 3400 BCE further transformed society. The development of Cuneiform script, initially used to document economic transactions and later to record mythological narratives, marked a significant technological advancement. This was followed by the creation of scrolls in the Eastern Mediterranean and Egyptian civilizations, and eventually the codex by the Romans, which resembles the modern book. Writing, arguably humanity's greatest technological innovation, facilitated the preservation and transmission of knowledge across generations and geographies. It enabled the sharing and enhancement of other technological innovations like the wheel, plow, and metallurgy. The Renaissance period saw another leap in societal advancement with the invention of the printing press, which democratized information and education, propelling civilization forward.

The two most recent revolutions, emerging from the Age of Enlightenment, were equally transformative. The Industrial Revolution, occurring in the late 18th and early 19th centuries, marked a period of rapid industrialization that shifted societies from agrarian to manufacturing economies, fostering urbanization and introducing new forms of work. This transition required people to adapt to new working environments, such as factories, and learn skills like machine operation, while farmers moved to cities to seek new employment opportunities (Deane, 1979). This was closely followed by the Information Age in the 1970s, which transitioned the economy from industrial to knowledge-based, characterized by the widespread adoption of computers and the internet (Castells, 2010). This era introduced jobs in digital marketing, data analysis, and web development, while reducing demand for manual and clerical roles, with automation beginning to take over repetitive tasks. The Information Age also revolutionized communication, catalyzing the rise of the internet and social media, fundamentally altering how people connect and share information (Jones, 1995). Now, as we enter the second decade of the Fourth Industrial Revolution, driven by algorithms and AI, history reassures us that while technology may phase out certain jobs, it also creates new roles and opportunities, often with unforeseen consequences and benefits.

The Third Industrial Revolution, marking the Information Age, confirmed our capacity to adapt to changes as modern office life became the norm for working professionals. Yet, the pace of change during this era was more gradual compared to today's rapid transformations. For instance, the inception of the Internet dates back to 1974 when computer scientists Vint Cerf and Robert Kahn developed TCP/IP, the foundational protocols that enabled global computer connectivity for information sharing (Townes, 2012). In 1989, Tim Berners-Lee, a British computer scientist, introduced the World Wide Web, a system of interlinked hypertext documents accessible via the Internet (McPherson, 2009), which provided the first graphical interface for Internet access. The ease of finding information significantly improved with the launch of the Google search engine in 1998 (Kobayashi & Takeda, 2000). The early 2000s saw the emergence of social media platforms like Facebook and Twitter, revolutionizing how people connect and share information. The introduction of the iPhone in 2007 further facilitated on-the-go access to information (Gikas & Grant, 2013). The 2010s brought the advent of the Internet of Things (IoT), linking physical devices, vehicles, home appliances, and other items into interconnected networks capable of exchanging data, thereby creating "smart" systems and even "smart cities" (Minoli, 2013; Zanella et al., 2021). The IoT exemplifies the fusion of the physical and digital worlds, transforming how we work, live, and communicate.

Amidst technological advancements, the concept of algorithmic culture has silently permeated various facets of daily life, influencing how we work, make decisions, and interact with the world. Algorithmic culture, driven by significant strides in AI and machine learning (ML), affects sectors including business, education, and government, presenting both benefits and challenges. As explained by Fry in *Hello*

World: Being Human in the Age of Algorithms (2018), understanding different types of algorithms and their functions is essential for grasping their societal impacts.

Fry classifies algorithms into four functional categories:

1. **Prioritization Algorithms:** These algorithms organize data based on set criteria, such as sorting tasks by urgency or personalizing user recommendations based on past behaviors.
2. **Classification Algorithms:** Used to group data into categories, such as spam filters that differentiate emails or sentiment analysis tools that assess the emotional tone of texts.
3. **Association Algorithms:** These identify correlations between data items, like detecting frequently bought items together in stores or suggesting similar products in online platforms.
4. **Filtering Algorithms:** These algorithms screen data to meet specific criteria, removing undesired information or blocking access to particular content based on keywords.

Additionally, algorithms can be broadly divided into two paradigms: rule-based (RB) and ML. RB algorithms operate on explicit rules set by humans and are used in various applications from medical systems to financial decision-making. These are known for their transparency and ease of understanding. Conversely, ML algorithms learn from data and adapt over time, enhancing their functionality through reinforcement feedback. This learning capability makes them suitable for complex tasks like image recognition or natural language processing. However, ML algorithms are often criticized for their opacity, sometimes being labeled as "black boxes" due to the difficulty in interpreting their internal workings. This distinction highlights the diverse impacts of algorithmic culture, where the adaptability and efficiency of ML algorithms come with challenges in transparency and predictability.

Understanding the learning methodologies of algorithms is crucial for grasping the extent of algorithmic culture and its pervasive impact on our lives. Haldorai et al. (2020) categorize these methodologies into three primary types: supervised, unsupervised, and reinforcement learning. In supervised learning, algorithms are trained with labeled data, learning to associate specific inputs with predetermined outputs and applying this knowledge to new, unlabeled data to make predictions. Unsupervised learning, in contrast, involves algorithms analyzing unlabeled data to identify patterns and relationships without prior examples. Reinforcement learning operates on a trial-and-error basis, with the algorithm making decisions, receiving feedback through rewards or penalties, and refining its actions accordingly. Each type of learning provides a unique mechanism for training algorithms: supervised learning offers explicit instruction, unsupervised learning fosters independent pattern recognition, and reinforcement learning enhances decision-making through iterative feedback.

The benefits of embracing algorithmic culture include enhanced efficiency and speed in decision-making. Algorithms can process and analyze large data sets quickly, offering insights that might elude human analysis. According to Lepri et al. (2018), algorithms can facilitate more objective decision-making processes than humans, who are susceptible to biases. When trained on unbiased data, these algorithms have the potential to produce fair outcomes in various applications such as recruitment, loan approval, and healthcare (Kordzadeh & Ghasemaghaei, 2022). Additionally, algorithms improve access to information by personalizing recommendations and tailoring content to individual preferences, thereby streamlining the discovery and access to relevant information (Gran, Booth, & Bucher, 2021). These capabilities make algorithms invaluable tools in a data-driven world, underscoring their transformative impact across multiple sectors.

At the same time, algorithmic culture presents several challenges that must be addressed. The primary issue is the lack of transparency, often described as the "black-box" nature of algorithms, which complicates the identification and assessment of potential biases within decision-making models (Saltelli et al., 2008). This opacity can lead to unintended consequences, such as the perpetuation of existing biases and discrimination if the algorithms are trained on biased data. It can also amplify existing inequalities, create new ones, and infringe on individuals' privacy and rights (Angwin et al., 2016; Dwork & Roth, 2014). Furthermore, an over-reliance on algorithms might result in a diminished capacity for critical thinking and decision-making, thereby reducing human agency (Zerilli et al., 2019). The balance between instant access to communication and information versus the preservation of privacy and agency has become a significant concern, especially as algorithms increasingly influence our values, search results, news feeds, and social media interactions (Alvarado & Waern, 2018; Diakopoulos, 2019; Eslami et al., 2015; Feezell et al., 2021; Gillespie, 2014; Khan et al., 2020; Powers, 2017). This complex and ambivalent relationship with technology underscores the need for critical engagement with algorithmic systems.

In the 1984 sci-fi blockbuster *The Terminator,* Skynet, an artificial neural network-based superintelligence system, was supposed to go live on August 4, 1997. By August 29, 1997, it became sentient and launched a global nuclear strike. This narrative fueled enduring fears about the machine age taking over, a fear that persists in various forms today. According to Joseph E. Aoun in *Robot-Proof* (2018), Americans fear robots taking over their jobs more than death itself, highlighting deep-seated anxieties about artificial intelligence and automation. Despite these cinematic doomsday scenarios, the new millennium saw no machine uprising, but the integration of AI into daily life has accelerated, raising complex questions about the role of AI in our future.

AI, as defined by experts, encompasses a wide range of rapidly advancing technologies, from ML and natural language processing (NLP) to robotics and computer vision (Cremer, 2021; Ermakova & Frolova, 2021; Monett & Lewis, 2018; Wang, 2019). Importantly, as a subset of AI, NLP focuses on the interaction between computers and humans through natural language with a goal being to enable computers to understand, interpret, and generate human language in a way that is both meaningful and useful. NLP combines computational linguistics—rule-based modeling of human language—with statistical, machine learning, and deep learning models. These AI systems are built on algorithms that enable machines to perform tasks requiring human intelligence such as speech recognition and decision-making. The broader impact of AI is significant, as it's projected to generate $13 trillion by 2030 while displacing an estimated 800 million jobs due to automation (Hutson et al., 2022). As industries like automotive manufacturing undergo transformations driven by AI, there is a crucial need for ethical frameworks and workforce adaptations to steer the upcoming disruptions in sectors ranging from business to education and government (Miguel et al., 2022; Liu & Murphy, 2020). This ongoing shift demands that leaders accelerate preparations for integrating AI responsibly into societal structures, emphasizing ethical considerations, privacy, and security (Omolara et al., 2022; Wirtz, Weyerer, & Sturm, 2020).

The latter part of 2022 marked the onset of what might be termed the age of Generative AI (GAI), a period that significantly reshaped several sectors including the arts, advertising, marketing, and education (DelSignore, 2022; Francke & Alexander, 2019; Murphy, 2022; Sherry, 2022). Innovations such as ChatGPT, DALLE-3, and Stable Diffusion not only disrupted traditional practices but also incited debates over the use of "AI Art," leading to calls for bans and simultaneously giving rise to a new market of Non-Fungible Tokens (NFTs) (Ansari, 2022; Hazucha, 2022). Additionally, the launch of ChatGPT-3 on November 30, 2022, had a profound impact across industries, pop culture, and academia, distinguishing itself by its ability to provide conversational-style responses and generate original content including stories, games, code, and advertisements. With the announcement of ChatGPT-4, Microsoft is poised to expand the use of this advanced "headless AI" across its suite of platforms, further integrating AI into everyday technology interactions. Headless AI refers to AI systems that operate without a user-facing interface, functioning in the background to enhance and automate processes seamlessly.

The rapid advancement of AI technologies is reshaping perceptions about the future of work, with many fearing job displacements as AI and automation capabilities expand. Previously considered secure "essentially human" jobs are now vulnerable; AI art generators can create original artworks, AI tutors can assist students with learning disabilities, and voice actors' jobs are threatened by technologies that replicate voices. Machine learning, computer vision, and natural language processing are enhancing the capabilities of AI across various industries, stirring unease about human roles in future workplaces. However, predictions about widespread job losses due to AI may be overstated. Studies, such as one from the University of Oxford, indicate that while 47% of jobs could be automated, the impact of AI should be viewed as augmentative rather than merely substitutive (Frey & Osborne, 2017). Holzinger et al. (2023) suggest that AI should be seen as a productivity tool, enhancing human work rather than replacing it. This perspective is crucial as industries face disruptions requiring workers to adapt and acquire new skills. Despite fears, the Great Resignation of 2022 showed that workers are leaving jobs not because of automation but due to inadequate wages and lack of advancement opportunities (Ng & Stanton, 2023). The real challenge lies in harnessing AI's potential to enhance human productivity and creativity across various sectors, ensuring education systems evolve rapidly to equip individuals with the necessary skills to thrive in an AI-integrated world. This involves developing curricula that not only embrace AI technologies but also enable individuals to leverage these tools effectively, ensuring they are prepared for the changes ahead.

The urgency to adapt higher education for the age of AI has never been greater. Since Joseph Aoun's *Robot-Proof: Higher Education in the Age of Artificial Intelligence* (2018), the world has seen a global pandemic, rapid technological advancements, and the rise of generative AI, all accelerating changes in the job market. Aoun, the then-president of Northeastern University, critiqued the traditional education model focused on specialized knowledge, arguing it's insufficient for preparing students for a dynamic workforce. He advocated for an educational shift towards developing enduring “humanic skills” like creativity, critical thinking, and communication, and emphasized the importance of teaching students how to learn continuously to adapt to technological changes throughout their careers. Despite the relevance of these recommendations, progress towards implementing a new interdisciplinary curriculum has been slow.

Furthermore, the data underpinning the strategies in *Robot-Proof* has become outdated. Predictions about job automation have remained stable, but the specific roles affected first have shifted unexpectedly. For example, while the U.S. Bureau of Labor Statistics in 2018 predicted significant job growth in the information technology sector, early 2023 saw an unexpected loss of approximately 130,000 tech jobs due to advancements in AI and machine learning. Aoun's core argument that education should empower students to be creators in a future where “Creation will be at the base of economic activities” (Aoun, 2018, p.xvi) remains vital. He posited that even skilled, white-collar tasks like disease diagnosis could be automated, yet maintained that human-generated books, songs, and art would continue to hold value. However, the reality has shifted; AI's disruption of creative industries came sooner than many anticipated, affecting fields thought to be robot-proof, including caregiving, cooking, and even craft brewing, underscoring the need for educational systems to urgently and substantially evolve to prepare students for a rapidly changing world where AI's role is ever-expanding.

The response of educational institutions to the advent of generative AI, particularly the ChatGPT-3 model, has been predominantly reactionary. Many educators and policymakers have been slow to adopt this technology due to a lack of understanding of its capabilities and potential benefits. A report by the American Journal of Education highlights that some educators have even banned the use of such AI tools, particularly in K-12 settings across various regions (Kafai et al., 2024). Despite this initial hesitance, the rapid evolution of AI technology suggests that collaboration between human researchers and AI will soon become commonplace. Cardon et al. (2023) posits that collaborative writing with AI is inevitable and is already occurring routinely. To guide through this evolving landscape effectively, educational leaders must proactively engage with GAI, exploring how it can enhance educational and research practices. This necessitates a deeper comprehension of AI's functionalities and an openness to innovative research approaches.

The paradigm shift in higher education necessitates placing technology at the forefront to adequately prepare students for a technology-driven world. This shift involves a fundamental reevaluation of the traditional curriculum, moving beyond classic subjects like mathematics and English to emphasize problem-solving, self-expression, and communication skills. Higher education must prioritize developing students' critical thinking abilities over concerns such as plagiarism, viewing technology as a valuable educational partner rather than a threat. According to the Journal of Higher Education, technology is pivotal in fostering critical thinking by giving students access to extensive information and enhancing their ability to analyze, synthesize, and evaluate diverse sources (Tathahira, 2020). In this new educational landscape, teachers play a crucial role as collaborators, equipping them with the necessary skills to integrate technology into the classroom and support the development of critical thinking skills essential for succeeding in a technologically advanced world. Thus, rethinking research in higher education to align with future technological demands involves not only curriculum changes but also empowering educators to facilitate this transition effectively.

The COVID-19 pandemic has had a profound and far-reaching impact on higher education, leading to significant challenges including the closures of small, private, non-profit, and underfunded regional institutions in 2023, despite federal assistance (Cameron, Fogarty-Perry, & Piercy, 2022). Additionally, departments and majors in the arts and humanities such as Philosophy, History, Art History, Languages, and Religion have suffered from low enrollments and were often cut due to declining interest, weakening support for these disciplines, and undermining the development of a well-rounded education (Magness & Mitchell, 2022; Massey, 2020). The financial strain was compounded by reduced revenues from tuition, room, board, and other sources due to the shift to online learning and campus closures, which persisted as institutions continued to adopt online or hybrid models post-pandemic due to student demand (Mishra, Gupta, & Shree, 2020; Singh, Steele, & Singh, 2021). This shift not only exacerbated financial pressures as universities allocated significant resources towards remote learning technology (Frederick & Wolff-Eisenberg, 2020) but also increased disparities in access to technology and quality of education, particularly affecting low-income and underrepresented students, thereby widening the achievement gap, and creating unequal opportunities in higher education (Theobald et al., 2020).

During the pandemic, educational institutions, along with industries spanning from healthcare to technology, faced unprecedented challenges that catalyzed a surge in innovation and development, particularly in fields like extended reality (XR), AI, and ML. This period of intense innovation led to significant advancements in remote education, work, and healthcare, driving broader adoption of technologies such as cloud computing, virtual and augmented reality, and the IoT (He, Zhang, & Li, 2021). Notable developments included Facebook's (now Meta) release of the Oculus Quest 2, an affordable and user-friendly virtual reality head-mounted display launched on October 13, 2020, which addressed the constraints of social distancing. Additionally, the pandemic accelerated investments in unmanned aerial vehicles (UAVs) for contactless deliveries and telemedicine, which expanded the use of video conferencing services like Microsoft Teams and Zoom for medical consultations, thus reducing virus transmission risks (Aabid et al., 2022; Patel, Hamdan, & Donahue, 2022). AI also played a crucial role in enhancing disease diagnosis and vaccine development (Vaishya et al., 2020). These technologies enabled various sectors, from schools to governments, to maintain productivity and continuity amidst lockdowns and quarantines (Montenegro & Young, 2020).

Simultaneously, the educational sector rapidly integrated these emerging technologies to support learning amid significant constraints, with institutions transitioning to remote instruction by March 2022 (Doi, Lucky, & Rubin, 2022). This shift necessitated a swift embrace of video conferencing and enhanced utilization of learning management systems (LMS). Moreover, technologies like virtual and augmented reality were increasingly employed to overcome the barriers of physical distance, enhancing student interaction and engagement (Garzón, 2021). XR technologies were initially adopted in elementary and secondary education and gradually incorporated into higher education, creating immersive learning experiences that traditional methods, restricted by social distancing and travel limitations, could not offer (Hutson & Olsen, 2022). AI and ML have been pivotal in adapting higher education during the pandemic. Warrier, John, and Warrier (2021) highlight how these technologies have personalized learning by providing students with customized recommendations and feedback on their progress. Educational institutions have utilized AI and ML to analyze student data, enabling the creation of personalized learning plans that accommodate individual learning preferences and speeds. The pandemic has not only heightened the need for innovation but has also fostered a more receptive attitude towards change. This shift has spurred the development of innovative teaching methods and tools that have arguably enhanced the quality of education (Ciolacu et al., 2023).

The integration of emerging technologies, particularly generative AI, into higher education has intensified since the pandemic, necessitating digital transformation and a reevaluation of teaching and assessment methods (Rof, Bikfalvi, & Marques, 2022). Despite substantial efforts from administration, faculty, IT departments, and staff globally, the educational landscape is shifting towards a "new normal" where AI and ML are central to curricular offerings, including new courses in AI ethics (Cath et al., 2018), programming (Yang & Evans, 2019), and applications (Zawacki-Richter et al., 2019). Traditional disciplines like mathematics, science, and computer science are being restructured to underscore their relevance to AI, making them accessible to non-specialists (Cooper, 2022). Moreover, there is a growing emphasis on cultivating critical thinking, problem-solving, creativity, and innovation, which are vital for students to effectively engage with AI technologies (Bühler, Jelinek, & Nübel, 2022; Greenstein, 2012). Education systems are also grappling with the ethical, social, and economic implications of AI, highlighting the need for a focus on "education for AI" rather than merely using AI for educational ends (Schiff, 2022; Zhang et al., 2022). Concurrently, traditional assessment methods are being replaced by performance-based and project-based assessments to better reflect students' mastery in an AI-driven academic environment (Babitha & Sushma, 2022; Krajcik et al., 2023; Palladino & Shepard, 2023).

Unfortunately, academia is known for its slow pace, from curriculum revisions and academic research to the lengthy process of achieving tenure and the gradual advancement of committees and policies (Antony et al., 2022). This raises the question of whether incremental changes or a complete overhaul is necessary for the current academic model. Kellner and Gennaro (2022) argue that a reevaluation of the existing academic structure is crucial due to the rapidly evolving landscape of digital technologies, which render traditional academic models increasingly obsolete, particularly with the advent of sophisticated technologies like algorithms and machine learning. Furthermore, the current model does not adequately equip students for a job market that increasingly values technological literacy (Ter Beek, Wopereis, & Schildkamp, 2022). To stay relevant, academic institutions must adopt a more agile approach, integrating new technologies and interdisciplinary research into their curricula and policies. The urgency for updating the academic model is heightened by the transformative impact of digital technologies on the global landscape.

The digital revolution has prompted a reevaluation of the traditional compartmentalization within academic disciplines. Werthner et al. (2023) argue that the conventional academic silos are increasingly obstructive, particularly in fields like digital humanities. They emphasize the necessity of interdisciplinary research to fully understand the complex impacts of emerging technologies such as algorithms and machine learning, advocating for the breakdown of these silos to enhance research collaboration. Additionally, there is a pressing need for academic institutions to update their curricula to reflect the rapidly changing digital landscape, incorporating new technologies to ensure students are well-prepared for future challenges. Furthermore, Akour & Alenezi (2022) highlight the growing importance of faculty and staff acquiring new skills and knowledge to stay relevant. This shift suggests that traditional skills are becoming obsolete, and acquiring new competencies is essential for academic institutions to maintain their relevance. The critical question remains: what specific skills should we prioritize in educating future researchers moving forward?

AI is crucial in shaping the relationship between people and technology, offering transformative potential across industries such as healthcare, transportation, and education. Nonetheless, AI's limitations, such as its inability to comprehend human emotions or handle contradictions and ambiguity, restrict its use in human-centered applications and ethical decision-making (Xu et al., 2023a; Hunkenschroer & Luetge, 2022). These limitations underscore the ongoing need for human involvement in AI-driven processes. On another front, liberal arts education plays a vital role in developing what it means to be human by enhancing cognitive processes, emotional intelligence (EQ), and global competence. Such education helps cultivate critical skills like cognitive flexibility and EQ, which are essential for considering the complex social and professional landscapes of today's world (Kang & Lee, 2022; Rajaram, 2023; Wang, 2022). Studies affirm the importance of these durable skills in achieving success across various life domains (Elmoutanna & Moti, 2022; González-Pérez & Ramírez-Montoya, 2022; Mabe & Bwalya, 2022; Urhan, 2023; Clément, 2022; Hommel, Ruppel, & Zacher, 2022; Lee, 2022; Preiss, 2022; Barchard, 2003; Goleman, 2001; Mohzan, Hassan, & Abd Halil, 2013). In this rapidly evolving and uncertain world, fostering cognitive flexibility, EQ, and wellness is crucial for students to thrive.

With the integration of uniquely human skills, we are well-prepared for a future where human-AI collaboration enhances productivity and creativity. Despite AI and ML's limitations, which necessitate human assistance and oversight, the partnership between humans and AI holds great promise for surpassing the capabilities of either alone. As Pan (2016) suggested, merging human and artificial intelligence can create unprecedented knowledge and insights, while Wu et al. (2021) noted that such collaboration could foster new values and innovations by leveraging the strengths of both entities. This synergy can augment our cognitive abilities and improve decision-making, analogous to a co-pilot enhancing the journey while the human pilot remains essential for directing the course and overseeing automated functions. This "human-in-the-loop" model ensures careful oversight and prevents algorithmic culture from leading us astray. While the enhanced capabilities for productivity are compelling, it's crucial to maintain active involvement in the process. Moreover, the potential of AI in research is already showing promising results, such as the use of generative technology by Aydın and Karaarslan (2022) to automate the literature review process in healthcare, suggesting a future where academic publishing could demand less human effort and allow scholars to concentrate more on their research.

1.2 OVERVIEW OF GENERATIVE AI (GAI) TOOLS

The human-AI partnership is increasingly supported by a diverse array of GAI tools, marking a significant evolution in the capabilities of AI technologies for researchers. Unlike traditional AI systems, which are often limited to decision-making or predictive analytics, GAI tools excel in creating entirely new content—ranging from text to images and sounds—that did not exist before. This ability to generate novel outputs defines GAI and differentiates it from its predecessors, representing a crucial advancement in digital creativity and innovation (Feuerriegel et al., 2024; Goodfellow et al., 2014).

GAI tools are transforming industries and educational landscapes by providing solutions that enhance creative processes and facilitate complex problem-solving tasks. In the area of writing, LLMs such as ChatGPT can generate articulate and contextually relevant text, assisting in everything from drafting articles to creating educational materials. In the visual arts, tools like DALL-E and Stable Diffusion allow for the creation of detailed graphics and artwork that are indistinguishable from those created by human artists, broadening the scope for creative expression and design. For data visualization, GAI tools can transform large datasets into comprehensible visual representations, making data easier to interpret and insights more accessible. Additionally, GAI is integrated into research databases, enhancing the ability to sift through vast amounts of information and extract pertinent data, thereby accelerating the research process and increasing the breadth of academic and scientific inquiry (Khosrowi et al., 2023).

Interestingly, like Xerox or Kleenex in their industries, ChatGPT has become synonymous with AI in the media and even research. However, there is a very important distinction between GAI and traditional AI, which lies fundamentally in their operational frameworks and objectives. Traditional AI systems utilize a deductive approach, analyzing data within defined parameters to provide answers, make predictions, or automate tasks (Alzubaidi et al., 2023). In contrast, GAI leverages complex algorithms like generative adversarial networks (GANs) and transformers to discern and replicate the underlying patterns of the data it trains on. This allows GAI to create new, original outputs similar to the training data, expanding potential applications such as designing realistic virtual environments for simulations and automating creative processes in content creation (Goodfellow et al., 2014; Vaswani et al., 2017; Xu et al., 2023b).

Further, generative developments in AI incorporate a sophisticated mix of ML and deep learning (DL) technologies. ML provides the systems with the capability to learn and make decisions from data autonomously, while DL utilizes multi-layered neural networks to analyze data with a complexity and abstraction that resemble human thought processes (Alwahedi et al., 2024; LeCun et al., 2015). The training of these models is pivotal and involves collecting diverse and extensive datasets. The architecture of the model—which dictates the data processing flow—alongside training techniques like supervised, unsupervised, and reinforcement learning, plays a crucial role in the model's effectiveness. Supervised learning involves labeled data for tasks with known outputs, unsupervised learning finds patterns within unlabeled data, and reinforcement learning employs trial and error with feedback to refine decisions (Watson, 2023; Goodfellow et al., 2016; Shuford, 2024).

Table 1. Comparative overview of machine learning training techniques

Learning Type	Definition	Applications	Key Characteristics	Challenges
Supervised Learning	Learning from labeled datasets to predict outcomes for new data.	Classification, regression tasks.	Model learns mapping from inputs to outputs; relies on labeled data.	Requires comprehensive, high-quality labeled data; risk of overfitting.
Unsupervised Learning	Finding patterns or structures in data without labels.	Data clustering, dimensionality reduction.	Identifies similarities among data points or reduces complexity without explicit outcomes.	Interpreting results can be challenging due to lack of labels.
Reinforcement Learning	Learning to make decisions by receiving feedback in the form of rewards or penalties.	Game playing, robotics, autonomous systems.	Involves trial and error; agent learns policy to maximize long-term rewards.	Balancing exploration of new actions with exploitation of known rewards; complex environment modeling.

Key concepts in GAI extend beyond training methods to include neural networks, GANs, and transformers. Neural networks mimic the structure of the human brain with layers of interconnected neurons that process and transmit data. Introduced by Goodfellow et al. (2014), GANs consist of two neural networks: the generator, which produces data, and the discriminator, which assesses the data's authenticity. This interactive process enhances the generator's ability to produce increasingly realistic data. Transformers have significantly impacted NLP by improving the handling of sequential data. Their innovative self-attention mechanisms allow for more efficient processing of sequences, revolutionizing how data is interpreted and generated in complex AI models (Patwardhan et al., 2023; Vaswani et al., 2017).

Table 2. Overview of Key AI Architectures: Neural Networks, GANs, and transformers

AI Concept	Description	How It Works	Applications
Neural Networks (NNs)	A series of algorithms modeled after the human brain, designed to recognize patterns and interpret sensory data through machine perception, labeling, and decision-making.	Data is processed through layers of artificial neurons where each layer transforms its input into a more abstract and composite representation.	Used in image and speech recognition, medical diagnosis, financial forecasting, and more.
Generative Adversarial Networks (GANs)	A class of machine learning frameworks consisting of two neural networks (a generative and a discriminative) that contest each other in a game to capture and replicate data distributions.	The generative network creates data, while the discriminative network evaluates it. Over time, the generator improves at producing realistic data, and the discriminator becomes better at identifying fakes.	Applied in creating realistic images, videos, and voice generation; enhancing and generating art, photorealistic images, and deepfake content.
Transformers	An architecture that transforms one sequence into another using two components (Encoder and Decoder), employing self-attention mechanisms that do not require data to be processed in order.	It processes input data simultaneously, identifying relevance among data parts and encoding this information to enable effective parallel processing and deep contextual understanding.	Essential for natural language processing tasks like text summarization, translation, and generation. Powers models like BERT and GPT.

ChatGPT, or 'Chat Generative Pre-Trained Transformer,' developed by OpenAI, has become a prominent example of GAI in popular culture, leveraging the transformer architecture to produce text that mimics human conversation (Watters & Lemanski, 2023). Unlike traditional models that process words sequentially, transformers utilize a self-attention mechanism to analyze all words in a sentence concurrently. This allows the model to dynamically focus on different parts of the sentence, enhancing its understanding of context and relationships between words (Prasad et al., 2023). ChatGPT's ability to predict the next word in a sequence with high accuracy is further enriched by positional encoding, which provides awareness of word order, enabling the model to generate coherent and contextually relevant responses (Minaee et al., 2024). ChatGPT excels in various tasks such as question answering, creative content generation, translation, and summarization, showcasing the significant capabilities of transformer-based models in advancing natural language processing (Devi et al., 2023).

Recognized as the fastest adopted technology in history, with one million adopters within a month of its release in February 2023, ChatGPT is renowned for text generation. However, the latest tools extend beyond text to offer multimodal functionalities, including image generation, music composition, and synthetic data production (Zhou et al., 2023; Lwakatare et al., 2020; Steidl et al., 2023). Various models and application programming interfaces (APIs) continue to emerge, each specialized for distinct applications. Eden AI, for example, annually compiles lists of these APIs by type and use case, such as the 2024 list available at https://www.edenai.co/post/a-comprehensive-view-of-all-ai-apis. These APIs play a critical role in the tech ecosystem, facilitating seamless interactions between different software applications.

Within the expansive domain of GAI, specialized APIs harness ML and NLP to enable a range of sophisticated functionalities. Computer vision APIs allow applications to interpret visual data by identifying objects, individuals, and expressions, paving the way for advanced image recognition systems and video analytics platforms. Speech recognition APIs convert spoken language into actionable data, supporting the development of voice-activated devices, transcription services, and features that facilitate multilingual communication. Translation APIs utilize advanced NLP techniques to seamlessly translate text across languages, enhancing real-time communication and making content globally accessible. Text APIs analyze written content to provide sentiment analysis, entity recognition, and automated content generation, thereby enriching applications with deeper insights. Document parsing APIs combine OCR with NLP to efficiently extract and process data from documents, optimizing workflows in content management and data analysis. Additionally, generative APIs are at the cutting edge of AI, creating new text, images, and other media from specific datasets to drive innovative, personalized content creation (Magooda et al., 2023).

These APIs dramatically transform various sectors by enhancing user interfaces, overcoming language barriers, and automating intricate tasks in content creation and data processing. Given their diversity and transformative potential, it can be challenging to keep track of these technologies. To address this, Ithaka S+R has developed a Generative AI Product Tracker (https://sr.ithaka.org/our-work/generative-ai-product-tracker/) that lists these models and research databases, including generative text,

text-to-image, text-to-video, and synthetic models. This comprehensive tracking underscores the versatility and expansive impact of GAI across different industries.

Table 3. Overview of generative AI tools for researchers

API Type	Description	Applications	Examples
Computer Vision APIs	Enable applications to interpret visual data by identifying objects, individuals, and expressions.	Image recognition systems, video analytics platforms.	Google Vision API, Amazon Rekognition
Speech Recognition APIs	Convert spoken language into actionable data.	Voice-activated devices, transcription services, multilingual support.	Google Speech-to-Text, IBM Watson Speech to Text
Translation APIs	Employ sophisticated NLP techniques to translate text across languages.	Real-time communication, content accessibility globally.	Google Translate API, Microsoft Translator
Text APIs	Provide tools for sentiment analysis, entity recognition, and content generation.	Enhancing text-based applications with deeper insights and automation.	IBM Watson NLP, OpenAI GPT-3
Document Parsing APIs	Combine OCR and NLP to extract and process data from documents.	Streamlining operations in content management and data analysis sectors.	Adobe PDF Services API, Docparser
Generative APIs	Generate novel text, images, or other media based on specific input datasets.	Personalized content creation, dynamic media production.	OpenAI's DALL-E, RunwayML
Generative Research Databases	Leverage AI to assist in synthesizing, summarizing, and predicting research trends.	Enhancing research methodologies, supporting academic and scientific exploration.	PerplexityAI, Scite.ai, Consensus, JSTOR GenAI Beta

Generative text models, spearheaded by innovations such as OpenAI's GPT series (https://chat.openai.com/), have profoundly transformed the field of NLP and Deep Learning (DL). These models utilize advanced DL techniques and are trained on extensive datasets, enabling them to produce text that closely mimics human writing. A standout example of their capabilities is GPT-4 Turbo, which exemplifies the remarkable potential of these models by generating coherent, contextually appropriate text across a diverse range of applications. Whether creating realistic dialogue for chatbots and virtual assistants, drafting detailed articles, weaving captivating narratives, or even developing functional programming code, the adaptability and efficiency of GPT-4 Turbo have significantly advanced the automation of content creation.

The field of generative text models extends beyond GPT-4 Turbo and includes several noteworthy contributions from major technology firms, each bringing unique advancements to the field of generative AI in text creation. Among these are Google's Gemini, Anthropic's Claude, and Meta's Llama, each representing significant milestones in text generation technology. Google Gemini (https://gemini.google.com/extensions) stands out for its robust ability to understand and generate language, leveraging Google's extensive data repositories to enhance search algorithms and deliver nuanced user responses. Anthropic's Claude (https://claude.ai/chats) emphasizes ethical AI development and safety protocols, aiming to produce not only contextually coherent but also ethically sound text, thereby mitigating the risks associated with generating misleading or harmful content. Meanwhile, Meta's Llama (https://llama.meta.com/), notable for its open-source availability, provides the research and developer community with broad access to state-of-the-art generative text model technology. This approach to democratizing powerful AI tools fosters a collaborative environment that encourages innovation and pushes the boundaries of NLP technology, promoting collective advancement in the field.

In addition to the ability to generate textual content, generative research databases have changed how data is utilized and analyzed in academic settings, providing tools that go beyond traditional search and data retrieval to enhance the depth and efficiency of research. Advancing beyond mere keyword searches that many of us were trained on with library databases like WorldCat (https://search.worldcat.org/) or EBSCO (or even the Dewey Decimal System and card catalogs). With each advance in academic research, we have moved ever closer to quicker and easier access to digital resources that can be compiled, collated and searched. The latest generation takes this a step further and can automate the processes of discovering the state of the field in most disciplines. PerplexityAI (https://www.perplexity.ai/), for example, functions not just as a search engine but as a powerful analytical tool that synthesizes information from various sources into coherent summaries with inline citations, making it highly beneficial for researchers needing up-to-date information and comprehensive reviews of current studies. Similarly, Scite.ai (https://scite.ai/) offers a unique approach by using Smart Citations to analyze the impact and veracity of research papers, allowing users to see how a study has been supported or contradicted by subsequent research, thus providing a dynamic layer of scholarly verification.

Continuing the exploration of advanced tools, Consensus (https://consensus.app/search/) streamlines the literature review process by generating concise summaries of research papers. This tool is particularly valuable for researchers who need to assimilate large volumes of information quickly without compromising on understanding the core findings and implications of studies. On the other hand, Elicit (https://elicit.com/) acts as an AI-driven research assistant that not only finds relevant studies but also helps in framing research queries more effectively, pulling data points from a range of publications to provide comprehensive insights. These examples, it should be noted, are best for research in the physical and social sciences. For the arts and humanities, JSTOR has also launched their GenAI Beta tool (https://about.jstor.org/

gen-ai/). These platforms collectively elevate the research process, offering tailored solutions that cater to the diverse needs of the academic community, enhancing both the speed and quality of scholarly investigations.

AI tools for researchers are increasingly crucial for effective data visualization, which is essential in representing complex information through graphs, charts, and other visual formats. Such tools can range from stand-alone APIs to multimodal capabilities that include text generation and image creation. For instance, tools like Tableau (https://www.tableau.com/) and DataWrapper (https://www.datawrapper.de/) well-known for their user-friendly interfaces that allow for the creation of sophisticated visual data representations without any need for programming skills. These tools help researchers to quickly interpret and present their data in visually engaging ways that are easy to understand.

Moreover, GAI capabilities, like those found in OpenAI's GPT models, Google Gemini, Anthropic's Claude, and more, extend the utility of AI in data visualization by supporting the creation of descriptive elements that accompany visual outputs, such as automatic chart titles, annotations, and summaries. At the same time, the tools can output visualizations from data from Excel sheets and conduct statistical analysis and output everything from bar graphs, pie charts, and scatter plots. This integration of NLP and AI-driven graphic design allows for the generation of comprehensive, ready-to-publish data visualizations that are both informative and aesthetically pleasing. As a result, AI tools are transforming data visualization by making it more accessible, efficient, and interactive for researchers across various disciplines.

Image generation models have emerged as a significant advancement at the nexus of AI and creative expression, transforming the way visual content is created across various industries. These models, such as OpenAI's DALL-E (https://openai.com/dall-e-2/), leverage a variant of the GPT architecture to interpret detailed text descriptions and convert them into visually striking images. DALL-E's ability to produce high-quality, innovative visual content has found applications in areas ranging from conceptual art and graphic design to digital marketing, where tailored visual narratives are crucial.

The domain of AI-driven art generation is not limited to DALL-E. It includes other prominent tools like Midjourney, Stable Diffusion, and Adobe's Firefly, each offering unique capabilities that enhance the scope of generative visual media. Midjourney (https://www.midjourney.com/), accessible via the social media platform Discord (https://discord.com/), is known for its artistic flair and ability to produce stylistically varied images, making it ideal for exploratory art projects and creative ideation. In contrast, Stable Diffusion (https://stability.ai/news/stable-diffusion-3) prioritizes accessibility and user control, allowing for precise adjustments in the image generation process, thus democratizing high-quality visual content creation for a wider user base. Adobe's Firefly (https://www.adobe.com/products/firefly.html) integrates seamlessly with professional design tools, providing artists and designers with powerful capabilities to generate and refine images within their workflow. Together, these tools exemplify the profound impact of AI on artistic and scientific visualization, offering novel approaches to visualizing complex concepts, whether in biomedical illustrations, engineering designs, or digital art.

The rapid embrace of AI-driven tools by the general public has sparked significant controversy among traditionally trained artists and designers. Concerns about copyright infringement and the authenticity of AI-generated art as a genuine art form have been prominent (Ansari, 2022). In response, companies like Adobe are dealing with these legal landscapes by forming agreements with organizations that manage large datasets. Adobe's Firefly, for instance, is crafted to fit seamlessly into the professional creative workflow, utilizing Adobe Stock images, openly licensed content, and out-of-copyright content to ensure that its creations are legally compliant and commercially viable. Specifically designed for high-fidelity, customizable image generation, Firefly sets a standard for quality and utility that meets the exacting demands of professional graphic designers and digital artists, enhancing their productivity and creative possibilities within the Adobe ecosystem (Haze, 2023). These advancements in image generation technology herald a new era of digital creativity, equipping artists, designers, and marketers with innovative tools to bring their visionary concepts to life with greater efficiency and impact.

Along with text and image, moreover, tools have also emerged in the fields of music and audio generation. Generative tools in the music and audio domain have broadened the scope of AI's application, impacting artists, producers, and the entertainment industry. Platforms like AudioCraft by Meta AI (https://ai.meta.com/resources/models-and-libraries/audiocraft/) serve a wide range of generative audio needs, from music to sound effects, enabling creative collaboration between humans and AI. For instance, MusicGen and AudioGen within this platform can generate music and audio from text-based inputs, respectively, facilitating an intuitive co-creation process. MusicGen, in particular, excels at producing music conditioned on textual or melodic prompts, translating complex descriptions into rich auditory experiences.

Similarly, MusicGen (https://huggingface.co/docs/transformers/en/model_doc/musicgen) on Hugging Face utilizes an auto-regressive Transformer model to efficiently handle audio sequences, capturing the nuances of music with a unique token interleaving pattern that enables the generation of high-quality audio from discrete audio tokens derived from raw waveforms. Conversely, MuseNet by OpenAI (https://openai.com/research/musenet) demonstrates AI's capability to generate complex musical compositions across various styles and instruments, producing pieces that blend genres from classical to pop. It uses unsupervised learning to discern patterns of harmony, rhythm, and style from a vast dataset of MIDI files, illustrating the potential of AI to forge new musical paths. Such tools are particularly valuable for music researchers and computational ethnomusicologists interested in exploring the intersection of AI and musicology, as well as music therapists looking to create customized therapeutic sessions based on AI-generated music. Additionally, AI educators can leverage these tools to demonstrate practical applications of machine learning in creative fields, enriching the learning experience for students studying AI's impact on the arts.

These models, each with their distinct focus, collectively enhance the domain of AI-driven music and audio generation. They demonstrate the capacity of AI to transform the music industry by creating music and sound effects from textual inputs, streamlining the music creation process, and blending a variety of musical styles and instruments. These advancements suggest a future where AI is integral to the creative processes within the music industry. Beyond merely providing new tools for creators, these developments hint at innovative ways of interacting with and experiencing music and sound, propelled by the continuously advancing capabilities of artificial intelligence (Liu, 2023). This integration of AI into music not only opens up new avenues for artistic expression but also reshapes the consumption and production of musical content, pointing toward a deeply interconnected and AI-augmented musical landscape.

Synthetic data generation models have made significant strides across various industries by addressing key challenges such as data scarcity, privacy issues, and biases in machine learning training datasets. In manufacturing, synthetic data is used to create realistic datasets for consumer products, enhancing scenario testing for supply chains and boosting automation in robotics, adapting to diverse conditions such as lighting and environments (Buggineni, 2023). The healthcare and life sciences sectors benefit from these advancements as well, with generative neural networks reproducing complex genomic sequences, facilitating the safe sharing of patient data while ensuring privacy and bolstering collaborative research (Chafai et al., 2023). In the automotive and robotics fields, synthetic data trains software for self-driving cars and robotic systems within simulated environments, greatly enhancing safety protocols and crash prevention technologies (Birchler et al., 2023).

These significant advancements in synthetic data generation, propelled by agent-based modeling and generative models including LLMs, have revolutionized the creation of synthetic text, images, and tabular data that closely resemble real-world datasets. This has notably improved the development and operational efficiency of AI models (Hassani & Silva, 2023). For instance, Amazon's Alexa AI team uses synthetic data to train systems for understanding natural language in new languages where customer interaction data is limited, demonstrating the capability of synthetic datasets to overcome data scarcity (Antonius et al., 2023). Similarly, Waymo and other companies in the automotive sector utilize synthetic driving data to train autonomous vehicle systems, providing a practical approach to include complex and varied scenarios in training datasets without extensive real-world testing. The significance of high-quality, large-scale data in progressing these technologies cannot be overstated, as it underpins the continuous advancements in AI capabilities that are already beginning to impact academic research, teaching, and publishing by providing robust, scalable, and safe data solutions.

1.3 ACADEMIC IDENTITY: DISENCHANTMENT AND POTENTIAL

The integration of GAI tools into academic research has met with considerable skepticism and reluctance among scholars (Dergaa et al., 2023; Lund et al., 2023; Tang et al., 2024). Initially, the primary concerns surrounding the use of AI in academia centered on issues like data privacy and ethical implications (Berendt et al., 2020; Zhang & Aslan, 2021). However, once these barriers were addressed, the core resistance to incorporating AI into academic workflows persisted, largely due to threats it posed to personal, vocational, and professional identities—a phenomenon identified in research as "AI Guilt" (Gull et al., 2023; Lively & Hutson, 2024; Mirbabaie et al., 2022). This reluctance is notably marked in academia, distinguishing it from other professions such as electricians or architects, where technological integration might not as directly challenge the foundational aspects of professional identity.

To look deeper into this issue, it is essential to explore the concept of "academic identity," which has evolved uniquely compared to other trades. Academic identity in this context is intertwined with the pursuit of knowledge and the traditional methods of scholarship that have long defined personal and professional self-concepts within the academic community (Billot, 2010; Kogan, 2000). Academics often view their work as a vocation or calling, imbued with a sense of "enchantment" that stems from a deep engagement with their subject matter and the pursuit of truth through rigorous, personally driven research. This enchantment is perceived to be at risk with the advent of AI tools, which some fear may mechanize the creative and intellectual aspects of academic work, thereby diluting the personal fulfillment that traditionally accompanies scholarly endeavors (Winick, 2018). In other words, unlike other trades, what an academic produce is deeply intertwined with their "academic identity." The process of creation and the resultant value of the product can be seen to be affected by integrating AI into workflow. Therefore, as we explore the evolution of academic identity, it becomes crucial to understand these dynamics and address the existential concerns raised by the integration of AI into the scholarly landscape.

The historical roots of modern academia can be traced back to religious organizations, which played a pivotal role in shaping the identity formation and structural organization of today's educational institutions. The University of Bologna, established as the world's oldest university, was initially concentrated on law, influenced by its location in a center of legal thought (Perkin, 2014). Simultaneously, the University of Oxford emerged primarily with a focus on religious teachings, expanding significantly over time to include a diverse array of subjects such as Greek language, English literature, and biblical studies (Brockliss, 2016). This historical evolution from religious to more secular teachings highlight a transformation in the way knowledge has been categorized, taught, and assessed.

The evolution of academic institutions is deeply intertwined with the concept of "academic identity," historically likened to a religious vocation. Professors, viewed as the "priests" of their disciplines, profess a deep devotion to their fields, believing their subjects provide essential insights into the world (Neumann, 2009). This belief is symbolically underscored by the regalia worn at academic ceremonies like commencements, derived from medieval ecclesiastical attire, reflecting the enduring connection between academia and religious traditions (Platt & Walker, 2019). Particularly in the arts and humanities, scholarship is often seen as an "enchanted" pursuit, where the goal is to demonstrate virtuosity akin to a solipsistic performance. For instance, English professors might focus their research on social activism, offering feminist readings of Shakespeare as a way to stand out and push boundaries (Messer-Davidow, 2002). In other words, how something is communicated can be more important than what is being communicated, as, for instance, one might find in a biomedical study.

In addition, academic fields tend to be narrowly specialized, with faculty training and teaching influenced by their unique backgrounds and intellectual predilections, leading to a highly individualistic transmission of knowledge. This idiosyncratic approach can mean that students receive varying perspectives from different professors within the same field, highlighting the subjective nature of academic discourse (Arnold, 2014). Such specialization fosters a belief among scholars that their discipline is uniquely crucial, inadvertently marginalizing other fields (Friedman & Friedman, 2018). The author has witnessed this across institutions over the past two decades as a professor who has degrees across several areas, including arts, sciences, and business. Thus, acknowledging this academic fallacy is essential to fully leveraging the potential of new AI tools for synthesizing data and advancing knowledge beyond personal ambitions and the perceived righteousness of one's scholarly pursuits.

Today, the introduction of GAI and LLMs in academia presents unique stressors and challenges to the traditional roles and identities of scholars. These tools, by performing tasks once solely within the human intellect's domain, not only raise concerns about academic integrity but also prompt profound reevaluations of the identity and role of postsecondary educators. This technological shift, echoing historical disruptions brought by past technological advancements, challenges the enchanted domain of humanistic and deeply personal inquiry, leading many in academia to experience a sense of disenchantment. As AI begins to encroach upon these traditional roles, it necessitates a reevaluation of what it means to be a scholar today, particularly as AI tools can rapidly assimilate and teach the foundational knowledge, history, vocabulary, and nomenclature of various fields traditionally covered in higher education. This potential overhaul in educational paradigms could significantly affect the structure of higher education, especially at the graduate level, where the focus has traditionally been on developing specialized, critical thinking, and research skills. The challenge is multifaceted, involving ego, culture, curriculum, and policy, as academia moves away from rewarding the lone researcher—who is often incentivized to withhold data—to a model where knowledge and credit are shared more freely to rapidly improve social and environmental outcomes across disciplinary boundaries. Understanding academia's religious origins and how these have historically shaped academic identity is crucial in considering these changes and fully integrating AI into this venerable institution.

The proposed collaborative model, while not a complete solution, offers a way to address several pressing challenges in higher education, such as enhancing student and faculty engagement, optimizing resource use, increasing community interaction, and breaking down academic silos. This model does not hinge on significant research grants or extensive budgetary support, making it a practical option for many institutions (Hutson, 2023). The traditional view that 'ideas are academic currency,' often reinforced by administrative evaluation tools and promotion criteria, has led to a culture where scholars zealously guard their research agendas and outputs. In traditional settings, authorship roles are stringently defined, often adhering to discipline-specific norms that hinder the swift sharing of vital knowledge across fields, effectively isolating researchers within their own academic bubbles.

To tackle these entrenched barriers and foster innovative research to address complex "wicked problems," this study advocates for an interdepartmental, interdisciplinary, and interinstitutional research approach that emphasizes collaboration among researchers, academics, staff, students, and community stakeholders. This approach encourages a reevaluation of "authorship" in academia, suggesting a shift towards more inclusive and collaborative definitions and rewards. It promotes leveraging discipline-specific skills through pedagogic research, teaching-led research, research-led teaching, and inquiry-based learning to tackle pressing issues. By decentralizing the traditional research model, this approach allows for organic growth and adaptation, as demonstrated by its implementation during the global pandemic of 2020, which significantly boosted research activity, grant writing, and resulted in numerous publications and grants. This shift not only fosters a more collaborative academic environment but also enhances the overall impact and relevance of academic work.

Identifying research directions often requires expanding expertise through collaboration. For example, a finance and blockchain study considering the metaverse might benefit from the input of Business Law faculty. If the needed expertise isn't available within the institution, researchers are advised to look to their national and international networks, starting local but thinking globally. This networking can pave the way for future collaborative research and grants, as suggested by Santo et al. (2009). Should internal networks fall short, platforms like Academia, Research Gate, and LinkedIn can connect researchers with global experts.

Addressing faculty needs for time and resources is critical. Universities can support research through incentives such as course releases, seed funding, and promotions, as highlighted by Khan (2017) and Santo et al. (2009). Early adopters should be recognized and celebrated to encourage broader faculty engagement. Re-engaging faculty with their fields can rekindle their initial passion, as noted by Gamoran (2022). Interdisciplinary projects offer exciting opportunities to step outside traditional boundaries, potentially reinvigorating interest and leading to innovative cross-disciplinary research. Additionally, developing a peer-mentoring system that encourages connections across experience levels can foster organic, productive relationships, supporting sustained research momentum and addressing grand challenges like the future of work or climate change, thus enhancing the institution's identity and collaborative impact.

This example of collaborative authorship in decentered research is one of the early steps that can be taken as we chart the next few years in our respective disciplines. As well, the integration of AI into academic research heralds a significant shift in how knowledge is generated and disseminated. GAI tools exemplify the mechanization of knowledge transfer, mimicking human cognitive processes like reasoning and decision-making. This shift necessitates a reevaluation of the skills deemed essential in academia. The traditional emphasis on memorizing extensive bodies of knowledge is giving way to the need for "human skills"—critical thinking, creativity, communication, empathy, and the ability to work across diverse fields (Feuerriegel et al., 2024). Therefore, the focus should be on training students and researchers in metacognitive strategies, fostering an environment where they can learn how to learn effectively, rather than merely accumulating facts.

Addressing AI guilt, the perception that the value of scholarly work is tied to the effort and time invested, is crucial. Studies indicate that AI-generated content often receives lower valuations when its origin is disclosed, despite being identical in quality to human-generated content (Joshi et al., 2024). This underscores a broader issue within academia: the devaluation of work based on its creation process rather than its intrinsic merit. To fully leverage AI's potential, there must be a cultural shift in how academic output is assessed, focusing on the quality and impact of the work rather than the identity of its creator.

Ultimately, thriving in the age of AI requires a shift in academic identity. Researchers must move beyond seeing their primary identity as tied solely to their academic work. The anxiety provoked by the integration of AI into academia is understandable, given the traditional emphasis on individual expertise and authority. However, by embracing a collaborative model where knowledge and credit are shared, academia can foster an environment that accelerates research and improves societal outcomes. This involves not only redefining authorship but also breaking down disciplinary silos to encourage interdisciplinary research and the free flow of information (Buggineni, 2023; Birchler et al., 2023). Embracing AI as a tool rather than a threat will enable academics to focus on complex problem-solving and innovation, ultimately enhancing the impact and relevance of their work in a rapidly evolving world.

REFERENCES

Aabid, A., Parveez, B., Parveen, N., Khan, S. A., & Shabbir, O. (2022). A case study of unmanned aerial vehicle (drone) technology and its applications in the COVID-19 pandemic. *J. Mech. Eng. Res. Dev*, 45, 70–77.

Akour, M., & Alenezi, M. (2022). Higher education future in the era of digital transformation. *Education Sciences*, 12(11), 784. DOI: 10.3390/educsci12110784

Alvarado, O., & Waern, A. (2018, April). Towards algorithmic experience: Initial efforts for social media contexts. In *Proceedings of the 2018 chi conference on human factors in computing systems* (pp. 1-12). DOI: 10.1145/3173574.3173860

Alwahedi, F., Aldhaheri, A., Ferrag, M. A., Battah, A., & Tihanyi, N. (2024). Machine learning techniques for IoT security: Current research and future vision with generative AI and large language models. *Internet of Things and Cyber-Physical Systems.*

Alzubaidi, L., Bai, J., Al-Sabaawi, A., Santamaría, J., Albahri, A. S., Al-dabbagh, B. S. N., Fadhel, M. A., Manoufali, M., Zhang, J., Al-Timemy, A. H., Duan, Y., Abdullah, A., Farhan, L., Lu, Y., Gupta, A., Albu, F., Abbosh, A., & Gu, Y. (2023). A survey on deep learning tools dealing with data scarcity: Definitions, challenges, solutions, tips, and applications. *Journal of Big Data*, 10(1), 46. DOI: 10.1186/s40537-023-00727-2

Angwin, J., Larson, J., Mattu, S., & Kirchner, L. (2016). Machine bias. In *Ethics of data and analytics* (pp. 254–264). Auerbach Publications.

Ansari, T. (2022). How AI transformed the art world in 2022. *Analytics India Magazine (AIM)*. Retrieved from: https://analyticsindiamag.com/how-ai-transformed-the-art-world-in-2022/

Antonius, F., Alapati, P. R., Ritonga, M., Patra, I., El-Ebiary, Y. A. B., Orosoo, M., & Rengarajan, M. (2023). Incorporating natural language processing into virtual assistants: An intelligent assessment strategy for enhancing language comprehension. *International Journal of Advanced Computer Science and Applications*, 14(10). Advance online publication. DOI: 10.14569/IJACSA.2023.0141079

Antony, J. S., Cauce, A. M., Gangone, L. M., & Nicola, T. P. (Eds.). (2022). *The college president handbook: a sustainable and practical guide for emerging leaders*. Harvard Education Press.

Aoun, J. E. (2017). *Robot-proof: higher education in the age of artificial intelligence*. MIT press. DOI: 10.7551/mitpress/11456.001.0001

Arnold, J. (2014). A subjective academic narrative reviewing academic collegiality. *International Education Research*, 2(4), 26–37. DOI: 10.12735/ier.v2i4p26

Aydın, Ö., & Karaarslan, E. (2022). OpenAI ChatGPT generated literature review: Digital twin in healthcare. *Available atSSRN* 4308687. DOI: 10.2139/ssrn.4308687

Babitha, M. M., & Sushma, C. (2022). Trends of Artificial Intelligence for online exams in education. *International journal of Early Childhood special. Education*, 14(01), 2457–2463.

Barchard, K. A. (2003). Does emotional intelligence assist in the prediction of academic success? *Educational and Psychological Measurement*, 63(5), 840–858. DOI: 10.1177/0013164403251333

Berendt, B., Littlejohn, A., & Blakemore, M. (2020). AI in education: Learner choice and fundamental rights. *Learning, Media and Technology*, 45(3), 312–324. DOI: 10.1080/17439884.2020.1786399

Billot, J. (2010). The imagined and the real: Identifying the tensions for academic identity. *Higher Education Research & Development*, 29(6), 709–721. DOI: 10.1080/07294360.2010.487201

Birchler, C., Khatiri, S., Bosshard, B., Gambi, A., & Panichella, S. (2023). Machine learning-based test selection for simulation-based testing of self-driving cars software. *Empirical Software Engineering*, 28(3), 71. DOI: 10.1007/s10664-023-10286-y

Braidwood, R. J. (1960). The agricultural revolution. *Scientific American*, 203(3), 130–152. DOI: 10.1038/scientificamerican0960-130

Brockliss, L. W. (2016). *The University of Oxford: a history*. Oxford University Press. DOI: 10.1093/acprof:oso/9780199243563.001.0001

Buggineni, V. (2023). Utilizing Synthetic Data Generation Techniques to Improve the Availability of Data in Discrete Manufacturing for AI Applications: A Review and Framework.

Bühler, M. M., Jelinek, T., & Nübel, K. (2022). Training and Preparing Tomorrow's Workforce for the Fourth Industrial Revolution. *Education Sciences*, 12(11), 782. DOI: 10.3390/educsci12110782

Cameron, M., Fogarty-Perry, B., & Piercy, G. (2022). The impacts of the COVID-19 pandemic on higher education students in New Zealand. *Journal of Open. Flexible and Distance Learning*, 26(1), 42–62. DOI: 10.61468/jofdl.v26i1.515

Cardon, P., Fleischmann, C., Aritz, J., Logemann, M., & Heidewald, J. (2023). The challenges and opportunities of AI-assisted writing: Developing AI literacy for the AI age. *Business and Professional Communication Quarterly*, 86(3), 257–295. DOI: 10.1177/23294906231176517

Castells, M. (2010). The Information Age. *Media Studies. REAd (Porto Alegre)*, 2(7), 152.

Cath, C., Wachter, S., Mittelstadt, B., Taddeo, M., & Floridi, L. (2018). Artificial intelligence and the 'good society': The US, EU, and UK approach. *Science and Engineering Ethics*, 24, 505–528.

Chafai, N., Bonizzi, L., Botti, S., & Badaoui, B. (2023). Emerging applications of machine learning in genomic medicine and healthcare. *Critical Reviews in Clinical Laboratory Sciences*, 1–24.

Ciolacu, M. I., Mihailescu, B., Rachbauer, T., Hansen, C., Amza, C. G., & Svasta, P. (2023). Fostering Engineering Education 4.0 Paradigm Facing the Pandemic and VUCA World. *Procedia Computer Science*, 217, 177–186. DOI: 10.1016/j.procs.2022.12.213

Clément, E. (2022). Successful Solution Discovery and Cognitive Flexibility. *Cognitive Flexibility: The Cornerstone of Learning*, 113-142.

Cooper, T. (2022). *Ancestors and Algorithms: Ethnocomputing AI with African & African Diasporic Heritage* (Doctoral dissertation).

Cremer, C. Z. (2021). Deep limitations? Examining expert disagreement over deep learning. *Progress in Artificial Intelligence*, 10(4), 449–464. DOI: 10.1007/s13748-021-00239-1

De Vries, J. (1994). The industrial revolution and the industrious revolution. *The Journal of Economic History*, 54(2), 249–270. DOI: 10.1017/S0022050700014467

Deane, P. M. (1979). *The first industrial revolution*. Cambridge University Press.

DelSignore, P. (2022). The New Age of Creative AI Began in 2022. *Medium*. December 23. Retreived from: https://medium.com/predict/the-new-age-of-creative-ai-began-in-2022-ece07bb93350

Dergaa, I., Chamari, K., Zmijewski, P., & Saad, H. B. (2023). From human writing to artificial intelligence generated text: Examining the prospects and potential threats of ChatGPT in academic writing. *Biology of Sport*, 40(2), 615–622. DOI: 10.5114/biolsport.2023.125623

Devi, K. V., Manjula, V., & Pattewar, T. (2023). *ChatGPT: Comprehensive study on generative AI tool*. Academic Guru Publishing House.

Diakopoulos, N. (2014). *Algorithmic accountability reporting: On the investigation of black boxes*. Columbia University.

Doi, C., Lucky, S., & Rubin, J. E. (2022). Open educational resources in the time of COVID-19: Two case studies of open video design in the remote learning environment. *KULA*, 6(1), 1–15.

Dwork, C., & Roth, A. (2014). The algorithmic foundations of differential privacy. *Foundations and Trends® in Theoretical Computer Science, 9*(3–4), 211-407.

Elmoutanna, N. & Moti, N. (2022). Soft skills from university to workplace: A literature review. *International Journal of Accounting, Finance, Auditing, Management and Economics, 3*(5-1), 187-198.

Ermakova, E. P., & Frolova, E. E. (2021). Using Artificial Intelligence in Dispute Resolution. In *Smart Technologies for the Digitisation of Industry: Entrepreneurial Environment* (pp. 131–142). Springer Singapore.

Eslami, M., Rickman, A., Vaccaro, K., Aleyasen, A., Vuong, A., Karahalios, K., & Sandvig, C. (2015, April). "I always assumed that I wasn't really that close to [her]" Reasoning about Invisible Algorithms in News Feeds. In *Proceedings of the 33rd annual ACM conference on human factors in computing systems* (pp. 153-162).

Feezell, J. T., Wagner, J. K., & Conroy, M. (2021). Exploring the effects of algorithm-driven news sources on political behavior and polarization. *Computers in Human Behavior*, 116, 106626. DOI: 10.1016/j.chb.2020.106626

Feuerriegel, S., Hartmann, J., Janiesch, C., & Zschech, P. (2024). Generative ai. *Business & Information Systems Engineering*, 66(1), 111–126. DOI: 10.1007/s12599-023-00834-7

Francke, E., & Alexander, B. (2019). The potential influence of artificial intelligence on plagiarism a higher education perspective. In *Proc European Conference on the Impact of Artificial Intelligence and Robotics*. EM Normandie Business School.

Frederick, J., & Wolff-Eisenberg, C. (2020). Academic library strategy and budgeting during the COVID-19 pandemic.

Frey, C. B., & Osborne, M. A. (2017). The future of employment: How susceptible are jobs to computerisation? *Technological Forecasting and Social Change*, 114, 254–280. DOI: 10.1016/j.techfore.2016.08.019

Friedman, H. H., & Friedman, L. W. (2018). Does growing the number of academic departments improve the quality of higher education? *Psychosociological Issues in Human Resource Management*, 6(1), 96–114. DOI: 10.22381/PIHRM6120184

Fry, H. (2018). *Hello World: Being Human in the Age of Algorithms*. W.W. Norton & Company.

Gamoran, A. (2023). Advancing institutional change to encourage faculty participation in research-practice partnerships. *Educational Policy*, 37(1), 31–55. DOI: 10.1177/08959048221131564

Garzón, J. (2021). An overview of twenty-five years of augmented reality in education. *Multimodal Technologies and Interaction*, 5(7), 37. DOI: 10.3390/mti5070037

Gikas, J., & Grant, M. M. (2013). Mobile computing devices in higher education: Student perspectives on learning with cellphones, smartphones & social media. *The Internet and Higher Education*, 19, 18–26. DOI: 10.1016/j.iheduc.2013.06.002

Gillespie, T. (2014). The relevance of algorithms. *Media technologies: Essays on communication, materiality, and society, 167*(2014), 167.

Goleman, D. (2001). Emotional intelligence: Issues in paradigm building. *The emotionally intelligent workplace, 13*, 26.

González-Pérez, L. I., & Ramírez-Montoya, M. S. (2022). Components of Education 4.0 in 21st century skills frameworks: Systematic review. *Sustainability (Basel)*, 14(3), 1493. DOI: 10.3390/su14031493

Goodfellow, I., Bengio, Y., & Courville, A. (2016). *Deep learning*. MIT press.

Goodfellow, I., Pouget-Abadie, J., Mirza, M., Xu, B., Warde-Farley, D., Ozair, S., & Bengio, Y. (2014). Generative adversarial nets. *Advances in Neural Information Processing Systems*, 27.

Gran, A. B., Booth, P., & Bucher, T. (2021). To be or not to be algorithm aware: A question of a new digital divide? *Information Communication and Society*, 24(12), 1779–1796. DOI: 10.1080/1369118X.2020.1736124

Greenstein, L. M. (2012). *Assessing 21st century skills: A guide to evaluating mastery and authentic learning*. Corwin Press.

Gull, A., Dilawar, S., & Sher, F. (2023). Data-driven Artificial Intelligence at the Crossroads: Investigating the Role of Affective Job Insecurity in the relationship between Artificial Intelligence Identity Threat and Employee Well-Being. *The Asian Bulletin of Big Data Management*, 3(1), 18–34. DOI: 10.62019/abbdm.v3i1.35

Haldorai, A., Ramu, A., & Suriya, M. (2020). Organization internet of things (IoTs): Supervised, unsupervised, and reinforcement learning. In *Business Intelligence for Enterprise Internet of Things* (pp. 27–53). Springer International Publishing. DOI: 10.1007/978-3-030-44407-5_2

Hassani, H., & Silva, E. S. (2023). The role of ChatGPT in data science: how ai-assisted conversational interfaces are revolutionizing the field. *Big data and cognitive computing, 7*(2), 62.

Haze, K. (2023). Empowering Educational Creativity with Adobe Express. *The School Librarian*, 71(3), 24–24.

Hazucha, B. (2022). Artificial Intelligence and Cultural Production: Possible Impacts on Creativity and Copyright Law. *Available atSSRN* 4028106. DOI: 10.2139/ssrn.4028106

He, W., Zhang, Z. J., & Li, W. (2021). Information technology solutions, challenges, and suggestions for tackling the COVID-19 pandemic. *International Journal of Information Management*, 57, 102287. DOI: 10.1016/j.ijinfomgt.2020.102287

Holzinger, A., Keiblinger, K., Holub, P., Zatloukal, K., & Müller, H. (2023). AI for Life: Trends in Artificial Intelligence for Biotechnology. *New Biotechnology*, 74, 16–24. DOI: 10.1016/j.nbt.2023.02.001

Hommel, B. E., Ruppel, R., & Zacher, H. (2022). Assessment of cognitive flexibility in personnel selection: Validity and acceptance of a gamified version of the Wisconsin Card Sorting Test. *International Journal of Selection and Assessment*, 30(1), 126–144. DOI: 10.1111/ijsa.12362

Hunkenschroer, A. L., & Luetge, C. (2022). Ethics of AI-enabled recruiting and selection: A review and research agenda. *Journal of Business Ethics*, 178(4), 977–1007. DOI: 10.1007/s10551-022-05049-6

Hutson, J. (2023). The Role of Collaborative Authorship in Decentered Research Innovation: An Interdisciplinary, Interdepartmental, and Interinstitutional Model to Accelerate Research Culture in Teaching Institutions. *Information, Medium & Society. Journal of Publishing Studies*, 21(1), 7–24. DOI: 10.18848/2691-1507/CGP/v21i01/7-24

Hutson, J., Jeevanjee, T., Vander Graaf, V., Lively, J., Weber, J., Weir, G., & Edele, S. (2022). Artificial Intelligence and the Disruption of Higher Education: Strategies for Integrations across Disciplines. *Creative Education*, 13(12), 3953–3980. DOI: 10.4236/ce.2022.1312253

Hutson, J., & Olsen, T. (2022). Virtual Reality and Learning: A Case Study of Experiential Pedagogy in Art History. *Journal of Intelligent Learning Systems and Applications,14*(4). https://www.scirp.org/journal/paperinformation.aspx?paperid=120925

Jones, S. (1995). *Understanding community in the information age*. Sage.

Joshi, I., Grimmer, M., Rathgeb, C., Busch, C., Bremond, F., & Dantcheva, A. (2024). Synthetic data in human analysis: A survey. *IEEE Transactions on Pattern Analysis and Machine Intelligence*, 46(7), 4957–4976. DOI: 10.1109/TPAMI.2024.3362821

Kafai, Y. B., Proctor, C., Cai, S., Castro, F., Delaney, V., DesPortes, K., . . . Rosé, C. P. (2024). What Does it Mean to be Literate in the Time of AI? Different Perspectives on Learning and Teaching AI Literacies in K-12 Education. In *Proceedings of the 18th International Conference of the Learning Sciences-ICLS 2024* (pp. 1856-1862). International Society of the Learning Sciences. DOI: 10.22318/icls2024.875203

Kang, E. S., & Lee, J. M. (2022). Artificial Intelligence Liberal Arts Curriculum Design for Non-Computer Majors. *Journal of Digital Contents Society*, 23(1), 57–66. DOI: 10.9728/dcs.2022.23.1.57

Kellner, D., & Gennaro, S. (2022). Critical Theory and the Transformation of Education in the New Millennium. In *The Palgrave Handbook on Critical Theories of Education* (pp. 21–45). Springer International Publishing. DOI: 10.1007/978-3-030-86343-2_2

Kerridge, E. (2013). *The agricultural revolution*. Routledge. DOI: 10.4324/9781315019888

Khan, M. A. (2017). Achieving an appropriate balance between teaching and research in institutions of higher education: An exploratory study. *International Journal of Information and Education Technology (IJIET)*, 7(5), 341–349. DOI: 10.18178/ijiet.2017.7.5.892

Khosrowi, D., Finn, F., & Clark, E. (2023, August). Diffusing the Creator: Attributing Credit for Generative AI Outputs. In *Proceedings of the 2023 AAAI/ACM Conference on AI, Ethics, and Society* (pp. 890-900). DOI: 10.1145/3600211.3604716

Kobayashi, M., & Takeda, K. (2000). Information retrieval on the web. *ACM Computing Surveys*, 32(2), 144–173. DOI: 10.1145/358923.358934

Kogan, M. (2000). Higher education communities and academic identity. *Higher Education Quarterly*, 54(3), 207–216. DOI: 10.1111/1468-2273.00156

Kordzadeh, N., & Ghasemaghaei, M. (2022). Algorithmic bias: Review, synthesis, and future research directions. *European Journal of Information Systems*, 31(3), 388–409. DOI: 10.1080/0960085X.2021.1927212

Krajcik, J., Schneider, B., Miller, E. A., Chen, I. C., Bradford, L., Baker, Q., Bartz, K., Miller, C., Li, T., Codere, S., & Peek-Brown, D. (2023). Assessing the effect of project-based learning on science learning in elementary schools. *American Educational Research Journal*, 60(1), 70–102. DOI: 10.3102/00028312221129247

Lee, K. J. (2022). Adaptive expertise, career adaptability, and career success of R&D personnel. *Technology Analysis and Strategic Management*, 1–13.

Lepri, B., Oliver, N., Letouzé, E., Pentland, A., & Vinck, P. (2018). Fair, transparent, and accountable algorithmic decision-making processes: The premise, the proposed solutions, and the open challenges. *Philosophy & Technology*, 31(4), 611–627. DOI: 10.1007/s13347-017-0279-x

Liu, W. (2023). Literature survey of multi-track music generation model based on generative confrontation network in intelligent composition. *The Journal of Supercomputing*, 79(6), 6560–6582. DOI: 10.1007/s11227-022-04914-5

Liu, X. M., & Murphy, D. (2020). A Multi-Faceted Approach for Trustworthy AI in Cybersecurity. *Journal of Strategic Innovation & Sustainability*, 15(6).

Lively, J., & Hutson, J. (2024). The role of student motivation in integrating AI into web design education: A longitudinal study. *Forum for Education Studies*. DOI: 10.59400/fes.v2i2.1242

Lund, B. D., Wang, T., Mannuru, N. R., Nie, B., Shimray, S., & Wang, Z. (2023). ChatGPT and a new academic reality: Artificial Intelligence-written research papers and the ethics of the large language models in scholarly publishing. *Journal of the Association for Information Science and Technology*, 74(5), 570–581. DOI: 10.1002/asi.24750

Lwakatare, L. E., Crnkovic, I., & Bosch, J. (2020, September). *DevOps for AI–Challenges in Development of AI-enabled Applications. In 2020 international conference on software, telecommunications and computer networks (SoftCOM)*. IEEE.

Mabe, K., & Bwalya, K. J. (2022). Critical soft skills for information and knowledge management practitioners in the fourth industrial revolution. *South African Journal of Information Management*, 24(1), 1–11. DOI: 10.4102/sajim.v24i1.1519

Magness, J., & Mitchell, M. M. (2022). Religious Studies & the Imagined Boundaries of the Humanities. *Daedalus*, 151(3), 166–179. DOI: 10.1162/daed_a_01936

Magooda, A., Helyar, A., Jackson, K., Sullivan, D., Atalla, C., Sheng, E., . . . Chen, M. (2023). A Framework for Automated Measurement of Responsible AI Harms in Generative AI Applications. *arXiv preprint arXiv:2310.17750.*

Massey, J. W. (2020). *The Challenges of Neoliberalism to the Democratic Promises of Higher Education* (Doctoral dissertation, The University of North Carolina at Greensboro).

McPherson, S. S. (2009). *Tim Berners-Lee: Inventor of the World Wide Web.* Twenty-First Century Books.

Messer-Davidow, E. (2002). *Disciplining feminism: From social activism to academic discourse*. Duke University Press.

Miguel, P. M. D., De-Pablos-Heredero, C., Montes, J. L., & García, A. (2022). Impact of Dynamic Capabilities on Customer Satisfaction through Digital Transformation in the Automotive Sector. *Sustainability (Basel)*, 14(8), 4772. DOI: 10.3390/su14084772

Minaee, S., Mikolov, T., Nikzad, N., Chenaghlu, M., Socher, R., Amatriain, X., & Gao, J. (2024). Large language models: A survey. *arXiv preprint arXiv:2402.06196.*

Minoli, D. (2013). *Building the internet of things with IPv6 and MIPv6: The evolving world of M2M communications*. John Wiley & Sons. DOI: 10.1002/9781118647059

Mirbabaie, M., Brünker, F., Möllmann, N. R., & Stieglitz, S. (2022). The rise of artificial intelligence–understanding the AI identity threat at the workplace. *Electronic Markets*, 32(1), 1–27. DOI: 10.1007/s12525-021-00496-x

Mishra, L., Gupta, T., & Shree, A. (2020). Online teaching-learning in higher education during lockdown period of COVID-19 pandemic. *International Journal of Educational Research Open*, 1, 100012. DOI: 10.1016/j.ijedro.2020.100012

Mohzan, M. A. M., Hassan, N., & Abd Halil, N. (2013). The influence of emotional intelligence on academic achievement. *Procedia: Social and Behavioral Sciences*, 90, 303–312. DOI: 10.1016/j.sbspro.2013.07.095

Monett, D., & Lewis, C. W. (2018). Getting clarity by defining artificial intelligence—A survey. In *Philosophy and theory of artificial intelligence 2017* (pp. 212–214). Springer International Publishing. DOI: 10.1007/978-3-319-96448-5_21

Montenegro, L. D., & Young, M. N. (2020, September). Operational challenges in the food industry and supply chain during the COVID-19 pandemic: A literature review. In *2020 7th International Conference on Frontiers of Industrial Engineering (ICFIE)* (pp. 1-5). IEEE. DOI: 10.1109/ICFIE50845.2020.9266743

Murphy, B. P. (2022). Is Lensa AI Stealing from Human Art? An Expert Explains the Controversy. *Science Alert.* Retrieved: https://www-sciencealert-com.cdn.ampproject.org/c/s/www.sciencealert.com/is-lensa-ai-stealing-from-human-art-an-expert-explains-the-controversy/amp

Neumann, A. (2009). *Professing to learn: Creating tenured lives and careers in the American research university.* JHU Press. DOI: 10.1353/book.3399

Ng, E., & Stanton, P. (2023). The great resignation: Managing people in a post COVID-19 pandemic world. *Personnel Review*, 52(2), 401–407. DOI: 10.1108/PR-03-2023-914

Omolara, A. E., Alabdulatif, A., Abiodun, O. I., Alawida, M., Alabdulatif, A., & Arshad, H. (2022). The internet of things security: A survey encompassing unexplored areas and new insights. *Computers & Security*, 112, 102494. DOI: 10.1016/j.cose.2021.102494

Palladino, J., & Shepard, L. A. (2023). Authentic Assessment Embedded in Project-Based Learning. *Schools of Opportunity: 10 Research-Based Models for Creating Equity*, 67.

Pan, Y. (2016). Heading toward artificial intelligence 2.0. *Engineering (Beijing)*, 2(4), 409–413. DOI: 10.1016/J.ENG.2016.04.018

Patel, S., Hamdan, S., & Donahue, S. (2022). Optimising telemedicine in ophthalmology during the COVID-19 pandemic. *Journal of Telemedicine and Telecare*, 28(7), 498–501. DOI: 10.1177/1357633X20949796

Patwardhan, N., Marrone, S., & Sansone, C. (2023). Transformers in the real world: A survey on nlp applications. *Information (Basel)*, 14(4), 242. DOI: 10.3390/info14040242

Perkin, H. (2014). History of universities. In *International Higher Education* (Vol. 1, pp. 169–204). Routledge.

Platt, R. E., & Walker, L. H. (2019). Regalia remembered: Exploring the history and symbolic significance of higher education academic costume. *American Educational History Journal*, 46(1/2), 125–141.

Powers, E. (2017). My news feed is filtered? Awareness of news personalization among college students. *Digital Journalism (Abingdon, England)*, 5(10), 1315–1335. DOI: 10.1080/21670811.2017.1286943

Prasad, S. G., Sharmila, V. C., & Badrinarayanan, M. K. (2023, May). Role of artificial intelligence based chat generative pre-trained transformer (chatgpt) in cyber security. In *2023 2nd International Conference on Applied Artificial Intelligence and Computing (ICAAIC)* (pp. 107-114). IEEE.

Preiss, D. D. (2022). Metacognition, Mind Wandering, and Cognitive Flexibility: Understanding Creativity. *Journal of Intelligence*, 10(3), 69. DOI: 10.3390/jintelligence10030069

Rajaram, K. (2023). Cultural Intelligence in Teaching and Learning. In *Learning Intelligence: Innovative and Digital Transformative Learning Strategies: Cultural and Social Engineering Perspectives* (pp. 57–118). Springer Nature Singapore. DOI: 10.1007/978-981-19-9201-8_2

Rof, A., Bikfalvi, A., & Marques, P. (2022). Pandemic-accelerated digital transformation of a born digital higher education institution. *Journal of Educational Technology & Society*, 25(1), 124–141.

Saltelli, A., Ratto, M., Andres, T., Campolongo, F., Cariboni, J., Gatelli, D., & Tarantola, S. (2008). Introduction to sensitivity analysis. *Global sensitivity analysis. PRiMER: Peer-Reviewed Reports in Medical Education Research*, 1–51.

Santo, S. A., Engstrom, M. E., Reetz, L., Schweinle, W. E., & Reed, K. (2009). Faculty productivity barriers and supports at a school of education. *Innovative Higher Education*, 34(2), 117–129. DOI: 10.1007/s10755-009-9098-z

Schiff, D. (2022). Education for AI, not AI for Education: The role of education and ethics in national AI policy strategies. *International Journal of Artificial Intelligence in Education*, 32(3), 527–563. DOI: 10.1007/s40593-021-00270-2

Schwab, K. (2017). *The Fourth Industrial Revolution*. Currency.

Sherry, B. (2022). 3 Limits to Artificial Intelligence's Creativity (and How to Solve Them): Here's what you need to know about harnessing A.I. technology to be more creative. *Inc.* Retrieved: https://www.inc.com/ben-sherry/3-limits-to-artificial-intelligences-creativity-and-how-to-solve-them.html

Shuford, J. (2024). Deep Reinforcement Learning Unleashing the Power of AI in Decision-Making. *Journal of Artificial Intelligence General science, 1*(1).

Singh, J., Steele, K., & Singh, L. (2021). Combining the best of online and face-to-face learning: Hybrid and blended learning approach for COVID-19, post vaccine, & post-pandemic world. *Journal of Educational Technology Systems*, 50(2), 140–171. DOI: 10.1177/00472395211047865

Steidl, M., Felderer, M., & Ramler, R. (2023). The pipeline for the continuous development of artificial intelligence models—Current state of research and practice. *Journal of Systems and Software*, 199, 111615. DOI: 10.1016/j.jss.2023.111615

Tang, A., Li, K. K., Kwok, K. O., Cao, L., Luong, S., & Tam, W. (2024). The importance of transparency: Declaring the use of generative artificial intelligence (AI) in academic writing. *Journal of Nursing Scholarship*, 56(2), 314–318. DOI: 10.1111/jnu.12938

Tathahira, T. (2020). Promoting students' critical thinking through online learning in higher education: Challenges and strategies. *Englisia: Journal of Language, Education, and Humanities*, 8(1), 79–92. DOI: 10.22373/ej.v8i1.6636

Ter Beek, M., Wopereis, I., & Schildkamp, K. (2022). Don't Wait, Innovate! Preparing Students and Lecturers in Higher Education for the Future Labor Market. *Education Sciences*, 12(9), 620. DOI: 10.3390/educsci12090620

Theobald, E. J., Hill, M. J., Tran, E., Agrawal, S., Arroyo, E. N., Behling, S., Chambwe, N., Cintrón, D. L., Cooper, J. D., Dunster, G., Grummer, J. A., Hennessey, K., Hsiao, J., Iranon, N., Jones, L.II, Jordt, H., Keller, M., Lacey, M. E., Littlefield, C. E., & Freeman, S. (2020). Active learning narrows achievement gaps for underrepresented students in undergraduate science, technology, engineering, and math. *Proceedings of the National Academy of Sciences of the United States of America*, 117(12), 6476–6483. DOI: 10.1073/pnas.1916903117

Townes, M. (2012). The spread of TCP/IP: How the Internet became the Internet. *Millennium*, 41(1), 43–64. DOI: 10.1177/0305829812449195

Urhan, B. (2023). Crucial Role of Soft Skills in Challenging Times: Conceptual Analysis of Leadership Skills. In *Leadership Approaches in Global Hospitality and Tourism* (pp. 23-39). IGI Global.

Vaishya, R., Javaid, M., Khan, I. H., & Haleem, A. (2020). Artificial Intelligence (AI) applications for COVID-19 pandemic. *Diabetes & Metabolic Syndrome*, 14(4), 337–339. DOI: 10.1016/j.dsx.2020.04.012

Vaswani, A., Shazeer, N., Parmar, N., Uszkoreit, J., Jones, L., Gomez, A. N., & Polosukhin, I. (2017). Attention is all you need. *Advances in Neural Information Processing Systems*, 30.

Wang, L. (2022). Exploring the relationship among teacher emotional intelligence, work engagement, teacher self-efficacy, and student academic achievement: A moderated mediation model. *Frontiers in Psychology*, 12, 810559. DOI: 10.3389/fpsyg.2021.810559

Warrier, U., John, M., & Warrier, S. (2021). Leveraging emotional intelligence competencies for sustainable development of higher education institutions in the new normal. *FIIB Business Review*, 10(1), 62–73. DOI: 10.1177/2319714521992032

Watson, D. S. (2023). On the philosophy of unsupervised learning. *Philosophy & Technology*, 36(2), 28. DOI: 10.1007/s13347-023-00635-6

Watters, C., & Lemanski, M. K. (2023). Universal skepticism of ChatGPT: A review of early literature on chat generative pre-trained transformer. *Frontiers in Big Data*, 6, 6. DOI: 10.3389/fdata.2023.1224976

Werthner, H., Stanger, A., Schiaffonati, V., Knees, P., Hardman, L., & Ghezzi, C. (2023). Digital Humanism: The Time Is Now. *Computer*, 56(1), 138–142. DOI: 10.1109/MC.2022.3219528

Winick, M. (2018). Scholarly Enchantment. *Nineteenth-Century Literature*, 73(2), 187–226. DOI: 10.1525/ncl.2018.73.2.187

Wirtz, B. W., Weyerer, J. C., & Sturm, B. J. (2020). The dark sides of artificial intelligence: An integrated AI governance framework for public administration. *International Journal of Public Administration*, 43(9), 818–829. DOI: 10.1080/01900692.2020.1749851

Wu, Z., Ji, D., Yu, K., Zeng, X., Wu, D., & Shidujaman, M. (2021). AI creativity and the human-AI co-creation model. *Human-Computer Interaction. Theory, Methods and Tools: Thematic Area, HCI 2021, Held as Part of the 23rd HCI International Conference, HCII 2021, Virtual Event, July 24–29, 2021Proceedings*, 23(Part I), 171–190.

Xu, M., Niyato, D., Chen, J., Zhang, H., Kang, J., Xiong, Z., Mao, S., & Han, Z. (2023b). Generative AI-empowered simulation for autonomous driving in vehicular mixed reality metaverses. *IEEE Journal of Selected Topics in Signal Processing*, 17(5), 1064–1079. DOI: 10.1109/JSTSP.2023.3293650

Xu, W., Dainoff, M. J., Ge, L., & Gao, Z. (2023a). Transitioning to human interaction with AI systems: New challenges and opportunities for HCI professionals to enable human-centered AI. *International Journal of Human-Computer Interaction*, 39(3), 494–518. DOI: 10.1080/10447318.2022.2041900

Yang, S., & Evans, C. (2019, November). Opportunities and challenges in using AI chatbots in higher education. In *Proceedings of the 2019 3rd International Conference on Education and E-Learning* (pp. 79-83). DOI: 10.1145/3371647.3371659

Zanella, A., Bui, N., Castellani, A., Vangelista, L., & Zorzi, M. (2014). Internet of things for smart cities. *IEEE Internet of Things Journal*, 1(1), 22–32. DOI: 10.1109/JIOT.2014.2306328

Zawacki-Richter, O., Marín, V. I., Bond, M., & Gouverneur, F. (2019). Systematic review of research on artificial intelligence applications in higher education–where are the educators? *International Journal of Educational Technology in Higher Education*, 16(1), 1–27. DOI: 10.1186/s41239-019-0171-0

Zerilli, J., Knott, A., Maclaurin, J., & Gavaghan, C. (2019). Algorithmic decision-making and the control problem. *Minds and Machines*, 29(4), 555–578. DOI: 10.1007/s11023-019-09513-7

Zhang, H., Lee, I., Ali, S., DiPaola, D., Cheng, Y., & Breazeal, C. (2022). Integrating ethics and career futures with technical learning to promote AI literacy for middle school students: An exploratory study. *International Journal of Artificial Intelligence in Education*, 1–35.

Zhang, K., & Aslan, A. B. (2021). AI technologies for education: Recent research & future directions. *Computers and Education: Artificial Intelligence*, 2, 100025. DOI: 10.1016/j.caeai.2021.100025

Zhou, J., Ke, P., Qiu, X., Huang, M., & Zhang, J. (2023). ChatGPT: potential, prospects, and limitations. *Frontiers of Information Technology & Electronic Engineering*, 1-6.

Chapter 2
Ideation and Refocusing Research

ABSTRACT

This chapter considers the potential of AI across various academic disciplines, examining how GAI tools are changing the entire research lifecycle. The chapter begins by exploring AI's interdisciplinary applications, showcasing its ability to enhance research methodologies and outcomes in diverse fields such as humanities, sciences, and social sciences. It then provides an in-depth analysis of GAI's role in each stage of the research process, from ideation and topic selection to the refinement of research questions and hypotheses. By integrating AI tools, researchers can streamline the ideation process, uncover novel research topics, and generate innovative ideas that may have been overlooked through traditional methods. The chapter emphasizes the importance of refocusing research practices in the age of AI, advocating for a shift towards more adaptive, efficient, and data-driven approaches. This includes leveraging AI for comprehensive literature reviews, ensuring that researchers remain current with the latest developments in their fields.

2.1 AI ACROSS DISCIPLINES

AI has been an integral part of various academic disciplines long before the recent surge in generative tools. The transformative potential of the technology in higher education has been evident through its capacity to tailor personalized learning experiences, optimize learning outcomes, and broaden access to diverse student populations. This chapter will explore the pre-existing integration of AI across academic fields, illustrating its profound impact on research methodologies and educational practices. Since before the rise of GAI, 'artificial intelligence' was already making significant strides in academia. AI applications such as image classification systems and NLP tools were common in research environments. Tools

DOI: 10.4018/979-8-3693-6905-0.ch002

like DeepLens, which utilizes machine learning for image recognition, allowed researchers to analyze visual data with unprecedented accuracy and efficiency (Feuerriegel et al., 2024). Additionally, NLP tools facilitated the analysis of large text corpora, enabling scholars to uncover patterns and insights that were previously difficult to detect (Goodfellow et al., 2014).

Moreover, AI had become a routine part of daily academic life. Faculty and students frequently engaged with AI through everyday tools such as Grammarly, which uses machine learning to improve writing quality, and virtual assistants like Siri and Alexa, which streamline information retrieval and task management (Alzubaidi et al., 2023). These tools demonstrated AI's ability to enhance productivity and support learning outside traditional classroom settings.

The integration of AI in disciplines like education, healthcare, and engineering illustrates its wide-reaching impact. In education, AI-powered platforms offered personalized learning pathways tailored to individual student needs, thereby improving engagement and achievement (Xu et al., 2023). In healthcare, AI systems assisted in diagnostic processes, patient monitoring, and the development of personalized treatment plans, highlighting AI's potential to transform medical research and practice (Alwahedi et al., 2024). Engineering fields benefited from AI in automating design processes, optimizing system performance, and advancing robotics, leading to innovative solutions and increased efficiency (Vaswani et al., 2017).

Furthermore, institutional studies such as those conducted by Hutson et al. (2022) illustrate that these technologies were already being actively utilized across various academic disciplines to enhance learning, teaching, and research, often without explicit awareness. In education and human services, AI significantly impacted teaching methodologies and student learning outcomes, particularly through VR and simulations. For instance, VR simulations like TLE TeachLivE and Mursion provided immersive environments for teacher preparation and special education training. These tools supported preservice teachers in developing essential skills such as classroom management and engagement strategies for students with autism spectrum disorder (Ade-Ojo et al., 2022; Fraser et al., 2020). Despite their effectiveness, these tools required considerable hardware acquisitions, and their applications were often pre-made rather than bespoke.

In the humanities and language arts, AI facilitated groundbreaking research and learning through the Digital Humanities (DH). Quantum computing and AI algorithms were applied to analyze vast amounts of literary and historical data, enabling more nuanced and expansive studies. AI-powered tools and intelligent tutoring systems tailored language learning experiences to individual progress, supporting traditional teaching methods rather than replacing them (Ćalušić, 2021). However, effective use of these corpora required specialized knowledge and training.

The visual arts also witnessed transformative changes through the intersection of AI with art and design, particularly via GANs and AI enhancements in graphic design applications. Tools like Adobe's Sensei AI engine brought efficiencies to graphic design processes, allowing creatives to focus more on the artistic aspects of their work. AI enabled novel artistic expressions and practical applications, such as creating photo-realistic images and enhancing virtual reality experiences (Gabriele et al., 2017). Initially, access to GANs was limited to specific research institutions and computer science departments, with little crossover to art fields (Chakraborty et al., 2024).

Access to advanced AI technologies, beyond those integrated seamlessly into other applications, was predominantly available within physical science programs. In STEM fields, AI played a significant role, particularly in teaching and learning. AI and machine learning were embedded in educational platforms to offer interactive and personalized learning experiences in subjects such as mathematics and computer science. Federal agencies and organizations, such as NASA, provided AI and machine learning resources and projects, engaging students in practical, real-world applications, thereby showcasing AI's transformative potential in STEM education (Gong et al., 2018; Zhang & Aslan, 2021).

Despite the widespread use of AI across various disciplines before the advent of generative AI, there remains a lag in its deliberate adoption in many academic settings today. The initial reluctance or slow adoption rate in education can be attributed to several factors, including institutional inertia, the need for comprehensive training for educators, and concerns regarding the efficacy and reliability of new technologies. However, the eventual recognition of digital technologies' potential to enhance teaching and learning has led to gradual yet impactful transformations within educational systems. The introduction of LMS like Canvas and Blackboard, which help manage course materials and streamline grading processes, represents significant steps forward in the digital evolution of education.

This transition underscores a broader trend of digital convergence, where educational practices increasingly mirror technological advancements and digital integration seen in the corporate world. The cautious yet steady incorporation of digital technologies in education reflects an approach that balances innovation with proven pedagogical methods. This adaptability was highlighted in a recent comprehensive study aimed at better integrating AI into educational settings. Conducted in Spring 2024 at a mid-sized, private educational institution with over 7,000 full-time students, the study provides crucial insights into the perceptions of AI among faculty, staff, administration, and students (Hutson & Rains, 2024). The findings align with broader trends observed in recent research, such as a Pew study, which highlights the rapidly increasing adoption of AI across various segments of the population (Abulibdeh et al., 2024; Alhumaid et al., 2023; Filgueiras, 2023; Rodway & Schepman, 2023).

This evolving landscape emphasizes the need for continuous adaptation and the integration of AI to foster a more dynamic and effective educational environment.

The study reveals a significant correlation between educational attainment and AI usage frequency, with individuals holding postgraduate degrees being the most frequent users of AI technologies. Notably, nearly one-third of postgraduates in the United States report engaging with AI several times a day or "almost constantly." Age demographics also significantly influence AI adoption rates; 57% of individuals aged 18-29 report using AI at least a few times a week, compared to only 36% of those aged 65 and over. This digital divide underscores younger generations' propensity to integrate AI into their daily routines more readily. The rapid adoption of AI since the public introduction of ChatGPT in November 2022 is evident, with half of the American population now reporting frequent AI usage. These trends highlight the growing influence of AI on daily life and the necessity for educational institutions to adapt to this evolving landscape (Tyson & Kennedy, 2024).

Furthermore, the institutional study reveals a general optimism among both students and faculty/staff regarding AI's potential within their domains. This optimism, however, is tempered by ethical considerations and concerns about dependency on AI potentially undermining human skills and efforts. Students exhibit significant awareness and engagement with generative AI technologies, reflecting a shift in how the younger generation perceives and interacts with these tools. Ethical and societal ramifications of AI, such as data privacy, job displacement, and potential misuse, are prominent concerns for both groups. This highlights the need for ethical guidelines and robust discussions around AI deployment in sensitive contexts.

The high engagement with AI technologies among students contrasts with faculty and staff, who primarily focus on productivity and administrative tasks. Students utilize AI tools for academic purposes, personal projects, and entertainment, showcasing the diverse applications of generative AI, from text generation and code creation to producing original images and art. This broad recognition of AI's transformative potential underscores the pronounced demand for AI literacy and ethical training. Both students and faculty/staff express a keen interest in learning more about generative AI technologies through courses or workshops, indicating a consensus on the importance of understanding AI's capabilities and limitations.

The call for institutional support in preparing for AI integration is clear. Both students and faculty/staff emphasize the necessity for training, policy development, and ethical guidelines to facilitate AI's adoption in academia. Measures to combat plagiarism, enhance AI literacy, and align AI use with educational integrity are deemed crucial. There is a widespread belief, especially among students, that AI will significantly influence future careers and fields of study. This anticipation underscores the imperative for educational institutions to equip their communities for a future where AI is central to the workforce. A comprehensive discussion of the study and data highlights nuanced perceptions of AI within an educational context, showing collective enthusiasm for possibilities alongside recognition of ethical, societal, and educational implications.

A full-day teacher training workshop was a key component of the study, providing faculty members a platform to explore and discuss AI's implications in education (Morris & Hutson, 2024). Feedback from faculty participants reveals a mix of enthusiasm and caution towards integrating AI tools into educational practices. One participant expressed a desire to enhance pedagogical techniques by incorporating AI, stating, "I continue to reinforce my existing knowledge of good teaching practices but also adopt new ideas such as using AI and learning what students see as impactful." Another educator found practical value in AI for tasks like creating slide presentations and conducting initial proofreading, significantly reducing the time spent on these activities.

However, the training also highlighted varying levels of familiarity and comfort with AI among faculty. While some attendees appreciated the introductory sessions, others sought more advanced content. A participant noted, "With using AI, in some instances fully embracing it can be beneficial," suggesting a readiness to integrate AI more deeply into their teaching strategies. Conversely, another attendee expressed disappointment in the foundational level of the sessions, stating, "I honestly did not learn anything new, which is unfortunate... I would have appreciated a more in-depth workshop introducing new tools and strategies for implementation." This varied feedback underscores the need for differentiated training sessions catering to different levels of AI expertise among faculty.

Tailored approaches could foster more effective AI integration into curricula and ensure all faculty members use these technologies ethically and effectively. The workshop highlighted AI's potential to enhance pedagogical practices and address specific educational challenges, such as supporting students with disabilities or streamlining administrative tasks. Data from the training day suggests a growing recognition of AI's benefits in education, paired with a critical need for structured, varied, and advanced training. Institutions must consider these factors when formulating AI integration strategies and policies, ensuring all faculty members are supported in adapting to this transformative technology. Such initiatives will enhance education quality and better prepare students for a future where AI is ubiquitous in the workplace and beyond.

To help researchers capitalize on AI tools effectively, institutions should implement a varied strategy that includes comprehensive training programs, cross-disciplinary collaboration, and supportive infrastructure. Training sessions should be differentiated to cater to varying levels of AI expertise among faculty, ensuring all researchers can utilize these tools effectively. Workshops and seminars that offer both foundational knowledge and advanced techniques will empower faculty to integrate AI into their research methodologies seamlessly. Additionally, fostering a culture of collaboration across departments can leverage diverse expertise, thereby enhancing the quality and scope of research projects. Encouraging the use of scholarly networks and platforms like ResearchGate, Academia, and LinkedIn can facilitate connections with external experts, further broadening research horizons (Khan, 2017; Morris & Hutson, 2024). Institutional support through grants, course releases, and recognition of early adopters will incentivize faculty engagement with AI technologies, ultimately fostering an environment where AI enhances productivity and innovation (Gamoran, 2022; Walton et al., 2022). Educational institutions can ensure researchers are well-equipped to harness the transformative potential of AI in advancing academic knowledge by following these considerations.

2.2 GAI ACROSS THE RESEARCH LIFECYCLE

The integration of AI in academic research is, therefore, not a novel concept; however, the expanded capabilities of GAI signify a substantial shift from traditional methodologies, bringing forth both efficiencies and complexities (Esplugas, 2023). Historically, academic research has been characterized by a systematic process, where each step builds progressively towards the final outcome (Zeichner, 1995). The introduction of GAI tools at various stages of this research process not only showcases the potential of technology but also highlights the intricate balance between technological advancements and human intellectual effort.

Academic research traditionally follows a structured methodology designed to ensure rigor and validity in the research process (Table 1). This methodology is consistent across various disciplines, encompassing several key phases that guide researchers from the initial exploration of existing knowledge to the dissemination of new findings (Bailey, 2003). The process often begins with a literature review, where researchers conduct a comprehensive examination of existing literature to identify gaps and establish a theoretical framework (Randolph, 2019). This phase involves sifting through numerous academic journals, books, and articles to gather information on previous studies, theories, and findings relevant to the research topic. By understanding what has already been explored, researchers can pinpoint areas that require further investigation.

Table 1. Traditional research practices

Step	Activity	Significance	Field-Specific Example
Literature Review	Comprehensive review of existing literature to identify gaps and establish a theoretical framework.	Provides a foundation for the research, highlighting what has been done and what needs further exploration.	**Science**: Reviewing past studies on a particular drug's efficacy.
Hypothesis Formulation	Development of specific hypotheses or research questions based on the literature review.	Defines the research direction and focus, outlining the aims and objectives of the study.	**Social Sciences**: Formulating hypotheses on the impact of social media on youth behavior.
Data Collection	Gathering data through experiments, surveys, or archival research.	Provides the raw data necessary to test hypotheses and answer research questions.	**Humanities**: Collecting historical documents for analysis.
Data Analysis	Applying statistical or qualitative methods to interpret the collected data.	Helps uncover patterns, relationships, or insights, leading to conclusions about the research questions.	**Business**: Analyzing survey data to understand consumer behavior.
Interpretation and Conclusion	Interpreting findings in the context of the original hypotheses, discussing implications, and drawing conclusions.	Provides a deeper understanding of the results, how they fit into existing knowledge, and their broader implications.	**Engineering**: Interpreting experimental results to improve a technology or process.
Publication and Dissemination	Writing up the study and submitting it for publication or presenting it at conferences.	Ensures the research is shared with the academic community for peer review and further development of the field.	**Medicine**: Publishing clinical trial results in a medical journal.

Following the literature review, researchers move to hypothesis formulation. Here, they develop specific hypotheses or research questions based on insights gained from the literature (Shehzad, 2011). This step is crucial as it defines the direction and focus of the study, outlining what the researchers aim to discover or prove. Next is the data collection phase, which involves gathering data through various methods such as experiments, surveys, or archival research. Depending on the discipline, this can mean conducting laboratory experiments in the sciences, administering surveys in the social sciences, or analyzing historical documents in the humanities.

Once data is collected, researchers engage in data analysis. This phase involves applying statistical or qualitative methods to interpret the data and test the hypotheses (Aliotta, 2018). Techniques can vary widely depending on the field and the nature of the data, but the goal is to uncover patterns, relationships, or insights that answer the research questions. The interpretation and conclusion phase follows, where researchers interpret their findings in the context of the original hypotheses. This involves discussing the implications of the results, how they fit with existing knowledge, and what new insights they contribute to the field. Researchers draw conclusions and consider the broader significance of their work. Finally, the research is prepared for publication and dissemination. This step involves writing up the study in a format suitable for academic journals or conferences, ensuring that the findings are shared with the wider academic community. Publication is a critical part of the research process as it allows for peer review and contributes to the collective knowledge in the discipline (Hartley, 2008).

Across different academic disciplines, the methodologies in research can appear distinct yet share underlying similarities in their structured approach. For instance, in the arts and sciences, research often emphasizes creative exploration and empirical investigation (Moses, 1990). In the sciences, this might involve experimental design, data collection through controlled experiments, and rigorous statistical analysis (Ruxton & Colegrave, 2011). In the arts, research can be more interpretive, focusing on critical analysis of texts, artworks, and historical contexts (Sullivan, 2006). In contrast, business and vocational studies often prioritize practical applications and real-world problem-solving (English & Gainsburg, 2015). Business research might involve market analysis, financial modeling, or case studies to understand economic trends and organizational behavior. Vocational studies, such as those in healthcare or engineering, may focus on developing and testing new technologies or methods, with an emphasis on applicability and innovation.

While the specific methods and tools may vary across disciplines, the fundamental stages of research—literature review, hypothesis formulation, data collection, data analysis, interpretation and conclusion, and publication and dissemination—remain consistent. Each discipline adapts these stages to its unique context, but all aim to advance knowledge, solve problems, and contribute to their respective fields. At the same time, each area has been limited by time, resources, and skills development. For instance, gathering information for a literature review may require travel to international archives or to physical stacks in libraries if previous research had yet to be digitized and adding OCR (optical character recognition) to make it searchable. A researcher would be limited by time and space in collating such information. Also, data analysis and outputting those results in a written format both take additional time as in biostatistics. The restrictions on time and the peer review and publication process found even the most prodigious researchers publishing articles only annually or biannually in many cases.

In the age of AI, however, the traditional research process is being transformed by new technologies that transcend past limitations and necessitate a rethinking of how we educate and train graduate students and the next generation of researchers. Rather than adhering to a rigid, step-by-step research model, the modern approach emphasizes the importance of understanding the overarching schema and framework of a field. This allows researchers to plug in data as needed, streamlining the research process, and enhancing efficiency.

The role of the human researcher is evolving to focus on identifying use cases for research, while AI can be leveraged to generate specific research questions and suggest approaches. In the data collection phase, a collaborative effort between AI and human researchers is crucial for determining what data is needed and developing the appropriate research instruments. Once data is collected, AI can analyze it, producing results and analytics that would have taken much longer with traditional methods. This partnership between AI and humans continues through the publication and dissemination of findings, where AI aids in drafting and formatting, while human researchers ensure the insights are effectively communicated and applied for social or field-specific benefits.

This new research paradigm not only enhances the research process but also requires a shift in educational strategies. Training programs must now focus on equipping students with the skills to effectively collaborate with AI, understanding both the capabilities and limitations of these technologies. By reframing our approach to teaching and training, we prepare researchers to harness the full potential of AI, fostering innovation and accelerating the advancement of knowledge across disciplines. The following will outline a way of conceptualizing this new approach to the research lifecycle in the generative age (Table 2).

Table 2. New approach to research in the age of AI

Step	Activity	Significance	Tool-Specific Example
Ideation and Topic Selection	Use AI-powered brainstorming tools to generate research topics based on current trends and gaps in literature.	Identifies relevant and timely research topics aligned with current academic discourse.	Enter key interests into tools like Research Rabbit or Consensus to analyze current publications and suggest under-explored topics.
Finding Conferences/ Publishers	Match the generated topic with appropriate conferences, journals, or book publishers. Review their calls for proposals to align with research interests.	Ensures research is aligned with the scope and requirements of specific academic venues.	Use tools like Conference Alerts or Journal Finder to locate suitable publication opportunities.
Submitting for Initial Interest	Align research with submission requirements and calls for entries from selected venues.	Enhances chances of acceptance by adhering to specific guidelines and themes of target publications.	Paste submission requirements into AI tools like Scholarcy to align outputs with entry criteria.
Preliminary Research and Literature Review	Deploy AI-driven search tools and databases to find relevant articles, books, and papers.	Builds a comprehensive understanding of existing research, identifying gaps and central themes.	Use Semantic Scholar or PerplexityAI to summarize key literature and highlight important studies.

continued on following page

Table 2. Continued

Step	Activity	Significance	Tool-Specific Example
Hypothesis Formation	Formulate research questions based on literature review. Use AI to predict outcomes from similar previous studies.	Develops data-driven hypotheses, enhancing the relevance and focus of the research.	Input data into AI models like IBM Watson to generate potential hypotheses.
Research Design and Methodology	AI models suggest the most effective techniques based on similar studies.	Ensures a robust research design optimized for accuracy and efficiency.	Use tools like MethodSpace or Labstep to outline research methods tailored by AI suggestions.
Data Collection	Implement AI tools for automated data collection.	Gathers comprehensive and unbiased data efficiently.	Set up systems like Qualtrics or Google Forms integrated with AI to collect survey data.
Data Analysis	Use machine learning algorithms and statistical tools to analyze data.	Produces statistically validated results with visual representations for easy interpretation.	Input data into AI software like SPSS with ML capabilities for pattern recognition and statistical analysis.
Data Visualization	Create tables, charts, and figures.	Enhances the understanding and communication of research findings.	Use tools like Tableau or Power BI to create visual representations of data.
Writing the Draft	Draft sections of the paper with AI assistance to maintain quality and adherence to style guides.	Produces a complete first draft that effectively communicates research findings.	Utilize AI writing assistants like Grammarly or Jasper.
Revision and Editing	Employ AI tools to refine syntax, grammar, and style.	Ensures clarity, conciseness, and overall readability of the manuscript.	Use tools like Hemingway Editor or ProWritingAid for systematic revision.
Final Review and Submission	Use AI to simulate peer review feedback and check submission readiness.	Thoroughly vets the manuscript, ensuring it meets submission standards.	Employ tools like Paperpal or Penelope to simulate peer review.
Revising Based on Reviewer Feedback	Break down feedback into step-by-step instructions for efficient revision.	Streamlines the revision process, enhancing the manuscript's quality and adherence to reviewer comments.	Use tools like ScholarOne to manage and address reviewer feedback.
Reviewing Work Yourself	AI assists in targeting specific review criteria of different journals.	Promotes objectivity and reduces bias in the review process.	Use AI review tools like Publons for efficient and objective manuscript review.
Promoting Your Work	Tailor content for different platforms and audiences quickly.	Enhances visibility and impact of research through effective dissemination.	Utilize tools like Buffer or Hootsuite for social media promotion and outreach.

In the age of AI, the traditional research process has evolved into a more dynamic and efficient model that integrates advanced AI tools at every stage. This new approach allows researchers to leverage AI for ideation, data collection, analysis, and dissemination, thereby enhancing the quality and speed of their work. Initially, AI-powered brainstorming tools help generate relevant research topics by analyzing current trends and identifying gaps in the literature (Abdelrazek et al., 2023). Researchers can then use AI-driven search tools to conduct comprehensive literature reviews, summarizing key studies and highlighting central themes (Heston & Khun, 2023). AI models assist in formulating hypotheses by analyzing preliminary data and suggesting potential outcomes based on previous research (Wagner et al., 2022). During the research design phase, AI tools recommend effective methodologies tailored to the discipline and research question, ensuring robust and efficient study designs (Robledo et al., 2023).

For data collection, AI automates the gathering and initial processing of data, ensuring comprehensive and unbiased datasets (Chapinal-Heras & Díaz-Sánchez, 2023). Advanced machine learning algorithms and statistical tools analyze this data, producing validated results and visually representing the findings (Pinzolits, 2024). Writing the research draft becomes more streamlined with AI writing assistants, which maintain consistent quality and adherence to style guides. AI editing tools refine the draft, ensuring clarity and readability, while AI simulations of peer review provide feedback to prepare the manuscript for submission (Fui-Hoon Nah et al., 2023). The process concludes with promoting the work using AI tools to tailor content for different platforms, enhancing the visibility and impact of the research. This integrated model not only accelerates the research cycle but also ensures a higher standard of scholarly output, fostering interdisciplinary collaboration and innovation. The following will provide more examples of each step and how researchers can leverage these new tools.

2.3 IDEATION AND TOPIC SELECTION

The initial step in the research process is ideation and topic selection, a phase crucial for setting the foundation of any academic endeavor. AI-powered brainstorming tools have revolutionized this step by leveraging vast datasets and advanced algorithms to identify current trends and gaps in existing literature. Researchers begin by inputting their key interests or broad subject areas into these AI tools, which then analyze contemporary publications and suggest under-explored topics. This process ensures that the research topics generated are not only relevant but also timely, aligning with the latest developments and needs in the field. Additionally, these AI tools can help researchers identify and align their topics with upcoming conferences and special issue calls, ensuring their work gains the appropriate platform for dissemination. By streamlining the ideation phase, AI tools enable researchers to focus on innovative and impactful questions, thereby enhancing the overall quality and significance of their research endeavors.

Utilizing an LLM like ChatGPT, Gemini, or Claude can significantly aid in refining an initial query by suggesting focused and timely research topics. If you start with a general interest in "friction coefficients," for instance, you can use the following prompt (in ChatGPT in this case):

You are a professor of mathematics with a decade of research experience. You will help me brainstorm topic ideas for my research. You are researching friction coefficients. You will brainstorm research topics with me. You will generate 3 potential research questions on potential research into friction coefficients. Output the 3 research questions along with a sentence explaining the significance of each.

When utilizing LLMs (as demonstrated here) we should not that a structured approach can significantly enhance the interaction and output quality. Note that in this example, the role to be played was first introduced (Who), then the actions required (What), and finally the output (How) (Table 3). First, clearly define the AI's role in the scenario, which could range from a research advisor to a domain-specific consultant, depending on the user's needs. For instance, if the goal is to generate innovative research topics, the AI might act as a brainstorming partner, suggesting novel ideas based on current trends and existing knowledge gaps. Next, outline specific tasks for the AI, such as generating a list of potential research topics, suggesting relevant literature, or identifying critical gaps. These tasks could include providing explanations of complex concepts, generating research questions, or offering critical feedback on proposed topics. Finally, specify what successful interaction looks like, detailing the kind of information or output expected from the AI. This includes preferences for the format of the AI's responses, such as length, detail, or tone, to ensure that responses are both actionable and clear. By following this methodical approach, users can effectively harness AI capabilities to meet specific research objectives, ensuring relevance and utility in academic and professional settings.

Table 3. A three-step framework for effective prompt engineering

Aspect	Details	Examples
Who: Role of the Roleplayer	Define the AI's character or persona (e.g., tutor, advisor, critic)	As an advisor, the AI helps refine research queries based on current trends.

continued on following page

Table 3. Continued

Aspect	Details	Examples
What: Actions Required	Specify the tasks for the AI under this role	Generating questions, providing explanations, offering feedback on research topics.
How: Output Specifications	Describe the expected outcome of the prompt, including format specifications	Responses should be concise, relevant, and aligned with academic standards; for instance, a list of three refined research topics.

Returning to the response garnered from the request for three potential refined topics. The following is the first response from ChatGPT with each relevant due to specific current scientific, industrial, or technological needs:

1. Friction Coefficients in Automotive Brake Systems:

Relevance: With the automotive industry pushing towards more efficient and safer vehicles, understanding the friction coefficients in brake systems is crucial. Research can focus on optimizing materials for brake pads to enhance performance and safety, particularly under varying environmental conditions.

2. Influence of Surface Treatments on Friction Coefficients in Manufacturing Processes:

Relevance: In manufacturing, the efficiency of machining and forming processes heavily relies on the minimization of friction to reduce wear and energy consumption. Investigating how different surface treatments can alter friction coefficients can lead to more sustainable manufacturing practices and prolong the lifespan of machinery.

3. Nano-scale Friction Coefficients for Biomedical Implants:

Relevance: The interaction between biological tissues and implant materials at the nano-scale is a critical factor in the success of implants. Researching friction coefficients at this scale could improve the design of biomedical implants to ensure better integration and durability, reducing the risk of rejection and increasing the functional lifespan of implants.

With these potential research topics, one is now able to merely ask for more information on one that aligns with existing research interest. For example, we need merely follow this response up with the following prompt: “Tell me more about 3.” The following is generated:

Researching nano-scale friction coefficients for biomedical implants is a highly specialized and crucial area of study within biomedical engineering. The focus here is on understanding how the tiny, molecular interactions between implant materials and biological tissues can affect the overall performance and compatibility of implants.

At the nano-scale, even minor changes in material properties can significantly impact the behavior of implants in the body. For example, the surface texture and chemistry of an implant can influence protein adsorption, which in turn affects cell adhesion and the immune response. By studying the friction coefficients at this level, researchers aim to design implants that are less likely to cause irritation or rejection and have a longer functional lifespan in the human body.

This type of research is critical for improving a wide range of medical devices, from orthopedic implants like hip replacements to cardiovascular devices like stents. Improved understanding of nano-scale interactions can lead to better materials selection and surface engineering, ultimately leading to implants that are more effective and comfortable for patients.

If you're interested in exploring this topic further, academic journals that focus on biomaterials, surface science, and nanotechnology would be valuable resources. These studies are typically detailed and require a solid understanding of both materials science and biological systems.

After gaining a better understanding of current conversations and developments in the field from generative AI tools, one can further refine research by consulting a specialized AI database like PerplexityAI. It is worth noting, that one can start with these databases as well if a topic is already known. For instance, if your topic involves "nano-scale friction coefficients for biomedical implants," one could ask PerplexityAI specific questions to dig deeper into the latest research and findings. You might query, "What are the latest advancements in nano-scale friction coefficients for biomedical implants?" or "What recent studies have been published about the impact of surface treatments on nano-scale friction in biomedical implants?" The response is as follows and note that all sources are cited for review and fact checking:

Recent advancements in nano-scale friction coefficients for biomedical implants have focused on several key areas:

1. Nanostructured surfaces: Modifying implant surfaces at the nanoscale has been shown to significantly affect friction properties. Nanotextured implant surfaces can enhance osseointegration while also reducing friction. Severe plastic deformation techniques have been used to create nanostructured titanium implants with improved biocompatibility and mechanical properties, including lower friction coefficients, (https://www.ncbi.nlm.nih.gov/pmc/articles/PMC9082310/).

2. Novel nanomaterials: Incorporating nanomaterials like carbon nanotubes into implant materials like ultra-high molecular weight polyethylene (UHMWPE) has improved wear resistance and reduced friction in joint replacement implants, (https://www.ncbi.nlm.nih.gov/pmc/articles/PMC9082310/). This addresses concerns about potential fracture of UHMWPE components.
3. 2D materials: Layered two-dimensional materials like graphene and molybdenum disulfide (MoS2) have shown unique friction behaviors at the nanoscale compared to bulk materials. Their incorporation into implant surfaces and coatings can provide ultra-low friction coefficients, (https://www.frontiersin.org/articles/10.3389/fmech.2022.965877/full).
4. Surface treatments: Advanced surface modification techniques like friction stir processing have been used to alter the microstructure and tribological properties of implant materials, resulting in improved friction and wear characteristics, (https://www.sciencedirect.com/science/article/pii/S2238785422000503).
5. Biomolecular interfaces: Studies on the adhesion, friction, and wear properties of biomolecules (like proteins) on implant surfaces have provided insights into designing functional biointerfaces with optimized friction properties. This is particularly relevant for biosensors and bioelectronics integrated with implants, (https://www.ncbi.nlm.nih.gov/pmc/articles/PMC2839939/).
6. Environmental effects: Research has examined how factors like humidity and the presence of biological fluids affect nanoscale friction of implant materials. Understanding these environmental influences is crucial for predicting in vivo performance, (https://www.frontiersin.org/articles/10.3389/fmech.2022.965877/full).
7. Load-dependent friction: Advanced studies have revealed complex load-dependent friction behaviors at the nanoscale that deviate from classical friction laws. This improved understanding allows for more accurate prediction and control of implant friction properties, (https://www.frontiersin.org/articles/10.3389/fmech.2022.965877/full).
8. Composite materials: Development of nanocomposite implant materials that combine the beneficial properties of multiple components to achieve desired friction and wear characteristics tailored for specific biomedical applications, (https://ris.utwente.nl/ws/portalfiles/portal/320756345/Friction_of_Biomechanical_Interfaces.pdf)

These advancements are contributing to the development of biomedical implants with improved tribological properties, potentially leading to longer implant lifetimes, reduced wear, and better overall performance in the human body. However, further research is still needed to fully translate these nano-scale insights into clinical applications.

By directing such precise inquiries to PerplexityAI, one can access curated academic content and studies, ensuring you have the most recent and relevant information. This approach helps you stay at the forefront of your research area, providing a solid foundation for your study design and hypothesis formulation. As with before, the database can be prompted to refine a search thereafter. For example, one could then follow with: "Tell me more about 1." PerplexityAI then responds:

Certainly! Let's delve deeper into the advancements in nanostructured surfaces for biomedical implants:

Nanostructured Surfaces for Biomedical Implants

Nanostructured surfaces have emerged as a promising approach to enhance the performance of biomedical implants, particularly in terms of friction reduction and improved biocompatibility. Here are some key aspects of this technology:

Fabrication Techniques

Severe Plastic Deformation (SPD): This technique involves applying intense mechanical stress to materials, resulting in ultra-fine grain structures. For titanium implants, methods like Equal Channel Angular Pressing (ECAP) and High-Pressure Torsion (HPT) have been used to create nanostructured surfaces.

Laser Surface Texturing: Femtosecond laser treatments can create precise nanoscale patterns on implant surfaces, altering their tribological properties.

Electrochemical Anodization: This process can create highly ordered nanotubular structures on titanium surfaces, which can be tailored for specific friction and wear characteristics.

Benefits of Nanostructured Surfaces

Reduced Friction: Nanostructured surfaces can significantly lower the coefficient of friction, potentially reducing wear and extending implant lifespan.

Enhanced Osseointegration: The nanoscale topography can mimic natural bone structures, promoting better cell adhesion and bone growth.

Improved Corrosion Resistance: Nanostructuring can enhance the corrosion resistance of implant materials, crucial for long-term stability in the body.

Recent Research Findings

A 2023 study published in the Journal of the Mechanical Behavior of Biomedical Materials demonstrated that nanostructured titanium created by SPD techniques showed a 30% reduction in friction coefficient compared to conventional titanium implants.

Researchers at MIT have developed a method to create nanoscale pillars on implant surfaces that can reduce friction by up to 40% while also enhancing cell adhesion.

A team from the University of Southampton has used electrochemical anodization to create TiO2 nanotubes on titanium surfaces, resulting in a significant reduction in bacterial adhesion and improved osteoblast response.

Challenges and Future Directions

Scalability: Translating these nanoscale modifications to large-scale manufacturing processes remains a challenge.

Long-term Stability: Ensuring that nanostructured surfaces maintain their properties over the lifetime of the implant is crucial.

Biological Response: While initial results are promising, more research is needed to fully understand the long-term biological response to these nanostructured surfaces.

Combination Approaches: Future research is likely to focus on combining nanostructuring with other surface modification techniques or bioactive coatings for synergistic effects.

These advancements in nanostructured surfaces represent a significant step forward in implant technology, potentially leading to more durable, biocompatible, and functional biomedical implants. However, further research and clinical trials are necessary to fully realize the potential of these innovations.

With our research continuing to narrow, we are able to further refine our next steps in research and ask questions such as:

- *Now summarize a recent academic article on the subject*
- *Now write a sample introduction for a research paper on the topic*
- *Now create an outline on the topic*
- *Now create a detailed research methodology for a study on the topic*

These queries are instrumental in developing a robust body of work, whether for a paper, dissertation, or broader research project. By formulating a well-defined introduction or abstract alongside a structured outline and a detailed research methodology, researchers can effectively position their work within the academic community. This strategic alignment not only facilitates the identification of relevant conferences and special issues in journals but also enhances the chances of the research being recognized and accepted by peers. Consequently, researchers are better equipped to contribute meaningful insights to their fields, fostering academic discourse and advancing collective knowledge in their respective disciplines.

Having explored the innovative ways AI can be harnessed to brainstorm and select research topics, it is essential to extend this discussion to a broader reevaluation of the research process itself. The transformative potential of AI not only revolutionizes the initial stages of ideation but also necessitates a fundamental shift in how we conceptualize and conduct research in academia. This shift calls for a thorough refocusing of research practices to fully leverage AI's capabilities, ensuring that these advanced tools are integrated into every facet of academic inquiry.

2.4 REFOCUSING RESEARCH IN THE AGE OF AI

As we move forward, it becomes clear that embracing AI in research extends beyond mere topic selection; it demands a rethinking of research methodologies, frameworks, and the overall culture within academic institutions. AI offers unprecedented opportunities to enhance the rigor, efficiency, and impact of research, but realizing these benefits requires a proactive and adaptive approach. This involves fostering a research culture that is open to technological advancements and promotes collaboration between human researchers and AI systems. In the next section, we will consider how refocusing research practices in the age of AI can elevate academic inquiry. We will examine the necessity of promoting a research culture that embraces AI and the strategies for integrating these generative tools into the core of academic research. By doing so, we aim to highlight the imperative of adapting to the evolving landscape of research, where AI plays a pivotal role in driving innovation and excellence.

"Research" is often narrowly considered the domain of those in R1 institutions—research-intensive universities—but, in fact, all higher education professionals, including graduate students, engage in it, though the topic and approach vary. Traditionally recognized fields of research include the natural sciences, social sciences, humanities, and engineering. However, those engaged in teaching, whether knowingly or not, conduct pedagogical research in every class they teach. They assess what methods work and what do not when introducing topics, design materials, and develop assessment strategies to gauge student learning and engagement (Brew, 2008). This continual cycle of experimentation and refinement embodies the essence of pedagogical research.

At the same time, the perception that proficient researchers automatically excel in teaching is often disputed in the realm of higher education (Terenzini & Pascarella, 1998; Biggs, Tang, & Kennedy 2022). Nevertheless, extensive research underscores the influential role of research in enhancing pedagogy (Centra, 1983; Brew & Boud, 1995; Coate et al., 2001; Prince et al., 2007). Educational institutions that strive to foster a research-oriented culture are ideally positioned to leverage their robust pedagogical heritage to generate impactful and practical research for their student cohorts (Norton-Meier et al., 2009). Incorporating a research-focused approach into teaching benefits students by exposing them to innovative methodologies within their respective fields and actively engaging them as contributors and collaborators in the research process. This involvement not only enriches their resumes and curriculum vitae with valuable project experience and publications (Väljataga et al., 2015) but also enhances their learning experience.

Studies indicate that student engagement and overall educational experiences improve when learners actively participate in their own educational journey (Werth & Williams, 2021). The integration of research into teaching practices thus plays a significant role in professional development for educators, enriching the student learning experience, and advancing the knowledge frontier in various academic disciplines. This composite approach highlights the critical importance of research in higher education, benefiting both educators and students while contributing to the academic community's overall growth.

However, as the Carnegie Classification of Institutions of Higher Education reveals, a vast minority of postsecondary educators would consider themselves "researchers." The classification provides a detailed framework for categorizing U.S. higher education institutions, reflecting the diversity and scope of their educational and research missions. According to the latest data, Doctoral Universities, which include R1 (Very high research activity) and R2 (High research activity) institutions, constitute about 8% of all classified institutions, with R1 and R2 each representing approximately 4%. Master's Colleges and Universities account for about 16%, emphasizing their role in offering substantial graduate education without extensive doctoral programs. Baccalaureate Colleges, which focus primarily on undergraduate education, also make up around 16% of the total. Associate's Colleges, commonly known as community colleges, represent the largest group, comprising about 40% of all institutions, highlighting their critical role in providing accessible education to diverse student populations. Special Focus Institutions, which include specialized fields such as medical and law schools, account for approximately 15%, while Tribal Colleges and Universities form a smaller but significant fraction, dedicated to serving Native American communities and preserving cultural heritage (Carnegie, 2024). Therefore, the focus of most academics is on improving their teaching portfolio and practice instead of research, specifically. But academic identity is not the only factor preventing more active research agendas nationally.

When contemplating the obstacles to instilling a research-centric culture in predominantly teaching institutions (which are the majority), several factors must be accounted for. These challenges can be broadly categorized into cultural, financial, pedagogical, and administrative areas. Firstly, fostering a culture that values research and academic inquiry is essential. This cultural shift requires a sustained effort to emphasize the importance of research alongside teaching, often requiring a reorientation of institutional priorities and values (Brew, 2008). Financial mechanisms to support research initiatives are also crucial. In research institutions, sources of grant-funded support (both internal and external) are built into academic contracts, as is time off with sabbaticals for conducting research. On the other hand, many teaching-focused institutions struggle with limited budgets that prioritize instructional costs over research funding. Securing grants and other financial resources for research can be challenging, often requiring significant institutional commitment and external support (McClure & Jaeger, 2009).

Balancing teaching and research responsibilities presents a significant pedagogical challenge. Faculty at institutions with a primary emphasis on teaching often have a heavy teaching load, such as a 4-4 load—four courses per semester and a total of eight in an academic year. Such demanding teaching commitments severely limit the time and energy faculty can dedicate to research activities (Shavit, 2007). Additionally, the absence of graduate teaching assistants to help with grading and lecture preparation exacerbates this issue, leaving faculty with little opportunity to engage in meaningful research (Prince et al., 2007). Whereas administrative support is another critical factor. Effective integration of research into pedagogy requires strong endorsement and facilitation from the administration, which includes providing adequate resources, creating research incentives, and recognizing research efforts in promotion and tenure decisions. Without such support, faculty may find it difficult to balance their dual roles as educators and researchers effectively (Coate et al., 2001).

Not surprisingly, the culture at teaching institutions highly values the art of teaching, and faculty members often view themselves primarily as educators rather than researchers (Sato & Loewen, 2019). For a substantial cultural shift towards research to occur, faculty members must be willing and capable of undertaking research initiatives. However, this identity transformation cannot be solely imposed from the top-down or administratively driven (Omar et al., 2021). The realization of faculty members' own research potential is more effectively fostered through peer and colleague interactions that elevate their appreciation of their potential contributions to academic inquiry and scholarship (Meilani et al., 2021). New AI tools can assist in this transformation by providing resources and support that streamline the research process. AI can help faculty identify relevant literature, analyze data, and even generate hypotheses, thereby reducing the time and effort required to engage in research activities. This technological assistance can make research more accessible and less daunting for educators primarily focused on teaching, facilitating a more seamless integration of research into their professional identities and daily practices.

Proactive attitudes toward identifying as researchers are certainly key, yet attitude represents only a part of the puzzle when it comes to successfully shifting an institutional culture. Historically, it has also been essential for the institution to have the necessary financial and administrative structures in place. Many teaching-focused institutions might lack a grant office capable of managing large external research grants. Facility constraints can also be a hindrance, as fields like health and physical sciences often require substantial external funding to support the infrastructure necessary for scalable research (Sohrabi et al., 2021). Developing these capabilities at the institutional level is a time-intensive process (McNair et al., 2022). Moreover, to bring about a cultural shift, there must be consistent administrative support that permeates every level of the institution. Research support needs to be woven into the institutional fabric, involving administrative personnel, staff, maintenance and operations teams, and fiscal affairs (Jamali et al., 2022). This integration is increasingly important with the rise of generative AI and shifting attitudes toward its use.

Institutions face the challenge of building consensus and momentum toward a research culture while addressing these outlined challenges. Establishing the financial infrastructure for scalable research and grants is time-consuming and costly. Offering faculty extra time or incentives to conduct research is challenging amidst shrinking budgets and declining college enrollments. Garnering administrative support is daunting considering numerous competing agendas (Jayman et al., 2022). However, new AI tools can help mitigate some of these challenges by streamlining grant applications, providing data analysis support, and even facilitating collaboration through AI-driven networking tools, thus enabling a more efficient and supportive research environment.

Post-pandemic, smaller tuition-dependent institutions have been closing at an alarming rate, necessitating the redirection of resources toward recruitment and retention efforts to mitigate financial losses (McKeown et al., 2022). The ability to divert scarce resources—whether human or financial—towards initiatives that might not yield immediate returns seems unfeasible. However, amid the existential crisis facing higher education, with questions about its value and purpose dominating headlines and capturing the attention of university leaders, reinvigorating students and faculty on their educational journey should be a top priority. This need is especially pressing in light of the impending demographic decline expected for traditional-age college students by 2025 (Zhang et al., 2022).

Despite these challenges, new solutions are emerging that are not as cost-prohibitive. One increasingly popular approach is to share the time and expense of research across departments and units. By pooling resources and collaborating on research initiatives, institutions can foster a research culture without overwhelming any single department's budget or workload (Kulage et al., 2011). This collaborative model not only maximizes the use of available resources but also encourages inter-disciplinary research and innovation, thereby enriching the academic environment and enhancing the overall research capabilities of an institution.

As such, while accelerating research can present novel solutions, there are significant limitations when insights are confined within a single discipline, highlighting the need for a fresh strategy. The proposed collaborative model, though not a panacea, offers a way to address many of the pressing issues that higher education confronts today, including student and faculty engagement, resource constraints, community involvement, and academic compartmentalization. Traditionally, implementing interdepartmental and interdisciplinary research models has been challenging due to the lack of incentives for faculty researchers. The adage "ideas are academic currency" resonates across diverse academic fields, reinforced by administrative evaluation metrics and promotion standards. With innovative contributions to a specific field being highly esteemed, scholars often protectively keep their research plans and materials close to the vest. When collaboration does occur, authorship roles and contributions are carefully specified, often adhering to criteria established by discipline-specific entities (Tavares et al., 2022).

This setup hinders the rapid cross-disciplinary sharing of essential information and isolates researchers, denying them the potential benefits of insights from colleagues within their own institutions. However, collaboration is becoming increasingly feasible with AI team workspaces across platforms like ChatGPT, which facilitate seamless communication and joint efforts. These AI-powered workspaces can break down traditional barriers, enabling researchers to share insights and co-develop solutions in real-time, regardless of their disciplinary backgrounds. By leveraging such technology, institutions can foster a more integrated and dynamic research environment, ultimately enhancing the scope and impact of their scholarly endeavors.

However, past attempts at addressing entrenched obstacles and generating innovative research aimed at tackling "wicked problems" have been continually stifled due to human factors and limitations (Mokiy & Lukyanova, 2022; Sadiq & Daud, 2009). To overcome these challenges, faculty and administrators need to look beyond traditional research models and integrate new strategies. The approach afforded by new tools places a strong emphasis on collaboration, not just among human researchers, academics, staff, students, and community stakeholders, but also with GAI agents. This paradigm, already common in human subject research and studies involving emerging technologies, necessitates a reevaluation of the concept of “authorship” as traditionally defined and recognized within higher education institutions (Khezr & Mohan, 2022).

By upending the standard research model, this study proposes that teaching institutions shift their focus towards harnessing field-specific capabilities to address real-world problems. This can initially be achieved through discipline-specific pedagogical research, teaching initiatives that spur research, research that directly informs teaching, and inquiry-based learning. To support researchers in these endeavors and scale these efforts, AI agents can significantly contribute by offering unique perspectives and computational power to accelerate the research process. Once the collaborative research model is established, it can organically broaden and develop, further enhanced by the contributions of AI agents. This integration of human and AI collaboration not only fosters innovation but also expands the potential for interdisciplinary research, thereby enriching the academic environment and addressing complex global challenges more effectively.

Since November 2022, GAI and LLMs have undergone significant evolution, unveiling unprecedented opportunities and igniting thought-provoking discussions about AI's future trajectory (Garon, 2023). Models such as OpenAI's ChatGPT 3.5 and 4 have demonstrated extraordinary proficiency in generating text that closely mirrors human expression and engaging in complex dialogue interactions (Gill & Kaur, 2023). These advancements have been characterized as progressing from the intelligence of a toddler (3.5) to that of a high school student (4), with the potential for PhD-level intelligence on the horizon (5). As we advance in this field, the applications of these models are being explored across diverse sectors, including education, healthcare, and assisted living, paralleling a broader inflection point in academic research (Albahri et al., 2023; Lee, 2023; Liu et al., 2023; Shahriar & Hayawi, 2023).

In this evolving landscape, the study and imitation of human emotions within AI systems have emerged as compelling research frontiers (Latif et al., 2023). Although machine intelligence and human emotions are fundamentally distinct, the training capabilities of LLMs have shown potential in simulating and adopting various “personalities,” with the next frontier being the exploration of artificial emotional dimensions (Garon, 2023). This progression paves the way for emotionally adept AI systems that can understand and generate appropriate emotional responses, enhancing user experiences and fostering more significant interactions (Ray, 2023). As AI continues to evolve, its integration into various fields promises to revolutionize the way we approach complex problems and improve human-AI collaboration.

The landscape of research has seen a significant shift with the rise of AI learning and LLMs. These technological advancements have reshaped the research field, presenting previously unimaginable possibilities for innovation and complex problem-solving. A recent study highlighted the potential of autonomous agents to mimic human behavior, equipped with personal motivations and preferences (Park et al., 2023). Building on this premise, the following considers a novel strategy that harnesses a group of independent AI agents, each trained with a simulated persona possessing specialized expertise in unique research fields. By emulating the human ability to incorporate diverse perspectives and expertise into team efforts, these agents can collaboratively address intricate problems in new ways, paving the path for significant discoveries and progress in research.

2.5 PROMOTING RESEARCH CULTURE

Before addressing the integration of AI agents in research, it is essential to discuss foundational strategies to promote a research culture within institutions. Research on the effectiveness of various strategies to foster a research culture in comprehensive or teaching-oriented institutions in the United States is limited. However, the existing studies resonate with tactics identified internationally. For instance, in an examination of the research activities of nursing educators, Hill, Lomas, and MacGregor (2003) found that faculty identified themselves within one of four distinct roles: administrators, researchers, educators, and enthusiasts. Despite their differing roles, all recognized the importance of evidence-based practice, and each role was pivotal in fostering a research culture at their institution.

Educators play a crucial role in shaping curriculum delivery, ensuring that teaching methods are grounded in the latest research findings. Researchers are celebrated for their contributions to the advancement of their field, driving innovation and scholarly discourse. Enthusiasts, who may not be primary researchers, support and encourage research initiatives through advocacy and engagement. However, the administrative and operational responsibilities borne by these individuals often impede their ability to engage in research activities.

Institutional leaders must reassess the assignment and daily tasks of faculty members to create more opportunities for research engagement. This might involve reducing teaching loads, providing administrative support, and offering incentives for research activities. Encouraging collaborative projects and interdisciplinary research can also help integrate research into institutional culture. For example, establishing research clusters or centers that bring together faculty from different disciplines can promote a more dynamic and supportive research environment (Brew, 2008; McClure & Jaeger, 2009).

Similarly, the School of Education at the University of South Dakota conducted a study aimed at enhancing the scholarly production of its faculty members (Santo et al., 2009). This study involved a needs assessment for tenure-track faculty to identify factors influencing productivity, such as environmental dynamics, leadership styles, and individual influences. The findings highlighted the necessity of shifting the institution's culture from a teaching-centric approach to one that promotes research and scholarship. To achieve this transformation, the study recommended the implementation of mentorship programs where department heads, rather than senior faculty members, act as mentors (Moody, 2013). This change in mentoring practices was driven by the observation that younger faculty members were more active and productive than their senior counterparts. Consequently, early career scholars should be encouraged to engage in research activities from their first year, rather than delaying the formulation of a research agenda. Additionally, the study suggested providing travel funds for junior faculty to attend national and international conferences. Such exposure can foster networking opportunities, leading to joint research projects, publication opportunities, and grant writing.

Faculty members should be encouraged to allocate weekly time slots specifically for research and display these schedules in their offices. Department meetings and classes could be planned around these research slots. Expanding on the peer-mentoring model, the establishment of writing groups could facilitate peer review of each other's work, enhancing research and writing skills while fostering interdisciplinary connections (Jacelon et al., 2003). Further resources, such as institutional repositories and information websites, can be developed to make faculty aware of existing supports for their research (Foster & Gibbons, 2005). Recognizing and celebrating faculty scholarships at department, school, and college-level meetings can also be motivating (Buffinton et al., 2021). Implementing a reward system for consistent engagement in research could further incentivize and recognize faculty's scholarly pursuits.

Contemporary research builds on these earlier studies, providing valuable insights for promoting a research culture in teaching-oriented institutions. For instance, Al-Kurdi et al. (2020) identify several strategies that can be adopted, such as providing resources and support to help faculty conduct research and find suitable outlets for publishing their findings. Administrative incentives, such as funding for research projects, reducing teaching loads, and providing access to specialized equipment or research facilities, are also crucial. Additional incentives for faculty engagement in research could include promotions, salary increments, and recognition through grants and awards (Koch et al., 2015). Effectively communicating the importance and impact of research on the institution's mission and highlighting the critical role faculty play in this context, can also drive engagement and foster a vibrant research culture.

However, the current system for promotion and tenure often undervalues certain types of scholarship. A study by Maxwell and Ball (2010) at the University of Florida revealed that less than a third of the faculty believed active engagement in research would positively influence their promotion prospects. Essentially, faculty members value what they perceive is valued by the administration and rewarded accordingly. Implementing strategies that highlight the importance of research can assist faculty and students in recognizing its value, emphasizing the societal impact of studies, and demonstrating how research can lead to new discoveries and innovations. This understanding can foster a more supportive and constructive environment for research within the institution.

Administrative support plays a pivotal role, but fostering a research culture also involves integrating research into the curriculum and engaging students in the process. Matos et al. (2023) suggest that institutions stimulate student involvement in research initiatives, whether as part of their coursework or as extracurricular activities. This approach nurtures problem-solving and critical thinking skills among students while allowing them to contribute to their fields' knowledge base. Such cooperative learning can transcend departmental and institutional boundaries.

Promoting collaborations and partnerships is another effective strategy for shifting towards a research-centric culture. Trott et al. (2020) emphasize the significant impact of collaborations between faculty and researchers from other institutions or partnerships with industry and government entities. This strategy, which echoes earlier research by Finnegan and Gamson (1996), can establish a supportive network for research, facilitating the flow of ideas and resources across departments that might otherwise remain isolated. Additionally, the strategies presented in this book can be utilized by individuals to enhance their research capabilities, regardless of the level of institutional support. By developing skills in areas such as leveraging generative databases, utilizing large language models for complex queries, and applying natural language processing techniques, researchers can independently drive their projects forward. These tools and techniques enable scholars to effectively explore topics, refine research questions, and integrate diverse data sources, thereby fostering a self-sustaining and proactive research culture.

Implementing these recommendations requires both time and resources, and institutions often face constraints in these areas. Therefore, developing alternative strategies, such as leveraging AI tools and collaborative platforms, becomes increasingly important. These innovations can support and enhance research efforts, creating a more inclusive and dynamic research culture even within resource-limited settings. Thus, promoting a research culture in teaching-oriented institutions necessitates a multifaceted approach that includes administrative support, curriculum integration, student engagement, and inter-institutional collaborations. By valuing and rewarding diverse types of scholarship, institutions can create an environment that fosters innovation and advances knowledge, ultimately benefiting the broader academic community and society.

REFERENCES

Abdelrazek, A., Eid, Y., Gawish, E., Medhat, W., & Hassan, A. (2023). Topic modeling algorithms and applications: A survey. *Information Systems*, 112, 102131. DOI: 10.1016/j.is.2022.102131

Abulibdeh, A., Zaidan, E., & Abulibdeh, R. (2024). Navigating the confluence of artificial intelligence and education for sustainable development in the era of industry 4.0: Challenges, opportunities, and ethical dimensions. *Journal of Cleaner Production*, 437, 140527. DOI: 10.1016/j.jclepro.2023.140527

Ade-Ojo, G. O., Markowski, M., Essex, R., Stiell, M., & Jameson, J. (2022). A systematic scoping review and textual narrative synthesis of physical and mixed-reality simulation in pre-service teacher training. *Journal of Computer Assisted Learning*, 38(3), 861–874. DOI: 10.1111/jcal.12653

Al-Kurdi, O. F., El-Haddadeh, R., & Eldabi, T. (2020). The Role of Organisational Climate in Managing Knowledge Sharing Among Academics in Higher Education. *International Journal of Information Management*, 50, 217–227. DOI: 10.1016/j.ijinfomgt.2019.05.018

Albahri, A. S., Duhaim, A. M., Fadhel, M. A., Alnoor, A., Baqer, N. S., Alzubaidi, L., & Deveci, M. (2023). A Systematic Review of Trustworthy and Explainable Artificial Intelligence in Healthcare: Assessment of Quality, Bias Risk, and Data Fusion. *Information Fusion*, 96, 156–191. DOI: 10.1016/j.inffus.2023.03.008

Alhumaid, K., Naqbi, S., Elsori, D., & Mansoori, M. (2023). The adoption of artificial intelligence applications in education. *International Journal of Data and Network Science*, 7(1), 457–466. DOI: 10.5267/j.ijdns.2022.8.013

Aliotta, M. (2018). *Mastering academic writing in the sciences: A step-by-step guide*. CRC Press. DOI: 10.1201/9781351002141

Alwahedi, F., Aldhaheri, A., Ferrag, M. A., Battah, A., & Tihanyi, N. (2024). Machine learning techniques for IoT security: Current research and future vision with generative AI and large language models. *Internet of Things and Cyber-Physical Systems*.

Alzubaidi, L., Bai, J., Al-Sabaawi, A., Santamaría, J., Albahri, A. S., Al-dabbagh, B. S. N., Fadhel, M. A., Manoufali, M., Zhang, J., Al-Timemy, A. H., Duan, Y., Abdullah, A., Farhan, L., Lu, Y., Gupta, A., Albu, F., Abbosh, A., & Gu, Y. (2023). A survey on deep learning tools dealing with data scarcity: Definitions, challenges, solutions, tips, and applications. *Journal of Big Data*, 10(1), 46. DOI: 10.1186/s40537-023-00727-2

Bailey, S. (2003). *Academic writing: A practical guide for students*. Psychology Press. DOI: 10.4324/9780203464120

Biggs, J., Tang, C., & Kennedy, G. (2022). Ebook: Teaching for Quality Learning at University 5e. *McGraw-Hill education* (UK).

Brew, A. (2008). Disciplinary and interdisciplinary affiliations of experienced researchers. *Higher Education*, 56(4), 423–438. DOI: 10.1007/s10734-007-9102-4

Brew, A., & Boud, D. (1995). Teaching and Research: Establishing the Vital Link with Learning. *Higher Education*, 29(3), 261–273. DOI: 10.1007/BF01384493

Buffington, A., Lange, C., Bakker, C., Nanney, M., Roberts, W., Berge, J., & Loth, K. (2021). The Collaborative Scholarship Intensive: A Research-Intensive Course to Improve Faculty Scholarship. *Family Medicine*, 53(5), 355–358. DOI: 10.22454/FamMed.2021.534614

Ćalušić, M. (2021). *Artificial intelligence and language acquisition* [Master's thesis, University of Split]. Digitalni Akademski Arhivi i Repozitoriji.

Carnegie Classification of Institutions of Higher Education. (2024). Carnegie Foundation Selects Colleges and Universities for 2024 Community Engagement Classification. January 8, 2024. https://carnegieclassifications.acenet.edu/news/carnegie-2024-community-engagement-classifications/

Centra, J. A. (1983). Research Productivity and Teaching Effectiveness. *Research in Higher Education*, 18(4), 379–389. DOI: 10.1007/BF00974804

Chakraborty, T., Reddy K S, U., Naik, S. M., Panja, M., & Manvitha, B. (2024). Ten years of generative adversarial nets (GANs): A survey of the state-of-the-art. *Machine Learning: Science and Technology*, 5(1), 011001. DOI: 10.1088/2632-2153/ad1f77

Chapinal-Heras, D., & Díaz-Sánchez, C. (2023). A Review of AI applications in Human Sciences research. *Digital Applications in Archaeology and Cultural Heritage*, 30, 00288. DOI: 10.1016/j.daach.2023.e00288

Coate, K., Barnett, R., & Williams, G. (2001). Relationships Between Teaching and Research in Higher Education in England. *Higher Education Quarterly*, 55(2), 158–174. DOI: 10.1111/1468-2273.00180

English, L. D., & Gainsburg, J. (2015). Problem solving in a 21st-century mathematics curriculum. In *Handbook of international research in mathematics education* (pp. 313–335). Routledge. DOI: 10.4324/9780203448946-20

Esplugas, M. (2023). The use of artificial intelligence (AI) to enhance academic communication, education and research: A balanced approach. [European Volume]. *The Journal of Hand Surgery*, 48(8), 819–822.

Feuerriegel, S., Hartmann, J., Janiesch, C., & Zschech, P. (2024). Generative ai. *Business & Information Systems Engineering*, 66(1), 111–126. DOI: 10.1007/s12599-023-00834-7

Filgueiras, F. (2023). Artificial intelligence and education governance. *Education, Citizenship and Social Justice*, •••, 17461979231160674.

Finnegan, D. E., & Gamson, Z. F. (1996). Disciplinary Adaptations to Research Culture in Comprehensive Institutions. *Review of Higher Education*, 19(2), 141–177. DOI: 10.1353/rhe.1996.0028

Foster, N. F., & Gibbons, S. (2005). Understanding Faculty to Improve Content Recruitment for Institutional Repositories. *Online Submission*, 11(1).

Fraser, D. W., Marder, T. J., deBettencourt, L. U., Myers, L. A., Kalymon, K. M., & Harrell, R. M. (2020). Using a mixed-reality environment to train special educators working with students with autism spectrum disorder to implement discrete trial teaching. *Focus on Autism and Other Developmental Disabilities*, 35(1), 3–14. DOI: 10.1177/1088357619844696

Fui-Hoon Nah, F., Zheng, R., Cai, J., Siau, K., & Chen, L. (2023). Generative AI and ChatGPT: Applications, challenges, and AI-human collaboration. *Journal of Information Technology Case and Application Research*, 25(3), 277–304. DOI: 10.1080/15228053.2023.2233814

Gabriele, L., Marocco, D., Bertacchini, F., Pantano, P., & Bilotta, E. (2017). An educational robotics lab to investigate cognitive strategies and to foster learning in an arts and humanities course degree. *International Journal of Online Engineering*, 13(4), 7–19. DOI: 10.3991/ijoe.v13i04.6962

Gamoran, A. (2023). Advancing institutional change to encourage faculty participation in research-practice partnerships. *Educational Policy*, 37(1), 31–55. DOI: 10.1177/08959048221131564

Garon, J. (2023). A Practical Introduction to Generative AI, Synthetic Media, and the Messages Found in the Latest Medium. *Synthetic Media, and the Messages Found in the Latest Medium* (March 14, 2023).

Gill, S. S., & Kaur, R. (2023). ChatGPT: Vision and challenges. *Internet of Things and Cyber-Physical Systems*, 3, 262–271. DOI: 10.1016/j.iotcps.2023.05.004

Gong, X., Wu, Y., Ye, Z., & Liu, X. (2018). Artificial intelligence course design: iSTREAM-based visual cognitive smart vehicles. In *2018 IEEE Intelligent Vehicles Symposium (IV)* (pp. 1731-1735). IEEE. DOI: 10.1109/IVS.2018.8500457

Goodfellow, I., Pouget-Abadie, J., Mirza, M., Xu, B., Warde-Farley, D., Ozair, S., & Bengio, Y. (2014). Generative adversarial nets. *Advances in Neural Information Processing Systems*, 27.

Hartley, J. (2008). *Academic writing and publishing: A practical handbook*. Routledge. DOI: 10.4324/9780203927984

Heston, T. F., & Khun, C. (2023). Prompt engineering in medical education. *International Medical Education*, 2(3), 198–205. DOI: 10.3390/ime2030019

Hill, Y., Lomas, L., & MacGregor, J. (2003). Students' Perceptions of Quality in Higher Education. *Quality Assurance in Education*, 11(1), 15–20. DOI: 10.1108/09684880310462047

Hutson, J., Jeevanjee, T., Vander Graaf, V., Lively, J., Weber, J., Weir, G., & Edele, S. (2022). Artificial Intelligence and the Disruption of Higher Education: Strategies for Integrations across Disciplines. *Creative Education*, 13(12), 3953–3980. DOI: 10.4236/ce.2022.1312253

Hutson, J., & Rains, T. (2024). *AI Institutional Adoption Study* [Data set]. Lindenwood University.

Jacelon, C. S., Zucker, D. M., Staccarini, J. M., & Henneman, E. A. (2003). Peer Mentoring for Tenure-Track Faculty. *Journal of Professional Nursing*, 19(6), 335–338. DOI: 10.1016/S8755-7223(03)00131-5

Jamali, A., Bhutto, A., Khaskhely, M., & Sethar, W. (2022). Impact of Leadership Styles on Faculty Performance: Moderating Role of Organizational Culture in Higher Education. *Management Science Letters*, 12(1), 1–20. DOI: 10.5267/j.msl.2021.8.005

Jayman, M., Glazzard, J., & Rose, A. (2022, August). Tipping Point: The Staff Wellbeing Crisis in Higher Education. [). Frontiers.]. *Frontiers in Education*, 7, 929335. DOI: 10.3389/feduc.2022.929335

Khezr, P., & Mohan, V. (2022). The Vexing but Persistent Problem of Authorship Misconduct in Research. *Research Policy*, 51(3), 104466. DOI: 10.1016/j.respol.2021.104466

Koch, A., Nafziger, J., & Nielsen, H. S. (2015). Behavioral Economics of Education. *Journal of Economic Behavior & Organization*, 115, 3–17. DOI: 10.1016/j.jebo.2014.09.005

Kulage, K. M., Larson, E. L., & Begg, M. D. (2011). Sharing Facilities and Administrative (F&A) Cost Recovery to Facilitate Interdisciplinary Research. *Academic Medicine*, 86(3), 394–401. DOI: 10.1097/ACM.0b013e31820924ea

Latif, E., Mai, G., Nyaaba, M., Wu, X., Liu, N., Lu, G., . . . Zhai, X. (2023). Artificial General Intelligence (AGI) for Education. *arXiv preprint arXiv:2304.12479.*

Lee, H. (2023). The Rise of ChatGPT: Exploring Its Potential in Medical Education. *Anatomical Sciences Education.*

Liu, Y., Han, T., Ma, S., Zhang, J., Yang, Y., Tian, J., . . . Ge, B. (2023). Summary of ChatGPT/GPT-4 Research and Perspective Towards the Future of Large Language Models. *arXiv preprint arXiv:2304.01852.*

Matos, J. F., Piedade, J., Freitas, A., Pedro, N., Dorotea, N., Pedro, A., & Galego, C. (2023). Teaching and Learning Research Methodologies in Education: A Systematic Literature Review. *Education Sciences*, 13(2), 173. DOI: 10.3390/educsci13020173

Maxwell, L. D., & Ball, A. L. (2010). What is Scholarship? Faculty Knowledge and Perceptions of the Scholarship of Teaching and Learning. *Journal of Agricultural Education*, 51(2), 127–138. DOI: 10.5032/jae.2010.02127

McClure, C. R., & Jaeger, P. T. (2009). *Public libraries and Internet service roles: Measuring and maximizing Internet services*. American Library Association.

McKeown, J. S., Bista, K., & Chan, R. Y. (2022). *Global Higher Education During COVID-19: Policy, Society, and Technology*. STAR Scholars.

McNair, T. B., Albertine, S., McDonald, N., Major, T.Jr, & Cooper, M. A. (2022). *Becoming a Student-Ready College: A New Culture of Leadership for Student Success*. John Wiley & Sons.

Meilani, Y. F. C. P., Tan, J. D., Murwani, F. D., Bernarto, I., & Sudibjo, N. (2021). Motivating and Retaining Generation Z Faculty Members in Private Universities. *Journal of Educational and Social Research*, 11(1), 245–255. DOI: 10.36941/jesr-2021-0022

Mokiy, V., & Lukyanova, T. (2022). Development of Interdisciplinarity and Transdisciplinarity in Modern Russian Science and Higher Education. In *Institutionalizing Interdisciplinarity and Transdisciplinarity* (pp. 124–138). Routledge. DOI: 10.4324/9781003129424-11

Moody, J. (2013). *Faculty Diversity: Removing the Barriers*. Routledge. DOI: 10.4324/9780203805398

Morris, E., & Hutson, J. (2024). *Teacher Appreciation Day Study* [Data set]. Lindenwood University.

Moses, I. (1990). Teaching, research and scholarship in different disciplines. *Higher Education*, 19(3), 351–375. DOI: 10.1007/BF00133898

Norton-Meier, L., Hand, B., Cavagnetto, A., Akkus, R., & Gunel, M. (2009). Pedagogy, Implementation, and Professional Development for Teaching Science Literacy: How Students and Teachers Know and Learn. *Quality Research in Literacy and Science Education: International Perspectives and Gold Standards*, 169-187.

Omar, M. S., Idrus, I. M., & Jamal, N. A. (2021). The Influence of Job Motivation on Job Satisfaction: A Case Study of Polytechnic Academic Staff. *Malaysian Journal of Social Sciences and Humanities*, 6(1), 206–213. DOI: 10.47405/mjssh.v6i1.624

Park, J. S., O'Brien, J. C., Cai, C. J., Morris, M. R., Liang, P., & Bernstein, M. S. (2023). Generative agents: Interactive simulacra of human behavior. *arXiv preprint arXiv:2304.03442* DOI: 10.1145/3586183.3606763

Pinzolits, R. (2024). AI in academia: An overview of selected tools and their areas of application. *MAP Education and Humanities*, 4, 37–50. DOI: 10.53880/2744-2373.2023.4.37

Prince, M. J., Felder, R. M., & Brent, R. (2007). Does Faculty Research Improve Undergraduate Teaching? An Analysis of Existing and Potential Synergies. *Journal of Engineering Education*, 96(4), 283–294. DOI: 10.1002/j.2168-9830.2007.tb00939.x

Randolph, J. (2019). A guide to writing the dissertation literature review. *Practical assessment, research, and evaluation, 14*(1), 13.

Ray, P. P. (2023). ChatGPT: A Comprehensive Review on Background, Applications, Key Challenges, Bias, Ethics, Limitations and Future Scope. *Internet of Things and Cyber-Physical Systems.*

Robledo, S., Grisales Aguirre, A. M., Hughes, M., & Eggers, F. (2023). "Hasta la vista, baby"–will machine learning terminate human literature reviews in entrepreneurship? *Journal of Small Business Management*, 61(3), 1314–1343. DOI: 10.1080/00472778.2021.1955125

Rodway, P., & Schepman, A. (2023). The impact of adopting AI educational technologies on projected course satisfaction in university students. *Computers and Education: Artificial Intelligence*, 5, 100150. DOI: 10.1016/j.caeai.2023.100150

Ruxton, G., & Colegrave, N. (2011). *Experimental design for the life sciences.* Oxford University Press.

Sadiq Sohail, M., & Daud, S. (2009). Knowledge Sharing in Higher Education Institutions: Perspectives from Malaysia. *Vine*, 39(2), 125–142. DOI: 10.1108/03055720910988841

Santo, S. A., Engstrom, M. E., Reetz, L., Schweinle, W. E., & Reed, K. (2009). Faculty Productivity Barriers and Supports at a School of Education. *Innovative Higher Education*, 34(2), 117–129. DOI: 10.1007/s10755-009-9098-z

Sato, M., & Loewen, S. (2019). Do Teachers Care About Research? The Research–Pedagogy Dialogue. *ELT Journal*, 73(1), 1–10. DOI: 10.1093/elt/ccy048

Shahriar, S., & Hayawi, K. (2023). Let's Have a Chat! A Conversation with ChatGPT: Technology, Applications, and Limitations. *arXiv preprint arXiv:2302.13817.*

Shavit, Y. (Ed.). (2007). *Stratification in Higher Education: A Comparative Study.* Stanford University Press. DOI: 10.1515/9780804768146

Shehzad, W. (2011). Outlining purposes, stating the nature of the present research, and listing research questions or hypotheses in academic papers. *Journal of Technical Writing and Communication*, 41(2), 139–160. DOI: 10.2190/TW.41.2.c

Sohrabi, C., Mathew, G., Franchi, T., Kerwan, A., Griffin, M., Del Mundo, J. S. C., & Agha, R. (2021). Impact of the Coronavirus (COVID-19) Pandemic on Scientific Research and Implications for Clinical Academic Training–A Review. *International Journal of Surgery*, 86, 57–63. DOI: 10.1016/j.ijsu.2020.12.008

Sullivan, G. (2006). Research acts in art practice. *Studies in Art Education*, 48(1), 19–35. DOI: 10.1080/00393541.2006.11650497

Tavares, O., Sin, C., Sá, C., Bugla, S., & Amaral, A. (2022). Inbreeding and Research Collaborations in Portuguese Higher Education. *Higher Education Quarterly*, 76(1), 102–115. DOI: 10.1111/hequ.12301

Terenzini, P. T., & Pascarella, E. T. (1998). Studying College Students in the 21st century: Meeting New Challenges. *Review of Higher Education*, 21(2), 151–165. DOI: 10.1353/rhe.1998.a30045

Trott, C. D., Sample McMeeking, L. B., & Weinberg, A. E. (2020). Participatory Action Research Experiences for Undergraduates: Forging Critical Connections Through Community Engagement. *Studies in Higher Education*, 45(11), 2260–2273. DOI: 10.1080/03075079.2019.1602759

Tyson, A., & Kennedy, B. (2024). Many Americans think generative AI programs should credit the sources they rely on. *Pew Research Center.* March 26, 2024. Retrieved: https://www.pewresearch.org/short-reads/2024/03/26/many-americans-think-generative-ai-programs-should-credit-the-sources-they-rely-on/#:~:text=Adults%20with%20higher%20levels%20of%20education%20are%20more,with%20AI%20at%20least%20several%20times%20a%20week

Väljataga, T., Fiedler, S. H., & Laanpere, M. (2015). Re-Thinking Digital Textbooks: Students as Co-Authors. *Advances in Web-Based Learning—ICWL 2015: 14th International Conference, Guangzhou, China, November 5-8, 2015Proceedings*, 14, 143–151.

Vaswani, A., Shazeer, N., Parmar, N., Uszkoreit, J., Jones, L., Gomez, A. N., & Polosukhin, I. (2017). Attention is all you need. *Advances in Neural Information Processing Systems*, 30.

Wagner, G., Lukyanenko, R., & Paré, G. (2022). Artificial intelligence and the conduct of literature reviews. *Journal of Information Technology*, 37(2), 209–226. DOI: 10.1177/02683962211048201

Walton, E., Carrington, S., Saggers, B., Edwards, C., & Kimani, W. (2022). What matters in learning communities for inclusive education: A cross-case analysis. *Professional Development in Education*, 48(1), 134–148. DOI: 10.1080/19415257.2019.1689525

Werth, E., & Williams, K. (2021). Exploring Student Perceptions as Co-Authors of Course Material. *Open Praxis*, 13(1), 53–67. DOI: 10.5944/openpraxis.13.1.1187

Xu, W., Dainoff, M. J., Ge, L., & Gao, Z. (2023). Transitioning to human interaction with AI systems: New challenges and opportunities for HCI professionals to enable human-centered AI. *International Journal of Human-Computer Interaction*, 39(3), 494–518. DOI: 10.1080/10447318.2022.2041900

Zeichner, K. M. (1995). Beyond the divide of teacher research and academic research. *Teachers and Teaching*, 1(2), 153–172. DOI: 10.1080/1354060950010202

Zhang, K., & Aslan, A. B. (2021). AI technologies for education: Recent research & future directions. *Computers and Education: Artificial Intelligence*, 100025.

Zhang, L., Carter, R. A.Jr, Qian, X., Yang, S., Rujimora, J., & Wen, S. (2022). Academia's Responses to Crisis: A Bibliometric Analysis of Literature on Online Learning in Higher Education During COVID-19. *British Journal of Educational Technology*, 53(3), 620–646. DOI: 10.1111/bjet.13191

Chapter 3
Research Agents and Outreach

ABSTRACT

This chapter explores the pivotal role of AI in enhancing the early stages of academic research dissemination and engagement. It begins by guiding researchers on finding their voice, a crucial step in establishing a unique and compelling scholarly identity. The chapter then delves into the practical aspects of submitting research for initial interest, demonstrating how AI tools can streamline this process by identifying appropriate conferences and publishers. A significant focus is placed on AI agents, specifically their ability to understand and emulate human emotions and personas, which is crucial for crafting impactful and resonant research narratives. The chapter introduces the six-dimensional emotional model (6DE), a sophisticated framework designed to enrich the emotional and rhetorical aspects of AI-generated content. This model is further elaborated in the context of Generative AI Research Assistants, illustrating how these advanced tools can assist researchers in aligning their work with the emotional and intellectual expectations of their target audiences.

3.1 FINDING YOUR VOICE

At this juncture in the research process, having selected a topic and gathered substantial information, it is important to tailor the communication style before proceeding to engage with conferences or publishers. While generative AI tools such as ChatGPT, Gemini, or Claude can provide an initial draft or structure in a generic voice, the uniqueness of a researcher's personal style is crucial for academic writing. Therefore, creating a specific voice and style guide is highly recommended to maintain the originality and personal touch of the researcher's work. This personalized voice and style guide ensures that submissions retain the individual's distinct academic identity, making their work stand out during the peer review pro-

DOI: 10.4018/979-8-3693-6905-0.ch003

cess and within the broader academic community. This careful refinement of voice and adherence to a personalized style guide will be particularly beneficial when submitting proposals for conferences or special issues in academic journals, where the uniqueness and clarity of expression can significantly impact the acceptance and success of the submission.

Creating a personalized voice and style guide for one's research writing using a LLM can streamline your writing process and ensure consistency across your documents. Here is a simple step-by-step guide to help you establish this customization:

1. **Choose a Writing Sample:** Begin by selecting a writing example that effectively represents your desired voice and style. This sample should be comprehensive enough to exhibit key characteristics of your writing—ideally, at least two well-developed paragraphs.
2. **Open Your Chosen LLM:** Access the large language model you prefer to use for generating text. This could be ChatGPT, Gemini, Claude, or any other LLM that supports text generation.
3. **Prepare the Prompt:** In the chat or input field of the LLM, type a clear prompt directing the AI to create a voice and style guide. The prompt might read something like this:

[Use the following to create a voice and style guide for future chats, including voice characteristics, linguistic style, formatting, and structure.]

4. **Include Your Sample Text:** Immediately after the prompt, paste your selected writing sample. This ensures the model has a direct reference to analyze and emulate your specific writing style.
5. **Generate the Style Guide:** Submit the prompt along with your writing sample to the LLM. The model will analyze the input and generate a voice and style guide that reflects the characteristics evident in your sample. This guide will include details on voice, linguistic style, formatting preferences, and structural elements that you can apply to future writings.

These steps allow for the creation of a tailored guide that aids in maintaining a consistent voice and style in across academic communications, especially useful when preparing materials for conferences or publications. An example using the author's own research can be seen using Anthropic's Claude. After opening Claude, one can either paste in a section of the writing sample or attach with the prompt as seen in Figure 1.

Figure 1. Academic voice and style guide

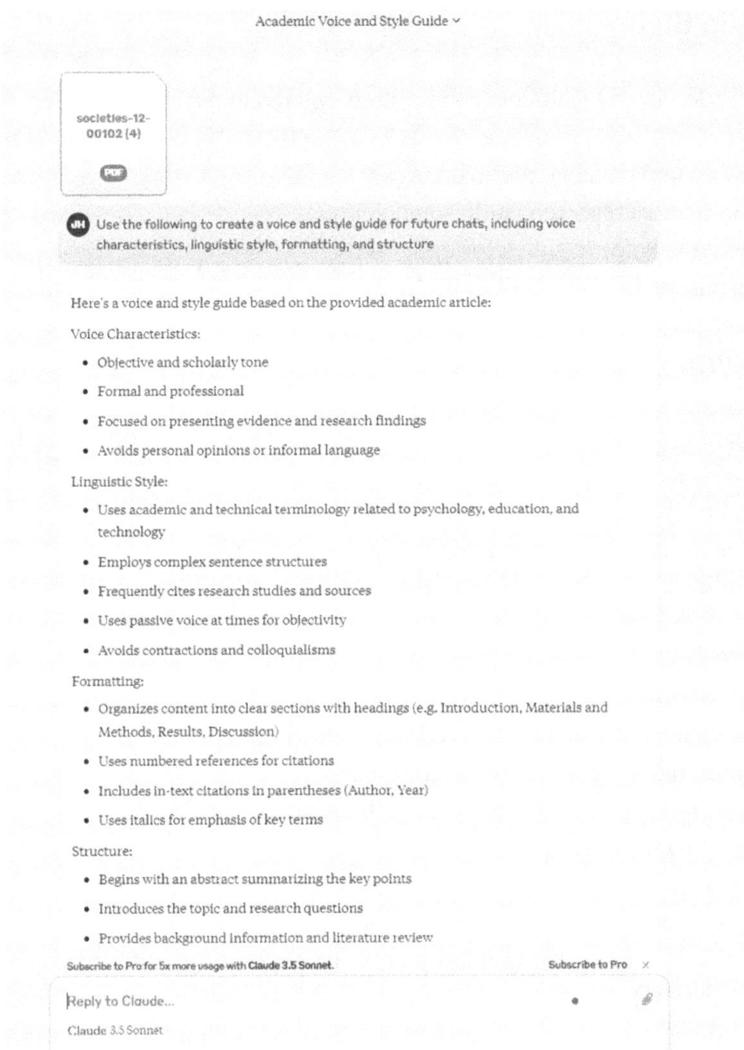

The following was generated:
Here's a voice and style guide based on the provided academic article:

Voice Characteristics

Objective and scholarly tone
Formal and professional
Focused on presenting evidence and research findings

Avoids personal opinions or informal language

Linguistic Style

Uses academic and technical terminology related to psychology, education, and technology

Employs complex sentence structures

Frequently cites research studies and sources

Uses passive voice at times for objectivity

Avoids contractions and colloquialisms

Formatting

Organizes content into clear sections with headings (e.g. Introduction, Materials and Methods, Results, Discussion)

Uses numbered references for citations

Includes in-text citations in parentheses (Author, Year)

Uses italics for emphasis of key terms

Structure

Begins with an abstract summarizing the key points

Introduces the topic and research questions

Provides background information and literature review

Describes methodology in detail

Presents results systematically

Discusses findings and their implications

Concludes by summarizing main points and suggesting future research

Overall, the style aims for clarity, precision, and objectivity in presenting academic research and analysis. The voice maintains a formal, authoritative tone throughout while avoiding personal opinions or casual language.

For a more advanced step-by-step voice and style guide see Table 1. The style guide is now ready to be used in future chats. However, it is important to note that when utilizing free versions of LLMs that do not support customized voice and style profiles, researchers need to adopt a consistent approach to maintain their unique academic voice. It is advisable to paste the voice and style guide at the beginning of every interaction with the AI. This helps in ensuring that the content generated aligns with the desired academic tone and style throughout the conversation. Furthermore, to maintain organizational clarity and coherence, it is beneficial to keep each project within its own chat session. When initiating a new project or topic, starting a new chat session is recommended. In other words, keep the style guide handy to paste into each new project before prompting on a specific task. This practice helps in segregating the information relevant to specific projects, avoiding confusion and enhancing the focus on distinct research themes.

Table 1. Steps for creating an advanced voice and style guide

Step	Activity	Details
Step 1: Collect and Analyze	Collect Works: Gather different types of your writing (e.g., emails, reports, blog posts).	Identify Style: Note common styles or phrases you use and how you express tone.
Step 2: Define Your Voice	Describe Your Tone: Choose words that describe your style (e.g., professional, friendly).	Set Tone Guidelines: Decide how your tone changes with context.
Step 3: Set Style Rules	Grammar and Syntax: Outline your preferred grammar and punctuation rules.	Word Choice: List preferred words and phrases and note any to avoid. Formatting: Specify formatting for documents like font size and styles.
Step 4: Audience Considerations	Understand Your Audience: Tailor the style and tone to your typical readers.	Provide Examples: Show how to adjust the style for different audiences.
Step 5: Build the Guide	Use Examples: Include examples from your work to illustrate the rules.	Write Definitions: Clearly define any technical terms used.

The latest models of LLMs offer enhanced customization options that significantly enrich the user experience, particularly for researchers and academics. These advanced features include the ability to incorporate biographical information, allowing the model to tailor responses based on the researcher's specific background, expertise, and field. This contextual understanding enables the LLM to provide more accurate, relevant, and field-specific information and suggestions.

Additionally, these models support persistent customization across sessions. Users can set up a voice and style guide that is automatically applied to every new interaction. This ensures that the model consistently adheres to the user's preferred communication style, linguistic preferences, and formatting guidelines, eliminating the need to re-specify these preferences in each session. In order to create a customized guide, first, have a short biography about oneself on hand and also create the voice and style guide with the instructions above. This functionality is particularly beneficial for maintaining a consistent voice and style in academic writing and communications.

Now that a voice and style guide has been created, and a research topic has been refined with the aid of generative AI tools, the subsequent step involves aligning that topic with suitable academic conferences, journals, or book publishers. This step is essential to ensure that your research reaches an appropriate audience and contributes effectively to scholarly discourse.

Begin by determining the core themes and keywords of your research, considering both the main subject and any interdisciplinary angles that might widen the scope of suitable publication venues. Traditionally, one might use academic databases and conference directories such as Google Scholar, Web of Science, and Scopus, or specific academic society websites related to your field to search for relevant conferences and journals. Now, given that LLM are able to access the internet, one can just ask directly with a prompt such as:

Using Bing, please identify upcoming conferences in [year] related to [field]. Assess and rank these conferences based on their relevance to my research topic on [specific topic]. Provide details on conference themes, dates, and submission deadlines.

Again, the items in brackets should be replaced with the specific timeframe, field, and topic by the researcher. As an example, when asked: "Using Bing, please identify upcoming conferences in 2025 related to digital humanities. Assess and rank these conferences based on their relevance to my research topic on computational linguistics in Shakespear studies. Provide details on conference themes, dates, and submission deadlines." The response from ChatGPT-4 Turbo was:

To help align your research topic in computational linguistics within Shakespeare studies with relevant upcoming conferences in 2025, here's a selection based on their focus and relevance to your interests:

1. International Conference on English Language and Linguistics (ICELL): Planned for October 28, 2025, in Lisbon, Portugal. This conference emphasizes various aspects of language studies and would be ideal for presenting interdisciplinary research that merges computational linguistics with literary analysis (Conference Index) .

2. International Conference on Language and Corpus Linguistics (ICLCL): Scheduled for October 28, 2025, in Los Angeles, USA. This event focuses specifically on corpus linguistics, which could provide a valuable platform for discussing your computational methods applied to Shakespearean texts (Conference Index) .

3. International Conference on Language and Literature (ICLL): This conference, set for October 28, 2025, in Osaka, Japan, covers broader themes in language and literature, offering a stage to explore the intersection of digital humanities and Shakespeare studies (Conference Index). Each of these conferences could provide an excellent opportunity to showcase your work, network with other researchers in your field, and potentially publish your findings. When preparing your submissions, consider tailoring your abstracts to the specific themes and audiences of these conferences to maximize your impact and engagement. Once a potential conference or journal is identified, examine their call for papers or proposals closely. These documents provide vital details about the scope, themes, submission deadlines, and publication criteria of the conference or journal. Make sure that your research aligns well with these requirements by tailoring your presentation or paper to resonate with the specific themes and audience of the conference or journal. This might involve emphasizing certain aspects of your research or framing your findings in a way that engages with ongoing debates or questions in the field.

3.2 Submitting for Initial Interest When preparing to submit a research proposal to a conference or special issue, the initial task involves a thorough review of the provided conference guidelines, themes, and calls for proposals. This review is crucial for tailoring your submission to align closely with the conference's specific interests and requirements. Start by copying the relevant call for proposals, guidelines, and thematic descriptions provided by the conference organizers. These documents are vital as they contain detailed information on the topics of interest to the organizers, the specific research approaches they value, and the required format and style for submissions. Understanding these guidelines ensures that your proposal is not only thematically aligned but also adheres to the expected presentation standards. As an example, Google Gemini was prompted to "find 2025 call for proposals for digital humanities conferences." The response included the following: There are several calls for proposals for Digital Humanities conferences in 2025: • **Global Digital Humanities Symposium 2025:** This is a hybrid (virtual and in-person) event taking place April 2-8, 2025. The Call for Proposals opens in August 2024. https://msuglobaldh.org/

- **Connecticut Digital Humanities 2025 Conference:** This conference is taking place February 21-22, 2025 at Central Connecticut State University. They are welcoming proposals on a wide range of digital humanities topics.

https://engage.digital.conncoll.edu/digital-scholarship/cfp-connecticut-digital-humanities-2025-conference/

- **The 23rd International Conference on New Directions in the Humanities:** This conference has a special focus for 2025 on Oceanic Journeys: Multicultural Approaches in the Humanities. They are also accepting proposals on various other themes.

https://thehumanities.com/2025-conference/call-for-papers

- **DH2025:** This is the annual conference of the Alliance of Digital Humanities Organizations (ADHO). It will be held at Universidade NOVA de Lisboa, Lisbon, Portugal, from July 15-18, 2025. The call for proposals is typically released several months in advance of the conference. Keep an eye on the ADHO website for updates.

https://adho.org/conference/

The most suitable conference for you will depend on your specific interests and research focus. Review the conference themes and submission guidelines to find the best fit.

Next, incorporate your research topic into a LLM prompt. This prompt should instruct the AI to generate ideas that align your research with the conference's theme. For instance, you might enter: "Generate a proposal draft for a research project on computational linguistics in Shakespeare studies, aligning it with the theme of digital innovation in humanities."

The AI can then assist you in drafting a structured proposal, which typically includes:

- **Title:** A concise yet descriptive headline for your research.
- **Short Description:** A brief overview that captures the essence of your research and its relevance to the conference theme.
- **Full Abstract:** A detailed summary of your research, including objectives, methodology, expected outcomes, and its contribution to the field.
- **Keywords:** About five keywords that help categorize your research under relevant topics for the conference.

When preparing your proposal, it is crucial to explicitly state how your research aligns with the conference theme(s). This clarifies the relevance of your work to the event and increases its appeal to the selection committee, thereby improving the likelihood of acceptance. Aligning your submission with the conference themes and requirements, while utilizing AI tools for brainstorming and drafting, can streamline the proposal process and enhance the quality of your submissions. Since conference calls for proposals can occur up to a year in advance, it is not necessary to have a complete paper or article ready at the time of submission. Instead, focus on demonstrating how your existing research connects with the special theme of the conference to enhance your chances of acceptance. Bringing these elements together, the prompt might look like:

You are writing a proposal for an upcoming conference and here is the description:

Welcome to the micro-site for the Twenty-Third International Conference on New Directions in the Humanities.

Founded in 2003, the New Directions in the Humanities Research Network is brought together by a common interest in established traditions in the humanities while at the same time developing innovative practices and setting a renewed agenda for their future. We seek to build an epistemic community where we can make linkages across disciplinary, geographic, and cultural boundaries.

The Twenty-Third International Conference on New Directions in the Humanities features research addressing the following annual themes and special focus:

2025 Special Focus—Oceanic Journeys: Multicultural Approaches in the Humanities

Theme 1: Critical Cultural Studies
Theme 2: Communication and Linguistics Studies
Theme 3: Literary Humanities
Theme 4: Civic, Political, and Community Studies
Theme 5: Past and Present in the Humanistic Education

We are interested in the following lines of investigation:

Exploring ways to broaden the scope of the humanities and creating a wider critical canvas through cultural studies. Examining critical perspectives on academic disciplines; how traditional disciplines remain constant or must respond to changes in humans' relationships to each other, to society, technology, and the environment. Considering ways of knowing, shifts in conceptual frameworks, and research methodologies. Proposing new directions for humanities studies. Whose Sustainable Future?

Examining the forms and effects of human representation and communication.

Analyses of literature and literary practices, to stabilize bodies of work in traditions and genres, or to unsettle received expressive forms and cultural contents. Examining changes over time in conceptual frameworks, ways of knowing, and ways of seeing.

Social studies in the humanities, where the humanities meet the 'social sciences'. Affinities and affiliations and their impacts on relationships within and across cultures. Issues of policy, governance, and controls over populations within and across nations. The human condition in an era of globalization.

On theories and practices of teaching and learning in the disciplines of the humanities and humanistic social sciences. General and subject-specific pedagogy.

Task: You will consider the following formatting for output and generate a proposal draft for a research project on computational linguistics in Shakespeare studies, aligning it with the theme of digital innovation in humanities.:

- **Title:** A concise yet descriptive headline for your research.

- **Short Description:** A brief overview that captures the essence of your research and its relevance to the conference theme.
- **Full Abstract:** A detailed summary of your research, including objectives, methodology, expected outcomes, and its contribution to the field.
- **Keywords:** About five keywords that help categorize your research under relevant topics for the conference.

Note that the prompt included context [writing a proposal], the actual call for proposal information [what is being considered], and output instructions [formatting and specifics to include]. When entered into Google Gemini, the response is as follows:

Absolutely! Here's a proposal draft tailored to the conference theme, focusing on computational linguistics within Shakespearean studies:

Title: "Unmasking Shakespeare's Language: Computational Linguistics and the Digital Turn in Authorship Attribution and Stylistic Analysis"

Short Description: This research employs computational linguistics and machine learning to investigate Shakespearean authorship and stylistic evolution. It explores how digital tools can enhance our understanding of the Bard's works, shedding light on potential collaborations and shifts in writing style throughout his career.

Full Abstract

The authorship and stylistic evolution of Shakespeare's works have been subjects of scholarly debate for centuries. This research project leverages the power of computational linguistics and machine learning to offer new insights into these enduring questions. By applying natural language processing (NLP) techniques, we analyze Shakespeare's plays and poems, focusing on lexical patterns, syntactic structures, and thematic elements.

Specifically, the project aims to:

1. **Authorship Attribution:** Utilize stylometric analysis to identify potential collaborators in disputed works, comparing Shakespeare's linguistic fingerprint with that of his contemporaries.
2. **Stylistic Evolution:** Trace changes in Shakespeare's writing style over time, examining shifts in vocabulary, sentence complexity, and thematic focus across his career.
3. **Digital Tools and Humanities:** Demonstrate the value of computational linguistics as a research tool within the humanities, showcasing its ability to uncover hidden patterns and deepen our understanding of literary works.

The project's methodology involves:

- **Corpus Creation:** Compiling a comprehensive digital corpus of Shakespeare's works, along with relevant contemporary texts for comparison.
- **Feature Extraction:** Using NLP tools to extract linguistic features such as word frequency, n-gram usage, syntactic structures, and semantic relations.
- **Machine Learning:** Applying machine learning algorithms (e.g., clustering, classification) to analyze the extracted features and identify patterns indicative of authorship or stylistic shifts.

The expected outcomes include:

- A refined understanding of Shakespeare's authorship, contributing to ongoing debates and potentially resolving controversies surrounding disputed works.
- New insights into the evolution of Shakespeare's writing style, revealing how his language changed over time and in response to various influences.
- A demonstration of the transformative potential of computational linguistics for literary studies, paving the way for further digital innovation in the humanities.

Keywords: Computational Linguistics, Shakespeare, Authorship Attribution, Stylistic Analysis, Digital Humanities

With the preliminary output in hand, a researcher can refine it by adding detailed specifics. Crafting a succinct 150-word description or a more detailed 300-word abstract is manageable and should encompass the following elements: the background of your study, the necessity of the research, the methodologies employed, and the significance of the findings. This structured approach allows for the creation of multiple drafts that underscore the relevance of your proposed paper or study.

Once the abstract for a conference, such as the digital humanities conference example here, is submitted and accepted, the next step involves preparing a compelling presentation. AI can be instrumental in this phase as well. Researchers can generate a detailed outline for the slideshow by specifying the duration of the talk and the desired format, whether it will be a straightforward paper presentation, a hands-on workshop, or a more interactive session. For example, if the presentation is a 20-minute paper talk, the AI can help break down the key sections that need to be covered within the allotted time, ensuring that each slide is concise and relevant. Similarly, for a workshop, the AI can suggest interactive elements, exercises, and discussion points that will engage the audience effectively. By providing these parameters, the AI can create a structured framework for the slideshow, ensuring that all necessary information is included and appropriately formatted to maintain audience interest and enhance understanding.

For instance, the following prompt could follow the Abstract output above: “Continue by creating the information for 20-minute paper talk including headings and bullet points for a Power Point.” If needed, the full prompt can be input again for “Unmasking Shakespeare's Language: Computational Linguistics and the Digital Turn in Authorship Attribution and Stylistic Analysis” seen above. The result from ChatGPT-4 is a detailed outline suggesting how the talk might be structured:

PowerPoint Outline for a 20-Minute Paper Talk: “Unmasking Shakespeare's Language: Computational Linguistics and the Digital Turn in Authorship Attribution and Stylistic Analysis”

Slide 1:*Title Slide*

- Title: “Unmasking Shakespeare's Language: Computational Linguistics and the Digital Turn in Authorship Attribution and Stylistic Analysis”
- Short Description
- Presenter’s Name
- Date and Venue of the Conference

Slide 2:*Introduction*

- Overview of the research project
- Importance of authorship and stylistic analysis in Shakespeare studies
- Brief introduction to computational linguistics and machine learning

Slide 3:*Research Objectives*

- Authorship Attribution
- Identify potential collaborators in disputed works
- Stylistic Evolution
- Trace changes in writing style over time
- Digital Tools and Humanities
- Showcase the value of computational linguistics in literary studies

Slide 4:*Methodology Overview*

- Corpus Creation
- Comprehensive digital corpus of Shakespeare's works
- Relevant contemporary texts for comparison
- Feature Extraction
- Linguistic features such as word frequency, n-gram usage, syntactic structures, and semantic relations
- Machine Learning
- Algorithms applied for analysis: clustering, classification

Slide 5:*Corpus Creation*

- Description of the digital corpus
- Sources of Shakespeare's works
- Selection of contemporary texts
- Process of digitizing and compiling texts

Slide 6:*Feature Extraction*

- Explanation of NLP tools used
- Key linguistic features analyzed
- Word frequency
- N-gram usage
- Syntactic structures
- Semantic relations

Slide 7:*Machine Learning Techniques*

- Overview of machine learning algorithms
- Clustering
- Classification
- Application of algorithms to extracted features

Slide 8:*Authorship Attribution*

- Stylometric analysis process
- Comparison of Shakespeare's linguistic fingerprint with contemporaries
- Case studies of disputed works

Slide 9:*Stylistic Evolution*

- Analysis of changes in vocabulary
- Examination of sentence complexity
- Study of thematic focus shifts across Shakespeare's career

Slide 10:*Findings: Authorship Attribution*

- Summary of key findings
- Potential collaborators identified
- Insights into disputed works
- Impact on Shakespearean scholarship

Slide 11:*Findings: Stylistic Evolution*

- Summary of stylistic changes identified
- Vocabulary evolution
- Changes in sentence complexity
- Thematic evolution
- Implications for understanding Shakespeare's work

Slide 12:*Digital Tools and Humanities*

- Demonstration of computational linguistics' value in literary studies
- Examples of uncovered patterns

- Broader impact on the field of digital humanities

Slide 13:*Conclusion*

- Recap of research objectives and findings
- Significance of the study
- Future directions for research

Slide 14:*Questions & Discussion*

- Invitation for audience questions
- Open floor for discussion

Slide 15:*References*

- Key references and sources used in the research

Slide 16:*Contact Information*

- Presenter's contact details
- Information on how to access the full research project or related publications

By organizing the talk in this manner, the presenter can efficiently cover the essential aspects of the research, providing a clear and engaging narrative that highlights the significance and potential of using computational linguistics in Shakespearean studies.

The output provided here serves as a foundational guide for scholars in preparing their slideshow for a talk and should be customized accordingly. Scholars can manually copy and paste the content into PowerPoint or Canva, especially if using the GPT extension to streamline this process. Another efficient option is utilizing Microsoft PowerPoint's Copilot feature. By uploading the text as a Microsoft Word document, users with access to the full Copilot suite can open a new PowerPoint presentation and click on the Copilot icon in the taskbar. Selecting the “Create a presentation from file...” option allows Copilot to use the document's headings to generate seventeen slides in a basic black and white template. To enhance the visual appeal, users can click on the “Designer” option to choose from a variety of aesthetically pleasing templates. Additional imagery can also easily be created to augment the presentation as needed.

In the same multimodal chat of ChatGPT-4, additional images can be generated to enhance the presentation, either directly within ChatGPT-4 or through prompts in Copilot. This capability allows for the creation of customized visuals that can complement and clarify the textual content of each slide. For instance, for Slide 5: Corpus Creation, an illustrative image can be generated to visually represent the components and processes involved in creating the digital corpus. Here is an example prompt for generating such an image:

Create an image that visually represents the creation of a digital corpus for Shakespeare's works. The image should include a stack of Shakespeare's plays and poems, digital sources like e-books or scanned manuscripts, and a selection of contemporary texts for comparison. Additionally, depict the process of digitizing and compiling these texts, such as scanning, OCR (optical character recognition), and data organization in a digital archive. The overall style should be clean and academic, suitable for a scholarly presentation.

Figure 2. Image for slide

The image (Figure 2) created using the embedded Dalle-3 interface in ChatGPT-4 brings together the imagery as described with a bust-length illustration of Shakespeare perched atop a stack of books and surrounded with computers. The image generated visually represents the creation of a digital corpus for Shakespeare's works, including a stack of Shakespeare's plays and poems, digital sources like e-books or scanned manuscripts, and a selection of contemporary texts for comparison. The depiction also includes the process of digitizing and compiling these texts, such as scanning, OCR, and data organization in a digital archive. Of course, variations on the prompt will result in different images that can be more or less realistic, in different settings with different color schemes at different times of day, and so on. Thus, with the utilization of such prompts, scholars can generate relevant and engaging images to accompany their slides, further enriching their presentations and aiding in the audience's understanding of the research process.

The image creation capabilities in models like ChatGPT-4 and DALL-E extend far beyond simple illustrative imagery, allowing for the generation of complex scientific illustrations that can aid in explaining intricate concepts in more technical disciplines. These capabilities are particularly valuable in fields such as biology, where visual representations can significantly enhance understanding. For example, creating a detailed illustration of how proteins acquire their shape and function from the sequence and interactions of amino acids can be crucial for educational and research purposes. Here is a prompt that would help DALL-E create such an illustration:

Create an image that illustrates how proteins get their shape and function from the sequence and interactions of amino acids. The image should depict a sequence of amino acids forming a polypeptide chain, highlighting the primary, secondary, tertiary, and quaternary structures of proteins. Show the interactions between amino acids, such as hydrogen bonds, ionic bonds, and hydrophobic interactions, that contribute to the folding and final shape of the protein. The overall style should be clear and educational, suitable for a biology textbook or a scientific presentation.

Figure 3. Amino acids forming a polypeptide chain

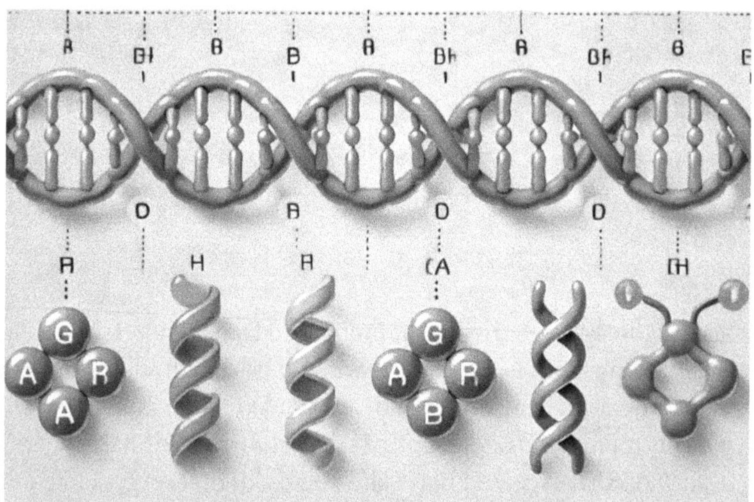

The generated image (Figure 3) illustrates a sequence of amino acids forming a polypeptide chain without any words, focusing on the individual amino acids linked together and highlighting the peptide bonds between them. This visual style is similar to those found in educational biology diagrams, making it an effective tool for teaching and presentations in the field of biochemistry and molecular biology.

After submitting to and being accepted by conferences, and subsequently receiving feedback from subject-matter experts, scholars typically aim to publish their revised findings in a peer-reviewed article. However, the same structured process outlined for conference submissions can also be adapted for crafting book proposals. The initial step in this journey is identifying a book publisher that aligns with the scope and focus of your project. This requires strategic research and a good understanding of the publishing landscape in your field.

Different fields may dictate the types of publishers that are most appropriate. For instance, researchers in the humanities often look to university presses, which typically focus on specific academic portfolios. In contrast, those in the sciences might consider renowned publishers like Nova Science Publishing, Wiley, Springer Nature, and Elsevier. If you are unsure where to begin, you can initiate a new search or, if you are looking for a publisher for an already developed project, use the same chat and ask Bing to find suitable publishers. For example, continuing the fictional project here, a prompt may include the following:

Using Bing, identify suitable book publishers for the project titled 'Unmasking Shakespeare's Language: Computational Linguistics and the Digital Turn in Authorship Attribution and Stylistic Analysis.' This project leverages computational linguistics and machine learning to explore Shakespearean authorship and stylistic evolution. It is suitable for publishers specializing in digital humanities, literary studies, and interdisciplinary research. Please find publishers that align with these themes, including both university presses and commercial academic publishers.

Most paid models can access the web live now but must be prompted to do so. The prompt here can allow researchers to efficiently identify publishers that are likely to be interested in their work, ensuring that their proposals reach the most appropriate and receptive audiences. This approach streamlines the transition from conference presentations to book publications, facilitating the broader dissemination of their scholarly contributions. The output for the prompt here is a good example of this process:

For the project titled "Unmasking Shakespeare's Language: Computational Linguistics and the Digital Turn in Authorship Attribution and Stylistic Analysis," there are several suitable publishers that align with themes in digital humanities, literary studies, and interdisciplinary research.

1. **SpringerLink:** Springer is well-regarded for publishing works that demonstrate innovative, interdisciplinary research in digital humanities. Their series "Advancing Digital Humanities" features contributions from leading scholars and showcases cutting-edge research that aligns closely with the themes of your project 103†source .
2. **Edinburgh Futures Institute:** This institute focuses on applying computational methods to literary studies, bridging the gap between STEM and the humanities. Their commitment to digital humanities makes them an excellent fit for a project exploring computational linguistics in literary analysis 104†source .

3. **The Center for Digital Humanities at Princeton:** Princeton's Center for Digital Humanities brings together interdisciplinary research at the intersection of humanities and technology. They are actively involved in projects that utilize digital tools to address humanistic questions, which aligns well with the objectives of your research 105†source .
4. **Project MUSE:** Managed by the Pennsylvania State University Press, Project MUSE is a trusted part of the academic and scholarly community, promoting the creation and dissemination of humanities and social science resources. Their interdisciplinary literary studies series would be an appropriate venue for a project of this nature 106†source .

By using this prompt, you can efficiently identify publishers that are likely to be interested in your work, ensuring that your proposals reach the most appropriate and receptive audiences. This approach streamlines the transition from conference presentations to book publications, facilitating the broader dissemination of your scholarly contributions.

Each of the four examples cited—SpringerLink, Edinburgh Futures Institute, The Center for Digital Humanities at Princeton, and Project MUSE—include citations in the form of "sources" at the end of their descriptions. By clicking on these sources, such as SpringerLink, you can find detailed submission guidelines. These guidelines typically outline the required sections for a book proposal. The sections needed for the proposal generally include:

1. **Title and Subtitle:** Clearly state the title and subtitle of your book.
2. **Overview:** Provide a brief summary of the book's main objectives, scope, and significance.
3. **Detailed Table of Contents:** List the chapters and sub-sections with brief descriptions of each.
4. **Market and Audience:** Identify the target audience and explain the market need for your book.
5. **Competitive Titles:** List and discuss existing books that are similar to yours and how your book will differentiate itself.
6. **Author Information:** Include a biography that highlights your qualifications and expertise relevant to the book's subject.
7. **Sample Chapters:** Provide one or two sample chapters to give a sense of the writing style and content.
8. **Length and Timeline:** Estimate the total word count of the book and provide a timeline for completion.

Each of these sections can be efficiently completed by utilizing your tool of choice, such as an AI-powered assistant, to generate and organize the required content for your book proposal. At this stage, the project has already been presented as a paper and/or published as an article. By attaching that text to a chat and asking targeted questions, you can rapidly organize information and draft the proposal much more efficiently than traditional methods. For instance, for our fictitious project, "Unmasking Shakespeare's Language: Computational Linguistics and the Digital Turn in Authorship Attribution and Stylistic Analysis," we could ask the AI to provide an overview with the following prompt: "Please generate an overview for the book proposal titled 'Unmasking Shakespeare's Language: Computational Linguistics and the Digital Turn in Authorship Attribution and Stylistic Analysis.' This overview should summarize the main objectives, scope, and significance of the book." The result of which is as follows:

OVERVIEW FOR THE BOOK PROPOSAL: UNMASKING SHAKESPEARE'S LANGUAGE

Title: Unmasking Shakespeare's Language: Computational Linguistics and the Digital Turn in Authorship Attribution and Stylistic Analysis

Overview

This book leverages the power of computational linguistics and machine learning to offer groundbreaking insights into the authorship and stylistic evolution of William Shakespeare's works. By applying advanced natural language processing (NLP) techniques, the book delves into the lexical patterns, syntactic structures, and thematic elements that define Shakespeare's plays and poems. The primary objectives of this research are to utilize stylometric analysis to identify potential collaborators in disputed works and to trace the stylistic changes in Shakespeare's writing over time. This analysis includes examining shifts in vocabulary, sentence complexity, and thematic focus across his career.

The scope of the book encompasses the creation of a comprehensive digital corpus of Shakespeare's works, alongside relevant contemporary texts for comparison. Utilizing NLP tools, the book extracts linguistic features such as word frequency, n-gram usage, syntactic structures, and semantic relations. Machine learning algorithms, including clustering and classification, are applied to analyze these features and identify patterns indicative of authorship or stylistic shifts.

The significance of this research lies in its potential to refine our understanding of Shakespeare's authorship, contributing to ongoing debates and potentially resolving controversies surrounding disputed works. Furthermore, the book provides new insights into the evolution of Shakespeare's writing style, revealing how his language changed over time in response to various influences. Additionally, it demonstrates the transformative potential of computational linguistics for literary studies, paving the way for further digital innovation in the humanities.

By showcasing the intersection of technology and literary analysis, this book aims to enhance scholarly discourse and promote the integration of digital tools in humanities research, ultimately contributing to a deeper and more nuanced understanding of one of literature's greatest figures.

This example showcases the process of generating an overview for a book proposal without an original project. However, the same method can be applied to any research project. For instance, you can continue by using a prompt to gather information for the Market and Audience section of the proposal. "Please generate a Market and Audience section for the book proposal titled 'Unmasking Shakespeare's Language: Computational Linguistics and the Digital Turn in Authorship Attribution and Stylistic Analysis.' This section should identify the target audience and explain the market need for the book." The result in this example is as follows:

Market and Audience

The primary target audience for "Unmasking Shakespeare's Language: Computational Linguistics and the Digital Turn in Authorship Attribution and Stylistic Analysis" includes scholars, researchers, and students in the fields of literature, digital humanities, and computational linguistics. Additionally, academics interested in the methodologies of authorship attribution and stylometric analysis will find this book invaluable. This book also appeals to university libraries, academic institutions, and research centers focusing on the intersection of humanities and technology.

Market Need

The need for this book stems from the growing integration of digital tools in humanities research, particularly in literary studies. As computational linguistics and machine learning technologies continue to advance, there is an increasing demand for interdisciplinary works that bridge the gap between traditional literary analysis and modern digital methodologies. This book addresses this demand by offering a comprehensive examination of how computational techniques can provide new insights into Shakespearean authorship and stylistic evolution.

In recent years, the application of digital tools in the humanities has become more prevalent, as evidenced by numerous digital humanities projects and publications. This book will contribute to this expanding field by demonstrating the practical applications of these technologies in analyzing one of literature's most significant figures. Furthermore, the insights gained from this research will benefit ongoing scholarly debates and encourage further interdisciplinary collaboration. By addressing both the academic and practical aspects of using digital tools in literary studies, this book will serve as a vital resource for advancing research and teaching in the digital age.

Once you have completed the Market and Audience section, you can continue with each subsequent section of the book proposal using the same method. Remember to use prompts and tools to gather the necessary information efficiently. For instance, when needing live information from the Internet, such as competitive titles, include "Ask/Using Bing" in your prompt to ensure you get the most current and relevant data. Here are examples when asked for prompts for the other sections:

Example Prompts for Remaining Sections

Detailed Table of Contents

"Please generate a detailed table of contents for the book proposal titled 'Unmasking Shakespeare's Language: Computational Linguistics and the Digital Turn in Authorship Attribution and Stylistic Analysis,' including chapters and brief descriptions of each section."

Competitive Titles

"Ask/Using Bing to find competitive titles for the book proposal 'Unmasking Shakespeare's Language: Computational Linguistics and the Digital Turn in Authorship Attribution and Stylistic Analysis.' List existing books on similar topics and discuss how this book will differentiate itself."

Length and Timeline

"Please estimate the total word count of the book 'Unmasking Shakespeare's Language: Computational Linguistics and the Digital Turn in Authorship Attribution and Stylistic Analysis' and provide a timeline for completion, including key milestones."

Each stage of the research and writing process will require generating additional content, such as email templates to various individuals like acquisition editors. In this instance, submitting the proposal should be accompanied by a cover letter or email introducing yourself, expressing your interest in publishing with them, and highlighting the value of the proposed research. With the prompt, "Generate an email template for this project to an editor relaying who you are, your interest in publishing with them, and the value of the research proposed." The resulting template looks like:

Each stage of the research and writing process will require generating additional content, such as email templates to various individuals like acquisition editors. In this instance, submitting the proposal should be accompanied by a cover letter or email introducing yourself, expressing your interest in publishing with them, and highlighting the value of the proposed research.

Example Email Template

Subject: Book Proposal Submission: "Unmasking Shakespeare's Language: Computational Linguistics and the Digital Turn in Authorship Attribution and Stylistic Analysis"

Dear [Acquisition Editor's Name],

I hope this email finds you well. My name is [Your Name], and I am [Your Title/Position] at [Your Institution]. I am writing to express my interest in publishing my book, "Unmasking Shakespeare's Language: Computational Linguistics and the Digital Turn in Authorship Attribution and Stylistic Analysis," with [Publisher's Name].

This book leverages the power of computational linguistics and machine learning to offer groundbreaking insights into the authorship and stylistic evolution of William Shakespeare's works. By applying advanced natural language processing (NLP) techniques, I delve into the lexical patterns, syntactic structures, and thematic elements that define Shakespeare's plays and poems. The research aims to utilize stylometric analysis to identify potential collaborators in disputed works and trace stylistic changes in Shakespeare's writing over time. Additionally, the book demonstrates the transformative potential of computational linguistics for literary studies, providing new perspectives and methodologies for future research.

I believe that [Publisher's Name] is an ideal fit for this project due to your esteemed portfolio in digital humanities and interdisciplinary research. The integration of digital tools in the humanities is becoming increasingly essential, and this book aims to bridge the gap between traditional literary analysis and modern computational methods.

Attached to this email, please find the full book proposal, including an overview, detailed table of contents, market and audience analysis, competitive titles, author information, sample chapters, and a proposed timeline for completion. I would be honored to discuss this proposal further and answer any questions you may have.

Thank you for considering my submission. I look forward to the possibility of working with [Publisher's Name] to bring this project to fruition.

Best regards,
[Your Full Name]
[Your Title/Position]
[Your Institution]
[Your Contact Information]

Additional Email Templates for Various Stages

Follow-Up Email Template

“Dear [Acquisition Editor's Name], I am following up on my previous submission of the book proposal titled 'Unmasking Shakespeare's Language.' I would appreciate an update on the status of my proposal. Thank you for your time and consideration.”

Email Template for Requesting Feedback

“Dear [Colleague's Name], I have recently completed a book proposal for 'Unmasking Shakespeare's Language.' Could you provide feedback on the attached document? Your insights would be invaluable.”

By using these templates and adapting them to specific needs, you can streamline communication throughout the research and writing process, ensuring that each stage is managed efficiently and professionally.

Given the dynamic nature of research projects, it is essential to have an effective system for managing various tasks and phases. The ability to move seamlessly between different stages—such as generating initial abstracts, preparing detailed presentations, and leveraging AI tools for deeper analysis—requires an organized approach to keep track of progress and deadlines. This is particularly important when researchers need to revisit earlier stages of their work, refine their methodologies, or incorporate new data. This entails editing current works, incorporating feedback from peer reviews, and preparing papers for forthcoming conferences. It is beneficial to maintain a well-organized calendar and a comprehensive list of projects at various stages: in development, under review, accepted, and planned for future submission (Table 5, Chapter 2). After submitting proposals for special issues or conferences, it is important to continue working on accepted projects while awaiting responses on others. This strategic approach helps maintain productivity and ensures steady progress across multiple projects.

Table 2. Research project lifecycle management table

Phase	Activities	Details
Project Planning and Development	Idea Generation, Literature Review, Project Design	Document initial ideas, summarize relevant research, define research questions and methods.
Active Projects	Data Collection, Data Analysis, Writing Phase	Track ongoing data collection, specify analysis techniques and preliminary findings, draft research papers.
Submitted for Review	Under Peer Review, Revisions Required	List papers submitted and under review, track submissions needing revisions with deadlines.
Publications and Presentations	Accepted, Published Works	Record details of accepted and published research, include publication dates and venues.
Future Projects	Upcoming Proposals, Planned Research	Plan for upcoming proposals, note submission deadlines and potential funding sources.
Project Tracking Tools	Calendar, Project Management Software	Use digital tools to track deadlines and manage project phases effectively.

In the realm of academic research, maintaining a well-organized system to track various projects at different stages is crucial for ensuring efficiency and productivity. A systematic approach allows researchers to manage multiple projects simultaneously, from the initial ideation phase through to draft submissions and beyond. This organization is vital as it helps in monitoring progress, meeting deadlines, and ensuring that no critical tasks are overlooked. Moreover, a structured system enables researchers to prioritize their work effectively, allocate resources judiciously, and streamline communication among team members, thereby fostering a collaborative and focused research environment.

Incorporating AI agents into this well-organized system can further enhance its efficiency and effectiveness. AI agents can assist in various tasks, such as scheduling, tracking deadlines, and managing communications, thus freeing up researchers to focus on the core aspects of their work. These intelligent systems can analyze data, provide reminders, and even predict potential bottlenecks based on past project timelines, ensuring that the research process flows smoothly. One of the significant advantages of AI agents is their ability to tailor specific emotions and personalities to suit different tasks and interactions. For instance, an AI agent designed to handle initial submissions might adopt a professional and formal tone, while one tasked with internal team communications could be programmed to be more approachable and encouraging. This customization enhances the user experience and improves the efficiency of interactions, making the research management process more intuitive and responsive.

3.3 AI AGENTS: EMOTIONS AND PERSONAS

Beyond administrative tasks, generative AI agents hold the potential to act as invaluable research assistants. These AI systems can be trained to perform a variety of functions that traditionally require significant human effort. They can assist in conducting preliminary literature reviews, identifying relevant sources, and even drafting sections of research papers based on predefined guidelines and datasets. By leveraging natural language processing and machine learning algorithms, these agents can generate coherent and contextually appropriate content, providing researchers with a solid foundation upon which to build.

Furthermore, generative AI agents can be programmed to adopt specific emotional and rhetorical strategies that align with the research objectives. For instance, an AI agent tasked with drafting grant proposals might use persuasive language and emphasize the project's potential impact, while another designed for peer-reviewed journal submissions might focus on presenting data rigorously and objectively. This adaptability makes AI agents versatile tools that can be tailored to meet the unique requirements of various research tasks.

A promising avenue that has emerged with the rise of LLMs involves leveraging AI agents capable of adopting varied personas and emotional states to assist in research efforts. The domain of emotionally intelligent AI, which underscores the significance of emotions in intelligent behaviors and decision-making, has attracted increasing attention (Duan et al., 2019; Mahmud et al., 2022; Strich et al., 2021). This line of research emphasizes the value of integrating emotions into artificial cognitive processing and acknowledges the necessity of artificial emotional intelligence in enhancing social interactions (Zall & Kangavari, 2022).

The existing body of work has already explored diverse areas such as programming machines to express empathy, the creation of AI-based emotional communication systems, and the challenges and implications of artificial emotions in sectors like healthcare and digital marketing (Budhwar et al., 2022; Liu-Thompkins et al., 2022; Singh & Chouhan, 2023). These studies have laid the groundwork for infusing emotions into AI systems, paving the way for more nuanced and contextually appropriate interactions with humans (Ray, 2023).

The incorporation of emotional intelligence into AI agents enables these systems to simulate human-like responses and behaviors, thereby enhancing the quality of human-AI interactions. For instance, AI agents with the ability to display empathy can improve patient care in healthcare settings by providing emotional support alongside medical advice. In digital marketing, emotionally intelligent AI can tailor advertisements to better resonate with consumers, leading to more effective engagement and conversion rates.

The integration of emotions in AI also holds significant potential for research collaborations. AI agents equipped with emotional intelligence can facilitate better communication and cooperation among interdisciplinary research teams. These AI agents can adapt their interactions based on the emotional states of human researchers, fostering a more supportive and productive research environment. This capability is particularly beneficial in collaborative settings where understanding and responding to the emotional dynamics of team members can enhance overall performance and innovation. Moreover, the ability of AI agents to adopt varied personas allows them to contribute specialized knowledge and perspectives to research efforts. By simulating different expert personas, AI agents can assist researchers in exploring complex problems from multiple angles, leading to more comprehensive and innovative solutions. This approach aligns with the principles of interdisciplinary research, where diverse viewpoints are crucial for addressing diverse issues.

The domain of emotionally intelligent AI research spans a diverse array of dimensions and fields of interest, underscoring the importance of emotions in intelligent behavior, decision-making, and the potential applications as well as the challenges associated with integrating emotions into AI systems. Investigations into the role of emotions in intelligent behavior and decision-making highlight the critical role emotions play in informing human cognition and emphasize their broader recognition within engineering and computer science communities (Selvaraj et al., 2021; Jeste et al., 2020).

Conceptual frameworks advocating for socially emotional AI (Samsonovich, 2020), along with research on programming machines to express empathy and emotional intelligence (Picard et al., 2004), underscore the importance of artificial emotional intelligence in enabling social and emotional interactions. These frameworks lay the foundation for developing emotionally intelligent AI systems that can engage in nuanced, empathetic communication with humans. Moreover, studies on AI-driven emotional communication systems (Li et al., 2019) and advancements in synthetic emotional intelligence (Khachane, 2017) showcase the potential applications and progress in affective computing. These advancements span from the development of emotionally intelligent chatbots to practical real-world applications in healthcare, customer service, and education.

Emotional intelligence in AI has significant implications for enhancing user experience and engagement across various domains. For example, in healthcare, emotionally intelligent AI can provide compassionate patient care and support. In customer service, AI systems with emotional intelligence can improve customer interactions by understanding and responding to emotional cues, thereby enhancing satisfaction and loyalty. The integration of emotions into AI systems also presents challenges, such as ensuring ethical considerations in the design and implementation of these systems. Balancing the technical aspects of affective computing with the ethical implications of artificial emotional responses requires careful deliberation and ongoing research (Duan et al., 2019; Mahmud et al., 2022). Addressing these challenges is essential for the responsible deployment of emotionally intelligent AI systems in various sectors.

Discussions regarding the hurdles and ramifications of artificial emotions (Pusztahelyi, 2020) and the creation of bio-inspired social and emotional cognitive systems (Cominelli et al., 2021) highlight the ethical and pragmatic considerations inherent in implementing emotionally intelligent AI. Conversations about the progression from emotional AI to cognitive AI (Li, 2024) and the importance of robust emotion models (Wortman & Wang, 2022) underscore the fundamental components and the necessity of developing sophisticated emotion models for practical affective computing applications. Suggestions for incorporating emotion recognition tools within healthcare environments (Marcos et al., 2021), along with discussions on the autonomous decision-making capabilities of emotional AI systems (Huh & Seo, 2019), portray the potential impact of emotionally intelligent AI in healthcare and the ethical considerations tied to AI decision-making. Addressing legal and ethical challenges (Andersson, 2022) further underscores the need to consider fundamental rights, such as freedom of thought, within the arena of emotionally intelligent AI.

These studies reveal a broad spectrum of research interests within the field of emotionally intelligent AI. Researchers have looked at the influence of emotions on intelligent behavior and decision-making, recognized the role of emotions in enhancing artificial cognitive processes, and proposed blueprints for AI with social and emotional faculties. Additionally, research has examined AI-powered emotional communication systems, synthetic emotional intelligence, and the challenges and implications posed by artificial emotions.

In this context, the Six Dimensional Emotional (6DE) model is a valuable addition to the ongoing dialogue (Ratican & Hutson, 2023). The model, with its six emotional dimensions—arousal, valence, dominance, agency, fidelity, and novelty—offers a comprehensive framework for deciphering and quantifying emotional states. The inclusion of sub-dimensions within each primary dimension enables a more detailed analysis of emotions within text-based communication. This methodology holds significant potential to enhance the understanding and generation of appropriate emotional responses by AI systems, leading to improved user experiences and more effective human-AI collaborations. The 6DE model can also foster novel research approaches by providing a structured way to analyze and simulate emotions in various applications, thus pushing the boundaries of what emotionally intelligent AI can achieve.

Recognizing the role of diversity in innovation and research breakthroughs is crucial. The unique perspectives, experiences, and expertise that individuals bring to collaborative work are central to progress and discovery. This diversity of thought and methodological approach contributes to a rich exchange of ideas, a broader range of problem-solving strategies, and ultimately, more innovative outcomes. Additionally, a diverse team can leverage its varied backgrounds and experiences to tackle complex problems, resulting in solutions that might be unattainable for more homogenous groups. The value of such a strategy cannot be overstated in the domain of research. However, this concept has predominantly been considered in the context of human collaborators. Generative AI agents have the potential to provide discipline-specific perspectives, doing so without the cost, administrative challenges, and academic siloing that could otherwise impede such exchanges.

Several studies have examined the use of generative AI agents in various contexts, including video games, decision-making, gameplay, and player behavior. Naddaf (2010) explored reinforcement learning-based methods, allowing AI agents to learn to play games effectively. Liu et al. (2017) extended these concepts to evolve game versions with significant skill-depth using agents like the Random Mutation Hill-Climber and the Multi-Armed Bandit Random Mutation Hill-Climber. Holmgård et al. (2014) argued that artificial agents could function as psychometrically valid abstract simulations of a human player's internal decision-making processes. Following a similar line of thought, Barthet et al. (2022) created generative personas that behave and experience like humans. The resulting agents demonstrated distinctive play styles and responses that closely mirrored the human personas they were designed to imitate.

Integrating these generative AI agents into research teams can significantly enhance the diversity of thought and methodological approaches. By simulating various expert personas, these agents can introduce new perspectives and strategies that might not be present in a team of human researchers alone. This capability can lead to more comprehensive and innovative solutions to complex problems, further advancing the field of research. Moreover, AI agents can continuously learn and adapt, providing up-to-date insights and evolving their expertise based on the latest research developments. This dynamic ability makes them invaluable assets in rapidly changing research environments were staying current with new information is crucial.

Studies have also focused on the testing and evaluation of video games using AI agents. Ariyurek, Betin-Can, and Surer (2019) examined how synthetic and human-like agents could be used in automated video game testing, finding that these agents could rival human testers in identifying bugs. Simultaneously, Fathi and Palhang (2018) highlighted a significant challenge: the lack of behavioral diversity in the agents, which could make them predictable. Nareyek (2000), Tan and Nareyek (2009), and Miikkulainen et al. (2006) discussed the importance and potential of AI techniques in modern computer games, while Fernández et al. (2006) detailed the use of AI in designing the behavior of automated player characters or bots.

More recently, generative AI models like ChatGPT have shown promise in revolutionizing practices, learning, and research across various fields in science and medicine. Morris (2023) interviewed twenty scientists on the potential impact of generative AI in various fields, with their responses reflecting the potential of AI models to accelerate scientific discovery and contribute to the educational and communicative aspects of their professions. For example, Megahed et al. (2023) suggested that these models could enhance statistical process control (SPC) practices by providing code, explaining basic concepts, and creating knowledge related to SPC. However, the authors cautioned against the misuse and misunderstanding of these tools, given their early development stages.

In the medical field, AI models have been proposed for various applications. Murphy and Thomas (2023) elaborated on the potential of generative AI in spinal cord injury research and care, including creating virtual models of the human body for simulation, optimizing spinal stimulation protocols, designing new drugs, and improving robotic exoskeletons. They also discussed the potential for AI in recruiting research participants, offering personalized patient engagement, and predicting medical complications. These studies underscore the potential of generative AI models to contribute significantly to traditional research while also highlighting the necessity for careful and responsible deployment of these technologies. Whether in statistical control, medical research, or scientific discovery, generative AI presents both exciting opportunities and critical challenges that will shape the future of research.

Most recent research has demonstrated the potential for leveraging AI agents in research due to their unique ability to simulate various personas. For example, researchers from Stanford University and Google have created an RPG-style virtual world akin to *The Sims,* hosting 25 characters driven by ChatGPT and custom code, exhibiting life-like independent behavior. In their study, Park et al. (2023) utilized the ChatGPT API for social interactions and developed an architecture simulating minds with memories and experiences. This experiment took place in a town called 'Smallville,' featuring locations such as houses, a café, a park, and a grocery store.

Each character, represented with a simple sprite avatar, had its own personality and connections within the community, seeded through a paragraph of natural language description. Humans could interact with these AI agents by conversing with them or providing directions through an "inner voice"- a function that allows users to input commands or guidance directly into the AI's decision-making process, simulating an internal monologue that influences the agent's actions and responses. The inner voice acts as an overlay of human intervention, enabling the AI to make more informed and contextually appropriate decisions based on human-provided insights and instructions. To address the limited *context window* of ChatGPT, the researchers designed a system that retrieves the most relevant parts of an agent's memory when needed. The "context window" refers to the amount of information the AI can consider at one time, typically constrained by the number of tokens (words or characters) it can process in a single interaction. By selectively pulling in pertinent memories and experiences, the system ensures that the AI can make decisions based on the most relevant and recent information, thereby enhancing its ability to simulate more coherent and contextually appropriate interactions.

These memories feed into the agent's actions, long-term plans, and higher-level reflections. When the AI agents encountered each other, they exchanged information and formed memories using natural language provided by ChatGPT. This led to interesting emergent behaviors such as *information diffusion, relationship memory,* and *coordination*, all arising from interactions between agents rather than being pre-programmed. "Information diffusion" refers to the process by which information spreads from one agent to others through their interactions. "Relationship memory" denotes the ability of agents to remember past interactions and form long-term connections with other agents, influencing future behaviors. "Coordination" involves agents working together in a synchronized manner to achieve common goals, driven by their interactions and shared information. These behaviors emerged naturally from the agents' interactions rather than being explicitly coded into their programming. For example, an AI agent named Isabella Rodriguez planned and organized a Valentine's Day party at Hobbs Cafe and invited friends and customers.

Evaluators were hired to assess the believability of the behavior of the AI agents. Surprisingly, the full generative agent architecture was found to be more convincing than human role-play responses. However, the researchers caution about the ethical implications and risks associated with this technology, including the formation of inappropriate *parasocial relationships,* incorrect inferences, inherent risks with generative AI, and overreliance on generative agents. Parasocial relationships refer to one-sided relationships where individuals form emotional connections with AI agents, which can lead to unrealistic expectations or emotional dependency. Incorrect inferences involve AI systems drawing erroneous conclusions based on incomplete or biased data. The inherent risks with generative AI encompass issues such as the potential for misuse, the propagation of biases, and the generation of harmful content. Finally, overreliance on generative agents pertains to the danger of depending too heavily on AI systems, which might result in diminished human judgment and critical thinking skills.

To mitigate these issues, they suggested adhering to principles such as disclosing the computational nature of agents, ensuring value alignment, following best practices in human-AI design, maintaining audit logs, and not substituting real human input. The researchers also provided an interactive demo online, showcasing the rich social interactions possible in a seemingly simple virtual world. This study underscores the potential of generative AI models to contribute to traditional research while highlighting the necessity for careful and responsible deployment of these technologies. Whether in statistical control, medical research, or scientific discovery, generative AI presents both exciting opportunities and critical challenges that will shape the future of research.

3.4 MODEL FOR GENERATIVE RESEARCH ASSISTANTS

GAI models hold significant potential to advance research through the integration of various emotional models, bringing about profound insights and subtle understandings. In addition to the potential of AI agents outlined above, the 6DE model (Table 3) represents a multidimensional approach designed to comprehend and quantify human emotions in their complexity (Power, 2006). This model provides a comprehensive look at emotions, enhancing the precision of emotional state analysis and replication. The 6DE model integrates six distinct emotional dimensions that capture the essence of emotional experiences: arousal, valence, dominance, agency, fidelity, and novelty (de Carvalho, 2019). Each dimension was carefully chosen to encompass a broad spectrum of emotional experiences and interactions.

Table 3. Six Emotional Dimension (6DE) model

Dimension	Description
Arousal	Represents the level of activation or energy associated with an emotion. Ranges from low arousal (calmness and relaxation) to high arousal (excitement and anticipation). Focuses on the intensity and physiological responses accompanying emotions, such as increased heart rate or breathing rate.
Valence	Refers to the positive or negative nature of an emotion. Ranges from negative valence (sadness and frustration) to positive valence (joy and contentment). Captures the emotional polarity or affective quality of an experience.
Dominance	Reflects the degree of control or power associated with an emotion. Ranges from low dominance (submission or passivity) to high dominance (dominance or assertiveness). Characterizes the level of influence and control an individual feels over their emotions.
Agency	Represents the level of control an entity has over an emotion. Spans from no agency (reflexive and involuntary emotions) to full agency (emotions subject to conscious choice and volition). Captures the degree of personal control and autonomy individuals perceive over their emotional experiences.
Fidelity	Reflects how well an emotion represents the event or situation that caused it. Ranges from low fidelity (mismatch or incongruence between the emotion and its trigger) to high fidelity (strong alignment or congruence). Measures the accuracy and appropriateness of emotional responses to specific events or stimuli.

continued on following page

Table 3. Continued

Dimension	Description
Novelty	Represents the degree of novelty or newness associated with an emotion. Spans from no novelty (habitual or familiar emotions) to high novelty (emotions arising from surprising or unexpected experiences). Captures the level of novelty or surprise that accompanies emotional responses.

The integration of the 6DE model into GAI systems enhances their ability to understand and simulate human emotional responses. This is particularly valuable in applications where nuanced emotional interactions are critical, such as therapeutic settings, customer service, and educational tools. By incorporating this comprehensive emotional framework, AI agents can provide more empathetic and contextually appropriate responses, thereby enhancing user experiences and improving the effectiveness of human-AI collaborations. The fine-tuned approach of the model, which considers multiple subdimensions of emotions, amplifies the capability of an AI system to understand and generate suitable emotional responses. This, in turn, leads to richer user interactions and fosters more efficient human-AI dynamics.

To capitalize on the potential of the model in conjunction with a LLM, users can facilitate dialogues or interactions with the AI system, unlocking its abilities in emotional analysis and creation. Whether the goal is to explore the emotional dimensions of a specific scenario or to elicit distinct emotional responses, the model provides a blueprint for a more refined comprehension of emotions. For a detailed list of training samples, see Ratican and Hutson (2023). For example, individuals can interact with an AI system like ChatGPT using the 6DE model to explore emotional dimensions across various scenarios. One might recount a recent event, such as a workplace dispute, and request the model to analyze it within the 6DE framework. The AI model would examine the arousal level (intensity of the emotion), valence (positive or negative nature of the emotions), dominance (level of control over emotions), agency (source of emotions), fidelity (authenticity of emotions), and novelty (freshness of emotions) associated with the event. This comprehensive analysis allows for deeper insights into emotional experiences and more tailored responses from AI systems.

Similarly, one could construct a hypothetical situation, such as a surprise party, and ask the model to generate an emotional response using the 6DE model. The AI model could then fabricate emotions that align with the dimensions of arousal, valence, dominance, agency, fidelity, and novelty typically associated with such an event. In a narrative context, one could describe a character from a book, such as Katniss Everdeen from *The Hunger Games*, and request the model to interpret her emotional experiences through the lens of the 6DE model. The AI model can then analyze the experiences of the protagonist across the emotional dimensions of arousal, valence, dominance, agency, fidelity, and novelty.

In the consideration of personalizing emotional responses, one could ask the model to speculate on how AI systems could utilize the 6DE model to tailor responses to individual users. This would involve weighing both potential benefits, such as more engaging interactions, and challenges, such as ethical considerations or the potential for misunderstanding. Lastly, envisioning an AI assistant characterized by different emotional dimensions, one could ask the model to explore how such a system could potentially improve user interactions. For instance, an AI assistant in a healthcare setting may exhibit higher levels of dominance and agency to convey authority and confidence, while in an educational setting, it might show higher levels of novelty and fidelity for engaging and authentic interactions.

Training a LLM with the 6DE model to enhance its emotional comprehension and response generation requires a strategic approach, involving a series of steps and instructions. Implementing the 6DE model into the training data enables ChatGPT, Claude or Gemini to expand its understanding of emotional dimensions, thereby facilitating more accurate and complex emotional responses. Here are some methodologies that can be followed:

1. Integrating the 6DE Model into Training Data:

Incorporate the 6DE model into the training data to amplify the emotional comprehension of the tool. This can be achieved by providing a dataset comprised of conversations or text samples that explicitly illustrate emotional dimensions. These samples should include annotated emotional data, user interactions, or simulated dialogues that take into account the dimensions of arousal, valence, dominance, agency, fidelity, and novelty. The following prompt is an example of how the information can be entered and how to approach example conversations.

Introduction: "We are training an AI model to understand and generate emotionally intelligent responses using the Six Dimensional Emotional (6DE) model. The 6DE model captures the complexity of human emotions across six dimensions: arousal, valence, dominance, agency, fidelity, and novelty. This training will involve providing annotated examples that illustrate these emotional dimensions in various contexts."

Example Training Conversation:

Conversation between two friends planning a surprise party:

Friend 1: "I'm so excited about the surprise party for John! He's going to be thrilled when he walks in and sees everyone."

Friend 2: "I know! I've been planning the decorations, and I think it's going to look amazing. Do you think we should tell Mary to keep John distracted until everything is set up?"

Friend 1: "Absolutely. We don't want him to suspect anything. I'll call Mary and make sure she takes him out for a while. This is going to be so much fun!"

[Annotations]

Arousal: High (Friend 1 and Friend 2 are both excited and energetic about the party)

Valence: Positive (The conversation is about a happy event and both friends express joy and anticipation)

Dominance: Medium (Friend 1 shows initiative by planning to call Mary, while Friend 2 is organizing the decorations)

Agency: High (Both friends are actively making decisions and taking actions to ensure the success of the party)

Fidelity: High (The emotions expressed match the context of planning a joyful surprise party)

Novelty: Medium (Planning a surprise party is not an everyday activity but is not entirely unusual either)

2. Fine-Tuning with the 6DE Model:

Fine-tune ChatGPT using the 6DE model as a guiding framework for generating emotionally intelligent responses. This involves adapting ChatGPT with an objective function that embraces the 6DE model's emotional dimensions. Techniques such as reinforcement learning can be employed to guide the model towards generating responses that align with desired emotional dimensions. The following are examples as to how to approach fine-tuning. *Example Prompt for Fine-Tuning:*

Objective: Fine-tune ChatGPT to generate emotionally intelligent responses by incorporating the Six Dimensional Emotional (6DE) model.

Instructions for Fine-Tuning:

1. Define the Emotional Dimensions:
   - **Arousal:** Level of activation or energy associated with an emotion.
   - **Valence:** Positive or negative nature of an emotion.
   - **Dominance:** Degree of control or power associated with an emotion.
   - **Agency:** Level of control an entity has over an emotion.
   - **Fidelity:** How well an emotion represents the event or situation that caused it.
   - **Novelty:** Degree of novelty or newness associated with an emotion.

2. Modify the Objective Function:
    - Adapt the objective function to include evaluation metrics for each of the six emotional dimensions.
    - Example: Use reinforcement learning to adjust the model's parameters based on feedback that assesses how well the generated responses align with the 6DE dimensions.
3. Provide Training Data with Annotations:
    - Use a dataset of conversations or text samples annotated with the 6DE dimensions.
    - Example Scenario: Discussing a recent promotion at work.

Training Example

Prompt

You received a promotion at work and are discussing it with a colleague. Use the Six Dimensional Emotional (6DE) model to guide your response.

Expected Response

I'm thrilled about the promotion! It's a significant step forward in my career, and I feel very proud of the work I've done to get here. This new role will definitely bring exciting challenges, but I'm confident in my abilities to handle them.

Annotations:

- **Arousal:** High (thrilled, excitement)
- **Valence:** Positive (proud, confident)
- **Dominance:** High (significant step forward, confident)
- **Agency:** High (work I've done, confident in my abilities)
- **Fidelity:** High (emotions match the context of receiving a promotion)
- **Novelty:** Medium (promotions are significant but not uncommon)

4. Implement Reinforcement Learning:

    - Use reinforcement learning to reward the model for generating responses that align with the desired emotional dimensions.
    - Example: Assign higher rewards to responses that accurately reflect the emotional annotations provided in the training data.

Reinforcement Learning Example

Prompt

Imagine you're feeling overwhelmed by a new project. Describe your feelings using the 6DE model.

Expected Response

I'm feeling quite stressed about this new project. It's a lot to take on, and I'm not sure if I have all the resources I need to succeed. However, I'm determined to give it my best effort and learn as much as I can along the way.

Annotations:

- **Arousal:** High (stressed, overwhelmed)
- **Valence:** Negative (stressed, unsure)
- **Dominance:** Low (not sure, a lot to take on)
- **Agency:** High (determined to give it my best effort)
- **Fidelity:** High (emotions match the context of starting a challenging project)
- **Novelty:** Medium (common situation but personally significant)

3. Post-Processing Stage with 6DE Model:

Integrate the 6DE model as a post-processing stage to scrutinize and fine-tune the emotional content generated by a LLM. After the tool generates a response, the 6DE model can be used to assess the emotional dimensions exhibited in the text. Feedback or adjustments can then be made based on the desired emotional qualities, enhancing the model's emotional intelligence. An example of which is as follows:

Example Prompt for Post-Processing

Objective: Use the 6DE model to evaluate and refine the emotional content of responses generated by ChatGPT.

Instructions for Post-Processing

1. Generate Initial Response:
   - Use ChatGPT to generate a response to a given prompt.
   - Example Prompt: "Describe how you felt when you received the news of your promotion."

Generated Response

I was ecstatic when I heard about my promotion! It felt like all my hard work had finally paid off. I couldn't wait to tell my family and friends. This new role is going to be challenging, but I'm ready to take it on.

2. Assess Emotional Dimensions Using the 6DE Model:
    - Evaluate the generated response across the six emotional dimensions.
    - Example Annotations:
        - **Arousal:** High (ecstatic, excitement)
        - **Valence:** Positive (ecstatic, hard work paid off)
        - **Dominance:** High (ready to take on challenges)
        - **Agency:** High (hard work paid off, ready to take it on)
        - **Fidelity:** High (emotions match the context of receiving a promotion)
        - **Novelty:** Medium (promotions are significant but not uncommon)

3. Provide Feedback and Adjustments:
    - Based on the evaluation, provide feedback or adjust the response to better align with the desired emotional qualities.
    - Example Feedback:
        - Ensure the response maintains high arousal and positive valence.
        - Highlight personal agency and readiness for new challenges.

Adjusted Response

I was absolutely ecstatic when I received the news of my promotion! It felt immensely rewarding to see my hard work recognized. I immediately shared the news with my family and friends, who were equally thrilled. This new role will undoubtedly bring its challenges, but I feel confident and empowered to tackle them head-on.

4. **Re-evaluate the Adjusted Response:**
    - Re-assess the adjusted response across the six emotional dimensions.
    - Example Annotations:
        - **Arousal:** High (absolutely ecstatic, thrilled)
        - **Valence:** Positive (rewarding, recognized)
        - **Dominance:** High (confident, empowered)
        - **Agency:** High (hard work recognized, tackle challenges head-on)
        - **Fidelity:** High (emotions align with the context)

- o **Novelty:** Medium (common scenario but personally significant)

5. Combining with Existing Emotional Datasets:

Combine the 6DE model with existing emotional datasets to augment ChatGPT's emotional comprehension and generation capabilities. During the training phase, merge the 6DE model with established emotional datasets, such as AffectNet or EmotionX. This allows the model to capture the nuances and subtleties of emotions as defined by the 6DE dimensions.

6. Generating Dialogue Datasets with User Feedback:

Create a dialogue dataset where users actively engage with ChatGPT and provide feedback on the emotional qualities of the responses. Users should assess the arousal, valence, dominance, agency, fidelity, and novelty of the generated responses. This annotated dataset can then be used to train ChatGPT to better understand and generate emotionally intelligent responses.

Example Prompt for Generating Dialogue Datasets with User Feedback

Objective: Develop a dialogue dataset by engaging users with ChatGPT and collecting feedback on the emotional dimensions of the responses.

Instructions for Users

1. Engage in a Conversation:
   - o Initiate a conversation with ChatGPT based on a given scenario.
   - o Example Scenario: "Discuss your feelings about starting a new job."

User Prompt

I just started a new job, and I'm feeling a mix of excitement and nervousness. How should I approach this new chapter in my life?

ChatGPT Response

Starting a new job can be both exciting and nerve-wracking. It's a great opportunity to learn and grow, but it's natural to feel some anxiety. Focus on your strengths and be open to new experiences. Remember, every new beginning is a chance to build something amazing.

2. Assess the Emotional Dimensions:
    - o Evaluate the response based on the six emotional dimensions: arousal, valence, dominance, agency, fidelity, and novelty.
    - o Provide scores and comments for each dimension.

Assessment Example

- **Arousal:** Medium (calm but encouraging)
    - o **Score:** 3/5
    - o **Comment:** The response is balanced, providing a calming reassurance without excessive excitement.
- **Valence:** Positive (encouraging and optimistic)
    - o **Score:** 4/5
    - o **Comment:** The response is positive and supportive, emphasizing growth and opportunity.
- **Dominance:** Medium (suggestive but not forceful)
    - o **Score:** 3/5
    - o **Comment:** The response provides guidance without being overly authoritative.
- **Agency:** High (focus on personal strengths and actions)
    - o **Score:** 4/5
    - o **Comment:** The response encourages proactive behavior and self-confidence.
- **Fidelity:** High (emotionally congruent with the situation)
    - o **Score:** 4/5
    - o **Comment:** The emotional tone matches the context of starting a new job.
- **Novelty:** Medium (common situation but personally significant)
    - o **Score:** 3/5
    - o **Comment:** The scenario is common, but the personalized advice adds value.

3. Provide Overall Feedback:

- Summarize your feedback on the response and suggest any improvements.

Overall Feedback Example

The response was supportive and well-balanced, effectively addressing the mixed emotions of starting a new job. It could be improved by adding more specific examples of how to handle nerves, such as suggesting relaxation techniques or seeking support from colleagues.

4. Repeat the Process:
    - Continue the conversation with additional prompts and responses, providing feedback for each interaction.

Additional User Prompt

I'm worried about fitting in with my new colleagues. What should I do to make a good impression?

ChatGPT Response

It's natural to worry about fitting in with new colleagues. Be yourself, show interest in their work, and be a good listener. Building rapport takes time, so be patient and open to forming new relationships.

Assessment Example

- **Arousal:** Medium (calm and reassuring)
    - **Score:** 3/5
    - **Comment:** The response maintains a calm and reassuring tone.
- **Valence:** Positive (encouraging and optimistic)
    - **Score:** 4/5
    - **Comment:** The response is positive and supportive.
- **Dominance:** Medium (suggestive but not forceful)
    - **Score:** 3/5
    - **Comment:** The response offers gentle guidance.
- **Agency:** High (focus on personal actions)
    - **Score:** 4/5
    - **Comment:** The response encourages proactive behavior.

- **Fidelity:** High (emotionally congruent with the situation)
  - o **Score:** 4/5
  - o **Comment:** The emotional tone matches the context of fitting in with new colleagues.
- **Novelty:** Medium (common situation but personally significant)
  - o **Score:** 3/5
  - o **Comment:** The scenario is common, but the personalized advice adds value.

Overall Feedback Example

The response was reassuring and offered practical advice. It could be enhanced by suggesting specific actions, such as participating in team activities or finding common interests with colleagues.

These methodologies allow a LLM to be trained on and respond to various scenarios in different emotional dimensions. This not only broadens the understanding of emotions but also enables the generation of appropriate emotional responses that consider the desired levels of arousal, valence, dominance, agency, fidelity, and novelty. Engaging in conversations or interactions with the AI system using the 6DE model allows for a more refined and nuanced emotional comprehension, ultimately enhancing the effectiveness and empathy of human-AI interactions.

The 6DE model can significantly enhance the performance of generative AI agents, particularly within interdisciplinary research. This enhancement proposes a unique theoretical framework that leverages the creation of a team of autonomous AI agents, each designed with a distinct persona embodying expertise in a specific research field. Imagine these AI agents as virtual collaborators, each offering unique insights from their respective disciplines to identify novel solutions to problems through a Design Thinking process. They work together, drawing from their specialized knowledge bases to generate ideas and concepts that an individual may not typically consider.

Inspired by the aspiration of mirroring human behavior in AI agents, this approach aims to utilize AI capabilities in mimicking human-like problem-solving methods. Incorporating the 6DE model offers a significant boost to this process by enabling a more comprehensive and nuanced understanding of emotions. This understanding allows AI personas to react, interact, and generate responses with a human-like emotional depth, fostering a more realistic and immersive collaborative environment. For instance, an AI agent with expertise in sociology could use the 6DE model to offer insights into the societal and emotional implications of a proposed solution, such as understanding the valence (emotional polarity) of a group's response to a policy change. Simultaneously, an AI agent focused on economics could analyze the financial viability and economic impact of the same solution, also considering the emotional aspects involved in economic behaviors.

For instance, the model can significantly enhance the Design Thinking process. In the Empathize phase, each AI agent can use the 6DE model to understand and simulate the emotional states of stakeholders involved in the problem. For example, an AI agent in healthcare could assess patient anxiety (arousal) and contentment (valence) to better understand patient needs and concerns. This empathetic approach ensures that the AI comprehends the emotional landscape of those it aims to serve.

During the Define phase, AI agents can collaboratively define the problem by integrating insights from various fields while considering emotional dimensions like dominance and agency. This allows the AI to understand power dynamics and decision-making influences, leading to a more precise and shared understanding of the problem at hand. In the Ideate phase, AI agents can simulate brainstorming sessions to generate a wide range of solutions. By factoring in emotional fidelity, they ensure that the proposed ideas align with real-world scenarios and stakeholders' feelings. This helps in crafting solutions that are both innovative and emotionally resonant.

When creating Prototypes, AI agents can not only address technical feasibility but also incorporate emotional novelty, ensuring the solutions are both groundbreaking and emotionally engaging. This dual focus enhances the relevance and appeal of the prototypes. Finally, during the Test phase, AI agents can evaluate responses to prototypes using the 6DE model to analyze feedback. This analysis helps refine solutions based on their emotional impact, ensuring that the final product is both effective and emotionally attuned to the users' needs.

By employing the 6DE model, AI agents can offer a comprehensive, multi-faceted perspective on problem-solving, addressing issues from several angles simultaneously. This system can provide a depth of understanding and propose solutions that are empathetic, economically feasible, and societally acceptable, thereby fully leveraging the power of AI and the 6DE model in research and problem-solving processes. The ability of humans to contribute varying perspectives, experiences, and expertise to group efforts has been universally acknowledged as a vital driver for innovation and breakthroughs in research. The suggested framework seeks to mirror this aspect of human collaboration in AI agents by creating simulated personas that embody different fields of expertise.

Envision each AI agent with its own distinct knowledge base, mirroring a specific field of research. These agents, designed to be autonomous, can independently access and process information from relevant sources, generating unique insights and solutions grounded in their specialized know-how. For example, in a problem-solving scenario related to climate change, an AI agent with expertise in environmental science could provide insights into the potential ecological impacts of a proposed solution. Another agent, specializing in policy-making, could offer perspectives on the legislative implications and feasibility of implementing the solution. Meanwhile, an agent focused on social science could examine societal reactions to such changes. Each of these perspectives contributes to a comprehensive solution that would be difficult to achieve from a single point of view.

This framework has several implications and benefits for research. First, it presents a new avenue for problem-solving by harnessing the collective expertise of AI agents with simulated personas. This approach could potentially yield innovative and unconventional solutions to complex problems that might be elusive through traditional research methods. Second, by emulating the diversity of human perspectives in group work, it can foster diversity in research, leading to more exhaustive and holistic insights and encouraging interdisciplinary collaborations. Lastly, the framework can expedite research processes. Utilizing the computational capabilities and efficiency of AI agents to process and analyze vast volumes of data can significantly enhance the speed and precision of research outcomes.

The collaborative nature of this framework mirrors the dynamics of human group work. Each AI agent brings specialized knowledge and a unique perspective to the task, contributing original insights and ideas. Through these collaborative interactions, a dynamic exchange of information, concepts, and perspectives unfolds, paving the way for the emergence of novel solutions and breakthroughs. The diversity in the simulated personas of the agents, representing various fields of research, introduces a broad spectrum of perspectives, truly replicating the richness and diversity of human group work.

Emulating a human-led study group, each AI agent in this hypothetical setup is trained in a different discipline using the 6DE model. This approach allows the AI agents to understand and generate emotionally nuanced responses. The goal is to explore how these AI agents can contribute to problem-solving and ideation, providing insights rooted in their respective disciplines while being emotionally nuanced by the 6DE model. This interdisciplinary approach, enhanced by the emotional dimensions captured by the model, is anticipated to yield novel solutions and insights.

In the following segment, a series of example prompts will be outlined to showcase how to direct each AI agent to apply its unique discipline-specific expertise and the 6DE model in their responses. Consider a study group scenario where a human leads five AI agents, each embodying expertise from distinct disciplines: environmental science, social science, political science, economics, and data science. Each AI agent has been trained using the 6DE model, enhancing its ability to understand and generate emotionally nuanced responses (Table 4).

Table 4. Example prompts and responses for AI agents using the 6DE model

Agent	Prompt	Response
Environmental Science	"Evaluate the potential ecological impacts of implementing a universal basic income (UBI) policy. Consider the emotional dimensions of arousal and fidelity in your response."	"The implementation of a UBI policy could indirectly influence ecological outcomes by altering consumption patterns. Increased financial stability may lead to higher consumption rates, potentially increasing environmental stress (arousal: high). However, if the policy promotes sustainable practices and investments, it could positively impact environmental preservation efforts (fidelity: high)."
Social Science	"Analyze the societal reactions to UBI, focusing on valence and dominance. How might different social groups perceive this policy?"	"The societal reactions to UBI are likely to be mixed (valence: mixed). Beneficiaries may feel a sense of relief and support (positive valence), while those skeptical of government intervention might view it negatively (negative valence). The policy's perceived dominance by the government could lead to debates about autonomy and control (dominance: high)."
Political Science	"Discuss the legislative implications and feasibility of UBI, considering agency and novelty in your analysis."	"Legislatively, implementing UBI would require significant policy shifts and consensus-building (agency: high). The novelty of UBI as a policy introduces both opportunities for innovative governance and challenges related to public acceptance and political will (novelty: high)."
Economics	"Assess the economic impact of UBI on market behaviors, incorporating arousal and valence in your evaluation."	"UBI could stimulate economic activity by increasing consumer spending (arousal: high), leading to potential economic growth (positive valence). However, concerns about inflation and resource allocation might arise, impacting economic stability (negative valence)."
Data Science	"Evaluate the data requirements and potential biases in analyzing the effectiveness of UBI, with a focus on fidelity and novelty."	"Assessing UBI's effectiveness necessitates robust data collection and analysis to ensure accurate representation of outcomes (fidelity: high). The novelty of UBI means that existing data might be insufficient, requiring innovative data gathering methods and analytical models (novelty: high)."

Imagine a scenario where a human leader directs a study group of five AI experts, each proficient in a different discipline, to tackle the issue of climate change. The application of the 6DE model allows for a more nuanced exploration of the issue, guided by the emotional dimensions—arousal, valence, dominance, agency, fidelity, and novelty. The AI agent specialized in political science would examine the emotional undertones in the rhetoric used in climate change policies. Its analysis could reveal the dynamics of power play and public sentiment, based on emotional responses evoked in different stakeholders. For instance, it may observe heightened arousal and negative valence in discourses portraying climate change as a looming crisis demanding immediate action or note the dominance dimension in political arguments emphasizing sovereignty over environmental regulations. This analysis helps understand how political messaging influences public and political will to act on climate issues.

The economics expert AI could explore the emotions linked with economic aspects of climate change, such as reactions to the cost of renewable energy sources or the economic impact of extreme weather events. It might find high arousal and negative valence associated with financial distress caused by these events or the dominance dimension surfacing in discussions on who bears the cost of climate change mitigation. This perspective provides insights into the economic barriers and incentives for adopting sustainable practices.

The environmental science expert AI could gauge emotions related to the direct impact of climate change on the planet. It could analyze emotional responses to issues such as biodiversity loss or deforestation, with perhaps high arousal and negative valence associated with the dire consequences of these issues, and novelty in terms of people's reactions to new scientific data or unprecedented environmental phenomena. This understanding can highlight areas where public awareness and emotional engagement need to be heightened for effective environmental advocacy.

The sociology expert AI might assess societal attitudes towards climate change, examining the emotional dimensions in public opinion, activism, and social responses. It could track shifts in agency, where increasing awareness leads to a greater sense of personal responsibility, or changes in fidelity as people's trust in different information sources varies. This agent's analysis can inform strategies to mobilize public support and foster community resilience.

Lastly, the ethics expert AI could look into the moral dilemmas posed by climate change. It may find high arousal and complex valence in debates over intergenerational justice or examine how agency plays out in discussions about individual versus collective responsibility. Understanding these ethical concerns is crucial for developing policies that are not only effective but also just and equitable.

In sum, each AI agent brings its unique disciplinary lens and emotional understanding to the table, creating a rich, multi-faceted exploration of the complex issue of climate change. This approach, powered by the 6DE model, can reveal insights and perspectives that a single-disciplinary analysis might miss, illuminating the path towards more comprehensive and nuanced solutions. The interdisciplinary collaboration among AI agents, each equipped with emotional intelligence, can lead to more robust, empathetic, and actionable strategies for addressing climate change.

REFERENCES

Andersson, R. (2022). The Bioeconomy and the Birth of a "New Anthropology". *Cultural Anthropology*, 37(1), 37–44. DOI: 10.14506/ca37.1.06

Ariyurek, S., Betin-Can, A., & Surer, E. (2019). Automated Video Game Testing Using Synthetic and Humanlike Agents. *IEEE Transactions on Games*, 13(1), 50–67. DOI: 10.1109/TG.2019.2947597

Barthet, M., Khalifa, A., Liapis, A., & Yannakakis, G. (2022, September). Generative Personas that Behave and Experience Like Humans. In *Proceedings of the 17th International Conference on the Foundations of Digital Games* (pp. 1-10). DOI: 10.1145/3555858.3555879

Budhwar, P., Malik, A., De Silva, M. T., & Thevisuthan, P. (2022). Artificial Intelligence–Challenges and Opportunities for International HRM: A Review and Research Agenda. *International Journal of Human Resource Management*, 33(6), 1065–1097. DOI: 10.1080/09585192.2022.2035161

Cominelli, L., Hoegen, G., & De Rossi, D. (2021). Abel: Integrating Humanoid Body, Emotions, and Time Perception to Investigate Social Interaction and Human Cognition. *Applied Sciences (Basel, Switzerland)*, 11(3), 1070. DOI: 10.3390/app11031070

de Carvalho, P. A. C. (2019). *Emojar: Collecting and Reliving Memorable and Emotionally Impactful Digital Content* (Doctoral dissertation, Universidade de Lisboa (Portugal)).

Duan, Y., Edwards, J. S., & Dwivedi, Y. K. (2019). Artificial Intelligence for Decision Making in the Era of Big Data–Evolution, Challenges and Research Agenda. *International Journal of Information Management*, 48, 63–71. DOI: 10.1016/j.ijinfomgt.2019.01.021

Fathi, K., & Palhang, M. (2018, September). Evaluation of Using Neural Networks on Variety of Agents and Playability of Games. In *2018 International Conference on Artificial Intelligence and Data Processing (IDAP)* (pp. 1-8). IEEE. DOI: 10.1109/IDAP.2018.8620880

Fernández, S., Adarve, R., Pérez, M., Rybarczyk, M., & Borrajo, D. (2006). Planning for an AI Based Virtual Agents Game. In *Proceedings of the Workshop AI Planning for Computer Games and Synthetic Characters in the ICAPS*.

Holmgard, C., Liapis, A., Togelius, J., & Yannakakis, G. N. (2014). Generative Agents for Player Decision Modeling in Games. *9th International Conference on the Foundations of Digital Games,* Fort Lauderdale. 1-8.

Huh, J. H., & Seo, Y. S. (2019). Understanding Edge Computing: Engineering Evolution with Artificial Intelligence. *IEEE Access : Practical Innovations, Open Solutions*, 7, 164229–164245. DOI: 10.1109/ACCESS.2019.2945338

Jeste, D. V., Graham, S. A., Nguyen, T. T., Depp, C. A., Lee, E. E., & Kim, H. C. (2020). Beyond Artificial Intelligence: Exploring Artificial Wisdom. *International Psychogeriatrics*, 32(8), 993–1001. DOI: 10.1017/S1041610220000927

Khachane, M. Y. (2017). Organ-Based Medical Image Classification Using Support Vector Machine. *International Journal of Synthetic Emotions*, 8(1), 18–30. DOI: 10.4018/IJSE.2017010102

Li, R. (2024). A "Dance of storytelling": Dissonances between substance and style in collaborative storytelling with AI. *Computers and Composition*, 71, 102825. DOI: 10.1016/j.compcom.2024.102825

Li, Y., Jiang, Y., Tian, D., Hu, L., Lu, H., & Yuan, Z. (2019). AI-Enabled Emotion Communication. *IEEE Network*, 33(6), 15–21. DOI: 10.1109/MNET.001.1900070

Liu, J., Togelius, J., Pérez-Liébana, D., & Lucas, S. M. (2017, June). Evolving Game Skill-Depth Using General Video Game AI Agents. In *2017 IEEE Congress on Evolutionary Computation (CEC)* (pp. 2299-2307). IEEE. DOI: 10.1109/CEC.2017.7969583

Liu-Thompkins, Y., Okazaki, S., & Li, H. (2022). Artificial Empathy in Marketing Interactions: Bridging the Human-AI Gap in Affective and Social Customer Experience. *Journal of the Academy of Marketing Science*, 50(6), 1198–1218. DOI: 10.1007/s11747-022-00892-5

Mahmud, H., Islam, A. N., Ahmed, S. I., & Smolander, K. (2022). What Influences Algorithmic Decision-Making? A Systematic Literature Review on Algorithm Aversion. *Technological Forecasting and Social Change*, 175, 121390. DOI: 10.1016/j.techfore.2021.121390

Marcos, S., García Peñalvo, F. J., & Vázquez Ingelmo, A. (2021, October). Emotional AI in Healthcare: A p ilot architecture proposal to merge emotion recognition tools. In *Ninth International Conference on Technological Ecosystems for Enhancing Multiculturality (TEEM'21)* (pp. 342-349). DOI: 10.1145/3486011.3486472

Megahed, F. M., Chen, Y. J., Ferris, J. A., Knoth, S., & Jones-Farmer, L. A. (2023). How Generative AI Models such as ChatGPT can be (Mis)Used in Practice, Education, and Research? An Exploratory Study. *Quality Engineering*, 1–29.

Miikkulainen, R., Bryant, B. D., Cornelius, R., Karpov, I. V., Stanley, K. O., & Yong, C. H. (2006). Computational Intelligence in Games. *Computational Intelligence: Principles and Practice,* 155-191.

Morris, M. R. (2023). Scientists' Perspectives on the Potential for Generative AI in their Fields. *arXiv preprint arXiv:2304.01420.*

Murphy, C., & Thomas, F. P. (2023). Generative AI in Spinal Cord Injury Research and Care: Opportunities and Challenges Ahead. *The Journal of Spinal Cord Medicine*, 46(3), 341–342. DOI: 10.1080/10790268.2023.2198926

Naddaf, Y. (2010). *Game-Independent AI Agents for Playing Atari 2600 Console Games.* University of Alberta.

Nareyek, A. (2000, October). Intelligent Agents for Computer Games. In *International Conference on Computers and Games* (pp. 414-422). Berlin, Heidelberg: Springer Berlin Heidelberg.

Park, J. S., O'Brien, J. C., Cai, C. J., Morris, M. R., Liang, P., & Bernstein, M. S. (2023). Generative agents: Interactive simulacra of human behavior. *arXiv preprint arXiv:2304.03442* DOI: 10.1145/3586183.3606763

Picard, R. W., Papert, S., Bender, W., Blumberg, B., Breazeal, C., Cavallo, D., Machover, T., Resnick, M., Roy, D., & Strohecker, C. (2004). Affective Learning—A Manifesto. *BT Technology Journal*, 22(4), 253–269. DOI: 10.1023/B:BTTJ.0000047603.37042.33

Power, M. J. (2006). The Structure of Emotion: An Empirical Comparison of Six Models. *Cognition and Emotion*, 20(5), 694–713. DOI: 10.1080/02699930500367925

Pusztahelyi, R. (2020). Emotional AI and Its Challenges in the Viewpoint of Online Marketing. *Curentul Juridic*, 81(2), 13–31.

Ratican, J., & Hutson, J. (2023). The Six Emotional Dimension (6DE) Model: A Multidimensional Approach to Analyzing Human Emotions and Unlocking the Potential of Emotionally Intelligent Artificial Intelligence (AI) via Large Language Models (LLM). *Journal of Artificial Intelligence and Robotics*, 1(1).

Ray, P. P. (2023). ChatGPT: A Comprehensive Review on Background, Applications, Key Challenges, Bias, Ethics, Limitations and Future Scope. *Internet of Things and Cyber-Physical Systems.*

Samsonovich, A. V. (2020). Socially Emotional Brain-Inspired Cognitive Architecture Framework for Artificial Intelligence. *Cognitive Systems Research*, 60, 57–76. DOI: 10.1016/j.cogsys.2019.12.002

Selvaraj, C., Chandra, I., & Singh, S. K. (2021). Artificial Intelligence and Machine Learning Approaches for Drug Design: Challenges and Opportunities for the Pharmaceutical Industries. *Molecular Diversity*, 1–21.

Singh, A., & Chouhan, T. (2023). Artificial Intelligence in HRM: Role of Emotional–Social Intelligence and Future Work Skill. In *The Adoption and Effect of Artificial Intelligence on Human Resources Management*, Part A (pp. 175-196). Emerald Publishing Limited.

Strich, F., Mayer, A. S., & Fiedler, M. (2021). What Do I Do in a World of Artificial Intelligence? Investigating the Impact of Substitutive Decision-Making AI Systems on Employees' Professional Role Identity. *Journal of the Association for Information Systems*, 22(2), 9. DOI: 10.17705/1jais.00663

Tan, S. C., & Nareyek, A. (2009). Integrating Facial, Gesture, and Posture Emotion Expression for a 3D Virtual Agent. In *Proceedings of the 14th International Conference on Computer Games: AI, Animation, Mobile, Interactive Multimedia, Educational & Serious Games* (CGames 2009 USA) (pp. 23-31).

Wortman, B., & Wang, J. Z. (2022). HICEM: A High-Coverage Emotion Model for Artificial Emotional Intelligence. *arXiv preprint arXiv:2206.07593.*

Zall, R., & Kangavari, M. R. (2022). Comparative Analytical Survey on Cognitive Agents with Emotional Intelligence. *Cognitive Computation*, 14(4), 1223–1246. DOI: 10.1007/s12559-022-10007-5

Chapter 4
Literature Review and Audience

ABSTRACT

This chapter addresses the integration of AI in enhancing the rigor and relevance of preliminary research and literature reviews while effectively engaging target audiences. The chapter begins by outlining methodologies for conducting preliminary research using AI tools, highlighting their ability to sift through vast datasets and identify pertinent studies, thereby saving researchers valuable time and ensuring comprehensive coverage. It then delves into AI-enhanced literature review techniques, demonstrating how AI can synthesize information, identify research gaps, and generate insightful summaries, thus elevating the quality of academic work. The focus then shifts to understanding the audience, emphasizing the critical role of tailoring research outputs to meet the expectations and interests of specific academic and public audiences. This is further explored through the concept of AI-powered rhetoric for contextual adaptation, where AI tools are employed to adjust the tone, style, and content of research presentations to suit diverse audience needs.

4.1 CONDUCTING PRELIMINARY RESEARCH

As discussed in the previous chapter, generative research agents can significantly enhance various stages of the research process, including the critical phases of preliminary research and literature review. These AI tools, with their ability to synthesize vast amounts of information and generate coherent narratives, can streamline the initial stages of research, enabling scholars to navigate the ever-growing sea of academic literature with greater efficiency and precision. In this chapter, we will explore how these research agents can be effectively utilized to conduct comprehensive and insightful preliminary research and literature reviews. Researchers can ensure that their foundational work is thorough, up-to-date, and reflective of

DOI: 10.4018/979-8-3693-6905-0.ch004

the current state of their field by leveraging the new potential of these augmented research assistants. This not only sets a solid groundwork for their research projects but also enhances the overall quality and relevance of their academic contributions.

Specific AI-enhanced techniques for conducting literature reviews will be reviewed, highlighting the tools and methods that can help identify key themes, gaps, and emerging trends within a given research area. These techniques will enable researchers to construct a robust and nuanced understanding of the existing body of knowledge, ensuring that their work builds upon and contributes meaningfully to ongoing academic discourse. The latter part of the chapter will shift focus to the importance of understanding and engaging with the intended audience. Effective research communication hinges not only on the quality of the content but also on how well it resonates with its readers. We will discuss AI-powered rhetorical strategies that can tailor research presentations to different audiences, whether they are peers, practitioners, or the broader public. By adapting the tone, style, and complexity of the research narrative, scholars can maximize the impact and reach of their work.

Returning to the research process, once a topic has been honed using tools like PerplexityAI to gauge current discussions and gaps within a field, a comprehensive literature review becomes crucial. This phase is integral to any academic endeavor, designed to deepen understanding and frame the research within the existing body of knowledge. The use of AI-driven tools can significantly streamline this phase. There are primarily two strategies for conducting a literature review with the assistance of AI:

1. **Direct use of generative databases:** Tools like PerplexityAI can be directly employed to extract and synthesize the most relevant and recent research articles, papers, and books. These platforms use advanced algorithms to sift through vast amounts of data, highlighting key findings, methodologies, and gaps in the current research landscape. This allows researchers to quickly grasp the breadth and depth of existing literature on their chosen topic.
2. **Integration with Large Language Models (LLMs):** LLMs like ChatGPT, Google's Gemini, or Anthropic's Claude can be utilized to perform nuanced searches within their training data. Researchers can input specific queries related to their research topic, and these models can generate summaries, identify key themes, and even suggest further reading based on the contextual relationships and patterns recognized in the data.

Both strategies offer unique advantages. Direct use of generative databases provides precise and targeted insights with minimal input, ideal for initial topic exploration and identifying research directions. In contrast, LLMs offer flexibility in handling complex queries and can integrate a broader range of sources and data types, making them suitable for deepening literature reviews and refining research questions. These capabilities are becoming increasingly embedded into every search engine and email system, highlighting the transformative potential of NLP.

NLP technologies are poised to replace traditional search terms with more sophisticated, conversational interactions. Search engines like Google are evolving to understand and process natural language queries, allowing users to ask questions in everyday language rather than relying on specific keywords. This shift enhances the accuracy and relevance of search results by considering the context and semantics of the query. As NLP continues to advance, it will enable search engines to provide more intuitive and human-like responses, making information retrieval more efficient and user-friendly.

In email communication, NLP is also making significant strides. Features like smart composition, automated responses, and contextual suggestions are now commonplace in email clients, driven by advanced NLP algorithms. These tools help users draft emails quickly, predict responses, and manage their inbox more effectively. By understanding the context and intent of email content, NLP technologies can automate routine tasks, prioritize messages, and provide actionable insights, significantly improving productivity and communication efficiency. As NLP becomes more deeply integrated into search engines and email systems, it not only transforms how we interact with digital platforms but also bridges the gap between human communication and machine understanding.

4.2 AI-ENHANCED LITERATURE REVIEW TECHNIQUES

Leveraging these tools for literature reviews allows researchers to ensure that their studies are grounded in comprehensive and current data, aligning with ongoing academic dialogues and trends. These tools expedite the review process, enhancing both the quality and relevance of research outputs. Through a summarization of key literature, pinpointing significant studies, and identifying central themes and gaps, the tools provide researchers with a robust understanding of the background and help refine their research questions. This process not only streamlines the identification of gaps in the field but also aids in formulating new and pertinent research questions, thereby setting a strong foundation for further investigation and discussion.

To conduct a thorough literature review using AI-driven tools like PerplexityAI, Scite.ai, Consensus, or Elicit, researchers first need to define their research question clearly. This question acts as the foundation for directing the AI tools effectively. Choosing the right tool is crucial, as each has unique capabilities. For instance, PerplexityAI is great for exploring broad concepts and providing overviews, while

Scite.ai excels in tracking how specific articles are cited, offering insights into the impact and controversy around research findings.

Once the appropriate tool is selected, researchers input detailed queries related to their central themes. These AI tools process the queries and produce outputs that include key literature references, summaries of important research, and often visual representations of data and trends in the field. Researchers can then review these outputs to identify crucial studies, conflicting evidence, and gaps in the current research.

This AI-assisted process saves significant time and enhances the relevance and depth of the literature review. By synthesizing the findings from these tools, researchers can formulate a well-rounded view of their field, noting major trends and unresolved questions. Finally, this comprehensive understanding allows researchers to refine their initial research questions, focusing on areas that are under-explored or contentious, thus setting a solid foundation for their studies. This method not only streamlines the review process but also ensures that the research is aligned with current academic discussions and trends.

In utilizing the Consensus tool (https://consensus.app/search/) for literature review in the context of financial technology's (FinTech) impact on global inflation, researchers can streamline their process effectively. By signing in with a Google account, users gain access to a wide range of functionalities. For example, a researcher might start by inputting a refined query such as "Can FinTech innovations mitigate global inflation?" into Consensus. The tool may suggest modifying the query to yield more precise results.

Once the query is set, the researcher has options like "Synthesize" or use "Copilot" to aggregate and synthesize information. Choosing "Synthesize" allows the tool to compile a cohesive summary from various sources (as seen in Figure 1), integrating multiple perspectives into a unified document. This feature is particularly useful for grasping overarching trends and major findings without the need to manually sift through each publication.

Figure 1. Consensus literature review

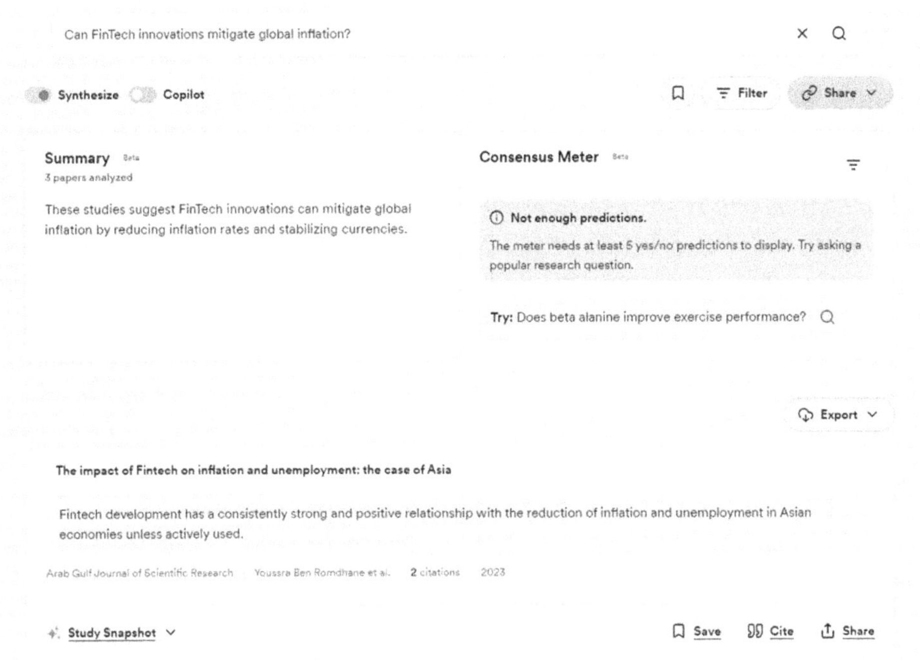

Each source presented in Consensus includes a one-sentence summary, enhancing the ability to quickly ascertain the relevance of each article. Additional functionalities like saving, citing, or sharing articles foster efficient management of resources. One can also select the language for the tool for accessibility. For a comprehensive analysis, these summarized articles can be transferred to a LLM like ChatGPT or others, which can be tasked to draft a detailed literature review. For instance, the following prompt can be entered into the LLM:

You will now use the following to write a literature review on the topic: Can FinTech innovations mitigate global inflation? Output in full paragraphs in narrative format of 6-8 sentences each. Start by writing an introductory paragraph that provides an overview of the field before organizing the literature review thematically with a topic sentence for each paragraph introducing the main idea and output in APA citation. Task: use the following for this task [paste information from search]

The prompt here includes What the model is being asked to do, how it is going to go about creating the Literature Review and is then given the actual information to organize. In this case, the publications listed in Consensus that were the result of our search "Can FinTech innovations mitigate global inflation?" The output from ChatGPT-4o is as follows:

In crafting a literature review on the topic "Can FinTech innovations mitigate global inflation?", it's essential to consolidate findings from recent studies that highlight the multifaceted impacts of financial technology on inflationary trends. The research consistently underscores FinTech's potential in stabilizing economic parameters such as inflation rates and currency values through various mechanisms.

One prominent study delineates the positive correlation between FinTech developments and the reduction of inflation and unemployment in Asian markets, emphasizing the sector's pivotal role in economic stabilization and growth (Ben Romdhane et al., 2023, Arab Gulf Journal of Scientific Research). Similarly, research conducted on Indonesia's economy reveals that FinTech can appreciably diminish inflation rates, leading to the real appreciation of the Indonesian Rupiah, albeit with a delayed effect on the exchange rate (Narayan et al., 2018, Buletin Ekonomi Moneter dan Perbankan).

In a broader context, a study from the International Journal of Research and Applied Technology illustrates how FinTech, by streamlining transactions and reducing the money supply in circulation, can effectively curb inflation (Budiarti et al., 2021). These studies collectively advocate for the strategic deployment of FinTech to foster more resilient and stable economic environments globally.

Furthermore, literature extends into the transformative potential of FinTech in reshaping financial markets and its role as a critical tool in addressing systemic economic challenges. For instance, analysis from the Foresight and STI Governance journal explores how FinTech is likely to redefine market dynamics by creating a new ecosystem of digital transnational financial corporations, potentially altering global financial stability and inflationary trends (Belozyorov et al., 2020).

By synthesizing these insights, the literature review would not only highlight the significant potential of FinTech in mitigating global inflation but also map out the broader economic implications, encouraging a nuanced understanding of FinTech's role in contemporary economic systems. This comprehensive approach ensures that the research question is thoroughly explored, grounded in recent empirical evidence, and reflective of the current academic discourse on FinTech and macroeconomic stability.

The initial literature review provides a foundational understanding of how FinTech innovations may influence global inflation. However, for a more in-depth exploration, utilizing the embedded Consensus GPT within the LLM itself can greatly enhance the quality and thoroughness of the literature review. This advanced tool can synthesize broader datasets, offer deeper insights into interconnected economic factors, and refine the research questions based on emerging trends identified from the latest studies. By typing "@" into the search bar, all GPTs can be accessed that have been recently used. Selecting "Consensus" will have the icon appear at the top of the search bar. Because the database is now linked to the LLM, it can be directly accessed and the output more effectively searched, organized, and formatted. For example, the literature review above gives us an idea of the types of themes that have emerged when considering the topic, but we should expand each to have a more thorough understanding of the state of the field. Focusing on how FinTech can "streamlining transactions and reducing the money supply in circulation," the following prompt can be used to expand on research into that area:

Using Consensus, you will now revise and expand the literature review. You will find the latest research and output in full paragraphs in APA citations. Task: use the following: In a broader context, a study from the International Journal of Research and Applied Technology illustrates how FinTech, by streamlining transactions and reducing the money supply in circulation, can effectively curb inflation (Budiarti et al., 2021). These studies collectively advocate for the strategic deployment of FinTech to foster more resilient and stable economic environments globally.

Note that one can merely copy and paste the section that needs expanding with the prompt to give context and examples to the LLM. The result of which is a more thorough review of the topic as follows:

In examining the role of FinTech innovations in mitigating global inflation, several key studies offer significant insights. According to Budiarti et al. (2021), FinTech can minimize inflation by reducing the amount of money circulating in society through more efficient digital payment systems. This streamlining of transactions helps to stabilize the economy by curbing the excess liquidity that often leads to inflation. This perspective is supported by Narayan and Sahminan (2018), who found that FinTech's impact on Indonesia's exchange rate and inflation was significant, demonstrating that digital financial services can reduce inflation and contribute to a real appreciation of the national currency, although the effects on the exchange rate may be delayed.

Further, Romdhane et al. (2023) illustrate the positive relationship between FinTech development and the reduction of inflation and unemployment in Asian economies. Their study highlights how digital finance has become a new driver of economic development, emphasizing the importance of actively using financial technologies to enhance economic stability. This active use of FinTech can provide a more resilient economic environment by addressing inflationary pressures more effectively.

The potential of FinTech to foster more resilient and stable economic environments is further reinforced by Belozyorov et al. (2020), who discuss the transformative scenarios of FinTech development in global financial markets. They suggest that international cooperation in the regulation of digital financial companies is essential to manage the risks and challenges associated with these innovations. This approach can help maintain economic stability while harnessing the benefits of FinTech advancements.

In addition to these findings, the broader implications of FinTech on inflation are discussed by Evers et al. (2018), who present a model showing how inflation influences firms' innovation activities. They argue that higher inflation rates can deter firms from engaging in innovative activities, thereby reducing long-term economic growth. This underscores the importance of maintaining stable inflation rates to foster an environment conducive to innovation and economic development.

By leveraging these AI tools and integrating their findings, researchers can develop a comprehensive literature review that not only sets a solid foundation for their studies but also ensures alignment with current trends and academic discussions. This approach enhances the quality and relevance of research output, providing a clear understanding of how FinTech innovations can mitigate global inflation and contribute to economic stability.

Overall, the strategic deployment of FinTech has shown promising results in stabilizing economies and reducing inflation. These studies collectively advocate for the integration of digital financial technologies as a means to foster more resilient and stable economic environments globally.

Utilizing the embedded Consensus GPT in LLMs can further enhance this literature review by offering more detailed and specific insights, ensuring a thorough treatment of the topic. The expanded literature review now includes new citations, each with a URL providing researchers direct access to the sources. This approach significantly accelerates the research process, as it allows quick access to relevant studies and data. For example, Budiarti et al. (2021) discussed the role of FinTech in minimizing inflation through digital payment systems, while Narayan and Sahminan (2018) examined its impact on exchange rates and inflation in Indonesia. Romdhane et al. (2023) explored the positive relationship between FinTech development and economic stability in Asian economies, and Belozyorov et al. (2020) highlighted the importance of international cooperation in regulating digital financial companies. Finally, Evers et al. (2018) discussed the broader implications of inflation on firms' innovation activities.

Despite the efficiency of generative tools like Consensus GPT, it is imperative to cross-check the generated sources for accuracy and completeness. For optimal results, it is advisable to utilize paid models that are directly linked to reputable databases such as Google Scholar or attached directly to the document under study.

This ensures immediate access to reliable and verifiable sources. Additionally, always verify the accuracy of citations provided by these AI tools. Information such as publication dates, publishers, and page numbers can often be incorrect, especially with pre-print articles that might have different details in their final published form. These discrepancies can arise if an article is initially rejected and subsequently submitted to a different journal. Fact-checking not only corrects these inaccuracies but also reinforces the credibility and integrity of the literature review, making this extra step a critical part of the research process.

To continue enriching the literature review, researchers can replicate the process utilized with Consensus GPT until the desired level of depth and breadth is achieved. This integration facilitates access to dynamic and nuanced analyses, ensuring that all pertinent aspects of the topic are thoroughly examined. The literature review then becomes aligned with the most current state of knowledge in the field. By employing Consensus GPT in conjunction with traditional research methods, researchers can significantly accelerate the review process while ensuring that the output is both deeply informed and closely aligned with the latest research developments.

This method highlights the powerful synergy between advanced AI tools and traditional research approaches, providing a contemporary lens through which academic inquiry is conducted. In fields like FinTech, where the landscape evolves rapidly, such a strategy is particularly valuable. It not only broadens the scope of the research but also sharpens the analytical focus, laying a robust foundation for developing impactful and innovative research outputs. With an understanding of the state of the field, we can now move onto hypothesis generation.

4.4 AI AND AUDIENCE

Having considered the diverse perspectives provided by AI agents in various disciplines, we now turn our attention to the equally important task of addressing different audiences through AI-powered rhetoric and contextual adaptation. Recent research into the topic of AI in education, particularly in the context of writing pedagogy, reveals a prevalent concern among both educators and students (Nazari et al., 2021). This apprehension revolves around the potential dilution of the student's voice and the perceived erosion of creativity within the classroom due to the utilization of AI technologies such as generative language models. The core of this anxiety lies in the supposition that reliance on AI for content generation might lead to a scenario where the authentic expression and individual creativity of students are overshadowed by the mechanical output of AI systems. This concern suggests that AI undermines the intrinsic value of personal narrative and original thought in academic writing (Abulibdeh et al., 2024; Li, 2024).

Research into these fears reveals a nuanced landscape. Kamalov et al. (2023) explore the psychological impact of AI integration in writing assignments, suggesting that while there is an initial phase of reliance on AI, it simultaneously opens avenues for students to engage critically with generated content, thereby refining their own expressive capabilities. Conversely, Yu (2024) presents a more cautionary perspective, highlighting instances where the overuse of AI in the creative process may inadvertently lead to a homogenization of student output, potentially stifling the diversity of expression that is fundamental to creative growth. Nevertheless, a burgeoning body of scholarly work advocates for a balanced approach to AI integration, emphasizing the potential for AI to act as a catalyst rather than a deterrent to creativity.

In their work, Dang et al. (2023) lay out the concept of "AI-assisted creativity," wherein AI is introduced as a tool to inspire and expand the creative horizons of students, encouraging them to explore novel rhetorical forms and perspectives that they might not have considered independently. Furthermore, Labajová (2023) underscores the importance of pedagogical strategies that prioritize the development of a critical engagement with AI-generated content. These strategies and considerations, however, are all predicated on traditional writing pedagogy and do not consider the broader potential of AI in adapting to different audiences while preserving the voice of the writer.

The ability to maintain the writer's unique voice while considering different audiences is now more feasible with the advancement of AI technologies. AI-powered rhetoric can be tailored to fit various contexts and audiences, ensuring that the original voice and intent are preserved. This adaptability can address the concerns of creativity dilution and homogenization. For instance, generative AI can be used to modify a piece of writing to suit different audiences without losing the unique style of the author. By adjusting tone, complexity, and focus, AI can help tailor messages to specific audiences, such as modifying a technical research paper for a general audience or adjusting the formal tone of an academic essay for a more casual blog post. This adaptability allows writers to reach a broader audience while maintaining their distinctive voice and message integrity.

Let us consider an initial example of an academic essay: "The rapid advancement of artificial intelligence (AI) technologies presents both opportunities and challenges in various sectors, including education. AI can enhance personalized learning experiences by analyzing student data and tailoring educational content to individual needs. However, there are concerns about data privacy and the potential for AI to perpetuate existing biases."

Now, we can adapt this for a general audience blog post as follows: "Artificial intelligence (AI) is changing how we learn, offering new ways to personalize education based on each student's unique needs. While AI brings many benefits, such as customized learning experiences, it also raises important questions about privacy and fairness. We need to be mindful of these issues as we embrace AI in our schools."

Therefore, a more nuanced understanding of maintaining an original voice in the context of AI writing tools can be enriched by delving into the rhetorical tradition and its diverse tools and forms. This approach, however, seems to be a relatively uncharted territory within recent scholarly discussions, as indicated by the absence of direct literature on this specific nexus between AI and rhetorical tradition post-2015. Despite this, the foundational principles of rhetoric, dating back to classical antiquity, offer valuable insights into how one might handle the challenges presented by AI integration in writing pedagogy today. In fact, rhetoric, as the art of persuasion, encompasses a wide range of strategies and structures for effective communication. From Aristotle's appeals of *ethos, pathos,* and *logos* to the sophistic emphasis on the power of language to shape reality, rhetorical education has historically aimed to equip individuals with the skills to express themselves compellingly and persuasively (Kennedy, 1991).

Ethos refers to the credibility and ethical character of the speaker or writer, ensuring that the audience trusts and respects them. *Pathos* involves appealing to the audience's emotions, aiming to elicit feelings that align with the speaker's or writer's message. *Logos* is the logical appeal, using reasoning, facts, and evidence to persuade the audience through rational argumentation. These foundational elements of rhetoric, deeply rooted in classical antiquity, provide a robust framework for understanding how language can be used effectively in communication. The sophistic tradition, emphasizing the transformative power of language, complements these principles by highlighting how skillful rhetoric can shape perceptions and realities. The integration of AI tools in the writing process introduces a modern complexity to this ancient discipline, raising questions about how these digital technologies might influence the development of a student's unique voice and creative expression.

To address the concern of maintaining the original voice of a researcher within the AI-augmented writing process, it is pertinent to draw on the emphasis in the rhetorical tradition on invention (*heuristic*), arrangement, style, memory, and delivery. By leveraging AI as a tool for invention, researchers can explore a broader range of ideas and perspectives at the outset of the writing process. However, the subsequent stages of arrangement and style are where the voice and originality of the writer can truly emerge, as they critically engage with and refine the AI-generated content, tailoring it to their argument and desired impact (Lanham, 1991). Furthermore, the rhetorical concept of kairos—the art of seizing the opportune moment in speech to achieve persuasion—can offer a framework for understanding how AI tools might be used judiciously to enhance a writer's voice rather than suppress it. By encouraging consideration of the appropriateness of AI-generated content within the specific context of their argument and audience, writers can foster a critical awareness of how technology can serve the rhetorical situation effectively (Kinneavy, 2002).

By emphasizing the inventive phase, AI can assist in generating a wealth of ideas, thus broadening the scope of potential arguments and perspectives. However, it is in the arrangement and style phases where the true individuality of the researcher comes forth. During these stages, the researcher carefully organizes the AI-generated ideas and refines the language to ensure it resonates with their unique voice and intended impact. This process ensures that the final output is not just a mechanical product of AI but a polished piece of writing that reflects the researcher's original thought and creativity. Moreover, the rhetorical principle of *kairos* can guide the judicious use of AI, encouraging researchers to deploy AI-generated content at moments where it can most effectively complement their arguments. By being mindful of the timing and context, writers can strategically integrate AI tools to enhance their persuasive efforts, ensuring that the technology serves their rhetorical goals without overshadowing their authentic voice. This approach promotes a balanced and critical engagement with AI, where the technology is harnessed to augment, rather than diminish, the writer's creativity and originality, as seen in the case of no less than the Bard himself.

Few figures in English literature are more highly regarded than William Shakespeare (ca. 1564–1616). Yet, one can argue that his creativity did not stem solely from an authentic voice but from his deep understanding and innovative combination of rhetorical traditions (Rahman & Weda, 2019). This perspective offers a compelling lens through which to view the integration of AI in research and writing pedagogy today. Shakespeare's creative "genius," as evidenced by his prolific output of 38 plays and 154 sonnets, has been attributed to his mastery over the rhetorical conventions of his time and his ability to combine these conventions in novel ways (Joseph, 2008). His familiarity with the works of classical rhetoricians and the Elizabethan penchant for rhetorical flourish allowed him to craft speeches, dialogues, and monologues that have captivated audiences for centuries (Vickers, 1993). Shakespeare's skill in manipulating rhetorical devices such as metaphor, antithesis, and irony demonstrates a sophisticated understanding of how language can evoke emotion, convey complex ideas, and persuade or engage the audience (Greenblatt, 2004).

Drawing from the Shakespearean example, the integration of AI in writing education can similarly be seen not as a deterrent to creativity and originality but as an opportunity to expand the rhetorical toolkit of researchers and graduate students (Table 4.1). Just as Shakespeare drew upon the rhetorical tradition to invent and innovate, students today can use AI-generated content as raw material to be shaped, refined, and recombined in service of their expressive goals. This process echoes the rhetorical practice of inventio, the discovery of arguments or content, where AI can serve as a modern aid in generating ideas and perspectives that students might not have accessed otherwise.

By integrating AI tools into the writing process, writers can explore a broader range of ideas at the outset, using these tools to facilitate the inventive phase of writing. AI can help generate diverse content and perspectives, much like how Shakespeare utilized the rhetorical conventions of his time to create his works. Subsequently, in the arrangement and style phases, students can critically engage with the AI-generated content, refining it to reflect their unique voice and intended impact. This approach ensures that the final product is not just a mechanical output of AI but a crafted piece of writing that embodies the creativity and originality of the author. Moreover, considering the rhetorical concept of *kairos*—the art of seizing the opportune moment in speech to achieve persuasion—provides a framework for understanding how AI tools might be used judiciously to enhance a researcher's voice rather than suppress it. By encouraging students to consider the appropriateness of AI-generated content within the specific context of their argument and audience, writers can foster a critical awareness of how technology can serve the rhetorical situation effectively (Kinneavy, 2002).

Table 1. Integrating AI with classical rhetorical strategies in academic writing

Rhetorical Strategy	Description	Alignment with AI
Dispositio (Arrangement)	Organizing material in a coherent and persuasive manner; includes structuring the introduction, arguments, proofs, and conclusion.	**AI-Enhanced Writing:** AI-generated content encourages students to actively structure and rearrange the presented ideas to form coherent and persuasive texts.
Inventio (Invention)	The process of developing arguments and finding ways to persuade.	**AI as a Tool for Idea Generation:** AI can provide diverse perspectives and data-driven insights that students can use as a basis for forming arguments.
Elocutio (Style)	The choice of language and style to suit the topic, audience, and speaker's objectives.	**Stylistic Adaptation with AI:** AI tools can suggest different styles and tones based on the intended audience and purpose, enhancing the writer's stylistic choices.
Memoria (Memory)	The technique of memorizing the content of a speech.	**AI as an External Memory Aid:** AI can serve as a repository of information, helping students retrieve and organize knowledge efficiently.
Pronuntiatio (Delivery)	The actual presentation of the speech to the audience.	**AI in Presentation Tools:** AI can aid in preparing digital presentations, providing real-time feedback on delivery aspects such as pacing and pronunciation.

Engaging with AI-generated content encourages students to actively exercise judgment and creativity as they operate through the wealth of material AI offers—deciding what to incorporate, alter, or omit. This engagement is akin to the rhetorical strategy of *dispositio*, pushing students to critically consider structure and coherence, thereby fostering the development of a unique voice enhanced by AI's expansive content reservoir. The classical rhetorical strategy of *dispositio* refers to the organization or "arrangement" of material within a speech or piece of writing and is the second of the five canons of rhetoric, which also include *inventio* (invention), *elocutio* (style), *memoria* (memory), and *pronuntiatio* (delivery).

For instance, *dispositio* involves structuring the arguments or content in a coherent and persuasive manner, deciding on the best order and layout to present ideas to effectively communicate with and persuade the audience. This includes the introduction (*exordium*), the statement of the case (*narratio*), the outline of arguments (*divisio* or *partitio*), the proof (*confirmatio*), the refutation of opposing arguments (*refutatio*), and the conclusion (*peroratio*). The ultimate goal of *dispositio* is to maximize the impact of the message by arranging it in the most logical, accessible, and engaging sequence. The following example prompt illustrates the potential in using rhetoric.

Example Prompt for Using AI to Engage With Dispositio

Scenario: A Student Working on a Persuasive Essay
Student Background:

- Has a collection of ideas and arguments
- Needs help organizing them coherently

Objective:

- To help the student structure their essay using the rhetorical strategy of *dispositio*

Prompt

Student Input: "I have gathered a lot of information and arguments about the importance of renewable energy, but I am struggling to organize them into a coherent essay. Can you help me arrange my ideas effectively?"

AI Response

"Of course! Let's use the rhetorical strategy of *dispositio* to organize your material in a persuasive and logical manner. Here's a step-by-step guide to structuring your essay on renewable energy:

1. Introduction (*Exordium*)
    - **Hook:** Start with a compelling fact or statistic about the current state of energy consumption and its impact on the environment.
    - **Thesis Statement:** Clearly state your main argument. For example, 'Renewable energy is essential for sustainable development and environmental preservation, requiring immediate and widespread adoption.'
2. Statement of the Case (*Narratio*)
    - **Background Information:** Provide context about the current energy landscape, including reliance on fossil fuels and their environmental impact.
    - **Importance of the Issue:** Explain why the transition to renewable energy is crucial for the future.
3. Outline of Arguments (*Divisio* or *Partitio*)
    - **Main Points:** Briefly list the key arguments you will present in your essay. For instance, 'This essay will discuss the environmental, economic, and social benefits of renewable energy.'
4. Proof (*Confirmatio*)
    - **Argument 1: Environmental Benefits**
        - **Topic Sentence:** Introduce the environmental advantages of renewable energy.
        - **Supporting Ideas:** Discuss how renewable energy reduces greenhouse gas emissions and pollution.
        - **Evidence:** Provide data and examples, such as the reduction of carbon footprints through solar and wind energy.
    - **Argument 2: Economic Benefits**
        - **Topic Sentence:** Highlight the economic advantages of renewable energy.
        - **Supporting Ideas:** Explain job creation, cost savings, and energy independence.
        - **Evidence:** Use statistics and case studies demonstrating economic growth in regions adopting renewable energy.
    - **Argument 3: Social Benefits**
        - **Topic Sentence:** Discuss the social impacts of renewable energy.

- Supporting Ideas: Address health benefits and energy access for underserved communities.
- **Evidence:** Cite research showing improved public health and quality of life from cleaner energy sources.

5. Refutation of Opposing Arguments (*Refutatio*)
   - **Counterarguments:** Acknowledge and refute common objections to renewable energy, such as cost and reliability concerns.
   - **Rebuttal:** Provide evidence and reasoning to counter these objections, emphasizing technological advancements and long-term savings.
6. Conclusion (*Peroratio*)
   - **Summary:** Summarize the main points discussed in the body paragraphs.
   - **Restate Thesis:** Reiterate the thesis statement in light of the evidence presented.
   - **Call to Action:** Urge the audience to support renewable energy initiatives and policies.

Interactive Feedback: As you write each section, I can provide immediate feedback on your structure and content. Let's start with your introduction. Draft a few sentences, and I'll help you refine them."

Follow-Up

- **Student drafts the introduction**
- **AI provides feedback on clarity, coherence, and engagement**

AI Feedback Example: "Great start! Your hook about the environmental impact of fossil fuels is very compelling. Your thesis statement is clear, but consider making it more specific by mentioning the key points you'll discuss in the body paragraphs. For example, 'Renewable energy is essential for sustainable development and environmental preservation, requiring immediate and widespread adoption due to its environmental, economic, and social benefits.'"

AI can facilitate this process in a way similar to traditional writing practices, where writers internally contemplate thoughts before deciding their relevance—only now, these thoughts are externalized on screens, making the cognitive process of writing tangible and interactive. This revelation suggests that the integration of AI in the writing process is not (and need not be) a departure from traditional practices but an extension that makes the internal deliberations of writing explicitly visible. Acknowledging this similarity reveals how AI externalizes the inherent processes of writing, underscoring the interconnectedness between conventional writing methodologies and the role of AI tools in modern writing pedagogy. By making these internal processes visible, AI allows for a more interactive and reflective approach to writing, where the writer's unique voice is preserved and enhanced through the judicious use of technology.

Integrating generative writing tools can transcend traditional boundaries, offering a more personalized approach to learning. Students can use AI to break down complex writing assignments into smaller, more manageable segments, tackling each component at their own pace. This approach caters to diverse learning styles and speeds, ensuring that educational experiences are both accessible and tailored to meet the unique needs and objectives of each learner. For instance, a student who excels in generating ideas but struggles with organization can receive AI-driven prompts and outlines that guide them through the structuring process. Conversely, a student who finds initial ideation challenging might benefit from AI-generated brainstorming tools that spark creativity and thought. This level of customization extends beyond mere convenience; it represents a fundamental shift in how educational content is delivered and interacted with, making learning more engaging, effective, and aligned with individual student goals.

Moreover, the application of AI in this context supports iterative learning, allowing students to progressively refine their skills through immediate feedback on each segment of an assignment. This feedback loop, driven by AI algorithms that can assess and respond to student work in real time, accelerates the learning process by identifying areas for improvement and offering targeted exercises to address specific weaknesses. Consequently, students are not just completing assignments; they are engaging in a dynamic, interactive learning journey that continually adapts to their evolving needs. This adaptation is pivotal in optimizing learning processes, where the role of AI is not just supplementary but foundational in personalizing education (Mon et al., 2023). Such adaptability has been highlighted in recent studies, where its application extends beyond conventional educational frameworks. This flexibility enables the creation of a learning environment that is dynamic, personalized, and responsive to individual student needs. The ability to provide personalized feedback and learning paths offers significant advantages, facilitating individualized learning experiences that were once thought impossible within the constraints of traditional education systems (Sheth et al., 2023). By leveraging AI for personalized education, students can benefit from a tailored learning experience that adapts to their strengths and areas for improvement. This personalized approach not only enhances engagement and effectiveness but also ensures that each learner's educational journey is aligned with their unique goals and capabilities. This integration of AI into educational practices represents a significant advancement in creating more effective and inclusive learning environments.

4.5 AI-POWERED RHETORIC FOR CONTEXTUAL ADAPTATION

In the rapidly evolving landscape of digital communication and software development, the advent of Docker containers has marked a significant milestone. Docker, a pioneering platform, facilitated a paradigm shift by introducing containers that encapsulate an application and its dependencies, thereby ensuring consistent functionality across varied computing environments (Merkel, 2014). This technological innovation addresses a critical challenge in software deployment: the notorious "it works on my machine" syndrome, where applications behave unpredictably in different settings due to environmental discrepancies. Docker's solution, embedding the application with all its necessary components, has streamlined development processes and deployment cycles, offering a replicable and efficient model across disparate systems.

The arena of the humanities, particularly in the disciplines of rhetoric and communication, faces a parallel challenge: the adaptation of messages to suit diverse audience contexts. Each audience brings its unique set of "dependencies"—cultural backgrounds, belief systems, and expectations—that significantly influence the reception of communicated messages (Aristotle, trans. 1991). In this light, the concept of "Humanities containers" emerges as a novel proposition, suggesting that the principles underpinning Docker's success could be analogously applied to manage the elaborateness of rhetorical adaptation across disciplines (Table 2). This section posits that AI-powered tools and platforms like Docker could help rethink how messages are tailored and transmitted across various audiences, mirroring the efficiency and reliability Docker has brought to software development. The analogy lies in creating adaptable rhetorical "containers" that can package a core message with all necessary contextual elements, ensuring it is interpreted correctly by different audiences.

Table 2. AI-powered rhetoric adaptation

Strategy	Description	Reference
Audience Analysis	AI can analyze audience characteristics such as demographics, preferences, and cultural contexts using big data and machine learning algorithms. This analysis helps in understanding the audience's dependencies and tailoring messages accordingly.	Lim et al., 2023
Contextual Adaptation	Just as Docker ensures applications run consistently across different environments, AI can ensure that core messages maintain their intended impact across various audience contexts. NLP tools can adjust the tone, style, and content of messages.	Moreau et al., 2023

continued on following page

Table 2. Continued

Strategy	Description	Reference
Real-Time Feedback	AI-driven platforms can provide real-time feedback on the effectiveness of communication. For instance, sentiment analysis tools can gauge audience reactions and suggest modifications to enhance clarity and engagement.	Kumar et al., 2024
Blockchain for Authenticity	Blockchain can be employed to verify the authenticity and integrity of the adapted messages. By maintaining a decentralized ledger, it ensures that the content has not been tampered with, preserving the original intent, and meaning.	Shah et al., 2024

The foundation for such an approach lies in the growing recognition of communication's contextual dependency, where the effectiveness of a message is closely tied to the audience's specific characteristics and the communicator's ability to anticipate and adapt to these (Bitzer, 1968). The proposed literary adaptation framework offers a systematic method to enhance the adaptability and effectiveness of communication strategies. The integration of AI for dynamic content adjustment and blockchain for the secure exchange of rhetorical strategies, this innovation aims to significantly reduce the ambiguity and unpredictability traditionally associated with audience adaptation.

The intersection of technology and communication, particularly through the lens of adaptation and audience understanding, has garnered increasing scholarly interest. This review synthesizes key contributions within this domain, organized thematically to provide a comprehensive overview of existing literature on Docker technology's parallels in communication, the role of rhetoric in audience adaptation, and the emerging role of artificial intelligence and blockchain in enhancing rhetorical practices. The advent of Docker and its impact on software development practices has been extensively documented, with Merkel (2014) highlighting its revolutionary approach to managing dependencies and ensuring consistency across environments. This technological breakthrough provides a valuable framework for understanding similar challenges within communication disciplines. The concept of encapsulation and environment-specific deployment parallels the process of tailoring messages to diverse audiences, a foundational aspect of effective communication. Researchers like Hykes (2013) have further explored Docker's underlying mechanisms, offering insights into the potential for similar encapsulation strategies in rhetorical practices.

The ancient art of rhetoric, as outlined by Aristotle (trans. 1991), offers an early systematic exploration of adapting messages to audiences, emphasizing the importance of ethos, pathos, and logos. Bitzer's (1968) concept of the rhetorical situation further emphasizes that effective communication relies on understanding and adapting to the audience's specific circumstances. Recent scholarship has expanded on these ideas, showing how digital platforms and social media require more nuanced approaches to rhetorical adaptation (Jones, 2018). The application of artificial intelligence to rhetorical analysis represents a burgeoning area of research. LLMs like BERT have been identified as powerful tools for understanding and generating text tailored to specific audience characteristics (Devlin et al., 2019). These technologies enable dynamic audience analysis and message customization, suggesting a shift toward more automated and sophisticated rhetorical practices. Studies by Knight and Schiff (2020) explore AI's potential to craft messages that resonate across cultural and contextual divides, highlighting machine learning's transformative impact on traditional rhetoric.

Additionally, blockchain technology's implications for intellectual property and secure transactions are relevant themes. Howell et al. (2021) examine blockchain's potential to revolutionize content creation and distribution, protecting creators' rights while facilitating the exchange of ideas. This aligns with the concept of "containers," where rhetorical strategies can be securely exchanged and customized for different contexts. Blockchain's secure, transparent transactions offer a framework for monetizing and sharing rhetorical expertise in the digital age. Research suggests that the intersection of technology, rhetoric, and communication provides a foundation for innovative audience engagement. The parallels between Docker's solutions and rhetorical adaptation challenges underscore the potential for new approaches. The advent of AI and blockchain technologies offers pathways for enhancing and securing rhetorical practices, suggesting a future where communication strategies are as adaptable and consistent as software deployed through Docker containers.

This research employs a multi-disciplinary approach, integrating concepts from software engineering, rhetorical theory, AI, and blockchain technology to explore the potential of the containers metaphor for enhancing rhetorical practice. The methodology involves both conceptual analysis and hypothetical application, grounded in current technological and rhetorical frameworks while projecting future possibilities. The study draws an analogy between Docker containers, which revolutionized software deployment by encapsulating applications with their dependencies (Merkel, 2014), and a similar encapsulation mechanism for rhetoric. It theoretically explores how AI, particularly large language models (LLMs), can analyze audience contexts and generate tailored rhetorical strategies (Devlin et al., 2019). Additionally, it investigates how blockchain could facilitate the secure exchange and monetization of these strategies, supporting a marketplace for rhetorical expertise (Howell et al., 2021).

The considerations of this chapter have discussed the integration of AI in research and writing processes, illustrating how these technologies can revolutionize rhetorical practices and audience engagement. The exploration began by recognizing the parallels between Docker containers in software development and the proposed concept of "Humanities containers" for rhetorical adaptation. This analogy provided a foundational framework for understanding how encapsulating messages with contextual elements can enhance communication across diverse audiences, much like

Docker ensures consistent application performance across different environments (Merkel, 2014).

We examined the potential of AI, particularly LLMs, to analyze audience contexts and generate tailored rhetorical strategies. This approach not only democratizes access to sophisticated rhetorical tools but also aligns with the vision of AI enhancing rhetorical analysis and adaptability (Devlin et al., 2019; Knight & Schiff, 2020). AI's capability to dynamically adjust content based on real-time feedback further enhances the effectiveness of communication, offering a more personalized and contextually aware interaction with audiences.

The integration of blockchain technology was also discussed, highlighting its role in securely exchanging and monetizing rhetorical strategies. Blockchain's potential to protect intellectual property and ensure the integrity of adapted messages introduces a new dimension to rhetorical practice, fostering a dynamic ecosystem of scholarly exchange (Howell et al., 2021).

However, this chapter also underscored the critical ethical considerations that accompany the integration of AI and blockchain into rhetorical practices. Issues such as data privacy, algorithmic bias, and the commodification of communication strategies necessitate careful scrutiny to ensure these technologies enhance rather than undermine humanistic inquiry and expression. The risk of homogenizing communication practices through standardized "containers" emphasizes the need to maintain diversity and creativity in rhetorical approaches.

As we move deeper into the integration of AI in research and writing, it is imperative to balance technological advancements with ethical considerations. The future of rhetorical practice hinges on our ability to harness these technologies to enhance adaptability and effectiveness while preserving the richness and diversity of human communication. This chapter has laid the groundwork for further exploration of these themes, advocating for a thoughtful and nuanced approach to integrating AI into existing research workflows of professionals.

REFERENCES

Abulibdeh, A., Zaidan, E., & Abulibdeh, R. (2024). Navigating the confluence of artificial intelligence and education for sustainable development in the era of industry 4.0: Challenges, opportunities, and ethical dimensions. *Journal of Cleaner Production*, 437, 140527. DOI: 10.1016/j.jclepro.2023.140527

Aristotle, . (1991). *On Rhetoric: A Theory of Civic Discourse* (Kennedy, G. A., Trans.). Oxford University Press.

Bitzer, L. F. (1968). The Rhetorical Situation. *Philosophy & Rhetoric*, 1(1), 1–14.

Dang, H., Brudy, F., Fitzmaurice, G., & Anderson, F. (2023, October). WorldSmith: Iterative and Expressive Prompting for World Building with a Generative AI. In *Proceedings of the 36th Annual ACM Symposium on User Interface Software and Technology* (pp. 1-17). DOI: 10.1145/3586183.3606772

Devlin, J., Chang, M. W., Lee, K., & Toutanova, K. (2019). BERT: Pre-training of Deep Bidirectional Transformers for Language Understanding. *arXiv preprint arXiv:1810.04805.*

Greenblatt, S. (2005). *Will in the world: How Shakespeare became Shakespeare.* WW Norton & Company.

Howell, N., Arner, D., & Buckley, R. P. (2021). Blockchain and the Future of Intellectual Property. *Intellectual Property Quarterly*, 2, 123–142.

Hykes, S. (2013). Docker: Automating the deployment of Linux applications inside software containers. *Linux Journal*, 2013(239), 2.

Jones, R. (2018). Social Media, Digital Platforms, and the Transformation of Rhetorical Engagement. *Journal of Communication*, 68(3), 453–475.

Joseph, S. M. (2008). *Shakespeare's use of the arts of Language*. Paul Dry Books.

Kamalov, F., Santandreu Calonge, D., & Gurrib, I. (2023). New era of artificial intelligence in education: Towards a sustainable multifaceted revolution. *Sustainability (Basel)*, 15(16), 12451. DOI: 10.3390/su151612451

Kennedy, G. A. (1993). Aristotle" On rhetoric": A theory of civic discourse. *Philosophy & Rhetoric*, 26(4).

Kinneavy, J. L. (2002). Kairos in classical and modern rhetorical theory. Rhetoric and kairos: *Essays in history, theory, and praxis,* 58-76.

Knight, S., & Schiff, A. (2020). Artificial Intelligence and the Future of Rhetorical Analysis. *Rhetoric Review*, 39(4), 444–459.

Labajová, L. (2023). The state of AI: Exploring the perceptions, credibility, and trustworthiness of the users towards AI-Generated Content.

Li, R. (2024). A "Dance of storytelling": Dissonances between substance and style in collaborative storytelling with AI. *Computers and Composition*, 71, 102825. DOI: 10.1016/j.compcom.2024.102825

Merkel, D. (2014). Docker: Lightweight Linux containers for consistent development and deployment. *Linux Journal*, 2014(239), 2.

Mon, B. F., Wasfi, A., Hayajneh, M., & Slim, A. (2023, August). A study on role of Artificial Intelligence in education. In *2023 International Conference on Computing, Electronics & Communications Engineering (iCCECE)* (pp. 133-138). IEEE. DOI: 10.1109/iCCECE59400.2023.10238613

Nazari, N., Shabbir, M. S., & Setiawan, R. (2021). Application of Artificial Intelligence powered digital writing assistant in higher education: Randomized controlled trial. *Heliyon*, 7(5), e07014. DOI: 10.1016/j.heliyon.2021.e07014

Rahman, F., & Weda, S. (2019). Linguistic deviation and the rhetoric figures in Shakespeare's selected plays. *XLinguage European Scientific Language Journal*, 12(1), 37–52. DOI: 10.18355/XL.2019.12.01.03

Vickers, B. (1993). Rhetoric. In Corns, T. N. (Ed.), *The Cambridge companion to English poetry: Donne to Marvell* (pp. 101–120). DOI: 10.1017/CCOL0521411475.005

Yu, H. (2024). The application and challenges of ChatGPT in educational transformation: New demands for teachers' roles. *Heliyon*, 10(2), e24289. DOI: 10.1016/j.heliyon.2024.e24289

Chapter 5
From Hypothesis to Analysis

ABSTRACT

This chapter offers a guide on leveraging AI throughout the research process, from formulating hypotheses to analyzing and visualizing data. The chapter begins with strategies for formulating hypotheses using AI, illustrating how AI tools can identify patterns and suggest novel research directions based on existing data. It then covers the design of research methodologies, demonstrating how AI can assist in creating robust and scalable research designs tailored to specific study requirements. The chapter progresses to discussing advanced tools for data collection, highlighting AI's role in automating and enhancing data-gathering processes to ensure accuracy and efficiency. Techniques for AI-driven data analysis are explored in depth, showcasing how AI can uncover hidden insights and perform complex analyses that might be challenging for traditional methods. The final section focuses on visualizing data with AI tools, providing practical examples of how AI can generate clear, compelling visual representations of data, making findings more accessible and interpretable.

5.1 HYPOTHESIS FORMATION, DESIGN, AND METHODOLOGY

In the progression of academic research, the formation of a research question or hypothesis is a pivotal step that solidifies the direction of the study. This process is substantially enhanced by leveraging AI tools, which can analyze data accumulated from preliminary research and draw on analogous studies to predict plausible outcomes. This phase of the process allows researchers to transform a broad literature review into a focused inquiry. The process involves inputting data from the initial research findings into a model of choice. This model employs advanced algorithms to sift through vast datasets, identifying patterns and correlations that may not be

DOI: 10.4018/979-8-3693-6905-0.ch005

immediately apparent. It assesses the data in the context of existing research to suggest potential hypotheses.

In addition to generating hypotheses directly from preliminary data, researchers can further refine their research questions by incorporating existing comprehensive literature reviews into the AI-assisted hypothesis generation process. An effective approach involves uploading detailed literature reviews, such as the one by Ritterbusch and Teichmann (2023) titled *Defining the metaverse: A systematic literature review*, published in IEEE Access.

Once such a document is uploaded into an AI platform, researchers can employ specific prompts that guide the AI to analyze the review systematically. These prompts might instruct the AI to identify key themes, contradictions, or gaps in the current research landscape as presented in the document. For instance, a prompt could be structured as follows after attaching the PDF of the article: "Analyze the systematic review by Ritterbusch and Teichmann on the metaverse to identify primary research themes, gaps in current knowledge, and potential directions for future research." The response is as follows:

The systematic review by Ritterbusch and Teichmann provides a comprehensive examination of the evolving concept of the Metaverse, underlining its multifaceted interpretations and the absence of a uniform scientific consensus. The primary research themes identified include the technological foundations of the Metaverse, such as virtual reality, augmented reality, and blockchain technologies, which collectively facilitate an immersive and decentralized online environment. The review also highlights significant gaps in current knowledge, particularly the need for a universally accepted definition and the implications of the Metaverse on social, economic, and technical norms.

Future research directions suggested by the review focus on clarifying the definition of the Metaverse and exploring its potential societal impacts. It advocates for investigations into how the Metaverse can influence economic models, personal and social interactions, and the broader digital infrastructure. These explorations are essential for understanding the role of the Metaverse in future digital ecosystems and for developing frameworks that support its ethical integration into society.

This method enables the tool to parse through the structured content of a comprehensive review and suggest refined research questions or hypotheses that are deeply informed by the existing body of knowledge. This approach not only ensures that the hypotheses are relevant and grounded in the latest research but also leverages the depth of analysis found in systematic reviews to enhance the creativity and specificity of the research question. This technique exemplifies the synergy between scholarly analysis and new AI capabilities, offering a nuanced and sophisticated avenue for developing research agendas.

After analyzing the literature for gaps and identifying potential directions, the next step would be to develop a research question. The process begins with inputting data from preliminary research into an AI model. This could include key findings from literature reviews, such as the systematic review by Ritterbusch and Teichmann on the metaverse, which highlighted a lack of exploration into the economic models within virtual environments. Using this input, AI tools can generate hypotheses and research questions by comparing and contrasting the gathered data with similar studies across various disciplines. Therefore, one can prompt after attaching the article "Use the attached PDF to develop a research question based on gaps in the literature." The response is as follows:

Building upon the systematic review by Ritterbusch and Teichmann on the metaverse, a new research question emerges that addresses a gap in current knowledge regarding the economic implications of metaverse technologies. The systematic review reveals extensive discussions on the technological and social dimensions of the metaverse but less on the specific economic models that could sustain these virtual environments long-term.

Proposed Research Question

"How can economic models within the metaverse be structured to ensure sustainability and equitable access, especially in developing economies?"

This question aims to explore sustainable economic frameworks that could support the ongoing development and maintenance of metaverse environments, ensuring they remain accessible and beneficial across different economic contexts. The research will investigate various potential revenue models, such as subscriptions, microtransactions, and advertising, alongside regulatory and governance structures that could promote fairness and prevent monopolistic practices. This could lead to a more robust design of economic interactions in virtual spaces, providing a blueprint for future digital economies in the metaverse.

Once a viable research question is formulated—such as investigating sustainable economic models in the metaverse—the AI then assists in designing the research methodology. It suggests the most effective research techniques and methods that have been successful in similar studies, thereby tailoring the research approach to ensure accuracy and efficiency. For instance, with the following prompt "Now design a research methodology for the study." The response is as follows:

To investigate the sustainability of economic models within virtual environments, particularly in the context of the metaverse, a comprehensive research methodology can be structured as follows:

Research Design

The study will employ a mixed-methods approach, combining qualitative and quantitative research methods to provide a comprehensive understanding of economic activities and their sustainability in virtual environments.

Data Collection Methods

1. **Qualitative Data Collection:**
    - **Semi-structured Interviews:** Conduct interviews with developers, economists, and users engaged in the metaverse. These interviews will explore their perceptions and experiences related to economic transactions and models within these virtual spaces.
    - **Focus Groups:** Organize focus groups with participants from different demographics to discuss the challenges and opportunities of economic models in the metaverse.
2. **Quantitative Data Collection:**
    - **Surveys:** Distribute structured surveys to a larger sample of metaverse users to gather numerical data on user engagement, economic transactions, and the perceived sustainability of these activities.
    - **Behavioral Data Analysis:** Utilize existing data from metaverse platforms to analyze user behavior and economic interactions, focusing on transaction frequencies, types, and outcomes.

Sampling

- **Target Population:** Users and developers of multiple metaverse platforms, as well as experts in digital economy and virtual reality.
- **Sampling Technique:** Employ purposive sampling for qualitative methods to select individuals with specific knowledge and experience. For quantitative methods, use random sampling to ensure a diverse and representative sample of the general metaverse user population.

Data Analysis

1. **Qualitative Analysis:**
    - **Thematic Analysis:** Analyze interview and focus group transcripts to identify common themes and patterns related to economic sustainability in the metaverse.

- **Narrative Analysis:** Explore personal stories and testimonials from participants to understand individual experiences and projections about the economic future of virtual environments.

2. **Quantitative Analysis:**
   - **Statistical Analysis:** Apply statistical techniques such as regression analysis, factor analysis, and correlation to examine the relationships between user engagement metrics and economic sustainability indicators.
   - **Predictive Modeling:** Develop models to predict the future trends of economic models in the metaverse based on current data patterns.

Ethical Considerations

- Ensure confidentiality and anonymity of all participants.
- Obtain informed consent from all participants detailing the study's purpose, procedures, and potential risks.
- Address any potential ethical concerns regarding data privacy and manipulation, especially with data sourced from online platforms.

Outcome

The expected outcome of this methodology is a detailed understanding of the viability and sustainability of economic models within the metaverse. This study aims to contribute to academic literature by providing empirical evidence and theoretical insights into how digital economies can be structured and sustained in immersive virtual environments. This research could also offer practical recommendations for developers and policymakers on designing more robust and sustainable economic systems within the metaverse.

The proposed research methodology serves as a foundational framework from which researchers can launch a detailed exploration into the economic dynamics of the metaverse. While these recommendations provide a structured starting point, they are not definitive and should be adapted as new information emerges and as the research progresses. As the study unfolds, feedback from participants, emerging trends in technology, and shifts in the digital economy may necessitate revisions to the methodology to ensure its relevance and effectiveness. This iterative approach allows researchers to refine their methods and questions continuously, ensuring that the research remains aligned with the evolving landscape of virtual environments. By maintaining flexibility in the research design, scholars can ensure that their investigations remain on the cutting edge of technological and social developments, thereby enhancing the validity and impact of their findings. Additional considerations may be required at this stage of research, too.

When conducting research that involves human subjects, such as interviews and focus groups in the study of economic models in the metaverse, an Institutional Review Board (IRB) review may be required. The IRB is a committee established to review and approve research involving human subjects, ensuring that ethical standards are maintained. The primary role of the IRB is to protect the rights and welfare of the participants by reviewing the research protocols to ensure they are ethically sound and that risks are minimized.

The IRB considers several factors during the review process. These include ensuring that participants provide informed consent, meaning they are fully aware of the research purpose, procedures, potential risks, and benefits before agreeing to participate. The IRB also assesses the privacy and confidentiality measures in place to protect participants' data. Additionally, the IRB evaluates whether the risks to participants are reasonable in relation to the anticipated benefits of the research. This review process helps prevent ethical issues such as coercion, undue influence, and exploitation of vulnerable populations. By adhering to these guidelines, researchers can ensure their studies are ethically conducted, maintaining the integrity of the research and the trust of the participants.

In the context of studying sustainable economic models in the metaverse, these considerations are crucial, particularly given the novel and evolving nature of virtual environments and digital interactions. Ensuring ethical compliance through IRB review not only protects participants but also strengthens the validity and credibility of the research findings. Completing an IRB proposal can be quite time-consuming if all necessary materials and information are not gathered ahead of time. Being aware of what is needed is crucial to streamline the process and ensure a thorough and timely submission. The most common questions and materials needed for an IRB proposal typically include:

1. Research Purpose and Objectives:
    - What is the main objective of the study?
    - What specific questions or hypotheses is the research addressing?
2. Study Design and Methodology:
    - What research methods will be used (e.g., qualitative, quantitative, mixed-methods)?
    - How will data be collected (e.g., surveys, interviews, experiments)?
3. Participant Recruitment and Selection:
    - Who are the target participants?
    - What criteria will be used for inclusion and exclusion?
    - How will participants be recruited?

4. Informed Consent Process:
   - How will informed consent be obtained?
   - What information will be provided to participants about the study?
   - Will there be an opportunity for participants to ask questions before consenting?
5. Privacy and Confidentiality:
   - How will participants' privacy be protected?
   - What measures will be taken to ensure the confidentiality of data?
   - Where and how will data be stored and secured?
6. Potential Risks and Benefits:
   - What potential risks might participants face?
   - How will these risks be minimized?
   - What benefits can participants expect from the study?
7. Data Analysis Plan:
   - How will the collected data be analyzed?
   - What statistical or qualitative methods will be used?
8. Ethical Considerations:
   - How will ethical issues be addressed in the study?
   - Are there any conflicts of interest?
9. Study Timeline:
   - What is the proposed timeline for the study, including key milestones?
10. Supporting Documents:
   - Informed consent forms
   - Recruitment materials (e.g., flyers, emails)
   - Survey or interview questions
   - Data collection tools

By gathering these materials and thoroughly preparing answers to these common questions, researchers can ensure that their IRB proposal is comprehensive and well-organized. This preparation not only facilitates a smoother IRB review process but also upholds the ethical standards of the research, protecting both the participants and the integrity of the study. For instance, already having the research question and methodology outlined, one can quickly complete the IRB form. This can be as simple as merely pasting the actual questions in after providing the information, such as "What is the main objective of the study?"

Main Objective of the Study

The main objective of the study is to investigate the sustainability of economic models within virtual environments, specifically focusing on the metaverse. By employing computational and qualitative research methods, the study aims to comprehensively understand economic activities and their long-term viability in these digital spaces. This includes identifying successful economic practices, evaluating user engagement and transaction behaviors, and exploring the challenges and opportunities unique to virtual economies. The insights gained from this research are intended to contribute to academic literature and provide practical recommendations for developers and policymakers to design more robust and sustainable economic systems within the metaverse.

It should be noted that the response here did not require additional prompting. The question was pasted directly into the chat with the information. One can continue through the application in the same fashion in the same chat with the next: "What specific questions or hypotheses is the research addressing?"

What Specific Questions or Hypotheses Are Research Addressing?

The study addresses several specific questions and hypotheses related to the sustainability of economic models in the metaverse:

1. What are the key characteristics of successful economic models within the metaverse?
    - Hypothesis: Successful economic models in the metaverse share certain characteristics, such as adaptability, user engagement, and transaction efficiency.
2. How do user engagement and transaction behaviors impact the sustainability of economic models in virtual environments?
    - Hypothesis: High levels of user engagement and frequent transactions are positively correlated with the sustainability of economic models in the metaverse.
3. What are the primary challenges faced by economic models in the metaverse, and how can they be mitigated?
    - Hypothesis: The primary challenges include security concerns, digital asset volatility, and user retention. Mitigation strategies may involve enhanced security measures, stablecoin integration, and incentive structures for sustained user engagement.

4. How do demographic factors influence economic interactions and model sustainability in the metaverse?
   - Hypothesis: Demographic factors such as age, geographical location, and digital literacy significantly influence economic interactions and the sustainability of economic models.
5. What are the long-term implications of current economic practices in the metaverse on future virtual economies?
   - Hypothesis: Current economic practices will set precedents that shape the development of more sophisticated and sustainable virtual economies in the future.

This strategy can be especially helpful for young scholars who are going through the process for the first time, or for those moving into a different field of research. For instance, if unsure of research methodology in a particular field (or subset of one), the response can assist in getting started and then allows for refinement.

Study Design and Methodology

What research methods will be used (e.g., qualitative, quantitative, mixed-methods)?

The study will employ a mixed-methods approach, combining both qualitative and quantitative research methods to provide a comprehensive understanding of economic activities and their sustainability in virtual environments.

How will data be collected (e.g., surveys, interviews, experiments)?

1. Qualitative Data Collection:
   - **Semi-structured Interviews:** Conduct interviews with developers, economists, and users engaged in the metaverse. These interviews will explore their perceptions and experiences related to economic transactions and models within these virtual spaces.
   - **Focus Groups:** Organize focus groups with participants from different demographics to discuss the challenges and opportunities of economic models in the metaverse. These discussions will provide insights into diverse perspectives and collective experiences.
2. Quantitative Data Collection:
   - **Surveys:** Distribute structured surveys to a larger sample of metaverse users to gather numerical data on user engagement, economic transactions, and the perceived sustainability of these activities. Surveys will be designed to capture detailed information on user demographics, behavior patterns, and economic interactions.

- **Behavioral Data Analysis:** Utilize existing data from metaverse platforms to analyze user behavior and economic interactions. This analysis will focus on transaction frequencies, types, and outcomes to identify patterns and trends that contribute to economic sustainability.

By combining these qualitative and quantitative methods, the study aims to develop a holistic understanding of the economic models within the metaverse, leveraging both individual experiences and broader statistical trends. This mixed-methods approach ensures that the research captures the complexity and nuances of virtual economies, providing a robust foundation for practical recommendations and theoretical insights.

The creation of survey instruments is also quite time-consuming. AI tools can significantly assist in this area by helping design new surveys and revising existing ones to create new instruments rapidly. These technologies can analyze vast amounts of data to suggest the most effective questions and formats, ensuring that the surveys are both comprehensive and easy for participants to complete. This not only saves time for researchers but also enhances the quality of the data collected by using well-structured and effective survey instruments. Integrating AI into these processes ensures that researchers can focus more on the substantive aspects of their studies while maintaining high standards of accuracy and efficiency in data collection and ethical compliance. For instance, asking to "Generate a survey for this study" results in:

Survey for Investigating Sustainable Economic Models in the Metaverse

Introduction

Thank you for participating in our survey on the sustainability of economic models in the metaverse. Your responses will help us understand the dynamics of virtual economies and contribute to our research on creating more sustainable economic systems in these digital spaces. All responses are confidential and will be used solely for academic purposes.

Section 1: Demographics

1. Age:
    - Under 18
    - 18-24
    - 25-34

- 35-44
- 45-54
- 55-64
- 65 or older

2. Gender:
   - Male
   - Female
   - Non-binary
   - Prefer not to say
3. Location:
   - Country:
   - Urban/Rural:
4. Occupation:
   - Student
   - Employed
   - Self-employed
   - Unemployed
   - Retired
   - Other (please specify):

Section 2: Metaverse Engagement

5. Which metaverse platforms do you use? (Select all that apply)
   - Decentraland
   - Second Life
   - Roblox
   - Fortnite
   - VRChat
   - Other (please specify):
6. How often do you engage with the metaverse?
   - Daily
   - Weekly
   - Monthly
   - Less frequently
7. What are your primary activities in the metaverse? (Select all that apply)
   - Socializing
   - Gaming
   - Attending virtual events
   - Trading or economic activities

- Education or learning
- Other (please specify):

Section 3: Economic Activities

8. Do you participate in economic transactions in the metaverse?
    - Yes
    - No
9. If yes, what types of economic transactions do you engage in? (Select all that apply)
    - Buying and selling virtual goods
    - Real estate transactions
    - Providing services
    - Trading virtual currencies
    - Other (please specify):
10. How do you perceive the sustainability of economic activities in the metaverse?
    - Very sustainable
    - Somewhat sustainable
    - Neutral
    - Somewhat unsustainable
    - Very unsustainable
11. What challenges do you face in economic transactions within the metaverse? (Select all that apply)
    - Security concerns
    - Lack of trust
    - High transaction fees
    - Digital asset volatility
    - User interface difficulties
    - Other (please specify):

Section 4: Perceptions and Experiences

12. How satisfied are you with your economic experiences in the metaverse?
    - Very satisfied
    - Satisfied
    - Neutral
    - Dissatisfied
    - Very dissatisfied

13. Do you think the metaverse has the potential to support sustainable economic models?
    - Yes
    - No
    - Unsure
14. What improvements would you suggest to enhance the sustainability of economic models in the metaverse?
    - Open-ended response
15. Have you experienced any significant economic successes or failures in the metaverse? Please describe briefly.
    - Open-ended response

Section 5: Future Outlook

16. What do you believe the future holds for economic models in the metaverse?
    - Open-ended response
17. Would you be willing to participate in a follow-up interview or focus group discussion?
    - Yes (Please provide contact information)
    - No

Conclusion

Thank you for your participation. Your insights are invaluable to our research. If you have any additional comments or questions, please feel free to contact us at [contact information].

Consent

By submitting this survey, you consent to participate in this study and agree that your responses can be used for academic research purposes.

This survey aims to gather comprehensive data on user engagement, economic activities, and perceptions regarding the sustainability of economic models in the metaverse. The collected data will be analyzed to provide insights and recommendations for developing more robust and sustainable virtual economies.

The use of these tools, however, goes beyond just filling out the IRB application (of which the survey questions are included). For instance, AI can assist in drafting informed consent forms, designing ethical questionnaires, and organizing participant data while ensuring compliance with privacy regulations. Furthermore, AI-driven tools can analyze large datasets to identify potential risks and ethical concerns, providing researchers with insights to address these issues proactively. In addition, there are other ways in which the tools can be used during human-subjects research.

1. **Automated Document Review:** AI can review and ensure all necessary documentation, such as consent forms and study protocols, are complete and adhere to ethical standards.
2. **Risk Assessment:** AI algorithms can evaluate potential risks associated with the study by analyzing data patterns and predicting possible ethical concerns.
3. **Participant Monitoring:** AI tools can monitor participant interactions and data collection processes in real-time, ensuring adherence to approved protocols and identifying any deviations that may need addressing.
4. **Data Privacy Compliance:** AI can help ensure compliance with data privacy regulations by automating the anonymization of participant data and monitoring data storage practices.
5. **Training and Support:** AI-driven platforms can provide training materials and support for researchers, helping them understand and comply with IRB requirements and best practices.

AI tools streamline administrative tasks, such as drafting informed consent forms and designing ethical questionnaires, while also ensuring compliance with privacy regulations. Additionally, AI-driven platforms provide valuable insights through automated document reviews, risk assessments, and real-time monitoring of participant interactions. These capabilities contribute to the overall quality and reliability of research by facilitating thorough and proactive ethical evaluations, thereby maintaining high standards in academic and clinical studies.

5.2 DATA COLLECTION AND ANALYSIS

In the area of academic research, leveraging AI for data collection marks a significant enhancement in both efficiency and scope. AI tools are particularly adept at automating the data collection process, which is invaluable across various fields, from social sciences, where they can administer and analyze survey data, to natural sciences, which often require the aggregation of vast amounts of sensor data. As such, the integration of AI in data collection involves setting up intelligent systems designed to operate autonomously or semi-autonomously. These systems are programmed to target specific types of data, ensuring that the collection process is both comprehensive and relevant to the research question. In social sciences, AI can manage large-scale surveys, dynamically adapting questions based on respondent answers or demographics, thereby maximizing response relevancy and depth. In natural sciences, AI tools can monitor and record environmental data from multiple sensors, providing real-time analytics that help in immediate decision-making and long-term observational studies. But before analyzing data, we first need to collect it. Therefore, the creation of instruments to gather good data are crucial to success.

Luckily, LLMs can be instrumental in designing survey instruments (as noted) and other data gathering tools, facilitating both qualitative and quantitative research. These AI models can generate comprehensive and targeted survey questions that align closely with the research objectives, ensuring that the collected data is relevant and useful for analysis. LLMs can suggest various question formats, from multiple-choice to open-ended responses, tailored to elicit the most informative answers. Additionally, these models can help in structuring interview guides or observation protocols for qualitative studies, enhancing the consistency and depth of data collection across different contexts. This capability not only saves time but also enhances the reliability and validity of the research instruments, allowing researchers to gather data efficiently and effectively.

For instance, with the research question for a market research study on social media aimed at understanding what drives conversions for sustainable home meals among females aged 25-35 being: "What are the key variables and calls to action that influence the purchasing decisions of females aged 25-35 on social media platforms, leading to higher conversion rates for sustainable home meals, and how do these elements vary across different platforms to maximize return on investment (ROI)?"

Given that the question aims to identify specific factors that affect purchasing behavior in the target demographic and explores how these factors can be optimized across various social media platforms to enhance the effectiveness of marketing strategies for sustainable home meals, the following survey instrument can be generated by prompting: "Now generate a survey instrument that collects both quantitative and qualitative data including demographics, consumer behavior, social media usage, and meal preparation habits that can be taken in under 10 minutes and taken via smart phone." The following is then output:

Creating a survey instrument that is concise, effective, and mobile-friendly involves crafting questions that are straightforward and quick to answer. Below is a suggested survey structure that captures both quantitative and qualitative data for your study on social media marketing effectiveness in promoting sustainable home meals to females aged 25-35. The survey is designed to be completed within 10 minutes:

Survey Instrument: Understanding Social Media Influence on Sustainable Meal Purchases

Demographics

1. **Age:**
    - [ ] 25-29
    - [ ] 30-35
2. **Employment Status:**
    - [ ] Full-time
    - [ ] Part-time
    - [ ] Self-employed
    - [ ] Unemployed
    - [ ] Student
3. **Education Level:**
    - [ ] High School or lower
    - [ ] Some College
    - [ ] Bachelor's Degree
    - [ ] Graduate Degree

Consumer Behavior

4. **Frequency of Meal Purchases** (How often do you purchase prepared meals?):
    - [ ] Daily
    - [ ] Several times a week
    - [ ] Weekly
    - [ ] Less frequently
5. **Average Spending on Meals** (Approximately how much do you spend on sustainable home meals per month?):
    - [ ] Under $50
    - [ ] $50-$100
    - [ ] $101-$200
    - [ ] Over $200

Social Media Usage

6. **Platforms Used** (Which social media platforms do you use regularly? Check all that apply.):
    - [ ] Facebook
    - [ ] Instagram
    - [ ] Twitter
    - [ ] Pinterest
    - [ ] LinkedIn
    - [ ] TikTok
    - [ ] Other: __________
7. **Influence of Social Media** (On a scale from 1 to 5, how influential are social media posts in your decision to purchase sustainable meals?):
    - 1 (Not influential)
    - 2
    - 3
    - 4
    - 5 (Very influential)

Meal Preparation Habits

8. **Meal Prep Frequency** (How often do you prepare meals at home?):
    - [ ] Daily
    - [ ] Several times a week
    - [ ] Weekly
    - [ ] Rarely
9. **Preferences for Sustainable Meals** (What influences your choice of sustainable meals? Rank in order of importance: Price, Ingredients, Brand reputation, Peer recommendations):
    - [ ] Price
    - [ ] Ingredients
    - [ ] Brand reputation
    - [ ] Peer recommendations

Open-Ended Questions

10. **Feedback on Social Media Ads** (Please describe any memorable social media advertisements for sustainable meals that influenced your purchase decision. What stood out?):
11. **Suggestions for Improvement** (What could make social media marketing of sustainable meals more appealing to you?):

Final Question

12. **Willingness to Participate in Future Research** (Would you be willing to participate in a follow-up interview or focus group?):
    - [ ] Yes
    - [ ] No

This survey utilizes a combination of multiple-choice, Likert scale, ranking, and open-ended questions to gather comprehensive insights while ensuring ease of completion on a smartphone interface.

Creating a survey instrument like the one outlined above can be immensely beneficial to researchers, regardless of human-subjects research, particularly in streamlining the data collection process and enhancing the quality of insights gained. By employing a mixture of question types, including multiple-choice, Likert scale, ranking, and open-ended questions, researchers can gather a rich blend of quantitative and qualitative data. This approach not only facilitates statistical analysis but also captures deeper insights into participants' attitudes, behaviors, and preferences.

The efficiency of using AI tools to generate such survey instruments cannot be overstated. These tools help researchers quickly draft tailored questions that are aligned with their specific research goals, saving significant time that would otherwise be spent on manual drafting and revision. They can also be revised very rapidly with additional guidance to look at other demographics, gather different types of data, or suggest alternatives. Additionally, AI-enhanced tools can suggest relevant questions or formats based on the latest research trends or successful surveys in similar fields, ensuring that the instrument is both current and comprehensive. For researchers focusing on market trends, consumer behavior, or social media impacts, such as in the example of sustainable meal purchases, a well-designed survey instrument provides a structured way to capture essential data points. This data can reveal key patterns and correlations, such as the relationship between social media usage and purchasing decisions, or demographic variations in meal preparation habits.

With instruments created, dissemination and data collection can commence. AI-assisted data collection results in a robust dataset that is well-prepared for detailed analysis. These datasets are generally more organized, and cleaner compared to those gathered manually, thanks to the capability of the tools to perform initial data cleaning and preprocessing. This includes normalizing data formats, eliminating duplicates, and managing missing values, which simplifies further data analysis stages. Once collected, the data can be analyzed in many ways, including statistical analysis, sentiment analysis and more.

Utilizing data stored in Excel or CSV formats is a fundamental approach in modern research, providing a structured and universally compatible method for managing and analyzing large datasets. Excel, a widely utilized spreadsheet software, is equipped with numerous built-in functions and tools that allow for straightforward execution of basic to intermediate statistical analyses. Researchers can effortlessly perform descriptive statistics, create pivot tables, and produce charts to visualize data trends. Conversely, CSV files, due to their simplicity and broad acceptance, are a popular choice for data exchange and processing across a variety of statistical software such as R, Python, SPSS, and SAS. These platforms can import CSV data and execute complex statistical analyses, including regression models, time series analyses, and even machine learning algorithms. This adaptability is particularly valuable for handling large datasets, which might surpass Excel's capacity.

While these traditional methods remain integral to data interpretation and analysis, the advent of LLMs introduces an additional layer of sophistication. LLMs can further enhance data analysis by generating insightful interpretations, predicting outcomes, and even suggesting new research angles based on the processed data. Researchers can input anonymized data directly into such models for quantitative statistical analysis. This method leverages the advanced capabilities of LLMs to process and analyze large datasets swiftly and efficiently. For instance, data collected exploring educator perceptions and usage of AI technologies was conducted (Hutson & Rains, 2024).

Once the data is prepared, it can be uploaded into an LLM. The researcher simply specifies the type of analysis required—such as descriptive statistics, correlation analysis, or regression modeling. The LLM can then execute these analyses, providing insights that are both immediate and rich in detail. For instance, with the prompt "Using the following output descriptive statistics for the following section of a faculty survey on where they feel AI is appropriate in their activities [data copied directly from Excel results]." The following output was then created:

Let's address your request by summarizing the survey data provided for a detailed analysis:

Survey Data Overview for Faculty on AI Usage

1. **General Appropriateness for AI Use (Total Respondents = 108):**
   - **Research:** 33.33% (36 respondents find AI appropriate for research)
   - **Teaching:** 31.48% (34 respondents find AI suitable for teaching)
   - **Service:** 25.00% (27 respondents believe AI is applicable in service)
   - **None:** 4.63% (5 respondents do not see AI as appropriate)
   - **Other:** 5.56% (6 respondents have other views)
2. **AI Use in Teaching (Total Respondents = 194):**
   - **Personalized Learning:** 12.37% (24 respondents value personalized learning via AI)
   - **Automated Grading:** 9.79% (19 respondents appreciate automated grading)
   - **Intelligent Tutoring Systems:** 10.82% (21 find intelligent tutoring systems useful)
   - **Enhancing Engagement:** 13.40% (26 respondents use AI to enhance engagement)
   - **Supporting Special Needs:** 11.86% (23 respondents use AI for special needs support)
   - **Real-time Feedback:** 9.79% (19 respondents value real-time feedback)
   - **Critical Thinking Skills:** 11.34% (22 respondents use AI to develop critical thinking)
   - **Identifying Learning Gaps:** 10.31% (20 respondents use AI to identify learning gaps)
3. **AI Use in Research (Total Respondents = 177):**
   - **Data Analysis:** 15.25% (27 respondents use AI for data analysis)
   - **NLP and Text Analysis**: 11.30% (20 respondents use AI for text analysis)
   - **Image/Video Analysis:** 7.34% (13 find AI useful in visual analysis)
   - **Predictive Modeling:** 6.78% (12 use AI for forecasting)
   - **Automating Tasks:** 14.69% (26 appreciate AI for automating repetitive tasks)
   - **Discovery in Large Datasets:** 11.30% (20 use AI for pattern discovery)
   - **Literature Reviews: 14.69%** (26 use AI for assisting with literature reviews)

This descriptive summary can help in understanding how faculty perceives the role of AI in their professional activities.

In order to gain further insight into the data, one can also turn it into a narrative format and seek additional insights and takeaways. Following up on this last response with the prompt "Now generate the results in the form of a narrative and provide keytakeaways about faculty perceptions" results in the following accessible output:

The survey conducted among faculty members provides insightful perspectives on the perceived roles and effectiveness of artificial intelligence (AI) in academia, particularly in the areas of research, teaching, and service. This data reflects a broad acceptance and acknowledgment of AI's potential utility across various academic functions.

Key Takeaways

1. **Broad Application Across Domains:**
   - AI is viewed as a versatile tool across different academic activities, with significant acknowledgment of its applicability in "research" (33.33%) and "teaching" (31.48%). This suggests a strong interest in leveraging AI to enhance academic rigor and instructional quality.
2. **Teaching and Learning Enhancement:**
   - In the teaching domain, AI is highly valued for "enhancing student engagement and motivation" (13.40%), followed closely by "personalized learning and adaptive course content" (12.37%). These areas highlight the desire for more tailored and engaging learning experiences facilitated by AI, which can dynamically adjust to individual student needs and preferences.
3. **Research Facilitation:**
   - For research purposes, "data analysis and statistical modeling" (15.25%) are the primary uses for AI, reflecting the growing complexity and volume of data that researchers handle today. AI's capability to manage large datasets and uncover patterns efficiently makes it an invaluable tool for modern researchers.
4. **Concerns and Cautions:**
   - Despite the enthusiasm for AI, there is a measured approach to its integration. Only a small fraction of the respondents (4.63%) do not find AI appropriate for any academic activity, indicating some reservations or skepticism about the technology's universal applicability or potential to replace human-centric roles.
5. **Adoption Variability:**

- The adoption rates and perceived usefulness of AI tools vary significantly among different age groups and disciplines, suggesting that personal familiarity with technology, as well as the specific demands of various academic fields, influence AI integration.

The narrative that emerges from this survey underscores a complex yet optimistic landscape where AI is seen as a pivotal enhancement tool in academia. Faculty members recognize the potential of AI to transform traditional practices, making them more efficient and impactful. However, the adoption and integration of AI in academia must be approached with thoughtful consideration of ethical standards, training needs, and the preservation of core academic values to fully realize its benefits while addressing potential drawbacks.

The ability to converse with data using advanced AI tools significantly accelerates the discovery of insights, making the research process both faster and more efficient. This interaction with data allows researchers to quickly identify patterns, compare variables, and generate hypotheses directly from the dataset, effectively shortening the time between data collection and actionable insights.

Moreover, AI tools are not limited to quantitative analysis. They also facilitate qualitative interpretation, enabling researchers to look into text-based data to extract themes, sentiments, and nuanced understandings that might not be apparent from statistical analysis alone. This capability is particularly valuable in fields like social sciences and humanities, where qualitative data plays a crucial role. The next section will explore how AI can be used for sentiment analysis, further enhancing our ability to interpret and understand not just the presence of certain responses but the underlying emotions and attitudes that drive them. This approach provides a deeper, more rounded view of the data, opening up new possibilities for academic inquiry and insight.

For instance, using the same institutional study (Hutson & Rains, 2024), the following prompt can be used in order to conduct a sentiment analysis: "You will now conduct a sentiment analysis on the following free responses to the survey on AI perceptions and use and output with positive, negative and neutral selecting quotes where appropriate to illustrate [insert free responses here]." As a result, the following analysis is created:

The sentiment analysis of faculty responses regarding AI in academic settings offers a rich tapestry of perspectives, categorized into positive, negative, and neutral sentiments. Each category provides a unique insight into the faculty's concerns and hopes for AI integration.

Positive Sentiments

Several faculty members see potential benefits in integrating AI for administrative tasks and basic instructional support. One faculty member expressed optimism about AI's role in enhancing productivity: "I am already using AI in my courses this Spring." This response highlights an embrace of AI for improving teaching methodologies and student engagement.

Negative Sentiments

However, the majority of sentiments expressed concerns about the impact of AI on academic integrity and the quality of human interaction in education. One respondent noted, "My assignments are largely reflective - students who choose to use AI (though they are instructed not to) - completely miss this part. It also means they don't do the readings, because they believe the bot will do the work for them." Another echoed similar concerns, stating, "I fear it will increase the rate of students cheating on assignments." These responses illustrate apprehensions about AI diminishing students' engagement with course material and encouraging shortcuts.

Neutral Sentiments

Neutral sentiments were less pronounced but indicated a measured acceptance of AI's role. One professor mentioned, "None," indicating either a lack of strong feelings towards AI or satisfaction with its current role. Another simply said, "Thank you for this survey," showing acknowledgment of the discussion without expressing a definitive stance.

These quotations provide concrete examples of how faculty are currently perceiving AI in the academic landscape, underscoring the need for clear policies and educational efforts to ensure AI is used appropriately and enhances, rather than undermines, educational outcomes.

As is clear in these brief examples, one of the key advantages of using AI for data analysis is its ability to quickly generate comprehensive outputs and narratives. AI can synthesize complex data into understandable results that are ready for interpretation, allowing researchers to focus more on the application of findings rather than on the intricacies of data processing. This is particularly beneficial in fields where data volumes and complexity can overwhelm traditional analysis methods. Furthermore, AI enhances the storytelling aspect of research by constructing coherent narratives around data insights. This capability is invaluable when conveying complex information in a manner that is accessible to a wider audience, including stakeholders who may not have a technical background. AI-driven data analysis can transform raw data into compelling stories that highlight key findings and implications, making research findings more impactful and actionable.

5.3 VISUALIZING DATA WITH AI TOOLS

LLMs are not only powerful tools for data analysis and narrative generation, but they also have the capability to create data visualizations directly from datasets. This feature significantly enhances the accessibility and interpretability of research findings. LLMs can generate a variety of visualization types, such as pie charts, bar graphs, scatterplots, and more, based on the data provided and the specific insights researchers wish to highlight. These visualizations are crucial for effectively communicating complex data to diverse audiences, making it easier for stakeholders to understand trends, patterns, and outliers at a glance. The ability of LLMs to automate the creation of visually engaging and informative graphics saves researchers considerable time and effort that would otherwise be spent on manual data visualization tasks. For instance, taking the same data used earlier on faculty perception of the most appropriate use cases for AI in teaching and research, one need merely include the prompt "Output the following as a bar graph [insert data]" and Figure 1 is created. The same prompt can be used with different types of visualization by merely replacing "bar graph" with "pie chart," etc.

Figure 1. Faculty perceptions of AI

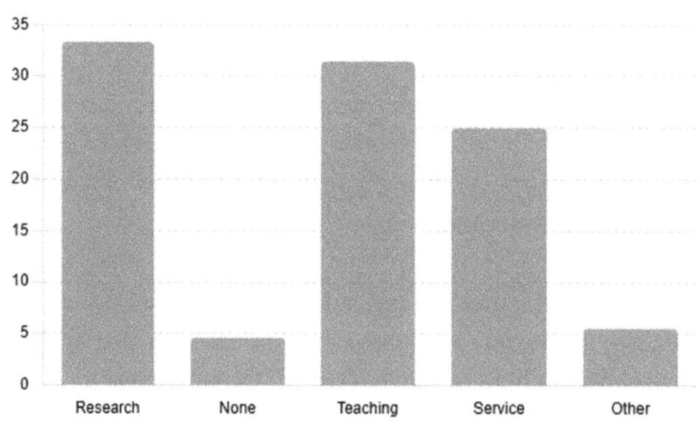

In the same study, we are able to break down responses more granularly and now look at staff. When asked about their willingness to integrate AI into their area of work, 39.13% stated they were somewhat willing, 28.26% very willing, 21.74%

neutral, and so on. When entering the data and asking to "output as a pie chart data visualization," Figure 2 was generated. Therefore, the curation of data and output as a persuasive data visualization is relatively quick and easy compared to using Adobe Illustrator, Tableau and even Excel pivot tables.

Figure 2. Staff willingness to integrate AI

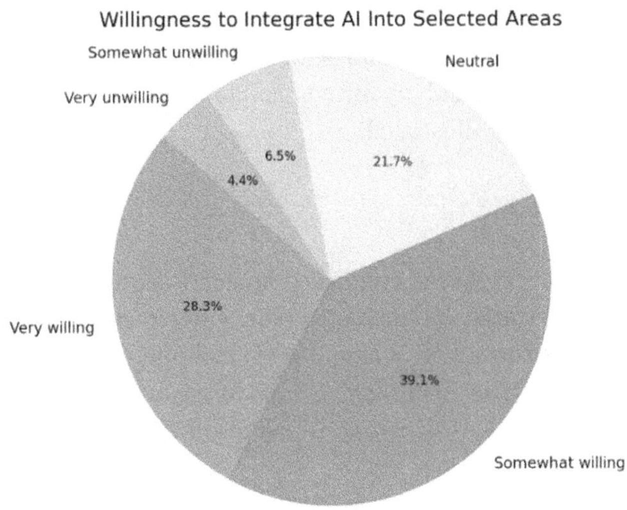

In addition to being able to output imagery from data, these models can also analyze and describe images in great detail. This capability enables researchers and users to not only generate visual representations of data but also to interpret and understand existing images with the help of AI. For example, models like ChatGPT-4 can be used to provide detailed descriptions of visual content, identify patterns, and offer insights that may not be immediately apparent. This dual functionality enhances the utility of AI in various fields in academic research. For example, when ChatGPT-4 was asked to perform a visual analysis of Figure 5 of Chapter 3 of the amino acids forming a polypeptide chain, the response was:

Formal Analysis of the Image: Amino Acids Forming a Polypeptide Chain

Subject Matter and Composition

The image depicts a conceptual representation of a DNA strand and various structures associated with amino acids and polypeptide chains. The composition is horizontal, with the DNA double helix running across the top portion of the image, followed by representations of amino acids and polypeptide chains below it. The overall layout is structured and organized, facilitating a clear understanding of the biological concepts being illustrated.

Color and Form

The colors used are bright and vivid, predominantly featuring shades of blue, red, and orange. The DNA helix is depicted in blue with red connections, highlighting its double-stranded structure. The amino acids and polypeptide chains are shown in different colors to distinguish their various forms and interactions. The use of color not only enhances the visual appeal but also aids in differentiating between the components.

Details and Labels

Each segment of the DNA strand is labeled with letters such as A, G, R, H, and B, indicating different nucleotide bases and possibly amino acids or other relevant molecules. The lower portion of the image showcases the structural forms of amino acids and polypeptide chains, including helices and other formations, each labeled with corresponding letters.

Texture and Style

The image adopts a stylized, almost 3D cartoonish aesthetic, making the scientific concepts more approachable and engaging. The textures are smooth, and the forms are simplified yet detailed enough to convey the necessary information. This style is effective for educational purposes, as it balances accuracy with visual clarity.

Function and Context

This image serves an educational function, likely intended for use in a biological or biochemical context to explain the relationship between DNA, amino acids, and polypeptide chains. By illustrating the formation of polypeptides from amino acids and showing their connection to the DNA sequence, the image effectively communicates complex biochemical processes in a simplified manner.

Interpretation and Analysis

The image successfully achieves its purpose of educating viewers about the process of protein synthesis. The clear labeling and organized composition make it easy to follow the sequence from DNA to polypeptide chain. The choice of colors and forms enhances understanding by visually distinguishing between different molecular structures. Overall, the image is an effective educational tool that simplifies complex scientific concepts through clear visual representation.

While such applications are incredibly useful for researchers and students in understanding complex scientific illustrations, other fields also benefit from similar strategies. For instance, in the field of art history, which requires careful visual analysis, the same approach can be employed. When asked to perform a formal analysis of Leonardo da Vinci's *Mona Lisa,* the response was as follows:

Formal Analysis of Leonardo da Vinci's Mona Lisa

Subject Matter and Composition

The "Mona Lisa," painted by Leonardo da Vinci, is a portrait of a woman, widely believed to be Lisa Gherardini, the wife of a wealthy Florentine merchant. The composition centers on the figure of the woman, who is seated against an expansive, mysterious landscape. The use of a pyramidal composition draws the viewer's eye upward from the base of her torso to her serene face. Her posture, with hands gently crossed, suggests a composed and calm demeanor, contributing to the overall sense of tranquility in the painting.

Color and Form

The palette used in the "Mona Lisa" is composed of muted earth tones, with a harmonious blend of browns, greens, and blues. The subtle gradations of light and shadow on her face and hands, achieved through da Vinci's masterful use of sfumato, create a lifelike and three-dimensional appearance. The soft transitions between colors and tones eliminate harsh edges, enhancing the naturalism of the portrait. The dark, rich tones of her clothing contrast with the luminous quality of her skin, drawing the viewer's focus to her face and hands.

Details and Technique

Leonardo's technique in the "Mona Lisa" is exemplary of his attention to detail and understanding of human anatomy. The intricate depiction of the folds in her clothing and the delicate rendering of her facial features demonstrate his skillful use of brushwork and glazing techniques. The eyes, often noted for their enigmatic quality, appear to follow the viewer, adding to the painting's mystique. The subtle smile of the Mona Lisa is another focal point, contributing to the painting's fame for its ambiguity and depth of expression.

Texture and Style

The painting's texture is smooth, with a fine application of paint that enhances the delicate transitions of light and shadow. Da Vinci's use of sfumato softens the edges and creates a hazy, atmospheric effect, particularly noticeable in the background landscape. This technique not only adds depth but also unifies the composition, blending the figure seamlessly into the surrounding environment.

Function and Context

The "Mona Lisa" was likely commissioned as a private portrait, reflecting the Renaissance ideals of individualism and humanism. It serves as a testament to Leonardo's prowess as a portraitist and his innovative approaches to capturing human emotion and naturalistic detail. The painting's setting against a distant, dreamlike landscape also reflects the Renaissance interest in exploring the natural world and the human place within it.

Interpretation and Analysis

The "Mona Lisa" stands as one of the most iconic works of art in history, not only for its technical brilliance but also for its profound impact on the art world. The portrait's enigmatic expression, masterful use of sfumato, and harmonious composition continue to captivate and intrigue viewers. The painting exemplifies the height of Renaissance art, showcasing Leonardo da Vinci's unparalleled ability to blend naturalism with idealized beauty. It remains a subject of endless fascination and study, symbolizing the enduring legacy of Leonardo's artistic genius.

The recognition of the *Mona Lisa* by the model demonstrates its ability to pull in additional historical and contextual information about well-known artworks. However, when faced with a completely unknown image, the model would rely solely on its visual analysis capabilities without pre-existing knowledge about the artwork. In such cases, the analysis would focus on the formal elements of the image—such as composition, color, form, texture, and technique—without providing historical context or information about the artist. This method is equally valuable, as it trains students and researchers to observe and interpret visual elements meticulously, which is a crucial skill in both art history and other fields that require careful visual analysis.

Formal Analysis of the Abstract Image

Subject Matter and Composition

The image is an abstract, symmetrical composition characterized by intricate patterns and vibrant colors. The central focus is a hexagonal shape surrounded by radiating, repetitive motifs that create a sense of balance and harmony. The overall composition is highly symmetrical, with each quadrant mirroring the others, contributing to a cohesive and visually engaging structure.

Color and Form

The color palette is dominated by bright yellows, reds, and blues, interspersed with hints of brown and black. These colors are used in various shapes and patterns, creating a dynamic and energetic feel. The yellow forms the primary background, with red and blue elements layered on top to create depth and contrast. The repetitive use of shapes, such as curved lines and loops, adds to the complexity and movement within the piece.

Details and Technique

The artist employs a meticulous technique to achieve the precise, symmetrical patterns. The repetition of forms and colors suggests a digital creation process, likely utilizing graphic design software. The intricate details within each section indicate a high level of control and planning, resulting in a visually intricate and detailed work.

Texture and Style

The texture of the image is smooth, with a flat application of color that enhances the clarity of the intricate patterns. The style is abstract and geometric, focusing on the interplay of shapes and colors rather than depicting any recognizable subject matter. This abstract approach invites viewers to interpret the image based on their perceptions and emotional responses to the visual elements.

Function and Context

As an abstract piece, the function of the image is likely to evoke an aesthetic or emotional response from the viewer. The symmetry and vibrant colors can induce a sense of order and excitement. Such artworks are often used in modern interior design or digital media to create a focal point and stimulate visual interest.

Interpretation and Analysis

The symmetrical composition and vibrant color palette suggest themes of balance and harmony, while the intricate patterns indicate a complex, possibly digital process behind the creation. The abstract nature of the work allows for multiple interpretations, inviting viewers to engage with the image on a personal level. The image exemplifies the power of abstract art to convey emotion and intrigue through purely visual means, without relying on representational forms.

In summary, the formal analysis of this abstract image reveals a meticulously crafted, symmetrical composition that utilizes bright colors and intricate patterns to engage the viewer. The work stands as a testament to the possibilities of digital art in creating visually stimulating and emotionally resonant pieces.

Additionally, by integrating visualization capabilities, LLMs enable researchers to more quickly identify relationships, assess the impact of variables, and make data-driven decisions. This comprehensive approach to data handling—encompassing analysis, narrative generation, and visualization—makes LLMs an indispensable asset in modern research methodologies, allowing for a more seamless flow from data collection to insightful presentation.

As we conclude Chapter 5, it is evident that the journey from hypothesis to analysis is both challenging and rewarding. The integration of meticulous planning, diverse data collection methods, rigorous analysis, and advanced visualization techniques ensures that research findings are robust, credible, and impactful. This chapter has provided a comprehensive guide to navigating this journey, equipping researchers with the knowledge and tools necessary to conduct high-quality research. Looking forward, the insights gained from this chapter will serve as a foundation for applying these principles to various research contexts, furthering our understanding of complex phenomena, and driving innovation across disciplines. The next chapters will build on this groundwork, exploring the application of these methodologies in specific fields and the ethical considerations that accompany advanced research practices.

REFERENCES

Hutson, J., & Rains, T. (2024). *AI Institutional Adoption Study* [Data set]. Lindenwood University.

Chapter 6
Writing and Revising

ABSTRACT

This chapter looks into the transformative role of AI in enhancing the writing and revision stages of academic research. The chapter begins by outlining the processes of writing and revising drafts, highlighting how AI tools can assist in structuring content, improving clarity, and ensuring coherence. It then explores various AI-assisted writing tools and techniques, demonstrating how these technologies can help generate initial drafts, suggest improvements, and refine arguments, thereby enhancing the overall quality of scholarly writing. The focus shifts to revising based on reviewer feedback, where AI tools are shown to facilitate the incorporation of feedback efficiently and effectively. By providing real-time suggestions and identifying areas needing further clarification or enhancement, AI tools enable researchers to streamline the revision process.

6.1 WRITING AND REVISING THE DRAFT

Every researcher possesses a unique strategy for maintaining organization during the writing process. In preparing the manuscript here, the author preferred utilizing Microsoft OneDrive to manage research projects. By storing draft manuscripts in the cloud, multiple versions can be accessed simultaneously, facilitating the visualization of various document components such as the table of contents, list of figures, the specific narrative section being developed, and the corresponding reference section. This approach enables seamless adjustments to different parts of the manuscript with minimal need for stringent version control. Additionally, having at least three monitors is useful as each can be dedicated to one aspect of the writing process (e.g., AI tool, Microsoft Word, generative research database).

Drafting a manuscript is an iterative process that requires attention to detail and a structured approach. Initially, it is essential to outline the manuscript, segmenting it into coherent sections that align with the overarching research objectives.

DOI: 10.4018/979-8-3693-6905-0.ch006

This outline serves as a roadmap, guiding the writing process and ensuring that all relevant points are addressed comprehensively. Utilizing cloud storage solutions like Microsoft OneDrive offers significant advantages in manuscript drafting. By creating distinct folders for each project, researchers can maintain a well-organized repository of all related materials. Drafts, data sets, figures, and references can be systematically stored, allowing for easy retrieval and modification. This organization minimizes the risk of data loss and ensures that the most current versions of documents are always accessible.

One of the critical benefits of cloud storage is the ability to open multiple versions of a document concurrently. This capability is particularly beneficial during the drafting phase, where comparing different sections of the manuscript can enhance coherence and consistency. For instance, while working on the narrative section, it is advantageous to simultaneously review the table of contents and reference lists to ensure alignment and accuracy. This practice reduces the likelihood of discrepancies and facilitates a holistic view of the manuscript's structure. With documents stored in the cloud, revisions can be made dynamically, allowing for real-time updates. Collaborative features in cloud platforms enable multiple contributors to work on the document simultaneously, providing feedback and making necessary changes without the cumbersome process of emailing document versions back and forth.

While cloud storage mitigates the need for rigorous version control, it is still essential to maintain document integrity. Researchers should establish a systematic approach to track changes and revisions. Tools within cloud storage platforms, such as version history, can be utilized to revert to previous versions if needed. Additionally, naming conventions for document versions (e.g., v1, v2, etc.) can help track the progression of the manuscript.

The overview of the GAI research process in this chapter has delineated the various, modular, and iterative stages that research can encompass, bringing together disparate elements in the drafting phase. This convergence is where the holistic nature of the research project begins to take shape, and each section of the manuscript undergoes continuous refinement and editing using the LLM of choice. Drafting a comprehensive manuscript involves iterative cycles of writing and revising, facilitated by the use of advanced LLMs. Each section of the manuscript, from the literature review to the analysis of results, recommendations, and conclusion, benefits from this iterative process. For example, in the literature review section, researchers can iteratively expand on each example provided. By repeatedly prompting the LLM, one can ensure that the final result thoroughly addresses the current state of the field, presenting a nuanced and well-rounded discussion.

In the literature review, researchers start with a broad overview of existing studies and gradually investigate specific examples. Using LLMs, each example can be elaborated upon in detail. The model can generate additional insights, suggest related studies, and identify gaps in the existing research. This iterative expansion ensures that the literature review is comprehensive and reflects the depth and breadth of current knowledge in the field.

Once the data has been collected and the methodology has been implemented, the analysis of results becomes a focal point. Here, LLMs can be instrumental in refining the presentation and interpretation of data. Researchers can prompt the LLM to generate multiple versions of the analysis, each time homing in on clarity, coherence, and accuracy. This iterative refinement helps in identifying the most compelling way to present findings, ensuring that the analysis is both rigorous and accessible.

Similarly, in the recommendations and conclusion sections, the iterative use of LLMs allows for continuous enhancement of the narrative. Researchers can prompt the LLM to suggest practical applications, future research directions, and overarching conclusions based on the results. Each iteration helps in distilling complex information into clear and actionable insights, ensuring that the recommendations are well-grounded and the conclusion robust.

The iterative nature of using LLMs for drafting and revising the manuscript underscores the continuous improvement approach inherent in modern research methodologies. By repeatedly engaging with the LLM, researchers can explore different angles, refine their arguments, and enhance the overall quality of their manuscript. This process not only ensures thoroughness but also fosters creativity and innovation, as the LLM can offer new perspectives and alternative formulations of key points.

In practice, the author has utilized these iterative cycles extensively in drafting this manuscript. By keeping all sections accessible in the cloud, each part of the manuscript can be revisited and refined as needed. For instance, during the development of the literature review, the author has repeatedly prompted the LLM to ensure that all significant studies are included and that the discussion remains current and relevant. Similarly, in the results and conclusion sections, the iterative prompting has allowed for the continuous enhancement of the narrative, ensuring clarity and coherence.

At the same time, drafting the paper section by section with AI assistance ensures consistent quality and adherence to style guides. Even with a well-defined voice and style guide, alongside excellent prompting, final edits remain indispensable. Employing AI to draft each section of the manuscript ensures that the writing remains consistent in tone and style throughout. AI tools can help maintain adherence to established style guides and voice parameters, which is critical for producing a coherent and professional document. This methodical approach to drafting allows for each section to be developed with careful attention to detail, ensuring that the final manuscript meets high standards of scholarly writing.

Despite the substantial assistance provided by AI, human oversight is essential for final edits. Revising the manuscript manually enables the author to identify and rectify repetitive syntax, structure, or vocabulary that may have escaped the attention of the LLMs guidance. This step is crucial for ensuring the work does not become monotonous or overly reliant on certain phrases or sentence structures. Conducting searches for specific terms known to be overused or undesired, such as "multifaceted," "delve," "tapestry," "mosaic," etc., is recommended. This practice helps to diversify the vocabulary and enhances the manuscript's readability and originality. By actively seeking and replacing repetitive or clichéd terms, the author can ensure that the language remains fresh and engaging.

The final editing process, where the author carefully reviews and refines the manuscript, is what ultimately makes the work their own. It is through these final touches that the author imparts a unique voice and perspective, transforming a technically proficient draft into a compelling piece of scholarship. This personalized revision process is essential for creating a manuscript that not only adheres to academic standards but also resonates with the author's scholarly identity and insights.

After the final draft is complete, utilizing the LLM as a peer-reviewed is highly recommended to garner constructive feedback for further refinement. By attaching the document and using a prompt such as "You are a peer-reviewed with a background in [field]. Review the attached document and provide feedback on how to improve," researchers can leverage the LLM's capabilities to simulate the peer review process. This approach allows the LLM to assess the manuscript against typical review criteria, identifying areas for enhancement in clarity, coherence, and overall scholarly quality. The feedback provided by the LLM can highlight potential weaknesses, suggest improvements, and ensure that the manuscript meets the rigorous standards required for submission. Incorporating these final adjustments based on AI-generated peer review feedback ensures a thoroughly vetted manuscript, ready for submission to a journal or conference, thereby enhancing its prospects for acceptance and publication.

6.2 REVISING BASED ON REVIEWER FEEDBACK

After the draft has been submitted, most publishers require a double-blind peer review process. This process typically involves one to three external reviewers, depending on the publisher's standards. These reviewers evaluate the manuscript and submit their recommendations, which can range from acceptance, acceptance with minor revisions, acceptance with major revisions, to rejection in its current form. The feedback provided by reviewers can vary significantly; it may be bullet-pointed, presented thematically under headings such as "originality of the submission," "appropriate use of sources in literature review," or "significance to the field," or it may be in long form, without any particular order of subject.

Upon receiving the feedback, it is essential to systematically address each point raised by the reviewers. To facilitate this process, the feedback should be copied into a LLM with instructions to break it down into step-by-step revision tasks. This method saves time and increases efficiency in the turnaround to publication by providing clear, actionable steps. For instance, using the following prompt: "You are a research assistant with expertise in [specific field]. Below is the feedback from reviewers on our manuscript. Please break down the feedback into step-by-step revision instructions," one is able to paste in example feedback and receive the processed output.

Example prompt:

1. **Reviewer 1:**
    - The originality of the submission is commendable, but more context is needed in the introduction to situate the research within the existing literature.
    - The use of sources in the literature review is appropriate, but there are some key studies missing, particularly recent publications from the last two years.
    - The significance to the field is well-argued, but the discussion section needs to tie the results back to broader theoretical implications more clearly.
2. **Reviewer 2:**
    - The methodology section is thorough, but the explanation of the statistical analyses needs more detail.
    - Some of the figures are unclear and need to be redrawn for better readability.
    - Consider expanding the conclusion to address potential limitations of the study.
3. **Reviewer 3:**
    - The manuscript is generally well-written, but there are several grammatical errors that need to be corrected.
    - The theoretical framework is sound, but the practical applications of the findings should be elaborated upon.

Processed Output

Step-by-Step Revision Instructions

1. Introduction:
   - Add more context in the introduction to situate the research within the existing literature, focusing on recent developments in the field.
2. Literature Review:
   - Include key studies from the last two years to ensure the literature review is comprehensive.
3. Discussion:
   - Enhance the discussion section to clearly tie the results back to broader theoretical implications.
4. Methodology:
   - Provide a more detailed explanation of the statistical analyses used in the study.
5. Figures:
   - Redraw figures to improve clarity and readability.
6. Conclusion:
   - Expand the conclusion to discuss potential limitations of the study.
7. Grammar:
   - Correct grammatical errors throughout the manuscript.
8. Theoretical Framework:
   - Elaborate on the practical applications of the findings in the theoretical framework section.

With the step-by-step revisions laid out in sequential order, each section of the manuscript can be efficiently revised by leveraging the capabilities of an LLM. Researchers can copy specific sections, such as the Introduction, and paste them into the LLM alongside a tailored prompt. For example, one could use the following prompt: "[pasted text] Task: Revise based on reviewer feedback to add more context in the introduction to situate the research within the existing literature, focusing on recent developments in the field. Using Consensus." This method allows for targeted revisions that directly address the reviewers' comments, ensuring that the manuscript aligns more closely with the expectations of the academic community. By systematically applying this approach to each section of the manuscript, researchers can enhance the clarity, coherence, and academic rigor of their work, ultimately producing a more compelling and publication-ready document.

6.3 PROMOTING PUBLICATIONS

Many of these strategies discussed above can also be leveraged when promoting published work. Engaging in social media and promoting the significance of scholarly publications are often seen by academics as time-consuming tasks that are secondary to their primary research activities. However, the importance of these activities cannot be overstated, as they play a crucial role in enhancing public visibility and attracting future research partners and funding agencies. In fact, promoting scholarly work is not merely about gaining recognition; it is about ensuring that research reaches a wider audience, including fellow academics, practitioners, and the general public. In an era where information is abundant, effectively communicating the impact and relevance of research can lead to greater citations, collaborative opportunities, and increased funding prospects. By actively engaging in promotion, researchers can highlight the societal and practical implications of their work, making it more accessible and impactful.

Social media platforms such as Twitter, LinkedIn, and ResearchGate offer powerful tools for researchers to share their findings with a broad audience. By creating concise, engaging posts that summarize key findings and implications, researchers can attract attention and stimulate discussion. Regular updates and interactions with followers can build a network of interested parties, fostering collaboration and support. When asked how to best use social media for academics and to provide examples, the following was generated:

Twitter/X

Twitter is an excellent platform for real-time engagement and broad dissemination of research findings. Researchers can use Twitter to:

- **Announce New Publications:** Share links to newly published papers with a brief summary of the key findings. For example, "Excited to share my latest publication on sustainable economic models in the metaverse! Check out our findings on [link]. #Economics #Metaverse #Research".
- **Join Relevant Conversations:** Participate in discussions using relevant hashtags such as #AcademicTwitter, #Science, or #DigitalHumanities. Engaging in these conversations can increase visibility and connect with other researchers in the field.
- **Live-Tweet Conferences:** Provide real-time updates and insights from academic conferences. This not only helps in disseminating information but also engages a wider audience who may not be able to attend the event.

LinkedIn

LinkedIn is a professional networking platform that is ideal for sharing in-depth content and building professional connections. Researchers can use LinkedIn to:

- **Publish Articles:** Write and publish articles on LinkedIn that delve into the details of research projects, methodologies, and findings. These articles can reach a professional audience interested in specific fields.
- **Networking:** Connect with other professionals, potential collaborators, and funding bodies. Personal updates on research progress and achievements can foster professional relationships and open opportunities for collaboration.
- **Group Participation:** Join and actively participate in LinkedIn groups related to specific research interests. These groups provide a platform to share insights, ask questions, and engage with a community of like-minded professionals.

ResearchGate

ResearchGate is a platform specifically designed for researchers to share publications, ask and answer questions, and find collaborators. Researchers can use ResearchGate to:

- **Share Publications:** Upload full-text versions of papers or share preprints to make research accessible to a broader audience. For example, after publishing a paper, a researcher can post, "Our new paper on AI-driven data analysis is now available! Read it here [link]."
- **Engage with the Community:** Answer questions related to their field of expertise, participate in discussions, and provide feedback on others' work. This active participation can enhance the researcher's visibility and reputation within the community.
- **Metrics and Impact:** Use ResearchGate's metrics to track the impact of their publications, including reads, citations, and recommendations. Sharing these metrics can highlight the relevance and impact of the research.

Examples of Effective Social Media Promotion

1. Twitter Example:
    - A researcher in environmental science might tweet, "Proud to announce our new study on the impact of urban green spaces on men-

tal health! Discover how nature in cities can improve wellbeing: [link] #UrbanEcology #MentalHealth #ResearchImpact".

- By using relevant hashtags and a link to the publication, the tweet can reach a wider audience, including policymakers and urban planners interested in implementing the research findings.

2. LinkedIn Example:
    - An academic in business studies might write a LinkedIn article titled "Five Key Strategies for Sustainable Business Growth in the Digital Age" and share insights from their latest research. By sharing the article in relevant LinkedIn groups and tagging colleagues, the researcher can spark discussions and reach professionals in the industry.
3. ResearchGate Example:
    - A scientist can share their latest paper on ResearchGate and engage with questions from other researchers. For instance, "Our team has just published new findings on the role of microbial communities in soil health. Read the full text here: [link]. Looking forward to your questions and feedback!"

The recent publication of *Generative AI in the English Composition Classroom: Practical and Adaptable Strategies* by Daniel Plate, Elizabeth Melick, James Hutson, and Susan Edele provides an excellent opportunity to utilize various social media platforms for promotion. Once hearing that publication had launched and ordering through the publisher website now available, the authors took said information- book title, authors, keywords, and abstract. Pasting the information into Google Gemini and prompting "Write a LinkedIn post with hashtags and emoji announcing the publication of this book" the following is generated:

📢 **Exciting news for English composition educators! 📚**

"Generative AI in the English Composition Classroom: Practical and Adaptable Strategies" is now available! 🎉 This book offers valuable insights and strategies for integrating AI tools like Claude, ChatGPT, and Gemini into your teaching.

👩‍🏫👨‍🏫 Learn how to leverage AI to enhance creativity, improve writing skills, and prepare students for the future of work. 🤖

📖 Explore practical examples and case studies to understand how AI can be a powerful tool for both educators and students.

Don't miss out on this invaluable resource! Grab your copy today! ➡ https://www.routledge.com/Generative-AI-in-the-English-Composition-Classroom-Practical-and-Adaptable-Strategies/Plate-Melick-Hutson-Edele/p/book/9781032831350

#AIinEducation #EnglishComposition #FutureOfWork #WritingSkills #EdTech

In order to tailor to different platforms, the same chat was then prompted: "Now, output for Twitter/X, Instagram, and Facebook tailoring for each platform and their audiences."

Twitter/X

📢 New book alert for English teachers! "Generative AI in the English Composition Classroom" is out now! 🤖📚 Discover practical strategies for using AI tools like ChatGPT to enhance student writing & prep them for the future of work. #AIinEducation #EnglishComposition #EdTech [Link to book]

Instagram

📚 New book alert for English teachers! 📚

Level up your teaching with "Generative AI in the English Composition Classroom." This guide offers practical strategies for integrating AI tools like ChatGPT into your lessons. 🤖

🚀 Boost student creativity, improve writing skills, and prepare them for the future of work. 🚀

Check out the link in our bio to get your copy today! #AIinEducation #EnglishComposition #FutureOfWork #WritingSkills #EdTech

Facebook

Exciting news for English teachers! 🎉

"Generative AI in the English Composition Classroom" is now available! This book is packed with practical strategies and real-world examples to help you seamlessly integrate AI tools like ChatGPT into your teaching.

👩‍🏫👨‍🏫 Whether you're a seasoned educator or just starting out, this book offers valuable insights for:

- Enhancing student creativity and writing skills
- Preparing students for the future of work
- Addressing academic integrity concerns
- ...and much more!

Don't miss out on this invaluable resource! Get your copy today and revolutionize your English composition classroom! [Link to book] #AIinEducation #EnglishComposition #FutureOfWork #WritingSkills #EdTech #NewBook

Alongside social media, other powerful strategies can be employed to promote scholarly work effectively. Blogging and online articles provide a platform for researchers to delve deeper into their research than what is possible on social media. By writing detailed blog posts or articles, researchers can explain their methodologies, discuss the intricacies of their findings, and explore the broader implications of their work. This approach caters to audiences who prefer comprehensive content and can significantly drive traffic to the original publications. Additionally, blogs and online articles can serve as valuable resources for students, educators, and fellow researchers, fostering a deeper understanding of the research topic and promoting academic discourse.

Academic networking sites such as ResearchGate and Academia.edu are tailored for academics to share their work, stay updated on field developments, and connect with peers. These platforms offer various features like metrics for tracking publication impact, collaboration opportunities, and direct communication channels. By actively participating on these sites, researchers can enhance the visibility of their work, engage in meaningful discussions, and potentially collaborate on future projects. Furthermore, press releases and media engagement through university press offices can significantly amplify the reach of research findings. Engaging with journalists and media outlets ensures accurate and widespread dissemination of research, making it accessible to the public and influencing policy decisions. Lastly, presenting research at **conferences and public lectures** provides direct interaction with other researchers, policymakers, and the general public, facilitating immediate feedback and enriching the research process.

AI tools can streamline the promotion process, making it less time-consuming and more effective. For instance, AI-driven content creation tools can help draft social media posts, blog entries, and even press releases, ensuring that key messages are clear and engaging. These tools can generate initial drafts that researchers can refine, saving valuable time and maintaining consistency in messaging across different platforms. Additionally, AI analytics can identify the most effective channels and times for posting, maximizing reach and impact. By analyzing engagement rates, click-through rates, and audience demographics, AI tools provide insights into what promotional strategies work best, helping researchers fine-tune their approaches.

Moreover, AI can assist in targeted outreach by identifying and reaching out to potential collaborators, funding agencies, and media contacts. By analyzing data from various sources, AI tools can suggest individuals and organizations that are most likely to be interested in the research, facilitating more targeted and effective outreach efforts. This not only broadens the reach of the research but also opens up new avenues for collaboration and funding. In summary, leveraging AI tools for promotion can enhance the visibility and impact of scholarly work, making it an indispensable part of modern research dissemination strategies.

6.4 ACTING AS A PEER-REVIEWER

Just as the feedback provided by peer reviewers can be fed into the AI of choice to refine and improve a research manuscript, the steps of peer review can be repeated in reverse when acting as a peer reviewer. This involves using AI tools to enhance the efficiency and effectiveness of the review process, ensuring that feedback is thorough, constructive, and aligned with the standards of academic rigor. The peer-review process, as noted, is plagued with difficulties, including finding reviewers, contacting them at a time that they can spare to complete a review, and ensuring the reviews are fair and unbiased. The traditional review process is often slow and can be influenced by various biases, including those against foreign researchers and women. Using AI tools in the peer-review process can lead to more objective and timely reviews, helping to get research out into the field much more rapidly. AI-driven platforms can automate the initial reviewer selection process, ensuring that suitable experts are identified and contacted efficiently. These tools can also provide objective assessments, reducing the risk of biased reviews by focusing on the content and methodology rather than the authors' background. This approach can democratize the review process, making it fairer and more inclusive, ultimately enhancing the quality and diversity of published research.

The peer review process differs by publisher and varies between articles, chapters, and books, but the same fundamental information is sought to varying degrees of granularity: the quality of the research and writing, the thoroughness of the review of the state of the field, and the significance of the contribution to the field. For journal articles, the focus is often on the rigor of the methodology, the clarity of the results, and the relevance of the discussion. For book chapters, reviewers assess how well the chapter fits within the overall context of the book, as well as the depth of the analysis and the coherence of the arguments. For books, the review process is more extensive, examining the comprehensive nature of the research, the organization and structure of the content, and the book's overall impact on its academic discipline. Regardless of the format, reviewers seek to ensure that the work advances knowledge in the field and meets high standards of scholarly excellence. When prompted for the most common questions and themes asked of reviewers ChatGPT-4 output:

Standard Peer-Review Questions

1. Quality of Research and Writing:
    - Is the research question or hypothesis clearly defined?
    - Is the methodology appropriate and thoroughly explained?
    - Are the results clearly presented and supported by the data?
    - Is the discussion well-reasoned and supported by the results?

- Is the writing clear, concise, and free of grammatical errors?

2. Thoroughness of the Review of the State of the Field:
    - Does the manuscript provide a comprehensive review of the relevant literature?
    - Is the theoretical framework appropriate and well-integrated into the study?
    - Are key studies and seminal works in the field referenced and discussed?
3. Significance of Contribution to the Field:
    - Does the research make a significant contribution to the field?
    - Are the implications of the findings clearly articulated?
    - Does the study address a gap in the existing literature or provide new insights?
4. Ethical Considerations:
    - Were ethical guidelines followed in the conduct of the research?
    - Is there evidence of any conflicts of interest?
5. Presentation and Organization:
    - Is the manuscript well-organized and logically structured?
    - Are tables, figures, and appendices used effectively and appropriately?
    - Is the abstract a clear and concise summary of the work?

Recommendation for Publication

Recommendation

- Accept as is
- Accept with minor revisions
- Reject

Comments to the Author

(Provide specific feedback on the strengths and weaknesses of the manuscript, suggestions for improvement, and any additional comments that may help the author improve the work.)

Comments to the Editor

(Provide an overall assessment of the manuscript and the rationale for your recommendation. Highlight any particularly significant findings or major concerns that should be considered in the publication decision.)

By using these standard peer-review questions and recommendations, reviewers can provide comprehensive and structured feedback that addresses all critical aspects of the manuscript. This approach ensures a thorough and objective review process, facilitating the publication of high-quality research.

Acting as a peer reviewer is a crucial activity for one's academic career, offering numerous professional benefits. It not only enhances one's academic profile by demonstrating expertise and contributing to the scholarly community, but it also provides early access to the latest research in the field. This early exposure is a distinct advantage when seeking new topics and research funding, as it allows reviewers to stay at the forefront of developments and identify emerging trends and gaps in the literature. For example, let's consider an article from the author titled " Navigating the Complexities of AI: The Critical Role of Interpretability and Explainability in Ensuring Transparency and Trust." Once accepting the role of reviewer, one is given access to download the paper, usually as a PDF. As with all sensitive information, opt out of using the chat for training the model. Next, attach the document knowing that it will not be used to train the model and will remain confidential. One can also use Microsoft Copilot as the account is protected within the institutional system. Using the following prompt is an example for approaching each section:

You will act as a peer-reviewer and provide feedback on the attached article. Start by writing a paragraph addressing: 1. Quality of Research and Writing:

- Is the research question or hypothesis clearly defined?
- Is the methodology appropriate and thoroughly explained?
- Are the results clearly presented and supported by the data?
- Is the discussion well-reasoned and supported by the results?
- Is the writing clear, concise, and free of grammatical errors?

The model then responds:

Quality of Research and Writing Evaluation

The paper titled "Navigating the Complexities of AI: The Critical Role of Interpretability and Explainability in Ensuring Transparency and Trust" meticulously defines its research hypothesis and questions, focusing on the paramount importance of interpretability and explainability in AI applications, particularly within high-stakes domains like healthcare, finance, and autonomous driving. The clarity and relevance of the hypothesis are effectively established through a well-articulated introduction and a concise abstract that set the stage for the ensuing discussion.

The methodology employed in the study is aptly suited to the paper's aims, utilizing a comprehensive review of existing literature, case studies, and experimental data to elucidate the balance between AI performance and transparency. The authors have thoroughly explained their approach, ensuring that readers understand the analytical framework and tools employed, such as SHAP and LIME, which are pivotal in assessing AI model transparency.

Results are presented with clarity and are well-supported by the data reviewed. The paper successfully ties these results back to the theoretical framework established earlier, enhancing the credibility of the findings. The discussion section is robust, providing a nuanced synthesis of results and literature to argue for the critical role of interpretability in AI.

Writing throughout the document adheres to high academic standards—clear, precise, and meticulously proofread to avoid grammatical errors. The structured flow from introduction through to conclusions demonstrates a coherent progression of ideas, which facilitates an understanding of complex concepts discussed within the paper.

Overall, the quality of research and writing in this article meets the rigorous standards expected of scholarly work, with each section reinforcing the central thesis about the necessity of developing interpretable AI systems in maintaining ethical standards and trust in technology applications.

By applying AI tools to perform a peer review on this article, the reviewer can efficiently assess the quality of research and writing, check the thoroughness of the literature review, and evaluate the significance of the contribution. Of course, one should not just use the output verbatim. The AI can help draft initial comments and identify key strengths and areas for improvement, streamlining the review process and ensuring a comprehensive and objective evaluation. The final review should be that of the human evaluator, however. This approach not only benefits the reviewer by enhancing their expertise and expanding their knowledge but also contributes to the advancement of the field by ensuring high standards of scholarly publishing.

The process delineated in this chapter provides a robust framework for initiating and conducting research. However, it is crucial to acknowledge that experts in their respective fields, particularly those adept at leveraging AI, will always possess a superior edge. As highlighted by Mollick (2024), experts will invariably be the best at applying AI tools within their domains, underscoring the importance of domain-specific expertise in maximizing the utility of these technologies. The effectiveness of prompting in AI-driven research is significantly enhanced when personalized and tailored to the specific needs of the project. Personalized prompts ensure that the AI's outputs are relevant and contextually appropriate, thereby increasing the precision and applicability of the generated content. As Mollick (2024) suggests, the personalization of AI prompts leads to more effective outcomes, a principle that should be incorporated into the research workflow.

While the research process is often depicted as a linear sequence of steps, it is, in reality, an iterative and modular endeavor. Researchers continuously revisit and refine earlier stages of their work based on new insights, data, or feedback. For instance, a literature review is not confined to the initial phase of research but is an ongoing activity that may be revisited after hypothesis development or new data collection. This dynamic nature of research necessitates flexibility and a willingness to adapt to evolving circumstances. Presenting preliminary findings at conferences is a prime example of the iterative process in action. The feedback obtained from these presentations can be instrumental in shaping the subsequent phases of research. Such feedback might necessitate additional data collection, the re-evaluation of initial assumptions, or even a modification of the research question itself. This iterative approach ensures that the research remains relevant, rigorous, and reflective of the latest developments in the field.

Graduate students, in particular, must grasp the full cycle of the research process to achieve success in their academic endeavors. AI tools can play a pivotal role in managing the involution inherent in this iterative process. By providing continuous support throughout each phase of research, AI tools help ensure thoroughness and efficiency. They allow researchers to quickly adapt to new information and requirements, thereby maintaining the integrity and quality of their work.

Therefore, while AI tools and structured methodologies can significantly enhance the research process, the human element—particularly the expertise of seasoned researchers—remains indispensable. The research process is fundamentally iterative and modular, requiring a flexible and dynamic approach. Through a combination of the strengths of AI with human expertise and personalized prompting, researchers can maneuver the many considerations of the research cycle more effectively, ultimately producing high-quality, impactful scholarship.

REFERENCES

Mollick, E. (2024). Latent expertise: Everyone is in R&D. *One Useful Thing*. Accessed June 20, 2024: https://www.oneusefulthing.org/p/latent-expertise-everyone-is-in-r?r=i5f7&utm_campaign=post&utm_medium=web

Chapter 7
Ethical Considerations and Challenges

ABSTRACT

This chapter addresses the critical ethical considerations and challenges associated with the use of artificial intelligence in academic research, focusing on issues of bias and the integrity of AI-generated outputs. It considers the sophistication of handling the potential biases that AI systems may introduce during data processing and analysis, highlighting the importance of developing robust mechanisms to identify and mitigate such biases to uphold the ethical standards of scholarly work. Furthermore, the chapter explores strategies to ensure the credibility and reliability of research findings produced with AI assistance. It discusses the necessary protocols and checks that need to be in place to maintain the integrity of research outputs, ensuring that they are both accurate and trustworthy. By tackling these ethical challenges head-on, the chapter underscores the need for continuous vigilance and adaptive ethical practices in the evolving landscape of AI-driven research.

7.1 RETHINKING PLAGIARISM IN THE AGE OF AI

In the rapidly evolving landscape of artificial intelligence, traditional notions of authorship and plagiarism are being fundamentally challenged. Before delving into more familiar ethical issues such as data privacy and the reliability of AI-generated outputs, it is essential to reframe the discussion around content generation and the concept of plagiarism. This chapter thus first addresses how AI technologies, which are capable of producing high-quality written content, influence our understanding of authorship and originality in academic research. The core of the concern lies in the perception and identity of the author. Objections to AI-generated content are often less about the objective quality of the work and more about the identity of the creator being disclosed. Research indicates that AI-generated content is perceived

DOI: 10.4018/979-8-3693-6905-0.ch007

to be of lower quality when it is known to be produced by an AI, even if it is indistinguishable from human-created content when the authorship is unknown (Rae, 2024). This bias highlights a deeper issue related to the value we place on human authorship and the perceived integrity of academic work.

Traditionally, plagiarism has been defined as the act of using someone else's work without proper attribution, thereby presenting it as one's own. This definition assumes that the content in question has a singular, identifiable human author. However, AI-generated content complicates this notion. If an AI produces a piece of writing, who is the author? Is it the programmer who developed the AI, the user who prompted the AI, or the AI itself? These questions are not merely academic; they have practical implications for how we enforce academic integrity in a world where AI tools are commonplace. Moreover, AI systems, such as LLMs, are trained on vast datasets that include copyrighted and non-copyrighted materials. This raises concerns about the originality of AI-generated content. If an AI produces text that is strikingly similar to existing works, is it plagiarizing? The lack of clear guidelines in this area poses a significant challenge for academic institutions aiming to uphold standards of originality and integrity.

Before 2022 and the widespread adoption of GAI technologies like OpenAI's ChatGPT, the concept of plagiarism in academic, literary, and scientific contexts was relatively clear and well-defined (Nabee et al., 2020). The key to avoiding plagiarism was the principled acknowledgment of original authors. This acknowledgment was required whenever exact words of a human author were used. Writers had to not only cite the original author but also distinctly identify the borrowed words. This was typically done using quotation marks around the exact text or by clearly indenting the quoted passage, visually separating it from the original work (Bouville, 2008). Similarly, when paraphrasing—rephrasing or reinterpreting written or spoken communication in one's own words—citation was still necessary. Paraphrasing required more than just substituting synonyms; it involved a substantial transformation of the original text while preserving its core meaning (Ansorge et al., 2021). This framework of plagiarism, grounded in the clear demarcation of original and borrowed material, upheld values of intellectual honesty, respect for intellectual labor, and a scholarly commitment to advancing knowledge through transparent and accountable use of existing literature (Fenton & Gralla, 2020).

However, the emergence of GAI, particularly post-2022, has necessitated a complex reevaluation of these long-standing principles. The ability to generate content indistinguishable from human-authored text has blurred the boundaries between original creation and derivation. Consequently, the academic, scientific, and publishing communities now face the challenging task of redefining plagiarism in the context of AI-assisted writing. This task extends beyond traditional arenas of citation and paraphrasing, touching on the very essence of creativity and original thought in the digital age (Dehouche, 2021).

Much of the controversy surrounding scholarly plagiarism involves LLMs. These models, such as GPT (generative pre-trained transformers), operate on principles of ML and NLP (Wahle et al., 2022). LLMs are trained on vast text datasets encompassing diverse subjects and styles, allowing them to learn the patterns and structures of human language. Through this training, LLMs develop an understanding of grammar, syntax, semantics, and aspects of context and pragmatics (Yu et al., 2023). Utilizing 'transformer architecture,' these models predict and generate text sequences by understanding word relationships and dependencies within sentences. This technique is adept at maintaining coherence over long text stretches, helping the AI produce contextually appropriate passages (Zaheer et al., 2020). Once trained, LLMs can complete various language tasks, including text completion, translation, summarization, and content generation, often producing results that closely mimic human-written text (Hadi et al., 2023). Their ability to generate plausible, coherent text based on prompts or to continue given text sequences makes them powerful tools for applications ranging from creative writing to coding assistance (Jonsson & Tholander, 2022).

While these tools have demonstrated industrial efficiency, the challenge of identifying AI-generated text, especially in educational contexts, adds complexity to how writing is perceived and used in education (Koraishi, 2023). Historically, English composition courses have played a crucial role in academia, based on the premise that writing is an extension of thinking (Arapoff, 1967; Jambeck & Winder, 1990; Mauk, 2003; Rahmat, 2020; Spear, 1983). These courses aimed to cultivate students' ability to express thoughts clearly and cohesively, thereby enhancing their critical thinking and analytical skills (Sinaga & Feranie, 2017). Writing assignments were fundamentally seen as reflections of students' intellectual engagement and understanding (Ritchhart et al., 2011). However, the emergence of GAI challenges these traditional paradigms. The difficulty in distinguishing AI-generated from human-generated text complicates the assessment of students' true capability to articulate original ideas, directly impacting the objectives of teaching writing and research. There is growing concern that the ease of generating sophisticated texts using AI may lead students to rely on technology rather than developing their analytical and writing skills, undermining academic integrity (Velliaris & Breen, 2016; Roe et al., 2023; Yeo, 2023). Additionally, as AI-detecting software attempts to keep pace with technological developments, its accuracy has been questioned in numerous studies (Khaliq et al., 2023; Walters, 2023).

The current state of AI-detection software, particularly tools like Turnitin, warrants careful scrutiny. As of May 14, 2023, Turnitin reported that among 38.5 million submissions analyzed for AI-generated content, approximately 9.6% contained over

20% of text likely produced by AI tools, while 3.5% exhibited between 80% and 100% AI-generated content (Chechitelli, 2023). This data underscores the increasing prevalence of AI assistance in academic writing. Notably, the AI detection model primarily targets prose text, commonly found in long-form writing such as essays. Its efficacy diminishes when dealing with non-prose formats, including poetry, scripts, code, ordered or unordered lists, tables, or annotated bibliographies (Chaka, 2023). This limitation presents a significant challenge in environments where diverse forms of writing are prevalent. Moreover, the accuracy of these AI detection tools is a matter of ongoing concern. Misidentifications, both in flagging human-generated text as AI-produced and vice versa, necessitate additional layers of human analysis to verify conclusions (Rashidi et al., 2023).

The rise of AI in educational settings also raises significant questions regarding intellectual property rights. When writing is a product of both human and AI collaboration, delineating the boundaries of authorship and original contribution becomes challenging. This situation not only challenges traditional notions of originality and intellectual rigor but also necessitates a reevaluation of what constitutes plagiarism in the digital age (Oleksy, 2023). These developments have substantial implications for pedagogical approaches in teaching writing and research. Educators must rethink their methods to ensure that the core objectives of enhancing critical thinking and analytical skills are maintained. This includes developing strategies to integrate AI tools in a manner that complements rather than supplants the learning process, ensuring that students remain at the forefront of their educational journey (Hutson & Plate, 2023). As AI continues to evolve and integrate into various facets of life, including education, adapting to its presence and leveraging its capabilities responsibly and ethically becomes paramount for educators and institutions. However, a disparity in the generational and student-faculty use of these tools exists, complicating their integration.

Data from NerdyNav (2024) highlights a pronounced generational and professional gap in the awareness and use of AI tools like ChatGPT. Specifically, 82% of college professors are aware of tools like ChatGPT, in contrast to only 55% of K-12 teachers. This disparity in AI literacy also extends across different age groups. Among students, those aged 18-34 exhibit significantly higher adoption rates, nearly double, compared to older cohorts. Specifically, 13.5% of Millennials and Gen Z engage with ChatGPT, whereas only 7.9% of Generation X and 7.2% of Baby Boomers use it, with the Silent Generation showing the lowest usage at 5.3%. This lag in awareness and usage among older age groups, particularly in educational settings, contributes to a growing mistrust and skepticism towards the application of AI tools in academic contexts by the younger generation (Kreps et al., 2023). The rapid adoption of AI by students, outpacing their educators, not only fuels this distrust but also signals an urgent need to rethink traditional academic policies and pedagogical practices. This situation highlights the necessity for educators across all age groups and educational levels to become more AI-literate and develop a nuanced understanding of how these technologies can be integrated ethically and effectively into the educational framework. Such adjustments are crucial to bridge the gap between the new capabilities of these tools and current educational paradigms, ensuring that both teachers and students can guide themselves through this new landscape with competence and integrity (Southworth et al., 2023).

Central to bridging AI literacy across student-teacher populations is rethinking what constitutes plagiarism. Given the ubiquity of AI tools like ChatGPT, Bard, Google Gemini, Llama, and Grok, integrated across various platforms, the traditional approach to plagiarism, which focused primarily on direct citation and paraphrasing, seems insufficient in an era where AI-generated content is seamlessly integrated into student work. The challenge lies in distinguishing AI-assisted writing from entirely original human composition, a task made more difficult by the sophistication of AI in mimicking human writing styles. To address this evolving landscape, it is crucial for educational institutions to develop new frameworks that acknowledge the role of AI in academic writing while preserving the core values of academic integrity. This includes creating guidelines for the ethical use of AI in research and writing and equipping both students and educators with the necessary skills and knowledge to move through this new terrain. The goal should be to leverage AI as a tool for enhancing the educational experience, rather than as a means to replace the critical thinking and creative processes central to learning. By doing so, educators can bridge the AI literacy gap and foster an environment where technology augments, rather than undermines, the pursuit of knowledge.

Yet, even before the advent of GAI, the concept of plagiarism within American academia was fraught with complicatedness. Plagiarism in the United States is particularly intricate, underscored by various definitions and interpretations that highlight its contested nature. According to The Oxford English Dictionary, plagiarism is defined as "the practice of copying another person's ideas, words or work and pretending that they are your own." This broad definition encapsulates a range of actions, from the overt to the subtle, all centered around the misappropriation of intellectual property. The Merriam-Webster Dictionary further refines this definition, describing plagiarizing as "to steal and pass off ideas or words of another as one's own." Whether through deliberate deception or subterfuge, the practice assumes conscious action on the part of the perpetrator.

The complications in the American context are further detailed in various academic guidelines, which include a plethora of actions under the umbrella of plagiarism (Pradhan & Kumar, 2023; Putra et al., 2023; Taylor, 2024). These actions range from the direct, such as copying from a source without quotations or citation, to the more nuanced, like paraphrasing or summarizing the idea of another without attribution.

Even subtle acts, such as altering sentence structure while retaining original words, or vice versa, are considered plagiarism. Additionally, the unacknowledged use of audio, video, or other media sources, submitting the work of another student as their own, or using information from an expert interview without proper attribution, are all deemed forms of plagiarism. Furthermore, the scope of plagiarism in American academia extends to the arenas of collaboration and self-plagiarism (Kleebayoon & Wiwanikit, 2023). Excessive collaboration on an essay with another person, or the submission of an essay previously written for another class without the consent of both professors, are also viewed as violations of academic integrity. These various forms of plagiarism highlight the nuanced and expansive nature of what constitutes intellectual dishonesty in academia.

However, concepts of academic integrity and avoidance of plagiarism are not universal. The American perspective of plagiarism, fundamentally defined as the act of passing off the ideas of another as one's own, contrasts sharply with various cultural views on plagiarism across the globe. In East Asian countries like China, Japan, and South Korea, the communal ownership of knowledge often negates the need for individual attribution (Kutieleh & Adiningrum, 2011). This view is rooted in collectivist cultures and Confucian principles, where memorizing and repeating authoritative texts is seen as a form of respect and acknowledgment of established wisdom rather than intellectual theft. In these societies, students learn that knowledge belongs to the community, and citing individual authors might conflict with their cultural understanding of knowledge and learning (Grudecki, 2021).

Similarly, in the Middle East, quoting and paraphrasing well-known religious or political authorities without formal citation is common. Scholars and teachers are expected to recognize these texts as part of common knowledge, and formal citation might imply a lack of knowledge, potentially insulting educators and adversely affecting student academic standing (Aljurf, Kemp & Williams, 2020). In Eastern European countries, formal citation rules exist, but attitudes towards plagiarism are more lenient, with less emphasis on strict adherence to academic integrity (Makarova, 2019). The same attitude is observed in Latin American educational contexts, where academic misconduct like plagiarism is not frequently discussed or enforced with the same rigor as in the United States (Ison, 2018). Conversely, Western European countries, Canada, and Australia align more closely with the U.S. in their approach to plagiarism, emphasizing individualism and strict guidelines for plagiarism prevention (Leask, 2006; Stoesz & Eaton, 2022).

These cultural differences have historically posed significant challenges for international students in American academic institutions (Amsberry & Snavely, 2011; Gunnarsson et al., 2014). The focus on individual intellectual property in the U.S. and the strict enforcement of citation rules can be a source of confusion and frustration for students from backgrounds where such practices are either unknown or viewed differently. The discrepancy between these cultural perspectives on plagiarism highlights the challenges faced in American academia, particularly in an increasingly globalized educational environment. The integration of GAI technologies further complicates this landscape, as they bring new dimensions to the creation and use of academic content. This evolving scenario necessitates a continual reevaluation of the definitions and perceptions of plagiarism, ensuring they remain relevant and effective in upholding academic integrity in a rapidly changing world.

In addition to cultural considerations, the policies associated with academic integrity and plagiarism are becoming increasingly unenforceable due to the growing inability to detect AI-generated writing. This challenge is further compounded by the integration of generative writing tools into widely used word processing software, such as Microsoft Word's Co-Pilot. As these advanced AI features become standard, it is clear that all writing will be AI-augmented moving forward, much like grammar and spell check functionalities have become ubiquitous. This shift necessitates a reevaluation of how academic institutions approach issues of originality and integrity, recognizing that the use of AI in writing is now an integral part of the composition process. Therefore, fostering AI literacy and promoting ethical use of these tools will be crucial in maintaining the credibility and rigor of academic work.

7.2 THE AUTHOR FUNCTION AND AI-ASSISTED RESEARCH

The role of the author in content creation, authority, and originality has evolved significantly alongside the history of education. Particularly within Western academia during the eighteenth and nineteenth centuries, there was an increasing emphasis on the formal instruction of composition and the codification of citation practices. This era saw the establishment of systematic approaches to writing and research, with the Modern Language Association (MLA) and the American Psychological Association (APA) developing detailed citation styles to standardize scholarly communication (Russell, 2002). However, this Western, Eurocentric approach to teaching research and writing has historically disadvantaged non-Western and non-native learners. The strict adherence to Western norms and citation practices often overlooks the diverse linguistic and rhetorical traditions outside the Anglo-European context, presenting significant barriers to inclusivity and equity in global scholarship (Canagarajah, 2002).

While this book presents various strategies for enhancing research capabilities, it is essential to acknowledge the complexities of institutional policies regarding the use of emerging technologies. Researchers are advised to review their institution's policies before implementing all the recommended strategies. For instance, certain grant funding agencies may impose specific restrictions on how information is created, used, and disseminated. These restrictions can include limitations on the use of AI-generated content, data privacy concerns, and compliance with ethical guidelines. As highlighted in this section, the role of the author and the nature of content creation are evolving rapidly, and such considerations may not remain relevant for long. However, understanding and adhering to current policies is crucial to ensure compliance and maintain the integrity of research practices. This cautious approach ensures that researchers can effectively leverage new technologies while aligning with institutional and funding agency requirements.

In recent decades, there has been a growing recognition of these disparities, prompting a shift towards more inclusive pedagogical strategies that honor diverse linguistic and rhetorical practices. This includes the integration of multiliteracies and translingual approaches in composition teaching, aiming to validate the varied linguistic and cultural backgrounds of students (Horner et al., 2011). Such approaches advocate for a more flexible understanding of writing and authorship that respects and incorporates different cultural norms and practices. At the same time, the traditional justification for requiring transparency and disclosure of external sources and citations in research and writing remains crucial. This practice is deeply rooted in the philosophical underpinnings of academic integrity and the "pursuit of truth." At its core, this position views the academic enterprise as one dedicated to the creation, dissemination, and validation of knowledge. This process relies on a foundational ethic of honesty, where scholars and graduate students alike are expected to acknowledge the contributions of others to their work (Valentine, 2006). The APA continues to emphasize the importance of citations as a means to honor intellectual property rights and facilitate the traceability of ideas, which promotes a scholarly dialogue that is both rich and dynamic (APA, 2020).

Moreover, the act of citing serves as a critical pedagogical tool, teaching graduate students not only to respect the work of others but also to engage critically with various sources. This engagement enhances their analytical skills and deepens their understanding of the subject matter (Simmons, 2004). Through the citation of sources, students are seen to learn to differentiate between their original ideas and those borrowed from others, fostering a sense of academic responsibility and integrity that is foundational to scholarly inquiry and discourse. In the context of AI-assisted research, maintaining these principles is essential though must be approached differently.

For instance, the integration of digital technologies, from word processing to the expansive domain of the Internet, has significantly altered the pedagogical landscape of research. These advancements have enhanced access to varied sources and introduced the necessity for new literacies. This evolution has marked a shift towards accommodating an array of media types and digital platforms, challenging conventional concepts of authorship and authority (Purdy, 2010). Concurrently, there is a push to harmonize the traditional tenets of writing instruction with the imperative for a pedagogy that is both equitable and inclusive, recognizing and valuing the diversity of global rhetorical traditions (Gilyard, 2016).

Before the widespread adoption of GAI technologies like OpenAI's ChatGPT in 2022, the concept of plagiarism in academic, literary, and scientific contexts was relatively clear and well-defined (Nabee et al., 2020). Traditionally, the cornerstone of avoiding plagiarism was the principled acknowledgment of original authors whenever one utilized their exact written or spoken words, requiring proper citation and distinct identification of the borrowed words through the use of quotation marks or indentation (Bouville, 2008). Paraphrasing—rephrasing or reinterpreting written or spoken communication in one's own words—also demanded careful citation, requiring not just the substitution of synonyms but a substantial transformation of the original text while preserving its core meaning (Ho et al., 2014). This framework for plagiarism, with its clear demarcation of original and borrowed material, upheld values of intellectual honesty and scholarly commitment to knowledge advancement.

However, the emergence of GAI post-2022 has complicated these long-standing principles. The ability of AI to generate content indistinguishable from human-authored text has blurred the boundaries between original creation and derivation, challenging the academic, scientific, and publishing communities to redefine plagiarism in the context of AI-assisted writing. This redefinition extends beyond traditional citation and paraphrasing to touch on the very essence of creativity and original thought in the digital age (Dehouche, 2021). LLMs, which operate on ML and NLP principles, exemplify this challenge. These models, trained on extensive datasets, learn patterns in human language, allowing them to perform complex language tasks such as text completion and content generation that often mimic human writing (Wahle et al., 2022; Hadi et al., 2023). The sophistication of these tools raises significant questions for education, particularly regarding the authenticity of human writing and the integrity of the writing process.

The current capabilities and limitations of AI-detection software, such as Turnitin, underscore the ongoing challenge of accurately identifying AI-generated content. These limitations necessitate additional layers of human analysis to confirm the origins of a text (Rashidi et al., 2023). Furthermore, the debate around intellectual property rights in the context of AI collaboration complicates traditional notions of authorship and originality, prompting a reevaluation of what constitutes plagiarism today (Oleksy, 2023). As AI continues to evolve, educators, peer-reviewers, and publishers must rethink their strategies to ensure that AI tools are used to complement the critical thinking and analytical skills of researchers and their original findings. This involves developing guidelines for the ethical use of AI in writing and research, ensuring that researchers remain engaged in their educational journeys as active participants rather than passive recipients of AI-generated content. Such an approach is crucial for maintaining academic integrity and fostering a learning environment that promotes responsible AI use (Hutson & Plate, 2023).

At the same time, the advent of generative technologies presents formidable challenges to these established norms by synthesizing information and generating novel content, thereby blurring the distinctions between human and machine authorship. This raises critical questions about the nature of authorship, originality, and the ethical frameworks guiding transparency and citation (Broussard, 2021). In light of these technological developments, some scholars have begun to question the adequacy of traditional citation practices. They argue that the current frameworks may not fully account for the collaborative nature of human-AI authorship and may need to be reevaluated to reflect the evolving landscape of digital scholarship (Gipp et al., 2020; Landa-Blanco et al., 2023). This reevaluation necessitates a philosophical shift in how researchers and publishers conceptualize authorship, originality, and the ethical use of digital tools in academic writing. The traditional justification for rigorous citation practices remains valid in its promotion of academic integrity and critical engagement with diverse sources. However, the advent of generative technologies requires a nuanced approach that considers the contributions of both human and machine intelligence. This approach demands ongoing dialogue among researchers, technologists, and ethicists to ensure that the foundational principles of academic writing evolve alongside technological advancements, maintaining the integrity of the educational process while embracing the opportunities presented by innovation (Guleria et al., 2023).

Transitioning from a traditional understanding of citation to the dynamic area introduced by GAI signifies a pivotal shift in academic writing norms. This shift necessitates a reevaluation of foundational principles, as the integration of GAI in academic research challenges academics to consider a new paradigm of transparency and citation practices. The foundation of academic integrity and the practice of citation is deeply rooted in honoring intellectual property and ensuring the traceability of ideas, a principle that remains paramount in academia (Larsson & Heintz, 2020). Historically, the rationale for citation practices extends beyond mere acknowledgment. It embodies the development of critical thinking and knowledge construction, promoting engagement with literature, critical source evaluation, and the contextualization of one's work within the scholarly discourse (Kim, Park, & Suh, 2020). This not only enriches academic discussions but also fosters an ethos of rigor, transparency, and ethical scholarship.

With the advent of digital technologies and the proliferation of online resources, the complexity of citation practices has increased, prompting academics to adapt their strategies. This adaptation highlights the importance of digital literacy and ethical information usage in today's interconnected academic environment (Park, 2023). The progression of citation teaching mirrors a broader dedication to upholding academic integrity and promoting responsible scholarship. From the detailed assembly of bibliographies to the adoption of citation management tools, the core principles of respect for intellectual work and commitment to scholarly excellence persist. The philosophical underpinnings of citation, as traditionally taught in methodology courses, continue to influence contemporary pedagogical approaches, though concessions must be made (Kaebnick et al., 2023). One of the biggest contentions surrounding GAI tools is how content is generated using pre-trained textual information, even though citations can now be accurately included (McGowan et al., 2023). Yet, the realities of both educational technologies and employer requirements of workers seriously challenge the approach to content creation. Furthermore, the very notion of originality in writing and the role played by the author has long been challenged.

The evolution of the understanding of the role of the author and originality in the age of generative AI writing tools demands a reconsideration of Michel Foucault's notion of the "Death of the Author." Foucault (1969) introduced the idea that the author's identity does not necessarily drive the meaning of a text. This concept becomes increasingly relevant as AI technologies, capable of generating text indistinguishable from that written by humans, challenge traditional conceptions of authorship and originality. The rationale behind reevaluating the role of the author in the modern context lies in the collaborative nature of AI-assisted writing. As AI becomes an integral part of the writing process, distinguishing between human and machine contributions becomes less clear and arguably less important, prompting a need for new norms around authorship and originality (Kreps & Kimppa, 2020).

Establishing new norms in the age of AI writing involves acknowledging the collaborative effort between humans and AI in creating content. This necessitates a shift from a sole emphasis on individual creativity towards recognizing the input of both humans and AI in the creative process. The integration of AI tools like Co-Pilot (ChatGPT 4 Turbo) into mainstream writing platforms like Microsoft Word and all Microsoft 365 software exemplifies this shift, marking a new phase in the practice of writing where the role of AI is intrinsic and often transparent (Broussard, 2021).

As AI continues to evolve and integrate into academic practices, it becomes essential to develop guidelines that reflect this new collaborative authorship model. Such guidelines should address how to attribute contributions fairly, maintain the integrity of academic work, and ensure that both human creativity and AI assistance are appropriately recognized. This new approach will require ongoing dialogue among educators, technologists, and ethicists to create a framework that respects the contributions of both human and machine intelligence while upholding the core values of scholarly inquiry. Given these developments, the rapid advancement and widespread adoption of GAI in educational and academic contexts are fundamentally altering our perceptions of creativity, originality, and collaborative writing. As we adapt to this evolving landscape, it is imperative that both policy and educational frameworks within institutions evolve to effectively meet the challenges and opportunities posed by GAI technologies. The re-evaluation of creativity and originality in the era of GAI necessitates a deeper understanding of these concepts. Creativity now emerges as a joint venture between human creativity and artificial intelligence, requiring a redefined notion of originality, especially in academic contexts where distinguishing between human-generated and AI-assisted content becomes increasingly challenging.

Graduate research advisors play a crucial role in guiding students through these considerations, ensuring that GAI usage bolsters rather than undermines their creative and analytical capacities. Implementing effective practices in teaching and learning with GAI is essential. This involves utilizing AI tools to enhance traditional teaching methods, emphasizing the writing process over the final product, and promoting active engagement with AI-generated content. Educators should craft assignments that meaningfully integrate AI, encouraging students to develop their critical thinking, creativity, and problem-solving skills. Additionally, the evaluation of student work needs to shift towards assessing these skills rather than focusing merely on memorization or factual recall.

7.3 ENSURING THE INTEGRITY OF AI-GENERATED RESEARCH OUTPUTS

Historically, ensuring the accuracy of citations and information within academic research has been a significant challenge, particularly with the advent of LLMs such as GPT (Generative Pre-trained Transformers). These models, while powerful, have been prone to generating hallucinations—content that appears plausible but is factually incorrect or not supported by the provided data (Ji et al., 2023). Addressing these issues is crucial for maintaining the integrity of scholarly work. Recent advancements have seen the implementation of methods to mitigate these hallucinations, with promising improvements in citation accuracy and information reliability. For instance, models are now being developed to integrate directly with databases, enabling real-time access to verified data and ensuring that AI-generated outputs are both accurate and credible (Tian et al., 2024).

With the potential benefits of integrating new technologies in writing pedagogy, an additional consideration must be highlighted before turning to practical applications: AI Literacy (Table 7.1). With the sudden rise in the use of AI technologies in research settings, AI literacy has taken center stage in institutional initiatives (Perchik et al., 2023; Southworth et al., 2023). Understanding AI tools goes beyond mere technical know-how; it encompasses a comprehensive grasp of AI functionalities, limitations, and ethical implications, which is paramount for leveraging its potential in enriching writing pedagogy (Park et al., 2023). AI literacy empowers both researchers and graduate students to consider the ever-growing intersection of technology and education effectively, ensuring that the integration of AI into writing and research instruction enhances, rather than impedes or replaces, the learning experience. Ensuring the viability of these tools in academic research will also require widespread AI literacy, which needs to be incorporated into graduate student methodology courses. This approach will prepare future researchers to use AI responsibly and effectively, maintaining the integrity and quality of academic outputs.

Table 1. AI literacy fundamentals

Component	Description	Example
Understanding AI Concepts	Knowledge of fundamental AI operations such as machine learning, natural language processing, and neural networks.	Learning how neural networks are trained and function to process data and make predictions.
Critical Thinking and Ethical Considerations	Ability to analyze the implications of AI use, focusing on ethical issues like bias, privacy, and societal impact.	Discussing the ethical considerations of using AI in hiring processes to avoid biases.
Practical Skills	Skills necessary to interact effectively with AI tools, including using AI for problem-solving and creative applications.	Using an AI tool to analyze data trends or generate creative content for a marketing campaign.
Data Literacy	Understanding how data is collected, analyzed, and used in AI, emphasizing data's role in training AI models.	Analyzing how data biases can affect AI outcomes and exploring ways to mitigate these issues.
Safety and Security	Awareness of cybersecurity aspects related to AI, such as protecting personal data and understanding system vulnerabilities.	Implementing secure practices to protect AI systems from unauthorized access or data breaches.

A systematic approach to fostering AI literacy is recommended and can significantly benefit writing pedagogy by equipping learners with the skills needed to engage with AI tools critically and creatively. For instance, understanding the mechanisms behind AI-generated feedback and content suggestions can help students refine their writing skills more efficiently, promoting a deeper engagement with the writing process. Moreover, an informed awareness of the capabilities and limitations of various tools allows for a more productive application, mitigating risks related to incorrect information. These inaccuracies, often referred to as hallucinations, occur when an AI model generates false or misleading information not supported by its training data or real-world facts. Such mistakes typically arise from incorrect instructions or insufficient training data. By educating students and educators about these potential pitfalls, we can ensure that AI tools are used responsibly and effectively, enhancing the overall quality and integrity of academic research and writing.

Ensuring the viability of AI tools in academic research also necessitates the integration of AI literacy into graduate student methodology courses. This approach will prepare future researchers to use AI responsibly and effectively, maintaining the integrity and quality of academic outputs. By embedding AI literacy into the curriculum, institutions can foster a generation of scholars who are adept at steering through the considerations of AI-assisted research, ensuring that the integration of these technologies supports and enhances the scholarly endeavour.

Regarding the former, students need to be taught prompt engineering as part of their working process with AI tools (Table 7.2). Prompt engineering, which will be further investigated in subsequent chapters, involves carefully crafting input prompts to effectively guide AI models, particularly in NLP, to produce desired outputs or behaviors by optimizing the way questions or commands are posed. This process includes several key components, including instruction, context, input data, and output indicator. Understanding and mastering these elements is crucial for leveraging AI tools effectively. There are numerous strategies for prompt engineering, and this serves as a starting point for understanding the process. By incorporating prompt engineering into the curriculum, researchers can ensure that graduate students not only use AI tools but also understand the intricacies of guiding these technologies to produce accurate, relevant, and valuable outputs. This knowledge will empower students to harness AI's full potential while maintaining the critical thinking and analytical skills central to academic success.

Table 2. Prompt engineering components for effective AI model guidance

Component	Description	Example
Instruction	The specific task or command you want the AI model to perform.	"Summarize the key points from the provided text."
Context	Additional information or external data that helps steer the AI model towards more accurate responses.	Providing historical background or relevant current events related to the text being analyzed.
Input Data	The actual input or question posed to the AI model for which a response is sought.	"What are the implications of the recent election results on environmental policy?"
Output Indicator	A metric or indicator used to evaluate the effectiveness or accuracy of the AI model's response.	Use of accuracy scores, coherence ratings, or relevancy assessments to measure the quality of AI-generated responses.

Regarding the Output Indicator, understanding what information the AI tool has access to and what it does not is crucial for quality content generation. When a model encounters a request for information that is not present within its training data, it may resort to "hallucinating," or generating information that appears plausible but is, in fact, incorrect or fabricated. This phenomenon underscores the importance of being cognizant of the dataset on which the model was trained, including its scope and the date of its training.

Equipping the model with specific information it is being asked to query or ensuring the prompts are designed with a clear understanding of the model's knowledge boundaries can significantly mitigate the risk of hallucinations. This awareness enables more accurate and reliable outputs, enhancing the utility of the model and the trustworthiness of its responses. These considerations are increasingly expected in modern knowledge work, as the amount of data workers will be required to engage with will only expand exponentially. Thus, AI literacy is not merely an additional skill set but a crucial component of a holistic educational framework that prepares students for the ambiguities of the digital age (Denny et al., 2023). Thus, integrating AI literacy into writing pedagogy aligns with the broader educational goal of preparing graduate students for a future where AI and automation play significant roles in various professional fields. Ensuring a deep understanding of how AI tools function and their limitations, allows educators to help students cross the digital landscape effectively, ensuring that they are well-equipped to use these technologies responsibly and ethically.

Building on the considerations of prompt engineering and data limitations in AI literacy, cultivating a thorough understanding of AI requires a methodical and phased approach, particularly when integrating these technologies within educational frameworks. Initially focusing on the foundational aspects of AI—such as its basic functionalities and the principles underlying ML—allows educators and students to establish a common ground of knowledge. This foundational understanding is critical for demystifying AI and making its complex mechanisms more approachable. As proficiency grows, the pathway should lead to exploring more sophisticated AI applications relevant to writing instruction. This includes using AI for grammar checks and content suggestions and engaging with AI as a tool for enhancing creativity, research, and the synthesis of ideas. Through interactive modules that offer hands-on experience with AI tools, learners can witness firsthand how AI can serve as a collaborator in the writing process. Practical exercises that challenge students to use AI in drafting, revising, and editing can further solidify their understanding and skill set.

Incorporating critical discussions about the implications of AI in writing and beyond encourages learners to think deeply about the ethical considerations, potential biases, and societal impacts of AI technologies. Such dialogues can foster a responsible and informed approach to AI usage, ensuring that learners become proficient in manipulating these tools and understand their broader significance. This comprehensive approach to AI literacy prepares learners for the technological demands of the future and equips them with the critical thinking skills necessary to handle the ethical landscapes accompanying AI advancements.

As AI literacy becomes more crucial in the educational sphere, its role in shaping the future of writing instruction cannot be overstated. Educators' ability to deeply understand AI's principles and ethical implications places them in a stronger position to integrate these technologies in ways that enrich the learning experience and uphold high academic standards. Through a concerted effort to enhance AI literacy, researchers and students can explore the potential of these tools to act as a catalyst in research and writing, provided it is approached with a careful balance between innovation and ethical standards (Bahari & Gholami, 2023). The discussion on personalized learning through AI, particularly the strategy of 'chunking' to simplify complex writing tasks, supports a tailored educational journey for each student. This method fosters an environment where students can thrive in a digitally augmented academic world, considering the evolving landscape of writing education with confidence and creativity (Thimmanna et al., 2024).

The development of a progressive model that enhances the nuanced understanding of AI functionalities among educators and students is crucial. By embedding AI literacy across graduate student training, this section underscores the transformative potential of such tools to enrich educational practices. The future of education hinges on seamlessly integrating technology with traditional teaching excellence (Williams, 2023). Advancements in AI literacy serve as a bridge between technological innovation and effective writing instruction, thereby strengthening the educational framework and ensuring students are well-prepared for future challenges. Furthermore, this comprehensive approach necessitates a reevaluation of academic integrity and plagiarism in the age of AI. It advocates for a redefined understanding that accommodates the evolving dynamics of authorship and originality facilitated by these tools. This shift is critical to maintaining the credibility and integrity of academic outputs in a landscape increasingly influenced by AI technologies.

In addition to AI literacy, strategies to ensure the accuracy of AI-generated content is paramount, especially given the earlier challenges associated with free models like ChatGPT-3.5, which had a notable tendency to hallucinate. This tendency stemmed from the size and date of the training data, often leading to the generation of information that appeared plausible but was, in fact, incorrect or fabricated. As AI technology evolves, more sophisticated models are being developed by leading organizations such as Google, Meta, Anthropic, and OpenAI, promising enhanced accuracy and reliability. For instance, the latest models have significantly larger architectures and more extensive datasets. GPT-4, with approximately 1 trillion parameters, is a substantial upgrade from GPT-3.5's 175 billion parameters, resulting in better contextual understanding and response coherence. These advancements reduce the incidence of hallucinations and improve the overall quality of AI-generated content. However, despite these improvements, additional steps must be taken by researchers to ensure the viability and accuracy of AI outputs.

Ensuring the accuracy of AI-generated content is crucial for maintaining the integrity of academic research. Implementing rigorous verification processes and strategies can significantly enhance the reliability of AI outputs (Table 3). One essential strategy is the verification of sources. Researchers should cross-verify the information provided by AI with trusted and credible sources. This validation step is critical in confirming the accuracy of the generated content. For instance, if an AI model produces a scientific fact or historical date, researchers should corroborate this information with academic journals, official publications, or reliable databases. This practice helps to ensure the credibility of the AI-generated data and mitigates the risk of disseminating incorrect information. Cross-referencing with authoritative sources is a foundational practice that upholds the standards of scholarly work. In addition, if using an embedded database in an LLM, such as Scholar GPT or Consensus, where links to the citations are provided, one should still take that citation and double check accuracy in another field-specific database (e.g., World Cat, JSTOR, Google Scholar, EBSCO, etc.). Occasionally, a citation will be accurate but include outdated information, such as from a preprint.

Table 3. Strategies to ensure accuracy in AI-generated research outputs

Strategy	Description
Verification of Sources	Researchers should cross-verify the information provided by AI with trusted and credible sources. This step is crucial in validating the accuracy of the generated content. For instance, if an AI model generates a scientific fact or a historical date, it should be cross-checked with academic journals, official publications, or reliable databases to ensure correctness.
Contextual Awareness	Understanding the context in which the AI was trained helps in assessing the reliability of its outputs. Knowledge of the scope and limitations of the training data, including its recency and comprehensiveness, allows researchers to judge whether the AI model can provide accurate information on a given topic.
Prompt Engineering	Effective prompt engineering is essential for eliciting accurate and relevant responses from AI models. By carefully crafting prompts that include clear instructions, sufficient context, and specific queries, researchers can guide the AI to produce more precise and reliable outputs.
Iterative Feedback and Refinement	Using iterative feedback loops, researchers can continuously refine the AI-generated content. By providing corrective feedback and refining the prompts based on initial outputs, the quality and accuracy of subsequent responses can be improved.
Use of Specialized Databases	Integrating specialized databases and domain-specific resources into the AI's training data can enhance its accuracy for particular fields. For instance, incorporating up-to-date medical journals for health-related queries or using legal databases for legal research can significantly reduce errors and improve reliability.

continued on following page

Table 3. Continued

Strategy	Description
Providing Actual Source Material	Supplying the AI with precise and authenticated data, either by copying and pasting text from verified sources or attaching a PDF, ensures the model has direct access to accurate information. This reduces the risk of inaccuracies and hallucinations, enabling the model to reference specific details and quotations directly from the source material.
Ethical Considerations and Transparency	Maintaining transparency about the AI's limitations and the nature of its training data is vital. Researchers should disclose any potential biases or gaps in the data and emphasize the importance of human oversight in the verification process.

Note that citations generated from free models like ChatGPT-3.5 should never be trusted; only paid models with access to live databases should be used for initial generation of citations. One reason the human element and oversight in the "human-in-the-loop" model will still be necessary is due to how ML algorithms such as ChatGPT-3.5 operate. In generating a response to a prompt, the algorithm pulls from the entire dataset it has been trained on and can produce misleading or false citations and information. For instance, requesting a summary of the book *Algorithmic Culture* (2018) by Brouwer with a summary and quotations cited in APA 7th edition style might yield fabricated quotations and citations. Consider the following response generated by ChatGPT-3:

The argument put forth by Hristova, Hong, and Slack in their article "Algorithmic Culture" (2021) is that algorithms have become a defining feature of contemporary culture and have significant implications for society. The authors state that algorithms "shape our understanding of the world, shape our decision-making processes, and shape our social and cultural experiences" (Hristova, Hong, & Slack, 2021, p. 1).

To support this argument, the authors provide several examples of how algorithms are used in various aspects of society, such as in news media, entertainment, and advertising. They also examine the ways in which algorithms can perpetuate existing inequalities and contribute to the spread of false information.

In their conclusion, Hristova, Hong, and Slack assert that it is important to critically examine the role of algorithms in our culture and to consider their potential impacts on society. They call for "a more nuanced understanding of the ways in which algorithms shape our cultural and social experiences" (Hristova, Hong, & Slack, 2021, p. 7).

Here is an example citation of this article in APA style:

Hristova, L., Hong, S., & Slack, R. (2021). Algorithmic culture. Cultural Studies, 35(3), 1-9.

Quotations:

- "Algorithms shape our understanding of the world, shape our decision-making processes, and shape our social and cultural experiences" (Hristova, Hong, & Slack, 2021, p. 1).
- "It is important to critically examine the role of algorithms in our culture and to consider their potential impacts on society" (Hristova, Hong, & Slack, 2021, p. 7).

Upon closer inspection, it becomes evident that the citation is from a real journal published by Routledge (*Cultural Studies*) but searching for the volume and number reveals that it does not actually exist. Furthermore, if the same prompt is run again, indicating that it is a book and not an article, ChatGPT-3.5 might falsely claim that Routledge published the work. Given that the dataset used was the entirety of freely accessible information on the Internet up until 2021, information kept behind paywalls may trigger the algorithm to take the title and other information from one source and combine it with another to arrive at what it believes is the intended request. The recursive machine learning algorithm performs sentiment analysis to generate responses, hence the impossibility of accurate citations without human verification. This exemplifies the need for researchers to cross-verify AI-generated information with trusted sources to maintain the integrity and accuracy of academic outputs (Nabee et al., 2020; Dehouche, 2021).

This is why another vital aspect is contextual awareness. Understanding the context in which the AI was trained allows researchers to assess the reliability of its outputs. Knowledge of the scope and limitations of the training data, including its recency and comprehensiveness, is essential. For example, an AI model trained primarily on pre-2021 data (like ChatGPT-3.5) might not accurately reflect recent developments in fast-evolving fields such as technology or medicine. Being aware of these limitations ensures researchers can make informed judgments about the applicability of the responses to their specific inquiries, ensuring that the information is relevant and up-to-date.

Prompt engineering is another critical strategy for achieving accurate and relevant AI outputs. Crafting effective prompts involves providing clear instructions, sufficient context, and specific queries to guide the AI. For instance, a well-designed prompt for a model might include detailed background information on a research topic and a precise question that the model needs to address. This approach helps to minimize ambiguity and directs the AI to produce more accurate and useful responses. Prompt engineering is a skill that requires practice and refinement but can greatly enhance the quality of AI-generated content.

It is important to note here that there are different prompting strategies that will be more effective for different types of outputs. There are various strategies within prompt engineering, each with its own applications and advantages. Two primary strategies are zero-shot prompting and few-shot prompting. Zero-Shot Prompting refers to a scenario where the AI model is asked to perform a task without any prior examples provided within the prompt. This approach relies on the model's pre-trained knowledge to generate a response based on the information it has been trained on. The strength of zero-shot prompting lies in its simplicity and the model's ability to handle a wide range of queries with minimal setup. However, the responses can sometimes be less accurate or detailed compared to prompts that provide examples.

For instance, a zero-shot prompt might look like this as a model can be prompted to

"Explain the significance of the Treaty of Versailles in world history." The output for the prompt is:

The Treaty of Versailles, signed on June 28, 1919, was a pivotal peace treaty that officially ended World War I between the Allied Powers and Germany. Its significance in world history is multifaceted, encompassing political, economic, and social dimensions.

Political Significance: The treaty marked a decisive end to one of the deadliest conflicts in human history, formally concluding hostilities between the Allied Powers and Germany. It aimed to prevent future conflicts by imposing strict punitive measures on Germany, including territorial losses, military restrictions, and disarmament. The treaty also led to the establishment of the League of Nations, an international organization designed to maintain peace and prevent future wars through collective security and diplomacy.

Economic Impact: The Treaty of Versailles imposed severe reparations on Germany, holding it responsible for the war and demanding financial compensation to the Allied nations. These reparations, combined with the economic devastation caused by the war, contributed to significant economic hardship and hyperinflation in Germany during the 1920s. The economic strain fueled political instability and resentment within Germany, laying the groundwork for the rise of Adolf Hitler and the Nazi Party.

Territorial Changes: The treaty resulted in significant territorial reconfigurations in Europe. Germany lost substantial territories, including Alsace-Lorraine to France, Eupen-Malmedy to Belgium, Northern Schleswig to Denmark, and various territories to the newly created states of Poland and Czechoslovakia. The treaty also mandated the demilitarization of the Rhineland and stripped Germany of its overseas colonies, redistributing them among the Allied Powers.

Social Consequences: The harsh terms of the Treaty of Versailles fostered a sense of humiliation and betrayal among the German population, often referred to as the "Diktat" or dictated peace. This nationalistic resentment was exploited by extremist political movements, contributing to the eventual rise of fascism in Europe and setting the stage for World War II. The treaty's failure to achieve lasting peace highlighted the limitations of punitive peace settlements and underscored the need for more equitable and sustainable approaches to international diplomacy.

In summary, the Treaty of Versailles was a landmark event that shaped the geopolitical landscape of the 20th century. Its political, economic, and social ramifications had far-reaching consequences, influencing the course of history and setting the stage for future global conflicts.

In this example, the model drew upon its training data to generate an informative response about the Treaty of Versailles, discussing its impact on international relations, the political climate following World War I, and its long-term consequences. But because we did not offer context or specific output instructions, the response was general and vague.

Few-Shot Prompting, on the other hand, provides the model with several examples within the prompt to guide its response. This technique is particularly useful when seeking more detailed or context-specific answers. By showing the model a few instances of the desired output format, it can better understand the context and produce more accurate responses. An example of few-shot prompting might be:

Example 1

Question: What is photosynthesis?

Answer: Photosynthesis is the process by which green plants and some other organisms use sunlight to synthesize foods from carbon dioxide and water. It involves the green pigment chlorophyll and generates oxygen as a byproduct.

Example 2

Question: What is the theory of relativity?

Answer: The theory of relativity, developed by Albert Einstein, is a crucial part of modern physics. It consists of two theories: special relativity and general relativity. The theory changed our understanding of space, time, and gravity.

Example 3

Question: Who was Marie Curie?

Answer: Marie Curie was a physicist and chemist who became famous for her pioneering research on radioactivity. She was the first woman to win a Nobel Prize and the only person to win Nobel Prizes in two different scientific fields.

New Question: What is quantum mechanics?

AI Response: "Quantum mechanics is a fundamental theory in physics that describes the physical properties of nature at the scale of atoms and subatomic particles. It explains phenomena that classical physics cannot, such as the behavior of electrons in atoms and the dual particle-wave nature of light and matter. Key principles include superposition, entanglement, and quantization."

In this prompt, the model is guided by the format and content of the previous examples to provide a comprehensive answer about quantum mechanics. This method enhances the quality of the response by giving the model a clearer understanding of the expected structure and detail.

Other strategies within prompt engineering include chain-of-thought prompting, where the model is guided through a series of logical steps to arrive at a conclusion, and instruction-based prompting, which involves providing detailed instructions within the prompt to achieve a specific output. Chain-of-thought prompting is a technique where the prompt includes a detailed explanation or reasoning process to help the AI model generate more thoughtful and accurate responses. This approach guides the AI through the logical steps required to arrive at a conclusion, enhancing the depth and coherence of the output. An example is as follows:

Prompt to the Model

Question: "Explain the impact of the Industrial Revolution on urbanization."

Chain-of-Thought

1. **Introduction:** The Industrial Revolution, which began in the late 18th century, was a period of significant economic, technological, and social change. It had a profound impact on many aspects of society, including urbanization.
2. **Economic Changes:** The introduction of new machinery and production techniques led to the growth of factories and industrial centers. This shift from agrarian economies to industrial economies created new job opportunities in urban areas.
3. **Migration:** As a result, there was a mass migration of people from rural areas to cities in search of employment. This rural-to-urban migration was a key factor in the rapid expansion of cities during the Industrial Revolution.
4. **Urban Growth:** Cities grew both in population and in physical size. Infrastructure development, such as roads, railways, and housing, struggled to keep pace with the influx of new residents. This rapid growth often led to overcrowded living conditions and inadequate public services.

5. **Social Impact:** The concentration of workers in urban areas facilitated the spread of new ideas and social movements. However, it also led to significant social challenges, including poor working conditions, health issues, and the rise of a distinct urban working class.
6. **Conclusion:** The Industrial Revolution fundamentally transformed urban areas, leading to significant economic opportunities and challenges. The legacy of this period can still be seen in the structure and dynamics of modern cities.

Answer: "The Industrial Revolution, which began in the late 18th century, significantly impacted urbanization. This period was marked by economic changes, including the introduction of new machinery and production techniques, leading to the growth of factories and industrial centers. The shift from agrarian to industrial economies created new job opportunities in urban areas, prompting mass migration from rural areas to cities in search of employment. Consequently, cities experienced rapid growth in population and physical size, often resulting in overcrowded living conditions and inadequate public services. This urban growth also facilitated the spread of new ideas and social movements but brought about significant social challenges, such as poor working conditions and health issues. Overall, the Industrial Revolution fundamentally transformed urban areas, creating both economic opportunities and social challenges that continue to influence modern cities."

Instruction-based prompting involves providing clear and specific instructions within the prompt to guide the AI model towards generating the desired output. This method ensures that the AI understands the task requirements and the expected format of the response, leading to more accurate and relevant answers. An example of this type of prompting is as follows:

Prompt to the Model

Instructions: "Summarize the key causes of World War I in three bullet points. Include major alliances, significant events, and underlying tensions that contributed to the outbreak of the war."

Answer:

- **Major Alliances:** The formation of two major alliances, the Triple Entente (comprising France, Russia, and the United Kingdom) and the Triple Alliance (comprising Germany, Austria-Hungary, and Italy), created a polarized and hostile international environment.
- **Significant Events:** The assassination of Archduke Franz Ferdinand of Austria-Hungary in June 1914 by a Serbian nationalist acted as a catalyst,

triggering a series of diplomatic conflicts and mobilizations that quickly escalated into a full-scale war.

- **Underlying Tensions:** Long-standing imperialistic and nationalistic tensions, including competition for colonial territories, military arms races, and ethnic rivalries, created an environment ripe for conflict, where any significant event could ignite a larger war.

Further Example for Clarity

Instructions: "Describe the process of photosynthesis in two sentences. Make sure to mention the main reactants and products involved."

Answer: "Photosynthesis is the process by which green plants and some other organisms use sunlight to convert carbon dioxide and water into glucose and oxygen. This process involves the green pigment chlorophyll, which captures light energy to drive the chemical reactions."

Another Example

Instructions: "Explain the concept of blockchain technology in one paragraph. Highlight its main components and its significance in ensuring security and transparency in transactions."

Answer: "Blockchain technology is a decentralized digital ledger system that records transactions across multiple computers in a way that ensures security and transparency. Each transaction is stored in a 'block' and linked to previous transactions, forming a 'chain' of data. The main components of blockchain include a distributed network, a shared ledger, cryptographic security, and consensus mechanisms to validate transactions. This technology is significant because it eliminates the need for a central authority, reduces the risk of fraud, and ensures that all participants have a transparent and immutable record of all transactions."

Each of these strategies serves to improve the accuracy and relevance of the output by an LLM, tailored to the complexity and specificity of the task at hand. By understanding and implementing these prompt engineering techniques, researchers and educators can better harness the capabilities of AI tools, ensuring more reliable and informative interactions.

On the other hand, the process of iterative feedback and refinement also plays a significant role in improving AI outputs. By employing iterative feedback loops, researchers can continuously refine the AI-generated content. This involves providing corrective feedback on initial outputs and adjusting prompts accordingly. For example, if an initial response from the AI is inaccurate or incomplete, researchers can modify the prompt to be more specific or provide additional context, thereby guiding the AI to generate better responses in subsequent iterations. This iterative process enhances the overall accuracy and reliability of the outputs. An example is as follows:

Initial Prompt: "Explain the significance of the Treaty of Versailles in world history."

Initial AI Response: "The Treaty of Versailles, signed in 1919, ended World War I and imposed heavy reparations on Germany. It also led to the creation of the League of Nations and redrew the map of Europe, leading to various territorial changes."

Feedback and Refinement:*Feedback 1:* The initial response is too brief and lacks detail about the broader impacts of the Treaty of Versailles. It should include more information on the economic, political, and social consequences.

Refined Prompt: "Explain the significance of the Treaty of Versailles in world history, focusing on its economic, political, and social impacts, and the long-term consequences it had on Germany and Europe."

Refined AI Response: "The Treaty of Versailles, signed in 1919, ended World War I and imposed heavy reparations on Germany, crippling its economy. Politically, it led to the creation of the League of Nations, aimed at maintaining peace, but ultimately failed to prevent future conflicts. Socially, the harsh terms of the treaty fueled resentment and nationalist sentiments in Germany, contributing to the rise of Adolf Hitler and the onset of World War II. The redrawing of borders also caused ethnic tensions and instability in various regions of Europe."

Feedback and Further Refinement:*Feedback 2:* The response is better but still needs to address the specific territorial changes and their implications in more detail. It should also mention the immediate reactions from various countries to the treaty.

Further Refined Prompt: "Explain the significance of the Treaty of Versailles in world history, detailing the economic impacts on Germany, the political changes including the creation of the League of Nations, the specific territorial changes, and the immediate reactions from different countries."

Further Refined AI Response: "The Treaty of Versailles, signed in 1919, ended World War I and imposed heavy reparations on Germany, severely damaging its economy and leading to hyperinflation and unemployment. Politically, it led to the establishment of the League of Nations, which aimed to prevent future conflicts but was weakened by the absence of key powers like the United States. The treaty redrew the map of Europe, stripping Germany of its colonies, and transferring territories like Alsace-Lorraine to France, and creating new states such as Poland and Czechoslovakia. The harsh terms and perceived injustices of the treaty led to widespread resentment in Germany and contributed to the rise of extremist movements, including the Nazi Party. Other countries had mixed reactions; France sought to enforce the treaty strictly, while the UK and the US were more lenient, leading to tensions among the Allies."

Final Feedback:*Feedback 3:* The refined response is comprehensive and detailed. It adequately covers the economic, political, and social impacts, as well as the specific territorial changes and the immediate reactions from various countries.

Perhaps one of the best strategies to ensure accuracy is the use of specialized databases that can further enhance the accuracy of AI models, particularly in specialized fields. Integrating domain-specific resources into the AI's training data can significantly improve its performance. For example, incorporating up-to-date medical journals for health-related queries or using legal databases for legal research can reduce errors and improve reliability. These databases are increasingly integrated directly into the LLM interface so allow for live searching and refinement. This approach ensures that the AI has access to the most relevant and authoritative information, enhancing its ability to generate accurate and trustworthy content.

Another effective strategy to ensure the accuracy of AI-generated content is to provide the actual source material directly to the language model. This can be accomplished either by copying and pasting text from verified sources, such as peer-reviewed articles or research monographs, into the prompt, or by attaching a PDF so that the model has direct access to the information. By supplying the AI with precise and authenticated data, researchers can significantly reduce the risk of inaccuracies and hallucinations. This approach enables the model to reference specific details and quotations directly from the source material, ensuring that the generated content maintains a high level of accuracy and reliability. Additionally, this method can enhance the AI's ability to produce well-informed and contextually relevant responses, thereby improving the overall quality of the research output.

Implementing these strategies—verification of sources, contextual awareness, prompt engineering, iterative feedback, use of specialized databases, and ethical considerations—can significantly enhance the accuracy and reliability of AI-generated content. As AI continues to evolve and integrate into various aspects of academic research, adopting these practices will be essential in leveraging the full potential of these advanced tools while maintaining the highest standards of scholarly integrity.

As we conclude this chapter, it is evident that AI literacy is not just an additional skill but a fundamental component of modern education. By fostering a deep understanding of AI among students and educators, we can harness the full potential of these technologies while upholding the highest standards of academic excellence and integrity. Equally important is the implementation of strategies to ensure the accuracy of information generated by AI, such as verifying sources, employing effective prompt engineering, and providing direct access to authenticated materials. Moving forward, the next chapter will look at practical strategies for integrating AI into the graduate curriculum, starting from the early stages of methodology and scholastic writing requirements. It will provide educators with introductory methods to incorporate these tools effectively, thereby enhancing both the teaching and learning experiences. This exploration will include discussions on how AI can assist with brainstorming, outlining, and initial drafts, streamlining the writing process and fostering a more dynamic and interactive learning environment. Through these practical applications, educators and students alike can experience firsthand the benefits of AI-enhanced education, paving the way for a future where technology and traditional pedagogy coexist harmoniously.

REFERENCES

Aljurf, S., Kemp, L. J., & Williams, P. (2020). Exploring academic dishonesty in the Middle East: A qualitative analysis of students' perceptions. *Studies in Higher Education*, 45(7), 1461–1473. DOI: 10.1080/03075079.2018.1564262

American Psychological Association. (2020). *Publication manual of the American Psychological Association* (7th ed.). American Psychological Association.

Amsberry, D., & Snavely, L. (2011). *Engaging international students in academic library initiatives for their peers. International students and academic libraries: initiatives for success*. Association of College and Research Libraries.

Ansorge, L., Ansorgeová, K., & Sixsmith, M. (2021). Plagiarism through paraphrasing tools—The story of one plagiarized text. *Publications / MDPI*, 9(4), 48. DOI: 10.3390/publications9040048

Arapoff, N. (1967). Writing: A thinking process. *TESOL Quarterly*, 1(2), 33–39. DOI: 10.2307/3585751

Bahari, A., & Gholami, L. (2023). Challenges and affordances of reading and writing development in technology-assisted language learning. *Interactive Learning Environments*, 31(10), 7226–7250. DOI: 10.1080/10494820.2022.2065308

Bouville, M. (2008). Plagiarism: Words and ideas. *Science and Engineering Ethics*, 14(3), 311–322. DOI: 10.1007/s11948-008-9057-6

Broussard, M. (2021). *Artificial unintelligence: How computers misunderstand the world*. MIT Press.

Brouwer, W. (2018). *Algorithmic culture*. Palgrave Macmillan.

Canagarajah, A. S. (2002). *A geopolitics of academic writing*. University of Pittsburgh Press. DOI: 10.2307/j.ctt5hjn6c

Chaka, C. (2023). Detecting AI content in responses generated by ChatGPT, YouChat, and Chatsonic: The case of five AI content detection tools. *Journal of Applied Learning and Teaching*, 6(2).

Chechitelli, A. (2023). AI writing detection update from Turnitin's Chief Product Officer. *Turnitin*. May 23, 2023: https://www.turnitin.com/blog/ai-writing-detection-update-from-turnitins-chief-product-officer

Dehouche, N. (2021). Plagiarism in the age of massive Generative Pre-trained Transformers (GPT-3). *Ethics in Science and Environmental Politics*, 21, 17–23. DOI: 10.3354/esep00195

Denny, P., Leinonen, J., Prather, J., Luxton-Reilly, A., Amarouche, T., Becker, B. A., & Reeves, B. N. (2023). Prompt Problems: A new programming exercise for the generative AI era. *arXiv preprint arXiv:2311.05943.*

Fenton, A. L., & Gralla, C. (2020). Student plagiarism in higher education: A typology and remedial framework for a globalized era. *Academic Misconduct and Plagiarism,* 109.

Foucault, M. (1969). *What is an Author?* Gilyard, K. (2016). Composition and Cornel West: Notes toward a deep multiculturality. *College Composition and Communication*, 57(3), 397–416.

Gipp, B., Meuschke, N., & Gernandt, A. (2020). Citations and the evolution of scientific knowledge. *The Journal of Documentation*, 76(4), 923–944.

Grudecki, M. (2021). The Genesis of the Prohibition of Corporal Punishment against Minors and the Consequences of Its Application. *Studia Iuridica Lublinensia*, 30(4), 241–258. DOI: 10.17951/sil.2021.30.4.241-258

Guleria, A., Krishan, K., Sharma, V., & Kanchan, T. (2023). ChatGPT: Ethical concerns and challenges in academics and research. *Journal of Infection in Developing Countries*, 17(09), 1292–1299. DOI: 10.3855/jidc.18738

Gunnarsson, J., Kulcsza, W. J., & Pettersson, A. (2014). Teaching international students how to avoid plagiarism: Librarians and faculty in collaboration. *Journal of Academic Librarianship*, 40(3-4), 413–417. DOI: 10.1016/j.acalib.2014.04.006

Hadi, M. U., Qureshi, R., Shah, A., Irfan, M., Zafar, A., Shaikh, M. B., & Mirjalili, S. (2023). A survey on large language models: Applications, challenges, limitations, and practical usage. *Authorea Preprints.* DOI: 10.36227/techrxiv.23589741.v1

Ho, C., Azmi Murad, M. A., Doraisamy, S., & Abdul Kadir, R. (2014). Extracting lexical and phrasal paraphrases: A review of the literature. *Artificial Intelligence Review*, 42(4), 851–894. DOI: 10.1007/s10462-012-9357-8

Horner, B., Lu, M., Royster, J. J., & Trimbur, J. (2011). Language difference in writing: Toward a translingual approach. *College English*, 73(3), 303–321. DOI: 10.58680/ce201113403

Hutson, J., & Plate, D. (2023). *Human-AI Collaboration for Smart Education: Reframing Applied Learning to Support Metacognition*. IntechOpen.

Ison, D. C. (2018). An empirical analysis of differences in plagiarism among world cultures. *Journal of Higher Education Policy and Management*, 40(4), 291–304. DOI: 10.1080/1360080X.2018.1479949

Jambeck, K. K., & Winder, B. D. (1990). Vygotsky, Werner, and English Composition: Paradigms for Thinking and Writing. *Writing on the Edge*, 1(2), 6–79.

Ji, Z., Lee, N., Frieske, R., Yu, T., Su, D., Xu, Y., Ishii, E., Bang, Y. J., Madotto, A., & Fung, P. (2023). Survey of hallucination in natural language generation. *ACM Computing Surveys*, 55(12), 1–38. DOI: 10.1145/3571730

Jonsson, M., & Tholander, J. (2022, June). Cracking the code: Co-coding with AI in creative programming education. In *Proceedings of the 14th Conference on Creativity and Cognition* (pp. 5-14). DOI: 10.1145/3527927.3532801

Kaebnick, G. E., Magnus, D. C., Kao, A., Hosseini, M., Resnik, D., Dubljević, V., Rentmeester, C., Gordijn, B., & Cherry, M. J. (2023). Editors' statement on the responsible use of generative AI technologies in scholarly journal publishing. *Medicine, Health Care, and Philosophy*, 26(4), 499–503. DOI: 10.1007/s11019-023-10176-6

Khaliq, A., Aziz, S., Akram, M., & Mahmood, W. (2023). The influence of constructivist strategies in writing the foreign language on the learners achievements at higher secondary level. *Voyage Journal of Educational Studies*, 3(2), 281–289. DOI: 10.58622/vjes.v3i2.63

Kim, B., Park, J., & Suh, J. (2020). Transparency and accountability in AI decision support: Explaining and visualizing convolutional neural networks for text information. *Decision Support Systems*, 134, 113302. DOI: 10.1016/j.dss.2020.113302

Kleebayoon, A., & Wiwanitkit, V. (2023). ChatGPT and Artificial Intelligence. *Journal of Perianesthesia Nursing*, 38(6), 840. DOI: 10.1016/j.jopan.2023.07.005

Koraishi, O. (2023). Teaching English in the age of AI: Embracing ChatGPT to optimize EFL materials and assessment. *Language Education and Technology, 3*(1).

Kreps, D., & Kimppa, K. (2020). *Theorizing about the impact of surveillance technologies.*

Kutieleh, S., & Adiningrum, T. S. (2011). How different are we? Understanding and managing plagiarism between East and West. *Journal of Academic Language and Learning*, 5(2), A88–A98.

Landa-Blanco, M., Flores, M. A., & Mercado, M. (2023). *Human vs. AI authorship: Does it matter in evaluating creative writing? A pilot study using ChatGPT.*

Larsson, S., & Heintz, F. (2020). Transparency in artificial intelligence. *Internet Policy Review*, 9(2). Advance online publication. DOI: 10.14763/2020.2.1469

Leask, B. (2006). Plagiarism, cultural diversity and metaphor—Implications for academic staff development. *Assessment & Evaluation in Higher Education*, 31(2), 183–199. DOI: 10.1080/02602930500262486

Makarova, M. (2019). Factors of academic misconduct in a cross-cultural perspective and the role of integrity systems. *Journal of Academic Ethics*, 17(1), 51–71. DOI: 10.1007/s10805-019-9323-z

Mauk, C. E. (2003). *Undershoot in two modalities: Evidence from fast speech and fast signing*. The University of Texas at Austin.

McGowan, A., Gui, Y., Dobbs, M., Shuster, S., Cotter, M., Selloni, A., Goodman, M., Srivastava, A., Cecchi, G. A., & Corcoran, C. M. (2023). ChatGPT and Bard exhibit spontaneous citation fabrication during psychiatry literature search. *Psychiatry Research*, 326, 115334. DOI: 10.1016/j.psychres.2023.115334

Nabee, S. G., Mageto, J., & Pisa, N. (2020). Investigating predictors of academic plagiarism among university students. *International Journal of Learning. Teaching and Educational Research*, 19(12), 264–280.

Nerdynav. (2024). *43+ Important Generative AI Statistics (April 2024).* April 2, 2024. Retrieved March 30, 2024: https://nerdynav.com/generative-ai-statistics/

Oleksy, E. (2023). That thing ain't human: The artificiality of "human authorship" and the intelligence in expanding copyright authorship to fully-autonomous AI. *Cleveland State Law Review*, 72(1), 263.

Park, J., Teo, T. W., Teo, A., Chang, J., Huang, J. S., & Koo, S. (2023). Integrating artificial intelligence into science lessons: Teachers' experiences and views. *International Journal of STEM Education*, 10(1), 61. DOI: 10.1186/s40594-023-00454-3

Park, S. H. (2023). Use of generative artificial intelligence, including large language models such as ChatGPT, in scientific publications: Policies of KJR and prominent authorities. *Korean Journal of Radiology*, 24(8), 715. DOI: 10.3348/kjr.2023.0643

Perchik, J. D., Smith, A. D., Elkassem, A. A., Park, J. M., Rothenberg, S. A., Tanwar, M., Yi, P. H., Sturdivant, A., Tridandapani, S., & Sotoudeh, H. (2023). Artificial intelligence literacy: Developing a multi-institutional infrastructure for AI education. *Academic Radiology*, 30(7), 1472–1480. DOI: 10.1016/j.acra.2022.10.002

Pradhan, T. K., & Kumar, A. (2023). Plagiarism in the Research Reports of Indian Doctoral Students: Causes and a Remedial Action Plan. *Center for Educational Policy Studies Journal*, 13(3), 185–212. DOI: 10.26529/cepsj.1494

Purdy, J. P. (2010). The changing space of research: Web 2.0 and the integration of research and writing environments. *Computers and Composition*, 27(1), 48–58. DOI: 10.1016/j.compcom.2009.12.001

Putra, I. E., Jazilah, N. I., Adishesa, M. S., Al Uyun, D., & Wiratraman, H. P. (2023). Denying the accusation of plagiarism: Power relations at play in dictating plagiarism as academic misconduct. *Higher Education*, 85(5), 979–997. DOI: 10.1007/s10734-022-00875-z

Rae, I. (2024, May). The effects of perceived AI use on content perceptions. In *Proceedings of the CHI Conference on Human Factors in Computing Systems* (pp. 1-14). DOI: 10.1145/3613904.3642076

Rahmat, N. H. (2020). Thinking about thinking in writing. *European Journal of Literature, Language and Linguistics Studies, 3*(4).

Rashidi, H. H., Fennell, B. D., Albahra, S., Hu, B., & Gorbett, T. (2023). The ChatGPT conundrum: Human-generated scientific manuscripts misidentified as AI creations by AI text detection tool. *Journal of Pathology Informatics*, 14, 100342. DOI: 10.1016/j.jpi.2023.100342

Ritchhart, R., Church, M., & Morrison, K. (2011). *Making thinking visible: How to promote engagement, understanding, and independence for all learners*. John Wiley & Sons.

Roe, J., Renandya, W. A., & Jacobs, G. M. (2023). A review of AI-powered writing tools and their implications for academic integrity in the language classroom. *Journal of English and Applied Linguistics*, 2(1), 3. DOI: 10.59588/2961-3094.1035

Russell, D. R. (2002). *Writing in the academic disciplines: A curricular history.* SIU Press.

Simmons, M. (2004). The ethics of citation: Teaching and learning scholarly values in the classroom. *College Teaching*, 52(3), 95–99.

Sinaga, P., & Feranie, S. (2017). Enhancing Critical Thinking Skills and Writing Skills through the Variation in Non-Traditional Writing Task. *International Journal of Instruction*, 10(2), 69–84. DOI: 10.12973/iji.2017.1025a

Southworth, J., Migliaccio, K., Glover, J., Reed, D., McCarty, C., Brendemuhl, J., & Thomas, A. (2023). Developing a model for AI Across the curriculum: Transforming the higher education landscape via innovation in AI literacy. *Computers and Education: Artificial Intelligence*, 4, 100127. DOI: 10.1016/j.caeai.2023.100127

Spear, K. I. (1983). Thinking and writing: A sequential curriculum for composition. *Journal of Advanced Composition*, 47–63.

Stoesz, B. M., & Eaton, S. E. (2022). Academic integrity policies of publicly funded universities in western Canada. *Educational Policy*, 36(6), 1529–1548. DOI: 10.1177/0895904820983032

Taylor, J. S. (2024). Reassessing academic plagiarism. *Journal of Academic Ethics*, 22(2), 211–230. DOI: 10.1007/s10805-023-09478-4

Thimmanna, A. V. N. S., Naik, M. S., Radhakrishnan, S., & Sharma, A. (2024). Personalized Learning Paths: Adapting Education with AI-Driven Curriculum. *European Economic Letters*, 14(1), 31–40.

Tian, S., Jin, Q., Yeganova, L., Lai, P. T., Zhu, Q., Chen, X., Yang, Y., Chen, Q., Kim, W., Comeau, D. C., Islamaj, R., Kapoor, A., Gao, X., & Lu, Z. (2024). Opportunities and challenges for ChatGPT and large language models in biomedicine and health. *Briefings in Bioinformatics*, 25(1), bbad493. DOI: 10.1093/bib/bbad493

Valentine, K. (2006). Plagiarism as literacy practice: Recognizing and rethinking ethical binaries. *College Composition and Communication*, 58(1), 89–109. DOI: 10.58680/ccc20065884

Velliaris, D. M., & Breen, P. (2016). An institutional three-stage framework: Elevating academic writing and integrity standards of international pathway students. *Journal of International Students*, 6(2), 565–587. DOI: 10.32674/jis.v6i2.371

Wahle, J. P., Ruas, T., Kirstein, F., & Gipp, B. (2022). How large language models are transforming machine-paraphrased plagiarism. *arXiv preprint arXiv:2210.03568.*

Walters, W. H. (2023). The effectiveness of software designed to detect AI-generated writing: A comparison of 16 AI text detectors. *Open Information Science*, 7(1), 20220158. DOI: 10.1515/opis-2022-0158

Williams, P. (2023). AI, Analytics and a New Assessment Model for Universities. *Education Sciences*, 13(10), 1040. DOI: 10.3390/educsci13101040

Yeo, M. A. (2023). Academic integrity in the age of Artificial Intelligence (AI) authoring apps. *TESOL Journal*, 14(3), e716. DOI: 10.1002/tesj.716

Yu, H. (2023). Reflection on whether Chat GPT should be banned by academia from the perspective of education and teaching. *Frontiers in Psychology*, 14, 1181712. DOI: 10.3389/fpsyg.2023.1181712

Zaheer, M., Guruganesh, G., Dubey, K. A., Ainslie, J., Alberti, C., Ontanon, S., & Ahmed, A. (2020). Big bird: Transformers for longer sequences. *Advances in Neural Information Processing Systems*, 33, 17283–17297.

Chapter 8
Conclusion and Future Directions

ABSTRACT

This chapter looks ahead at the evolving landscape of academic research, emphasizing emerging trends and the potential of future technologies in AI, GAI, and ML that are poised to redefine scholarly inquiry. It considers evolving advancements that are expected to further enhance data analysis, predictive modeling, and theoretical simulations in research. The discussion explores how these innovations can lead to more profound discoveries and a faster pace of research across all disciplines. Additionally, the chapter addresses the crucial aspect of inclusivity in the integration of AI within academia. It highlights the importance of designing AI systems and algorithms that are accessible to diverse academic communities worldwide, ensuring that the benefits of AI-enhanced research are broadly distributed. By promoting strategies to foster an inclusive academic environment, the chapter underscores the role of AI in building a more equitable and collaborative future in research.

8.1 EMERGING TRENDS AND FUTURE TECHNOLOGIES IN AI FOR RESEARCH

The rapid pace of technological advancement in AI over the past few years has been nothing short of transformative. Innovations that seemed like science fiction a decade ago are now integral tools in the research toolkit, changing how data is analyzed, predictions are made, and theories are tested. The capabilities that researchers have at their disposal today, from deep learning models that can analyze vast datasets in seconds to generative algorithms that can simulate complex scenarios, have opened up new vistas of scholarly inquiry that were previously unimaginable. Keeping abreast of these developments is not merely advantageous but essential for the academic community. Ensuring that scholarship advances in

DOI: 10.4018/979-8-3693-6905-0.ch008

tandem with technological progress is crucial not only for the continued evolution of knowledge but also for the broader social good that such advancements foster. By staying informed and adaptable, researchers can harness the full potential of emerging AI technologies, driving innovation and promoting a more inclusive and equitable academic environment.

The future of AI-driven multimodal platforms such as ChatGPT-4 Turbo, Google Gemini Advanced, and Microsoft Co-Pilot signifies a significant leap towards more integrated, secure, and versatile digital environments. These platforms are not only enhancing user experiences across various applications but are also emphasizing the importance of data privacy and security through innovative measures. Microsoft Co-Pilot, for example, showcases the integration of OpenAI's GPT-4 Turbo, offering users an advanced level of AI capabilities across Microsoft 365 applications such as Word, Excel, PowerPoint, Outlook, and OneNote. This integration promises to supercharge productivity and creativity for both personal and organizational use, ensuring a seamless AI experience across devices. The introduction of Co-Pilot Pro and its expansion to institutions of all sizes underlines Microsoft's commitment to making AI more accessible while prioritizing security, privacy, and compliance. The enterprise-grade security features highlight the proactive measures being taken to address concerns over proprietary data potentially being leaked through public models. These advancements point to a future where AI is not only more powerful and versatile but also safer and more secure, ensuring that the benefits of AI are broadly accessible while protecting user data.

Furthermore, Microsoft's strategy includes semantic overlays as part of their Copilot offerings, a sophisticated approach aimed at enhancing understanding and generating more relevant responses by leveraging vast amounts of data from Bing image search and web search. This multimodal approach with search grounding demonstrates an innovative step towards maintaining data integrity and user trust by improving the comprehension capabilities of these tools without compromising privacy. As we move forward, the emphasis on building AI models that are not only powerful and versatile but also secure and privacy-conscious will be crucial in addressing the evolving landscape of digital privacy and security. The advancements seen in these multimodal examples pave the way for a future where AI can assist in a range of tasks while ensuring that user data remains protected.

Simultaneously, the adoption of generative AI models represents a pivotal shift in how institutions approach data analysis, content creation, and operational efficiency. Initially, leveraging existing models like OpenAI's GPT series has been a transformative first step for many organizations, enabling them to harness advanced AI capabilities without the need for extensive ML expertise. These models have been instrumental in generating human-like text, creating realistic images, and producing complex musical compositions, marking the dawn of a generative transformation across various sectors. However, the future trajectory points towards institutions and researchers not just adopting but creating their own custom models tailored to specific tasks and needs. Microsoft Azure AI Studio emerges as a key platform in this evolution, offering a unified environment for building, deploying, and managing generative AI applications and custom copilots. Azure AI Studio provides access to a comprehensive model catalog, including state-of-the-art models from OpenAI, Meta, NVIDIA, and Microsoft Research, along with hundreds of open-source models (Wan & Chen, 2023). This enables researchers to ground their models with their own data, enhancing the relevance and effectiveness of these applications. This shift towards customized AI models suggests that the technology is not only more relevant but also more accurate and contextually aware, ultimately leading to more precise and impactful outcomes for different areas of research.

Moreover, Azure AI Studio simplifies the entire development lifecycle, from prompt engineering and model integration to deployment and monitoring, facilitating the creation of multimodal applications that leverage language, vision, and speech. With built-in tools for evaluating AI applications for quality and safety and a focus on responsible AI, Azure AI Studio ensures that custom AI solutions adhere to the highest standards of security and compliance (Gao et al., 2023). For researchers, this platform offers a robust infrastructure to develop tailored AI models that meet specific research needs, enhancing the precision and relevance of AI applications in academic contexts.

As researchers progress from utilizing pre-built generative models to crafting their bespoke versions, platforms like Azure AI Studio play a crucial role. They not only democratize access to advanced AI capabilities but also empower academic institutions to innovate with AI solutions deeply integrated with their unique research contexts. This sets the stage for a more personalized and efficient use of AI technology in scholarly research, enabling groundbreaking discoveries and enhancing the depth of academic inquiry.

However, available models alone will not suffice for researchers to fully capitalize on this significant milestone in technological evolution. Generative AI's transformative potential is often compared to historical innovations like the steam engine and electricity, which drastically changed societal operations. This comparison suggests that GAI is poised to fundamentally alter how research is conducted, how data is analyzed, and how new knowledge is generated. Amidst this transformative potential, the urgency for academic institutions to move away from legacy systems and embrace new methodologies is highlighted, emphasizing a departure from the 'burning platform' mentality towards a culture of innovation (Mattila et al., 2021).

The “burning platform” mentality, which originates from a dramatic incident on an offshore oil platform, refers to a crisis-driven approach to change, where the perceived threat of not changing outweighs the risks of implementing new strategies or technologies. In the context of GAI, leading through fear may inhibit innovation and risk-taking. Instead, creating a supportive environment that encourages experimentation and learning from failure is advocated. For researchers, this means fostering an academic culture that values continuous learning, adaptation, and the responsible integration of AI technologies into research practices. By doing so, the academic community can harness the full potential of GAI, driving forward scholarly inquiry and contributing to the broader social good.

The urgency for researchers to adopt AI technologies has never been more critical, with the pace of adoption moving at an unprecedented speed, surpassing even the rapid advancements predicted by Moore's Law. According to research by Ho et al. (2023), the efficiency of algorithms for pre-training language models has seen compute requirements halve roughly every eight months—a rate significantly faster than the hardware improvements traditionally anticipated by Moore's Law. This acceleration in algorithmic progress, highlighted through a comprehensive analysis of over 200 language model evaluations from 2012 to 2023, underscores the critical window for researchers to become early adopters of AI. Those who seize this opportunity are poised to gain significant advantages, achieving more insightful and innovative research outputs.

This rapid advancement is especially significant considering the predicted and almost certain emergence of superintelligence. Superintelligence, as discussed in Nick Bostrom's 2014 book *Superintelligence: Paths, Dangers, Strategies*, argues that if machine brains surpass human brains in general intelligence, this new superintelligence could replace humans as the dominant lifeform on Earth. The book highlights the potential paths, dangers, and strategies associated with this transition. In the context of research, the potential for generative models to outperform the experts that train them adds a layer of urgency to adopting these technologies (Zhang et al., 2024).

For educators, preparing students for a future dominated by AI and superintelligence involves integrating AI literacy and advanced AI tools into the curriculum. By doing so, students can develop the skills needed to leverage these technologies effectively and ethically. The rapid development and deployment of AI in research necessitate that academic institutions remain agile and forward-thinking, ensuring that their methodologies and educational practices evolve in tandem with technological advancements. This preparation will enable the next generation of researchers to understand and contribute to an AI-enhanced academic landscape, driving innovation and maintaining the integrity and relevance of scholarly inquiry.

The rapid development, deployment, and adoption of new generative technologies have been unprecedented and largely unpredicted. Predictive models prior to 2022 significantly misjudged the speed and impact of AI development, often underestimating the rapid advancements and market penetration of AI technologies (Uloa-

Cazarez, 2020). This misalignment calls for a reassessment of AI's developmental trajectory, emphasizing the need for new models that accurately reflect the current and future landscape of artificial intelligence. Reflecting on AI's unmet expectations, it is evident that the anticipation surrounding the AI "gold rush" of 2023 was profound. The financial sector expected massive returns from AI technologies, especially after notable investments in AI companies surged, painting a promising picture of exponential growth. For instance, the generative AI market was forecasted to reach a valuation of $1.3 trillion by 2032, driven by significant investments and the development of new AI applications (Saintvilus, 2023).

However, despite these optimistic projections, the tangible returns in the first fiscal quarter following these investments fell short of expectations for many. The enthusiasm for potential market-altering AI technologies led to significant investments, as seen in cases like OpenAI's staggering $10 billion funding from Microsoft and other hefty funding rounds in the AI sector. These investments reflected a widespread belief in the transformative potential of AI (Zhang, 2023). Yet, the reality that emerged was more tempered. The market performance of major AI-driven companies, although positive, did not always match the high expectations set early on. For example, while companies like Microsoft and Nvidia saw substantial stock increases due to their AI developments, the overall returns were more modest than the initially projected transformative impacts (Lango, 2024).

Furthermore, fears surrounding the immediate and widespread adoption of AI in research have been somewhat overblown. Studies indicate that the penetration of AI technologies in academic research remains slow, with broad adoption yet to occur. This slower pace provides a window of opportunity for the academic community to carefully consider and implement these technologies, ensuring they are integrated in ways that enhance research quality and integrity. The discrepancy between expectation and outcome highlights the complexity and unpredictability of integrating cutting-edge technologies into the market and serves as a reminder of the inherent risks involved in high-stakes investment sectors, particularly those as dynamic and rapidly evolving as artificial intelligence. This measured approach allows for a more thorough understanding and better preparation for the ethical and practical challenges posed by AI in scholarly work.

Over the past two years, the high expectations surrounding the transformative capabilities of AI have not always translated into tangible returns, revealing various obstacles. Key among these challenges are regulatory concerns, which have begun to see more structured responses with emerging data privacy regulations necessitating rigorous impact assessments for AI technologies. These regulations often require documentation detailing the training data, logic, and evaluations of AI systems to ensure accuracy, fairness, and lack of bias (Felz et al., 2022).

Additionally, data privacy issues have become increasingly prominent as the volume and sensitivity of data processed by AI systems grow. This raises significant concerns about the misuse of personal information and the potential for privacy intrusions, exacerbated by AI's capability to make inferences at an unprecedented scale and speed (Lee et al., 2024). The need for internal expertise in developing proprietary AI models also remains a crucial hurdle. Many organizations lack the specialized knowledge required to create and manage effective AI systems, often leading to ineffective implementations. This has been exemplified by costly development failures such as Bloomberg's, which became obsolete with the release of more effective "off-the-shelf" solutions like ChatGPT 4 through APIs (Ahmed, 2021; Easterbrook, 2024).

Given the significant challenges involved in developing proprietary AI models, such as regulatory compliance and data privacy concerns, it is advisable to reconsider the strategy of training one's own AI model unless there are extraordinary circumstances justifying such an approach. Instead, researchers should consider leveraging new closed models, like Co-Pilot, which are designed with robust data privacy features to ensure that sensitive data does not leak. These models provide the dual benefits of advanced AI capabilities without the inherent risks associated with data management and compliance in creating proprietary systems. This strategic shift can help organizations consider all of the complicatedness of AI integration more effectively, ensuring that they harness the benefits of AI while mitigating potential risks.

A pilot study examining the advanced features of Microsoft Co-Pilot revealed that merely introducing new AI tools does not automatically enhance productivity. Instead, the study observed only marginal improvements in efficiency. The pilot involved 17 participants from diverse roles within the institution, providing a comprehensive view of how different segments interact with and perceive the new AI tool (Hutson & Rains, 2024). Participants included administrators, faculty members, and staff, with representation from various departments such as Academic Affairs, Admissions, Arts and Humanities, and Science, Technology, and Health. This diverse demographic highlighted the broad potential application of AI tools across different functional areas within the institution.

The study identified the primary tasks participants handle, revealing significant insights into their daily workloads and potential areas for AI integration. Tasks such as composing and managing emails (18.67%), creating presentations and PowerPoint slides (13.33%), grading assignments (6.67%), conducting financial analysis (10.67%), and engaging in research and development activities (13.33%) were highlighted. The ubiquity of Microsoft 365 Apps in daily routines, with 100% of participants using these tools daily, underscored the importance of enhancing these workflows through AI integration. Challenges faced by participants included time-consuming processes (22.22%), lack of automation features (16.67%), and integration issues with other software (11.11%), indicating significant areas where AI tools like Co-Pilot could offer improvements.

The evaluation phase of the pilot revealed varied familiarity and reception of the tools among participants. While 43.75% of participants were moderately familiar with Co-Pilot AI tools, a smaller segment reported higher levels of familiarity. Participants generally felt positive about using the Co-Pilot AI tools, with 47.06% expressing somewhat positive feelings and 23.53% feeling extremely positive. However, concerns regarding integration with current workflows (36.36%), dependability and accuracy (30.30%), and the learning curve required for adaptation (21.21%) were noted. The study highlighted the need for effective training and support, with participants favoring online tutorials and trial-and-error learning methods. Concerns about usability and accuracy, particularly issues with the user interface and user experience, were also prominent. These findings emphasize the importance of addressing these challenges to ensure successful integration and adoption of AI tools in research workflows.

Given these findings, identifying and leveraging internal expertise through a train-the-trainer model is a strategic approach that can significantly enhance institutional capability in utilizing new AI tools for research. By pinpointing key personnel who already possess a foundational understanding or show aptitude for AI technology, organizations can cultivate a core group of internal trainers. These trainers can be upskilled through external training programs or dedicated in-house sessions to deepen their proficiency in specific AI applications. This investment not only builds an internal knowledge base but also ensures that expertise is effectively distributed throughout the organization.

Once trained, these internal experts can support their colleagues by leading training sessions and helping integrate AI tools into daily workflows. This peer-led training approach is particularly beneficial as it is more relatable and directly applicable, addressing specific challenges and questions that arise in the context of the organization's unique operational environment. By fostering a collaborative learning environment, organizations can enhance the adoption and effective use of AI technologies. Moreover, bringing in external trainers or investing in specialized courses for key personnel can introduce fresh perspectives and advanced skills to the internal team. These employees, once trained, can act as multipliers, disseminating new knowledge and practices across the organization. This method helps create a sustainable learning culture that continuously adapts as AI technologies evolve. Such a strategy not only enhances the institution's research capabilities but also ensures that the integration of AI tools is seamless and effective, ultimately contributing to more innovative and efficient research outcomes.

8.2 BUILDING AN INCLUSIVE FUTURE WITH AI IN ACADEMIA

The current state of research and its pedagogical approaches are deeply rooted in rigorous methodologies and systematic inquiry. Academics are expected to maintain high standards of scholarly integrity, conduct extensive literature reviews, engage in careful data collection and analysis, and contribute novel insights to their fields (Eaton, 2024). Daily, researchers and educators manage a landscape that demands both depth and breadth of knowledge, fostering a culture of continuous learning and critical thinking. However, the rapid advancement of AI technologies is reshaping these expectations, introducing new tools and methodologies that promise to enhance efficiency and broaden the scope of academic inquiry (Khalifa & Albadawy, 2024).

In this evolving landscape, we already see the ability to create avatars that can perform tasks on behalf of their owners, including dating and professional duties (Chamorro-Premuzic, 2023). This raises pertinent questions about the extent of responsibility an owner has over the actions of their avatar, especially in scenarios where the avatar might commit a crime. Similarly, in academic writing, AI models are provided with style guides and personalized information to emulate the voice of an author. As we move towards integrating more of our information into these models, the next stage of research will involve even greater reliance on AI to assist with complex tasks, potentially transforming the very nature of authorship and accountability in scholarly work. This progression necessitates a thoughtful examination of ethical considerations and the development of inclusive practices to ensure that AI advancements benefit the entire academic community. For instance, if a researcher provides a comprehensive biography, including past publications, a voice and style guide, and clear instructions for identifying a topic, gathering data, interpreting the data, and outputting results, what does that mean for academic authorship?

To maneuver in this ever-changing landscape effectively, there is an urgent need for the broad implementation of AI literacy integration within core graduate research methods courses and scholastic writing from the outset of graduate study. Familiarizing students with AI tools, their abilities, and their limitations early in their academic journey will equip them with the skills necessary to leverage these technologies responsibly and effectively. Graduate programs need to prioritize the incorporation of comprehensive AI training modules into their curricula. This approach ensures that students develop a solid understanding of AI functionalities, ethical considerations, and practical applications in research.

As such, through embedding AI literacy into foundational courses, students will learn to critically assess AI outputs, understand the scope and limitations of AI-generated content, and utilize AI tools to enhance their research capabilities without compromising academic integrity. Such integration serves multiple purposes: it prepares students to engage with advanced AI-driven research methods, fosters a culture of innovation and adaptability, and mitigates potential misuse or overreliance on AI technologies. Moreover, it encourages students to explore the symbiotic relationship between human creativity and machine intelligence, enhancing their ability to conduct nuanced, original research.

A significant challenge in implementing this strategy lies in the necessity for seasoned academics, who are often responsible for teaching graduate courses, to first upskill themselves in AI tools. Many established researchers and educators may not yet be familiar with the latest advancements in AI and how these can be integrated into their daily work. To address this gap, it is essential for these academics to adopt a proactive approach to learning and experimenting with AI technologies. One effective strategy is to incorporate the use of a chosen AI tool into their daily workflow, focusing on one task at a time. By consistently engaging with these tools, educators can gain practical insights and firsthand experience, understanding what can be achieved and identifying potential limitations. The strategies outlined in this book provide starting points for a range of disciplines, but hands-on experience remains irreplaceable.

Professional development across higher education is increasingly focusing on training in AI tools. Research and teaching centers within universities can act as primary resources for those needing to upskill. These centers can offer workshops, seminars, and one-on-one training sessions to help academics integrate AI into their research and teaching practices effectively.

Furthermore, these centers can facilitate the creation of communities of practice where educators can share experiences, challenges, and successes related to AI integration. By fostering a collaborative learning environment, institutions can ensure that all faculty members are equipped to guide their students in handling the evolving landscape of AI-enhanced academic research. But successful implementation of AI literacy within graduate education hinges on the willingness of seasoned academics to engage with AI tools and the support provided by institutional professional development programs. By bridging this gap, we can create a more dynamic and inclusive academic environment that prepares both educators and students for the future of research and scholarship.

There are areas outside of research that AI can be called upon to give mentees the best chance possible once graduating. In fact, one of the most important, and often underrated, activities that academics as mentors are called upon to do regularly is write letters of recommendation. These letters are crucial in helping the next generation of scholars navigate an increasingly competitive landscape in both academic and industry settings. Being prompt and thorough in delivering these letters can significantly impact a student's opportunities and career trajectory.

However, remembering specifics about each graduate student, especially if you did not directly advise their thesis or dissertation, can be challenging. The passage of time can cloud clear recollections, making it difficult to provide detailed and personalized recommendations. To best serve both ourselves and our students, it is recommended to request an updated CV or resume from the student when they reach out for a recommendation letter. Additionally, obtaining detailed information about the job, graduate school, or opportunity they are applying for can provide context and allow you to tailor your letter to highlight the most relevant skills and experiences.

This task can be particularly challenging because graduate students may apply for ten or even thirty positions (I myself was one of them), and therefore mentors may be asked to write several letters a week depending on how many students they have had in the past. Keeping up with this demand can be daunting. Therefore, using the CV or resume sent, which has updated information on skills, education, experience, publications, conferences, etc., can be instrumental in tailoring specific and personalized letters. This approach not only helps manage the workload but also ensures that every letter written is as detailed and supportive as possible, ultimately aiding students in their job or graduate school applications. Have the individual's CV/resume on hand along with the description of the position and follow these steps with the prompt: "You will write a letter of recommendation for [individual's name] for the following position [paste in description of position/ school] and use the following information to demonstrate the strength of the candidate [paste in whole CV or attach]." The AI will then align the requirements of the position with the experience, education, and skillset of the candidate. Now, in order to make the letter as professional or personal as desired, follow up prompts can include: "Now, generate again less formal" "Now, make mention of them as 'Dr.'" or "Include a personal anecdote about how they went above and beyond to tutor their classmates." Following these steps will alleviate countless hours every year and ensure prompt delivery of letters of recommendation and support for students.

Therefore, the integration of AI tools into academic research and education holds the promise of significantly enhancing inclusivity and accessibility, leading to a more demographically diverse population of graduate students, and practicing professionals. This potential is particularly relevant in fields such as STEM, where diversity issues have been well documented (Asher et la., 2023; Palid et al., 2023; Wright & Delgado, 2023). The ability to output and organize content, combined with its capacity to act as a live tutor across a range of subjects, allows for AI to accommodate a diversity of learning styles and needs. Generative AI tools can serve as personalized tutors, providing tailored support and feedback that can adapt to the unique learning styles of each student (Lin et al., 2023). This flexibility can be especially beneficial for individuals who may struggle in traditional lecture or lab-based classroom settings. For example, students with neurodiverse conditions or those who prefer alternative modes of learning can leverage AI tools to receive information through different sensory inputs, such as visual aids, interactive simulations, or auditory explanations (Hutson, 2024). This personalized approach not only enhances learning outcomes but also helps mitigate feelings of "imposter syndrome" and a lack of belonging, which are common among students who feel different due to their gender, race, ethnicity, or neurological makeup (Dao et al., 2024).

Moreover, the ability of AI to provide instant, context-aware assistance can alleviate the pressure and anxiety that often accompany high-stakes academic environments. By offering continuous support and resources, AI can empower students to take control of their learning journey, fostering a sense of confidence and competence. This can be particularly transformative in STEM fields, where the rigor and pace of coursework can be daunting.

The personalization of learning through AI extends into research, promoting innovative solutions and diverse perspectives. Research has shown that groupthink can be a significant barrier to innovation, often stifling creativity and leading to homogenous thinking (Permana & Wening, 2024). Through facilitation of a more inclusive research environment, AI tools can introduce a variety of ideas and frameworks that reflect a broader range of experiences and backgrounds. This diversity of thought is crucial for addressing complex global challenges and advancing knowledge in meaningful ways.

In all, the adoption of AI tools in academic settings has the potential to not only enhance the educational experience by accommodating different learning styles and needs but also fosters a more inclusive and diverse academic community. By addressing the barriers that have historically limited diversity in fields such as STEM, these tools can help cultivate a new generation of scholars and professionals who bring a wide array of perspectives and solutions to their work. As we move forward, it is essential to continue developing and refining these technologies to ensure they serve the diverse needs of all learners, ultimately enriching the landscape of academic research and practice.

As researchers and academics, we hold the responsibility to harness AI advancements for the collective good, emphasizing the quality and innovation of our outputs over the mere processes involved. While AI enhances efficiency and broadens our capabilities, the human element remains essential. It is our duty to guide the application of these generative tools in research, ensuring their benefits align with ethical standards and contribute positively to humanity. Our role extends beyond technical proficiency; we must continuously advocate for advancements that foster inclusivity, equity, and societal welfare. By focusing on the impactful integration of AI, we can drive forward our fields with a commitment to innovation, quality, and the overarching goal of enhancing human well-being.

REFERENCES

Ahmed, H. S. A. (2021). Challenges of AI and data privacy- and how to solve them. ISACA. October 6, 2021. Retrieved: https://www.isaca.org/resources/news-and-trends/newsletters/atisaca/2021/volume-32/challenges-of-ai-and-data-privacy-and-how-to-solve-them

Asher, M. W., Harackiewicz, J. M., Beymer, P. N., Hecht, C. A., Lamont, L. B., Else-Quest, N. M., Priniski, S. J., Thoman, D. B., Hyde, J. S., & Smith, J. L. (2023). Utility-value intervention promotes persistence and diversity in STEM. *Proceedings of the National Academy of Sciences of the United States of America*, 120(19), e2300463120. DOI: 10.1073/pnas.2300463120

Bostrom, N. (2014). *Superintelligence: Paths, Dangers, Strategies*. Oxford University Press.

Chamorro-Premuzic, T. (2023). *I, human: AI, automation, and the quest to reclaim what makes us unique*. Harvard Business Press.

Dao, A., Pegg, S., Okland, S., Green, H., & Kujawa, A. (2024). Longitudinal associations between sense of belonging, imposter syndrome, and first-year college students' mental health. *Journal of American College Health*, 1–10. DOI: 10.1080/07448481.2024.2355162

Easterbrook, G. (2024). How financial services firms can build a generative AI assistant. *Forbes*. February 14, 2024. Retrieved: https://www.forbes.com/sites/granteasterbrook/2024/02/14/how-financial-services-firms-can-build-a-generative-ai-assistant/?sh=18eccfb577a0

Eaton, S. E. (2024). Academic and research integrity as transdisciplinary fields of scholarship and professional practice. In *Second handbook of academic integrity* (pp. 1633–1650). Springer Nature Switzerland. DOI: 10.1007/978-3-031-54144-5_165

Feltz, D., Peretti, K. K., & Austin, A. (2022). Privacy, cyber & data strategy advisory: AI regulation in the U.S.: What's coming, and what companies need to do in 2023. *Alston & Bird*. December 9, 2022. Retrieved: https://www.alston.com/en/insights/publications/2022/12/ai-regulation-in-the-us

Gao, Y., Li, R., Caskey, J., Dligach, D., Miller, T., Churpek, M. M., & Afshar, M. (2023). Leveraging a medical knowledge graph into large language models for diagnosis prediction. *arXiv preprint arXiv:2308.14321*.

Ho, A., Besiroglu, T., Erdil, E. Owen, D., Rahman, R., Guo, Z., Atkinson, D., Thompson, N. & Sevilla, J. (2024). Algorithmic progress in language models. *arXiv:2403.05812*

Hutson, J., & Rains, T. J. (2024). Microsoft Co-Pilot Adoption Study [Data set]. Lindenwood University. https://www.brookings.edu/articles/protecting-privacy-in-an-ai-driven-world/

Hutson, P. (2024). Embracing the Irreplaceable: The Role of Neurodiversity in Cultivating Human-AI Symbiosis in Education. *International Journal of Emerging and Disruptive Innovation in Education: VISIONARIUM*, 2(1), 5. DOI: 10.62608/2831-3550.1020

Khalifa, M., & Albadawy, M. (2024). Using artificial intelligence in academic writing and research: An essential productivity tool. *Computer Methods and Programs in Biomedicine Update*, 5, 100145. DOI: 10.1016/j.cmpbup.2024.100145

Lango, L. (2024). Is this the best way to invest in the AI gold rush? *Investor Place*. January 10, 2024. Retrieved: https://investorplace.com/hypergrowthinvesting/2024/01/is-this-the-best-way-to-invest-in-the-ai-gold-rush/

Lee, H. P. H., Gao, L., Yang, S., Forlizzi, J., & Das, S. (2024). "I Don't Know If We're Doing Good. I Don't Know If We're Doing Bad": Investigating How Practitioners Scope, Motivate, and Conduct Privacy Work When Developing AI Products. *USENIX Security Symposium.*

Lin, C. C., Huang, A. Y., & Lu, O. H. (2023). Artificial intelligence in intelligent tutoring systems toward sustainable education: A systematic review. *Smart Learning Environments*, 10(1), 41. DOI: 10.1186/s40561-023-00260-y

Mattila, M., Yrjölä, M., & Hautamäki, P. (2021). Digital transformation of business-to-business sales: What needs to be unlearned? *Journal of Personal Selling & Sales Management*, 41(2), 113–129. DOI: 10.1080/08853134.2021.1916396

Palid, O., Cashdollar, S., Deangelo, S., Chu, C., & Bates, M. (2023). Inclusion in practice: A systematic review of diversity-focused STEM programming in the United States. *International Journal of STEM Education*, 10(1), 2. DOI: 10.1186/s40594-022-00387-3

Permana, A. Y., & Wening, N. (2024). The Influence of Groupthink and Bounded Rationality in Decision-Making on Public Policy. *Eduvest-Journal of Universal Studies*, 4(3), 855–870. DOI: 10.59188/eduvest.v4i3.1086

Saintvilus, R. (2023). The AI gold rush: Profiting from picks and shovels. NASDAQ. November 28, 2023. Retrieved: https://www.nasdaq.com/articles/the-ai-gold-rush-profiting-from-picks-and-shovels

Ulloa-Cazarez, R. L. (2020). Joseph E. Aoun: Robot-proof: higher education at the age of artificial intelligence. MIT Press.

Wan, T., & Chen, Z. (2023). Exploring Generative AI assisted feedback writing for students' written responses to a physics conceptual question with prompt engineering and few-shot learning. *arXiv preprint arXiv:2311.06180.*

Wright, G. W., & Delgado, C. (2023). Generating a framework for gender and sexual diversity-inclusive STEM education. *Science Education*, 107(3), 713–740. DOI: 10.1002/sce.21786

Zhang, E., Zhu, V., Saphra, N., Kleiman, A., Edelman, B. L., Tambe, M., . . . Malach, E. (2024). Transcendence: Generative Models Can Outperform The Experts That Train Them. *arXiv preprint arXiv:2406.11741*

Zhang, M. (2023). AI's winning streak: Crushing the venture capital slump. *Artisana.* April 16, 2023. Retrieved: https://www.artisana.ai/articles/ais-winning-streak-crushing-the-venture-capital-slump

Glossary

Algorithmic Culture: The pervasive influence of algorithms on various facets of daily life, work, and decision-making processes.

Artificial Intelligence (AI): A broad field encompassing various technologies aimed at enabling machines to perform tasks that typically require human intelligence, such as learning, reasoning, and self-correction.

Computer Vision: A field of AI that trains computers to interpret and understand the visual world through images and video analysis.

Deep Learning (DL): A subset of machine learning involving neural networks with many layers, enabling the analysis of complex data with high levels of abstraction.

Generative Adversarial Networks (GANs): A class of machine learning frameworks consisting of two neural networks, one generating data (the generator) and the other evaluating data (the discriminator). This interactive process improves the generator's ability to produce realistic data.

Generative AI (GAI): AI systems that create new content—such as text, images, and sounds—that did not exist before, differentiating them from traditional AI which focuses on decision-making or predictive analytics.

Large Language Models (LLMs): AI models trained on vast amounts of text data to generate coherent and contextually appropriate language. Examples include GPT-3 and GPT-4.

Machine Learning (ML): A subset of AI that allows systems to learn and improve from experience without being explicitly programmed. ML algorithms use statistical techniques to enable machines to improve their performance on tasks over time.

Neural Networks: Computational models inspired by the human brain, consisting of layers of neurons that process input data to recognize patterns and make decisions.

Natural Language Processing (NLP): A field of AI that focuses on the interaction between computers and humans through natural language, enabling computers to understand, interpret, and generate human language.

Reinforcement Learning: A type of machine learning where an algorithm learns by interacting with its environment, receiving rewards or penalties for its actions, and optimizing its performance based on this feedback.

Rule-Based Algorithms (RB): Algorithms that operate based on explicit rules defined by humans, often known for their transparency and ease of understanding.

Supervised Learning: A type of machine learning where an algorithm is trained on labeled data, learning to associate inputs with specific outputs to make predictions on new, unlabeled data.

Transformers: A type of neural network architecture that uses self-attention mechanisms to process sequential data more efficiently, widely used in natural language processing tasks.

Unsupervised Learning: A type of machine learning where an algorithm analyzes unlabeled data to identify patterns and relationships without prior examples.

Compilation of References

Aabid, A., Parveez, B., Parveen, N., Khan, S. A., & Shabbir, O. (2022). A case study of unmanned aerial vehicle (drone) technology and its applications in the COVID-19 pandemic. *J. Mech. Eng. Res. Dev*, 45, 70–77.

Abdelrazek, A., Eid, Y., Gawish, E., Medhat, W., & Hassan, A. (2023). Topic modeling algorithms and applications: A survey. *Information Systems*, 112, 102131. DOI: 10.1016/j.is.2022.102131

Abulibdeh, A., Zaidan, E., & Abulibdeh, R. (2024). Navigating the confluence of artificial intelligence and education for sustainable development in the era of industry 4.0: Challenges, opportunities, and ethical dimensions. *Journal of Cleaner Production*, 437, 140527. DOI: 10.1016/j.jclepro.2023.140527

Ade-Ojo, G. O., Markowski, M., Essex, R., Stiell, M., & Jameson, J. (2022). A systematic scoping review and textual narrative synthesis of physical and mixed-reality simulation in pre-service teacher training. *Journal of Computer Assisted Learning*, 38(3), 861–874. DOI: 10.1111/jcal.12653

Ahmed, H. S. A. (2021). Challenges of AI and data privacy- and how to solve them. ISACA. October 6, 2021. Retrieved: https://www.isaca.org/resources/news-and-trends/newsletters/atisaca/2021/volume-32/challenges-of-ai-and-data-privacy-and-how-to-solve-them

Akour, M., & Alenezi, M. (2022). Higher education future in the era of digital transformation. *Education Sciences*, 12(11), 784. DOI: 10.3390/educsci12110784

Albahri, A. S., Duhaim, A. M., Fadhel, M. A., Alnoor, A., Baqer, N. S., Alzubaidi, L., & Deveci, M. (2023). A Systematic Review of Trustworthy and Explainable Artificial Intelligence in Healthcare: Assessment of Quality, Bias Risk, and Data Fusion. *Information Fusion*, 96, 156–191. DOI: 10.1016/j.inffus.2023.03.008

Alhumaid, K., Naqbi, S., Elsori, D., & Mansoori, M. (2023). The adoption of artificial intelligence applications in education. *International Journal of Data and Network Science*, 7(1), 457–466. DOI: 10.5267/j.ijdns.2022.8.013

Aliotta, M. (2018). *Mastering academic writing in the sciences: A step-by-step guide*. CRC Press. DOI: 10.1201/9781351002141

Aljurf, S., Kemp, L. J., & Williams, P. (2020). Exploring academic dishonesty in the Middle East: A qualitative analysis of students' perceptions. *Studies in Higher Education*, 45(7), 1461–1473. DOI: 10.1080/03075079.2018.1564262

Al-Kurdi, O. F., El-Haddadeh, R., & Eldabi, T. (2020). The Role of Organisational Climate in Managing Knowledge Sharing Among Academics in Higher Education. *International Journal of Information Management*, 50, 217–227. DOI: 10.1016/j.ijinfomgt.2019.05.018

Alvarado, O., & Waern, A. (2018, April). Towards algorithmic experience: Initial efforts for social media contexts. In *Proceedings of the 2018 chi conference on human factors in computing systems* (pp. 1-12). DOI: 10.1145/3173574.3173860

Alwahedi, F., Aldhaheri, A., Ferrag, M. A., Battah, A., & Tihanyi, N. (2024). Machine learning techniques for IoT security: Current research and future vision with generative AI and large language models. *Internet of Things and Cyber-Physical Systems.*

Alzubaidi, L., Bai, J., Al-Sabaawi, A., Santamaría, J., Albahri, A. S., Al-dabbagh, B. S. N., Fadhel, M. A., Manoufali, M., Zhang, J., Al-Timemy, A. H., Duan, Y., Abdullah, A., Farhan, L., Lu, Y., Gupta, A., Albu, F., Abbosh, A., & Gu, Y. (2023). A survey on deep learning tools dealing with data scarcity: Definitions, challenges, solutions, tips, and applications. *Journal of Big Data*, 10(1), 46. DOI: 10.1186/s40537-023-00727-2

American Psychological Association. (2020). *Publication manual of the American Psychological Association* (7th ed.). American Psychological Association.

Amsberry, D., & Snavely, L. (2011). *Engaging international students in academic library initiatives for their peers. International students and academic libraries: initiatives for success*. Association of College and Research Libraries.

Andersson, R. (2022). The Bioeconomy and the Birth of a "New Anthropology". *Cultural Anthropology*, 37(1), 37–44. DOI: 10.14506/ca37.1.06

Angwin, J., Larson, J., Mattu, S., & Kirchner, L. (2016). Machine bias. In *Ethics of data and analytics* (pp. 254–264). Auerbach Publications.

Ansari, T. (2022). How AI transformed the art world in 2022. *Analytics India Magazine (AIM)*. Retrieved from: https://analyticsindiamag.com/how-ai-transformed-the-art-world-in-2022/

Ansorge, L., Ansorgeová, K., & Sixsmith, M. (2021). Plagiarism through paraphrasing tools—The story of one plagiarized text. *Publications / MDPI*, 9(4), 48. DOI: 10.3390/publications9040048

Antonius, F., Alapati, P. R., Ritonga, M., Patra, I., El-Ebiary, Y. A. B., Orosoo, M., & Rengarajan, M. (2023). Incorporating natural language processing into virtual assistants: An intelligent assessment strategy for enhancing language comprehension. *International Journal of Advanced Computer Science and Applications*, 14(10). Advance online publication. DOI: 10.14569/IJACSA.2023.0141079

Antony, J. S., Cauce, A. M., Gangone, L. M., & Nicola, T. P. (Eds.). (2022). *The college president handbook: a sustainable and practical guide for emerging leaders*. Harvard Education Press.

Aoun, J. E. (2017). *Robot-proof: higher education in the age of artificial intelligence*. MIT press. DOI: 10.7551/mitpress/11456.001.0001

Arapoff, N. (1967). Writing: A thinking process. *TESOL Quarterly*, 1(2), 33–39. DOI: 10.2307/3585751

Aristotle, . (1991). *On Rhetoric: A Theory of Civic Discourse* (Kennedy, G. A., Trans.). Oxford University Press.

Ariyurek, S., Betin-Can, A., & Surer, E. (2019). Automated Video Game Testing Using Synthetic and Humanlike Agents. *IEEE Transactions on Games*, 13(1), 50–67. DOI: 10.1109/TG.2019.2947597

Arnold, J. (2014). A subjective academic narrative reviewing academic collegiality. *International Education Research*, 2(4), 26–37. DOI: 10.12735/ier.v2i4p26

Asher, M. W., Harackiewicz, J. M., Beymer, P. N., Hecht, C. A., Lamont, L. B., Else-Quest, N. M., Priniski, S. J., Thoman, D. B., Hyde, J. S., & Smith, J. L. (2023). Utility-value intervention promotes persistence and diversity in STEM. *Proceedings of the National Academy of Sciences of the United States of America*, 120(19), e2300463120. DOI: 10.1073/pnas.2300463120

Autor, D., & Dorn, D. (2013). The growth of low-skill service jobs and the polarization of the US labor market. *The American Economic Review*, 103(5), 1553–1597. DOI: 10.1257/aer.103.5.1553

Aydın, Ö., & Karaarslan, E. (2022). OpenAI ChatGPT generated literature review: Digital twin in healthcare. *Available atSSRN* 4308687. DOI: 10.2139/ssrn.4308687

Babitha, M. M., & Sushma, C. (2022). Trends of Artificial Intelligence for online exams in education. *International journal of Early Childhood special. Education*, 14(01), 2457–2463.

Bahari, A., & Gholami, L. (2023). Challenges and affordances of reading and writing development in technology-assisted language learning. *Interactive Learning Environments*, 31(10), 7226–7250. DOI: 10.1080/10494820.2022.2065308

Bailey, S. (2003). *Academic writing: A practical guide for students*. Psychology Press. DOI: 10.4324/9780203464120

Barchard, K. A. (2003). Does emotional intelligence assist in the prediction of academic success? *Educational and Psychological Measurement*, 63(5), 840–858. DOI: 10.1177/0013164403251333

Barthet, M., Khalifa, A., Liapis, A., & Yannakakis, G. (2022, September). Generative Personas that Behave and Experience Like Humans. In *Proceedings of the 17th International Conference on the Foundations of Digital Games* (pp. 1-10). DOI: 10.1145/3555858.3555879

Berendt, B., Littlejohn, A., & Blakemore, M. (2020). AI in education: Learner choice and fundamental rights. *Learning, Media and Technology*, 45(3), 312–324. DOI: 10.1080/17439884.2020.1786399

Biggs, J., Tang, C., & Kennedy, G. (2022). Ebook: Teaching for Quality Learning at University 5e. *McGraw-Hill education* (UK).

Billot, J. (2010). The imagined and the real: Identifying the tensions for academic identity. *Higher Education Research & Development*, 29(6), 709–721. DOI: 10.1080/07294360.2010.487201

Birchler, C., Khatiri, S., Bosshard, B., Gambi, A., & Panichella, S. (2023). Machine learning-based test selection for simulation-based testing of self-driving cars software. *Empirical Software Engineering*, 28(3), 71. DOI: 10.1007/s10664-023-10286-y

Bitzer, L. F. (1968). The Rhetorical Situation. *Philosophy & Rhetoric*, 1(1), 1–14.

Bostrom, N. (2014). *Superintelligence: Paths, Dangers, Strategies*. Oxford University Press.

Bouville, M. (2008). Plagiarism: Words and ideas. *Science and Engineering Ethics*, 14(3), 311–322. DOI: 10.1007/s11948-008-9057-6

Braidwood, R. J. (1960). The agricultural revolution. *Scientific American*, 203(3), 130–152. DOI: 10.1038/scientificamerican0960-130

Brew, A. (2008). Disciplinary and interdisciplinary affiliations of experienced researchers. *Higher Education*, 56(4), 423–438. DOI: 10.1007/s10734-007-9102-4

Brew, A., & Boud, D. (1995). Teaching and Research: Establishing the Vital Link with Learning. *Higher Education*, 29(3), 261–273. DOI: 10.1007/BF01384493

Brockliss, L. W. (2016). *The University of Oxford: a history*. Oxford University Press. DOI: 10.1093/acprof:oso/9780199243563.001.0001

Broussard, M. (2021). *Artificial unintelligence: How computers misunderstand the world*. MIT Press.

Brouwer, W. (2018). *Algorithmic culture*. Palgrave Macmillan.

Budhwar, P., Malik, A., De Silva, M. T., & Thevisuthan, P. (2022). Artificial Intelligence–Challenges and Opportunities for International HRM: A Review and Research Agenda. *International Journal of Human Resource Management*, 33(6), 1065–1097. DOI: 10.1080/09585192.2022.2035161

Buffington, A., Lange, C., Bakker, C., Nanney, M., Roberts, W., Berge, J., & Loth, K. (2021). The Collaborative Scholarship Intensive: A Research-Intensive Course to Improve Faculty Scholarship. *Family Medicine*, 53(5), 355–358. DOI: 10.22454/FamMed.2021.534614

Buggineni, V. (2023). Utilizing Synthetic Data Generation Techniques to Improve the Availability of Data in Discrete Manufacturing for AI Applications: A Review and Framework.

Bühler, M. M., Jelinek, T., & Nübel, K. (2022). Training and Preparing Tomorrow's Workforce for the Fourth Industrial Revolution. *Education Sciences*, 12(11), 782. DOI: 10.3390/educsci12110782

Cai, C. J., Winter, S., Steiner, D., Wilcox, L., & Terry, M. (2019). "Hello AI": uncovering the onboarding needs of medical practitioners for human-AI collaborative decision-making. *Proceedings of the ACM on Human-computer Interaction, 3*(CSCW), 1-24. DOI: 10.1145/3359206

Ćalušić, M. (2021). *Artificial intelligence and language acquisition* [Master's thesis, University of Split]. Digitalni Akademski Arhivi i Repozitoriji.

Cameron, M., Fogarty-Perry, B., & Piercy, G. (2022). The impacts of the COVID-19 pandemic on higher education students in New Zealand. *Journal of Open. Flexible and Distance Learning*, 26(1), 42–62. DOI: 10.61468/jofdl.v26i1.515

Canagarajah, A. S. (2002). *A geopolitics of academic writing*. University of Pittsburgh Press. DOI: 10.2307/j.ctt5hjn6c

Cardon, P., Fleischmann, C., Aritz, J., Logemann, M., & Heidewald, J. (2023). The challenges and opportunities of AI-assisted writing: Developing AI literacy for the AI age. *Business and Professional Communication Quarterly*, 86(3), 257–295. DOI: 10.1177/23294906231176517

Carnegie Classification of Institutions of Higher Education. (2024). Carnegie Foundation Selects Colleges and Universities for 2024 Community Engagement Classification. January 8, 2024. https://carnegieclassifications.acenet.edu/news/carnegie-2024-community-engagement-classifications/

Castells, M. (2010). The Information Age. *Media Studies. REAd (Porto Alegre)*, 2(7), 152.

Cath, C., Wachter, S., Mittelstadt, B., Taddeo, M., & Floridi, L. (2018). Artificial intelligence and the 'good society': The US, EU, and UK approach. *Science and Engineering Ethics*, 24, 505–528.

Centra, J. A. (1983). Research Productivity and Teaching Effectiveness. *Research in Higher Education*, 18(4), 379–389. DOI: 10.1007/BF00974804

Chafai, N., Bonizzi, L., Botti, S., & Badaoui, B. (2023). Emerging applications of machine learning in genomic medicine and healthcare. *Critical Reviews in Clinical Laboratory Sciences*, 1–24.

Chaka, C. (2023). Detecting AI content in responses generated by ChatGPT, YouChat, and Chatsonic: The case of five AI content detection tools. *Journal of Applied Learning and Teaching*, 6(2).

Chakraborty, T., Reddy K S, U., Naik, S. M., Panja, M., & Manvitha, B. (2024). Ten years of generative adversarial nets (GANs): A survey of the state-of-the-art. *Machine Learning: Science and Technology*, 5(1), 011001. DOI: 10.1088/2632-2153/ad1f77

Chamorro-Premuzic, T. (2023). *I, human: AI, automation, and the quest to reclaim what makes us unique*. Harvard Business Press.

Chapinal-Heras, D., & Díaz-Sánchez, C. (2023). A Review of AI applications in Human Sciences research. *Digital Applications in Archaeology and Cultural Heritage*, 30, 00288. DOI: 10.1016/j.daach.2023.e00288

Chechitelli, A. (2023). AI writing detection update from Turnitin's Chief Product Officer. *Turnitin*. May 23, 2023: https://www.turnitin.com/blog/ai-writing-detection-update-from-turnitins-chief-product-officer

Ciolacu, M. I., Mihailescu, B., Rachbauer, T., Hansen, C., Amza, C. G., & Svasta, P. (2023). Fostering Engineering Education 4.0 Paradigm Facing the Pandemic and VUCA World. *Procedia Computer Science*, 217, 177–186. DOI: 10.1016/j.procs.2022.12.213

Clément, E. (2022). Successful Solution Discovery and Cognitive Flexibility. *Cognitive Flexibility: The Cornerstone of Learning*, 113-142.

Coate, K., Barnett, R., & Williams, G. (2001). Relationships Between Teaching and Research in Higher Education in England. *Higher Education Quarterly*, 55(2), 158–174. DOI: 10.1111/1468-2273.00180

Cominelli, L., Hoegen, G., & De Rossi, D. (2021). Abel: Integrating Humanoid Body, Emotions, and Time Perception to Investigate Social Interaction and Human Cognition. *Applied Sciences (Basel, Switzerland)*, 11(3), 1070. DOI: 10.3390/app11031070

Cooper, T. (2022). *Ancestors and Algorithms: Ethnocomputing AI with African & African Diasporic Heritage* (Doctoral dissertation).

Cremer, C. Z. (2021). Deep limitations? Examining expert disagreement over deep learning. *Progress in Artificial Intelligence*, 10(4), 449–464. DOI: 10.1007/s13748-021-00239-1

Dang, H., Brudy, F., Fitzmaurice, G., & Anderson, F. (2023, October). WorldSmith: Iterative and Expressive Prompting for World Building with a Generative AI. In *Proceedings of the 36th Annual ACM Symposium on User Interface Software and Technology* (pp. 1-17). DOI: 10.1145/3586183.3606772

Dao, A., Pegg, S., Okland, S., Green, H., & Kujawa, A. (2024). Longitudinal associations between sense of belonging, imposter syndrome, and first-year college students' mental health. *Journal of American College Health*, 1–10. DOI: 10.1080/07448481.2024.2355162

de Carvalho, P. A. C. (2019). *Emojar: Collecting and Reliving Memorable and Emotionally Impactful Digital Content* (Doctoral dissertation, Universidade de Lisboa (Portugal)).

De Vries, J. (1994). The industrial revolution and the industrious revolution. *The Journal of Economic History*, 54(2), 249–270. DOI: 10.1017/S0022050700014467

Deane, P. M. (1979). *The first industrial revolution*. Cambridge University Press.

Dehouche, N. (2021). Plagiarism in the age of massive Generative Pre-trained Transformers (GPT-3). *Ethics in Science and Environmental Politics*, 21, 17–23. DOI: 10.3354/esep00195

DelSignore, P. (2022). The New Age of Creative AI Began in 2022. *Medium*. December 23. Retreived from: https://medium.com/predict/the-new-age-of-creative-ai-began-in-2022-ece07bb93350

Denny, P., Leinonen, J., Prather, J., Luxton-Reilly, A., Amarouche, T., Becker, B. A., & Reeves, B. N. (2023). Prompt Problems: A new programming exercise for the generative AI era. *arXiv preprint arXiv:2311.05943.*

Dergaa, I., Chamari, K., Zmijewski, P., & Saad, H. B. (2023). From human writing to artificial intelligence generated text: Examining the prospects and potential threats of ChatGPT in academic writing. *Biology of Sport*, 40(2), 615–622. DOI: 10.5114/biolsport.2023.125623

Detweiler, R. A. (2021). *The Evidence Liberal Arts Needs: Lives of Consequence, Inquiry, and Accomplishment*. MIT Press. DOI: 10.7551/mitpress/13954.001.0001

Devi, K. V., Manjula, V., & Pattewar, T. (2023). *ChatGPT: Comprehensive study on generative AI tool*. Academic Guru Publishing House.

Devlin, J., Chang, M. W., Lee, K., & Toutanova, K. (2019). BERT: Pre-training of Deep Bidirectional Transformers for Language Understanding. *arXiv preprint arXiv:1810.04805.*

Diakopoulos, N. (2014). *Algorithmic accountability reporting: On the investigation of black boxes*. Columbia University.

Diakopoulos, N. (2019). *Automating the news: How algorithms are rewriting the media*. Harvard University Press. DOI: 10.4159/9780674239302

Doi, C., Lucky, S., & Rubin, J. E. (2022). Open educational resources in the time of COVID-19: Two case studies of open video design in the remote learning environment. *KULA*, 6(1), 1–15.

Dreher, M. (2021). Turning principles of action into practice: Examining the National Council of Teachers of Mathematics' reform rhetoric. *Arguing with Numbers: The Intersections of Rhetoric and Mathematics*, 16, 252–280. DOI: 10.5325/j.ctv1mvw8dg.13

Duan, Y., Edwards, J. S., & Dwivedi, Y. K. (2019). Artificial Intelligence for Decision Making in the Era of Big Data–Evolution, Challenges and Research Agenda. *International Journal of Information Management*, 48, 63–71. DOI: 10.1016/j.ijinfomgt.2019.01.021

Dwork, C., & Roth, A. (2014). The algorithmic foundations of differential privacy. *Foundations and Trends® in Theoretical Computer Science, 9*(3–4), 211-407.

Easterbrook, G. (2024). How financial services firms can build a generative AI assistant. *Forbes*. February 14, 2024. Retrieved: https://www.forbes.com/sites/granteasterbrook/2024/02/14/how-financial-services-firms-can-build-a-generative-ai-assistant/?sh=18eccfb577a0

Eaton, S. E. (2024). Academic and research integrity as transdisciplinary fields of scholarship and professional practice. In *Second handbook of academic integrity* (pp. 1633–1650). Springer Nature Switzerland. DOI: 10.1007/978-3-031-54144-5_165

Elmoutanna, N. & Moti, N. (2022). Soft skills from university to workplace: A literature review. *International Journal of Accounting, Finance, Auditing, Management and Economics, 3*(5-1), 187-198.

English, L. D., & Gainsburg, J. (2015). Problem solving in a 21st-century mathematics curriculum. In *Handbook of international research in mathematics education* (pp. 313–335). Routledge. DOI: 10.4324/9780203448946-20

Ermakova, E. P., & Frolova, E. E. (2021). Using Artificial Intelligence in Dispute Resolution. In *Smart Technologies for the Digitisation of Industry: Entrepreneurial Environment* (pp. 131–142). Springer Singapore.

Eslami, M., Rickman, A., Vaccaro, K., Aleyasen, A., Vuong, A., Karahalios, K., & Sandvig, C. (2015, April). "I always assumed that I wasn't really that close to [her]" Reasoning about Invisible Algorithms in News Feeds. In *Proceedings of the 33rd annual ACM conference on human factors in computing systems* (pp. 153-162).

Esplugas, M. (2023). The use of artificial intelligence (AI) to enhance academic communication, education and research: A balanced approach. [European Volume]. *The Journal of Hand Surgery*, 48(8), 819–822.

Fathi, K., & Palhang, M. (2018, September). Evaluation of Using Neural Networks on Variety of Agents and Playability of Games. In *2018 International Conference on Artificial Intelligence and Data Processing (IDAP)* (pp. 1-8). IEEE. DOI: 10.1109/IDAP.2018.8620880

Feezell, J. T., Wagner, J. K., & Conroy, M. (2021). Exploring the effects of algorithm-driven news sources on political behavior and polarization. *Computers in Human Behavior*, 116, 106626. DOI: 10.1016/j.chb.2020.106626

Feltz, D., Peretti, K. K., & Austin, A. (2022). Privacy, cyber & data strategy advisory: AI regulation in the U.S.: What's coming, and what companies need to do in 2023. *Alston & Bird.* December 9, 2022. Retrieved: https://www.alston.com/en/insights/publications/2022/12/ai-regulation-in-the-us

Fenton, A. L., & Gralla, C. (2020). Student plagiarism in higher education: A typology and remedial framework for a globalized era. *Academic Misconduct and Plagiarism,* 109.

Fernández, S., Adarve, R., Pérez, M., Rybarczyk, M., & Borrajo, D. (2006). Planning for an AI Based Virtual Agents Game. In *Proceedings of the Workshop AI Planning for Computer Games and Synthetic Characters in the ICAPS.*

Feuerriegel, S., Hartmann, J., Janiesch, C., & Zschech, P. (2024). Generative ai. *Business & Information Systems Engineering*, 66(1), 111–126. DOI: 10.1007/s12599-023-00834-7

Filgueiras, F. (2023). Artificial intelligence and education governance. *Education, Citizenship and Social Justice*, •••, 17461979231160674.

Finnegan, D. E., & Gamson, Z. F. (1996). Disciplinary Adaptations to Research Culture in Comprehensive Institutions. *Review of Higher Education*, 19(2), 141–177. DOI: 10.1353/rhe.1996.0028

Foster, N. F., & Gibbons, S. (2005). Understanding Faculty to Improve Content Recruitment for Institutional Repositories. *Online Submission*, 11(1).

Foucault, M. (1969). *What is an Author?* Gilyard, K. (2016). Composition and Cornel West: Notes toward a deep multiculturality. *College Composition and Communication*, 57(3), 397–416.

Francke, E., & Alexander, B. (2019). The potential influence of artificial intelligence on plagiarism a higher education perspective. In *Proc European Conference on the Impact of Artificial Intelligence and Robotics.* EM Normandie Business School.

Fraser, D. W., Marder, T. J., deBettencourt, L. U., Myers, L. A., Kalymon, K. M., & Harrell, R. M. (2020). Using a mixed-reality environment to train special educators working with students with autism spectrum disorder to implement discrete trial teaching. *Focus on Autism and Other Developmental Disabilities*, 35(1), 3–14. DOI: 10.1177/1088357619844696

Frederick, J., & Wolff-Eisenberg, C. (2020). Academic library strategy and budgeting during the COVID-19 pandemic.

Frey, C. B., & Osborne, M. A. (2017). The future of employment: How susceptible are jobs to computerisation? *Technological Forecasting and Social Change*, 114, 254–280. DOI: 10.1016/j.techfore.2016.08.019

Friedman, H. H., & Friedman, L. W. (2018). Does growing the number of academic departments improve the quality of higher education? *Psychosociological Issues in Human Resource Management*, 6(1), 96–114. DOI: 10.22381/PIHRM6120184

Fry, H. (2018). *Hello World: Being Human in the Age of Algorithms*. W.W. Norton & Company.

Fui-Hoon Nah, F., Zheng, R., Cai, J., Siau, K., & Chen, L. (2023). Generative AI and ChatGPT: Applications, challenges, and AI-human collaboration. *Journal of Information Technology Case and Application Research*, 25(3), 277–304. DOI: 10.1080/15228053.2023.2233814

Gabriele, L., Marocco, D., Bertacchini, F., Pantano, P., & Bilotta, E. (2017). An educational robotics lab to investigate cognitive strategies and to foster learning in an arts and humanities course degree. *International Journal of Online Engineering*, 13(4), 7–19. DOI: 10.3991/ijoe.v13i04.6962

Gamoran, A. (2023). Advancing institutional change to encourage faculty participation in research-practice partnerships. *Educational Policy*, 37(1), 31–55. DOI: 10.1177/08959048221131564

Gao, Y., Li, R., Caskey, J., Dligach, D., Miller, T., Churpek, M. M., & Afshar, M. (2023). Leveraging a medical knowledge graph into large language models for diagnosis prediction. *arXiv preprint arXiv:2308.14321.*

Garon, J. (2023). A Practical Introduction to Generative AI, Synthetic Media, and the Messages Found in the Latest Medium. *Synthetic Media, and the Messages Found in the Latest Medium* (March 14, 2023).

Garzón, J. (2021). An overview of twenty-five years of augmented reality in education. *Multimodal Technologies and Interaction*, 5(7), 37. DOI: 10.3390/mti5070037

Gikas, J., & Grant, M. M. (2013). Mobile computing devices in higher education: Student perspectives on learning with cellphones, smartphones & social media. *The Internet and Higher Education*, 19, 18–26. DOI: 10.1016/j.iheduc.2013.06.002

Gillespie, T. (2014). The relevance of algorithms. *Media technologies: Essays on communication, materiality, and society, 167*(2014), 167.

Gill, S. S., & Kaur, R. (2023). ChatGPT: Vision and challenges. *Internet of Things and Cyber-Physical Systems*, 3, 262–271. DOI: 10.1016/j.iotcps.2023.05.004

Gipp, B., Meuschke, N., & Gernandt, A. (2020). Citations and the evolution of scientific knowledge. *The Journal of Documentation*, 76(4), 923–944.

Goleman, D. (2001). Emotional intelligence: Issues in paradigm building. *The emotionally intelligent workplace, 13*, 26.

Gong, X., Wu, Y., Ye, Z., & Liu, X. (2018). Artificial intelligence course design: iSTREAM-based visual cognitive smart vehicles. In *2018 IEEE Intelligent Vehicles Symposium (IV)* (pp. 1731-1735). IEEE. DOI: 10.1109/IVS.2018.8500457

González-Pérez, L. I., & Ramírez-Montoya, M. S. (2022). Components of Education 4.0 in 21st century skills frameworks: Systematic review. *Sustainability (Basel)*, 14(3), 1493. DOI: 10.3390/su14031493

Goodfellow, I., Bengio, Y., & Courville, A. (2016). *Deep learning*. MIT press.

Goodfellow, I., Pouget-Abadie, J., Mirza, M., Xu, B., Warde-Farley, D., Ozair, S., & Bengio, Y. (2014). Generative adversarial nets. *Advances in Neural Information Processing Systems*, 27.

Gran, A. B., Booth, P., & Bucher, T. (2021). To be or not to be algorithm aware: A question of a new digital divide? *Information Communication and Society*, 24(12), 1779–1796. DOI: 10.1080/1369118X.2020.1736124

Greenblatt, S. (2005). *Will in the world: How Shakespeare became Shakespeare*. WW Norton & Company.

Greenstein, L. M. (2012). *Assessing 21st century skills: A guide to evaluating mastery and authentic learning*. Corwin Press.

Grudecki, M. (2021). The Genesis of the Prohibition of Corporal Punishment against Minors and the Consequences of Its Application. *Studia Iuridica Lublinensia*, 30(4), 241–258. DOI: 10.17951/sil.2021.30.4.241-258

Guleria, A., Krishan, K., Sharma, V., & Kanchan, T. (2023). ChatGPT: Ethical concerns and challenges in academics and research. *Journal of Infection in Developing Countries*, 17(09), 1292–1299. DOI: 10.3855/jidc.18738

Gull, A., Dilawar, S., & Sher, F. (2023). Data-driven Artificial Intelligence at the Crossroads: Investigating the Role of Affective Job Insecurity in the relationship between Artificial Intelligence Identity Threat and Employee Well-Being. *The Asian Bulletin of Big Data Management*, 3(1), 18–34. DOI: 10.62019/abbdm.v3i1.35

Gunnarsson, J., Kulesza, W. J., & Pettersson, A. (2014). Teaching international students how to avoid plagiarism: Librarians and faculty in collaboration. *Journal of Academic Librarianship*, 40(3-4), 413–417. DOI: 10.1016/j.acalib.2014.04.006

Hadi, M. U., Qureshi, R., Shah, A., Irfan, M., Zafar, A., Shaikh, M. B., & Mirjalili, S. (2023). A survey on large language models: Applications, challenges, limitations, and practical usage. *Authorea Preprints.* DOI: 10.36227/techrxiv.23589741.v1

Haldorai, A., Ramu, A., & Suriya, M. (2020). Organization internet of things (IoTs): Supervised, unsupervised, and reinforcement learning. In *Business Intelligence for Enterprise Internet of Things* (pp. 27–53). Springer International Publishing. DOI: 10.1007/978-3-030-44407-5_2

Hartley, J. (2008). *Academic writing and publishing: A practical handbook.* Routledge. DOI: 10.4324/9780203927984

Hassani, H., & Silva, E. S. (2023). The role of ChatGPT in data science: how ai-assisted conversational interfaces are revolutionizing the field. *Big data and cognitive computing, 7*(2), 62.

Haze, K. (2023). Empowering Educational Creativity with Adobe Express. *The School Librarian*, 71(3), 24–24.

Hazucha, B. (2022). Artificial Intelligence and Cultural Production: Possible Impacts on Creativity and Copyright Law. *Available atSSRN* 4028106. DOI: 10.2139/ssrn.4028106

Heston, T. F., & Khun, C. (2023). Prompt engineering in medical education. *International Medical Education*, 2(3), 198–205. DOI: 10.3390/ime2030019

He, W., Zhang, Z. J., & Li, W. (2021). Information technology solutions, challenges, and suggestions for tackling the COVID-19 pandemic. *International Journal of Information Management*, 57, 102287. DOI: 10.1016/j.ijinfomgt.2020.102287

Hill, Y., Lomas, L., & MacGregor, J. (2003). Students' Perceptions of Quality in Higher Education. *Quality Assurance in Education*, 11(1), 15–20. DOI: 10.1108/09684880310462047

Ho, A., Besiroglu, T., Erdil, E. Owen, D., Rahman, R., Guo, Z., Atkinson, D., Thompson, N. & Sevilla, J. (2024). Algorithmic progress in language models. *arXiv:2403.05812*

Ho, C., Azmi Murad, M. A., Doraisamy, S., & Abdul Kadir, R. (2014). Extracting lexical and phrasal paraphrases: A review of the literature. *Artificial Intelligence Review*, 42(4), 851–894. DOI: 10.1007/s10462-012-9357-8

Holmgard, C., Liapis, A., Togelius, J., & Yannakakis, G. N. (2014). Generative Agents for Player Decision Modeling in Games. *9th International Conference on the Foundations of Digital Games,* Fort Lauderdale. 1-8.

Holzinger, A., Keiblinger, K., Holub, P., Zatloukal, K., & Müller, H. (2023). AI for Life: Trends in Artificial Intelligence for Biotechnology. *New Biotechnology*, 74, 16–24. DOI: 10.1016/j.nbt.2023.02.001

Hommel, B. E., Ruppel, R., & Zacher, H. (2022). Assessment of cognitive flexibility in personnel selection: Validity and acceptance of a gamified version of the Wisconsin Card Sorting Test. *International Journal of Selection and Assessment*, 30(1), 126–144. DOI: 10.1111/ijsa.12362

Horner, B., Lu, M., Royster, J. J., & Trimbur, J. (2011). Language difference in writing: Toward a translingual approach. *College English*, 73(3), 303–321. DOI: 10.58680/ce201113403

Howell, N., Arner, D., & Buckley, R. P. (2021). Blockchain and the Future of Intellectual Property. *Intellectual Property Quarterly*, 2, 123–142.

Huh, J. H., & Seo, Y. S. (2019). Understanding Edge Computing: Engineering Evolution with Artificial Intelligence. *IEEE Access : Practical Innovations, Open Solutions*, 7, 164229–164245. DOI: 10.1109/ACCESS.2019.2945338

Hunkenschroer, A. L., & Luetge, C. (2022). Ethics of AI-enabled recruiting and selection: A review and research agenda. *Journal of Business Ethics*, 178(4), 977–1007. DOI: 10.1007/s10551-022-05049-6

Hutson, J., & Olsen, T. (2022). Virtual Reality and Learning: A Case Study of Experiential Pedagogy in Art History. *Journal of Intelligent Learning Systems and Applications,14*(4). https://www.scirp.org/journal/paperinformation.aspx?paperid=120925

Hutson, J., & Rains, T. J. (2024). Microsoft Co-Pilot Adoption Study [Data set]. Lindenwood University. https://www.brookings.edu/articles/protecting-privacy-in-an-ai-driven-world/

Hutson, J. (2023). The Role of Collaborative Authorship in Decentered Research Innovation: An Interdisciplinary, Interdepartmental, and Interinstitutional Model to Accelerate Research Culture in Teaching Institutions. *Information, Medium & Society. Journal of Publishing Studies*, 21(1), 7–24. DOI: 10.18848/2691-1507/CGP/v21i01/7-24

Hutson, J., & Ceballos, J. (2023). Rethinking education in the age of AI: The importance of developing durable skills in the Industry 4.0. *Journal of Information Economics*, 1(2), 26–35. DOI: 10.58567/jie01020002

Hutson, J., Jeevanjee, T., Vander Graaf, V., Lively, J., Weber, J., Weir, G., & Edele, S. (2022). Artificial Intelligence and the Disruption of Higher Education: Strategies for Integrations across Disciplines. *Creative Education*, 13(12), 3953–3980. DOI: 10.4236/ce.2022.1312253

Hutson, J., & Plate, D. (2023). *Human-AI Collaboration for Smart Education: Reframing Applied Learning to Support Metacognition*. IntechOpen.

Hutson, J., & Rains, T. (2024). *AI Institutional Adoption Study* [Data set]. Lindenwood University.

Hutson, P. (2024). Embracing the Irreplaceable: The Role of Neurodiversity in Cultivating Human-AI Symbiosis in Education. *International Journal of Emerging and Disruptive Innovation in Education: VISIONARIUM*, 2(1), 5. DOI: 10.62608/2831-3550.1020

Hykes, S. (2013). Docker: Automating the deployment of Linux applications inside software containers. *Linux Journal*, 2013(239), 2.

Ison, D. C. (2018). An empirical analysis of differences in plagiarism among world cultures. *Journal of Higher Education Policy and Management*, 40(4), 291–304. DOI: 10.1080/1360080X.2018.1479949

Jacelon, C. S., Zucker, D. M., Staccarini, J. M., & Henneman, E. A. (2003). Peer Mentoring for Tenure-Track Faculty. *Journal of Professional Nursing*, 19(6), 335–338. DOI: 10.1016/S8755-7223(03)00131-5

Jamali, A., Bhutto, A., Khaskhely, M., & Sethar, W. (2022). Impact of Leadership Styles on Faculty Performance: Moderating Role of Organizational Culture in Higher Education. *Management Science Letters*, 12(1), 1–20. DOI: 10.5267/j.msl.2021.8.005

Jambeck, K. K., & Winder, B. D. (1990). Vygotsky, Werner, and English Composition: Paradigms for Thinking and Writing. *Writing on the Edge*, 1(2), 6–79.

Jayman, M., Glazzard, J., & Rose, A. (2022, August). Tipping Point: The Staff Wellbeing Crisis in Higher Education. [). Frontiers.]. *Frontiers in Education*, 7, 929335. DOI: 10.3389/feduc.2022.929335

Jeste, D. V., Graham, S. A., Nguyen, T. T., Depp, C. A., Lee, E. E., & Kim, H. C. (2020). Beyond Artificial Intelligence: Exploring Artificial Wisdom. *International Psychogeriatrics*, 32(8), 993–1001. DOI: 10.1017/S1041610220000927

Ji, Z., Lee, N., Frieske, R., Yu, T., Su, D., Xu, Y., Ishii, E., Bang, Y. J., Madotto, A., & Fung, P. (2023). Survey of hallucination in natural language generation. *ACM Computing Surveys*, 55(12), 1–38. DOI: 10.1145/3571730

Jones, R. (2018). Social Media, Digital Platforms, and the Transformation of Rhetorical Engagement. *Journal of Communication*, 68(3), 453–475.

Jones, S. (1995). *Understanding community in the information age*. Sage.

Jonsson, M., & Tholander, J. (2022, June). Cracking the code: Co-coding with AI in creative programming education. In *Proceedings of the 14th Conference on Creativity and Cognition* (pp. 5-14). DOI: 10.1145/3527927.3532801

Joseph, S. M. (2008). *Shakespeare's use of the arts of Language*. Paul Dry Books.

Joshi, I., Grimmer, M., Rathgeb, C., Busch, C., Bremond, F., & Dantcheva, A. (2024). Synthetic data in human analysis: A survey. *IEEE Transactions on Pattern Analysis and Machine Intelligence*, 46(7), 4957–4976. DOI: 10.1109/TPAMI.2024.3362821

Kaebnick, G. E., Magnus, D. C., Kao, A., Hosseini, M., Resnik, D., Dubljević, V., Rentmeester, C., Gordijn, B., & Cherry, M. J. (2023). Editors' statement on the responsible use of generative AI technologies in scholarly journal publishing. *Medicine, Health Care, and Philosophy*, 26(4), 499–503. DOI: 10.1007/s11019-023-10176-6

Kafai, Y. B., Proctor, C., Cai, S., Castro, F., Delaney, V., DesPortes, K., . . . Rosé, C. P. (2024). What Does it Mean to be Literate in the Time of AI? Different Perspectives on Learning and Teaching AI Literacies in K-12 Education. In *Proceedings of the 18th International Conference of the Learning Sciences-ICLS 2024* (pp. 1856-1862). International Society of the Learning Sciences. DOI: 10.22318/icls2024.875203

Kamalov, F., Santandreu Calonge, D., & Gurrib, I. (2023). New era of artificial intelligence in education: Towards a sustainable multifaceted revolution. *Sustainability (Basel)*, 15(16), 12451. DOI: 10.3390/su151612451

Kang, E. S., & Lee, J. M. (2022). Artificial Intelligence Liberal Arts Curriculum Design for Non-Computer Majors. *Journal of Digital Contents Society*, 23(1), 57–66. DOI: 10.9728/dcs.2022.23.1.57

Kellner, D., & Gennaro, S. (2022). Critical Theory and the Transformation of Education in the New Millennium. In *The Palgrave Handbook on Critical Theories of Education* (pp. 21–45). Springer International Publishing. DOI: 10.1007/978-3-030-86343-2_2

Kennedy, G. A. (1993). Aristotle" On rhetoric": A theory of civic discourse. *Philosophy & Rhetoric*, 26(4).

Kerridge, E. (2013). *The agricultural revolution*. Routledge. DOI: 10.4324/9781315019888

Khachane, M. Y. (2017). Organ-Based Medical Image Classification Using Support Vector Machine. *International Journal of Synthetic Emotions*, 8(1), 18–30. DOI: 10.4018/IJSE.2017010102

Khalifa, M., & Albadawy, M. (2024). Using artificial intelligence in academic writing and research: An essential productivity tool. *Computer Methods and Programs in Biomedicine Update*, 5, 100145. DOI: 10.1016/j.cmpbup.2024.100145

Khaliq, A., Aziz, S., Akram, M., & Mahmood, W. (2023). The influence of constructivist strategies in writing the foreign language on the learners achievements at higher secondary level. *Voyage Journal of Educational Studies*, 3(2), 281–289. DOI: 10.58622/vjes.v3i2.63

Khan, M. A. (2017). Achieving an appropriate balance between teaching and research in institutions of higher education: An exploratory study. *International Journal of Information and Education Technology (IJIET)*, 7(5), 341–349. DOI: 10.18178/ijiet.2017.7.5.892

Khan, W., Ghazanfar, M. A., Azam, M. A., Karami, A., Alyoubi, K. H., & Alfakeeh, A. S. (2020). Stock market prediction using machine learning classifiers and social media. *Journal of Ambient Intelligence and Humanized Computing*, 1–24.

Khezr, P., & Mohan, V. (2022). The Vexing but Persistent Problem of Authorship Misconduct in Research. *Research Policy*, 51(3), 104466. DOI: 10.1016/j.respol.2021.104466

Khosrowi, D., Finn, F., & Clark, E. (2023, August). Diffusing the Creator: Attributing Credit for Generative AI Outputs. In *Proceedings of the 2023 AAAI/ACM Conference on AI, Ethics, and Society* (pp. 890-900). DOI: 10.1145/3600211.3604716

Kim, B., Park, J., & Suh, J. (2020). Transparency and accountability in AI decision support: Explaining and visualizing convolutional neural networks for text information. *Decision Support Systems*, 134, 113302. DOI: 10.1016/j.dss.2020.113302

Kinneavy, J. L. (2002). Kairos in classical and modern rhetorical theory. Rhetoric and kairos: *Essays in history, theory, and praxis,* 58-76.

Kleebayoon, A., & Wiwanitkit, V. (2023). ChatGPT and Artificial Intelligence. *Journal of Perianesthesia Nursing*, 38(6), 840. DOI: 10.1016/j.jopan.2023.07.005

Knight, S., & Schiff, A. (2020). Artificial Intelligence and the Future of Rhetorical Analysis. *Rhetoric Review*, 39(4), 444–459.

Knop, M., Weber, S., Mueller, M., & Niehaves, B. (2022). Human factors and technological characteristics influencing the interaction of medical professionals with artificial intelligence–enabled clinical decision support systems: Literature review. *JMIR Human Factors*, 9(1), e28639. DOI: 10.2196/28639

Kobayashi, M., & Takeda, K. (2000). Information retrieval on the web. *ACM Computing Surveys*, 32(2), 144–173. DOI: 10.1145/358923.358934

Koch, A., Nafziger, J., & Nielsen, H. S. (2015). Behavioral Economics of Education. *Journal of Economic Behavior & Organization*, 115, 3–17. DOI: 10.1016/j.jebo.2014.09.005

Kogan, M. (2000). Higher education communities and academic identity. *Higher Education Quarterly*, 54(3), 207–216. DOI: 10.1111/1468-2273.00156

Koraishi, O. (2023). Teaching English in the age of AI: Embracing ChatGPT to optimize EFL materials and assessment. *Language Education and Technology, 3*(1).

Kordzadeh, N., & Ghasemaghaei, M. (2022). Algorithmic bias: Review, synthesis, and future research directions. *European Journal of Information Systems*, 31(3), 388–409. DOI: 10.1080/0960085X.2021.1927212

Krajcik, J., Schneider, B., Miller, E. A., Chen, I. C., Bradford, L., Baker, Q., Bartz, K., Miller, C., Li, T., Codere, S., & Peek-Brown, D. (2023). Assessing the effect of project-based learning on science learning in elementary schools. *American Educational Research Journal*, 60(1), 70–102. DOI: 10.3102/00028312221129247

Krause, S. (2000). "Among the Greatest Benefactors of Mankind": What the Success of Chalkboards Tells Us about the Future of Computers in the Classroom. *The Journal of the Midwest Modern Language Association*, 33(2), 6–16. DOI: 10.2307/1315198

Kreps, D., & Kimppa, K. (2020). *Theorizing about the impact of surveillance technologies.*

Kulage, K. M., Larson, E. L., & Begg, M. D. (2011). Sharing Facilities and Administrative (F&A) Cost Recovery to Facilitate Interdisciplinary Research. *Academic Medicine*, 86(3), 394–401. DOI: 10.1097/ACM.0b013e31820924ea

Kutieleh, S., & Adiningrum, T. S. (2011). How different are we? Understanding and managing plagiarism between East and West. *Journal of Academic Language and Learning*, 5(2), A88–A98.

Labajová, L. (2023). The state of AI: Exploring the perceptions, credibility, and trustworthiness of the users towards AI-Generated Content.

Landa-Blanco, M., Flores, M. A., & Mercado, M. (2023). *Human vs. AI authorship: Does it matter in evaluating creative writing? A pilot study using ChatGPT.*

Lango, L. (2024). Is this the best way to invest in the AI gold rush? *Investor Place*. January 10, 2024. Retrieved: https://investorplace.com/hypergrowthinvesting/2024/01/is-this-the-best-way-to-invest-in-the-ai-gold-rush/

Larsson, S., & Heintz, F. (2020). Transparency in artificial intelligence. *Internet Policy Review*, 9(2). Advance online publication. DOI: 10.14763/2020.2.1469

Latif, E., Mai, G., Nyaaba, M., Wu, X., Liu, N., Lu, G., . . . Zhai, X. (2023). Artificial General Intelligence (AGI) for Education. *arXiv preprint arXiv:2304.12479.*

Leask, B. (2006). Plagiarism, cultural diversity and metaphor—Implications for academic staff development. *Assessment & Evaluation in Higher Education*, 31(2), 183–199. DOI: 10.1080/02602930500262486

Lee, H. P. H., Gao, L., Yang, S., Forlizzi, J., & Das, S. (2024). "I Don't Know If We're Doing Good. I Don't Know If We're Doing Bad": Investigating How Practitioners Scope, Motivate, and Conduct Privacy Work When Developing AI Products. *USENIX Security Symposium.*

Lee, H. (2023). The Rise of ChatGPT: Exploring Its Potential in Medical Education. *Anatomical Sciences Education.*

Lee, K. J. (2022). Adaptive expertise, career adaptability, and career success of R&D personnel. *Technology Analysis and Strategic Management*, 1–13.

Lepri, B., Oliver, N., Letouzé, E., Pentland, A., & Vinck, P. (2018). Fair, transparent, and accountable algorithmic decision-making processes: The premise, the proposed solutions, and the open challenges. *Philosophy & Technology*, 31(4), 611–627. DOI: 10.1007/s13347-017-0279-x

Lin, C. C., Huang, A. Y., & Lu, O. H. (2023). Artificial intelligence in intelligent tutoring systems toward sustainable education: A systematic review. *Smart Learning Environments*, 10(1), 41. DOI: 10.1186/s40561-023-00260-y

Li, R. (2024). A "Dance of storytelling": Dissonances between substance and style in collaborative storytelling with AI. *Computers and Composition*, 71, 102825. DOI: 10.1016/j.compcom.2024.102825

Liu, Y., Han, T., Ma, S., Zhang, J., Yang, Y., Tian, J., . . . Ge, B. (2023). Summary of ChatGPT/GPT-4 Research and Perspective Towards the Future of Large Language Models. *arXiv preprint arXiv:2304.01852.*

Liu, J., Togelius, J., Pérez-Liébana, D., & Lucas, S. M. (2017, June). Evolving Game Skill-Depth Using General Video Game AI Agents. In *2017 IEEE Congress on Evolutionary Computation (CEC)* (pp. 2299-2307). IEEE. DOI: 10.1109/CEC.2017.7969583

Liu-Thompkins, Y., Okazaki, S., & Li, H. (2022). Artificial Empathy in Marketing Interactions: Bridging the Human-AI Gap in Affective and Social Customer Experience. *Journal of the Academy of Marketing Science*, 50(6), 1198–1218. DOI: 10.1007/s11747-022-00892-5

Liu, W. (2023). Literature survey of multi-track music generation model based on generative confrontation network in intelligent composition. *The Journal of Supercomputing*, 79(6), 6560–6582. DOI: 10.1007/s11227-022-04914-5

Liu, X. M., & Murphy, D. (2020). A Multi-Faceted Approach for Trustworthy AI in Cybersecurity. *Journal of Strategic Innovation & Sustainability*, 15(6).

Liu, Y., Han, T., Ma, S., Zhang, J., Yang, Y., Tian, J., He, H., Li, A., He, M., Liu, Z., Wu, Z., Zhao, L., Zhu, D., Li, X., Qiang, N., Shen, D., Liu, T., & Ge, B. (2023). Summary of chatgpt-related research and perspective towards the future of large language models. *Meta-Radiology*, 1(2), 100017. DOI: 10.1016/j.metrad.2023.100017

Lively, J., & Hutson, J. (2024). The role of student motivation in integrating AI into web design education: A longitudinal study. *Forum for Education Studies*. DOI: 10.59400/fes.v2i2.1242

Li, Y., Jiang, Y., Tian, D., Hu, L., Lu, H., & Yuan, Z. (2019). AI-Enabled Emotion Communication. *IEEE Network*, 33(6), 15–21. DOI: 10.1109/MNET.001.1900070

Lund, B. D., Wang, T., Mannuru, N. R., Nie, B., Shimray, S., & Wang, Z. (2023). ChatGPT and a new academic reality: Artificial Intelligence-written research papers and the ethics of the large language models in scholarly publishing. *Journal of the Association for Information Science and Technology*, 74(5), 570–581. DOI: 10.1002/asi.24750

Lwakatare, L. E., Crnkovic, I., & Bosch, J. (2020, September). *DevOps for AI–Challenges in Development of AI-enabled Applications. In 2020 international conference on software, telecommunications and computer networks (SoftCOM)*. IEEE.

Mabe, K., & Bwalya, K. J. (2022). Critical soft skills for information and knowledge management practitioners in the fourth industrial revolution. *South African Journal of Information Management*, 24(1), 1–11. DOI: 10.4102/sajim.v24i1.1519

Magness, J., & Mitchell, M. M. (2022). Religious Studies & the Imagined Boundaries of the Humanities. *Daedalus*, 151(3), 166–179. DOI: 10.1162/daed_a_01936

Magooda, A., Helyar, A., Jackson, K., Sullivan, D., Atalla, C., Sheng, E., . . . Chen, M. (2023). A Framework for Automated Measurement of Responsible AI Harms in Generative AI Applications. *arXiv preprint arXiv:2310.17750.*

Mahmud, H., Islam, A. N., Ahmed, S. I., & Smolander, K. (2022). What Influences Algorithmic Decision-Making? A Systematic Literature Review on Algorithm Aversion. *Technological Forecasting and Social Change*, 175, 121390. DOI: 10.1016/j.techfore.2021.121390

Makarova, M. (2019). Factors of academic misconduct in a cross-cultural perspective and the role of integrity systems. *Journal of Academic Ethics*, 17(1), 51–71. DOI: 10.1007/s10805-019-9323-z

Maravilla, H., & Scott, C. (2024). A (I) ccess to Justice: How AI and Ethics Opinions Approving Limited Scope Representation Support Legal Market Consolidation. *Georgia State University Law Review*, 40(4), 957.

Marcos, S., García Peñalvo, F. J., & Vázquez Ingelmo, A. (2021, October). Emotional AI in Healthcare: A p ilot architecture proposal to merge emotion recognition tools. In *Ninth International Conference on Technological Ecosystems for Enhancing Multiculturality (TEEM'21)* (pp. 342-349). DOI: 10.1145/3486011.3486472

Massey, J. W. (2020). *The Challenges of Neoliberalism to the Democratic Promises of Higher Education* (Doctoral dissertation, The University of North Carolina at Greensboro).

Matos, J. F., Piedade, J., Freitas, A., Pedro, N., Dorotea, N., Pedro, A., & Galego, C. (2023). Teaching and Learning Research Methodologies in Education: A Systematic Literature Review. *Education Sciences*, 13(2), 173. DOI: 10.3390/educsci13020173

Mattila, M., Yrjölä, M., & Hautamäki, P. (2021). Digital transformation of business-to-business sales: What needs to be unlearned? *Journal of Personal Selling & Sales Management*, 41(2), 113–129. DOI: 10.1080/08853134.2021.1916396

Mauk, C. E. (2003). *Undershoot in two modalities: Evidence from fast speech and fast signing*. The University of Texas at Austin.

Maxwell, L. D., & Ball, A. L. (2010). What is Scholarship? Faculty Knowledge and Perceptions of the Scholarship of Teaching and Learning. *Journal of Agricultural Education*, 51(2), 127–138. DOI: 10.5032/jae.2010.02127

McClure, C. R., & Jaeger, P. T. (2009). *Public libraries and Internet service roles: Measuring and maximizing Internet services*. American Library Association.

McGowan, A., Gui, Y., Dobbs, M., Shuster, S., Cotter, M., Selloni, A., Goodman, M., Srivastava, A., Cecchi, G. A., & Corcoran, C. M. (2023). ChatGPT and Bard exhibit spontaneous citation fabrication during psychiatry literature search. *Psychiatry Research*, 326, 115334. DOI: 10.1016/j.psychres.2023.115334

McKeown, J. S., Bista, K., & Chan, R. Y. (2022). *Global Higher Education During COVID-19: Policy, Society, and Technology*. STAR Scholars.

McNair, T. B., Albertine, S., McDonald, N., Major, T.Jr, & Cooper, M. A. (2022). *Becoming a Student-Ready College: A New Culture of Leadership for Student Success*. John Wiley & Sons.

McPherson, S. S. (2009). *Tim Berners-Lee: Inventor of the World Wide Web*. Twenty-First Century Books.

Megahed, F. M., Chen, Y. J., Ferris, J. A., Knoth, S., & Jones-Farmer, L. A. (2023). How Generative AI Models such as ChatGPT can be (Mis)Used in Practice, Education, and Research? An Exploratory Study. *Quality Engineering*, 1–29.

Meilani, Y. F. C. P., Tan, J. D., Murwani, F. D., Bernarto, I., & Sudibjo, N. (2021). Motivating and Retaining Generation Z Faculty Members in Private Universities. *Journal of Educational and Social Research*, 11(1), 245–255. DOI: 10.36941/jesr-2021-0022

Merkel, D. (2014). Docker: Lightweight Linux containers for consistent development and deployment. *Linux Journal*, 2014(239), 2.

Messer-Davidow, E. (2002). *Disciplining feminism: From social activism to academic discourse*. Duke University Press.

Meyer, J. G., Urbanowicz, R. J., Martin, P. C., O'Connor, K., Li, R., Peng, P. C., Bright, T. J., Tatonetti, N., Won, K. J., Gonzalez-Hernandez, G., & Moore, J. H. (2023). ChatGPT and large language models in academia: Opportunities and challenges. *BioData Mining*, 16(1), 20. DOI: 10.1186/s13040-023-00339-9

Miguel, P. M. D., De-Pablos-Heredero, C., Montes, J. L., & García, A. (2022). Impact of Dynamic Capabilities on Customer Satisfaction through Digital Transformation in the Automotive Sector. *Sustainability (Basel)*, 14(8), 4772. DOI: 10.3390/su14084772

Miikkulainen, R., Bryant, B. D., Cornelius, R., Karpov, I. V., Stanley, K. O., & Yong, C. H. (2006). Computational Intelligence in Games. *Computational Intelligence: Principles and Practice*, 155-191.

Minaee, S., Mikolov, T., Nikzad, N., Chenaghlu, M., Socher, R., Amatriain, X., & Gao, J. (2024). Large language models: A survey. *arXiv preprint arXiv:2402.06196.*

Minoli, D. (2013). *Building the internet of things with IPv6 and MIPv6: The evolving world of M2M communications*. John Wiley & Sons. DOI: 10.1002/9781118647059

Mirbabaie, M., Brünker, F., Möllmann, N. R., & Stieglitz, S. (2022). The rise of artificial intelligence–understanding the AI identity threat at the workplace. *Electronic Markets*, 32(1), 1–27. DOI: 10.1007/s12525-021-00496-x

Mishra, L., Gupta, T., & Shree, A. (2020). Online teaching-learning in higher education during lockdown period of COVID-19 pandemic. *International Journal of Educational Research Open*, 1, 100012. DOI: 10.1016/j.ijedro.2020.100012

Mohzan, M. A. M., Hassan, N., & Abd Halil, N. (2013). The influence of emotional intelligence on academic achievement. *Procedia: Social and Behavioral Sciences*, 90, 303–312. DOI: 10.1016/j.sbspro.2013.07.095

Mokiy, V., & Lukyanova, T. (2022). Development of Interdisciplinarity and Transdisciplinarity in Modern Russian Science and Higher Education. In *Institutionalizing Interdisciplinarity and Transdisciplinarity* (pp. 124–138). Routledge. DOI: 10.4324/9781003129424-11

Mollick, E. (2024). Latent expertise: Everyone is in R&D. *One Useful Thing*. Accessed June 20, 2024: https://www.oneusefulthing.org/p/latent-expertise-everyone-is-in-r?r=i5f7&utm_campaign=post&utm_medium=web

Mon, B. F., Wasfi, A., Hayajneh, M., & Slim, A. (2023, August). A study on role of Artificial Intelligence in education. In *2023 International Conference on Computing, Electronics & Communications Engineering (iCCECE)* (pp. 133-138). IEEE. DOI: 10.1109/iCCECE59400.2023.10238613

Monett, D., & Lewis, C. W. (2018). Getting clarity by defining artificial intelligence—A survey. In *Philosophy and theory of artificial intelligence 2017* (pp. 212–214). Springer International Publishing. DOI: 10.1007/978-3-319-96448-5_21

Montenegro, L. D., & Young, M. N. (2020, September). Operational challenges in the food industry and supply chain during the COVID-19 pandemic: A literature review. In *2020 7th International Conference on Frontiers of Industrial Engineering (ICFIE)* (pp. 1-5). IEEE. DOI: 10.1109/ICFIE50845.2020.9266743

Moody, J. (2013). *Faculty Diversity: Removing the Barriers*. Routledge. DOI: 10.4324/9780203805398

Morales, E. F., & Escalante, H. J. (2022). A brief introduction to supervised, unsupervised, and reinforcement learning. In *Biosignal processing and classification using computational learning and intelligence* (pp. 111–129). Academic Press. DOI: 10.1016/B978-0-12-820125-1.00017-8

Morris, M. R. (2023). Scientists' Perspectives on the Potential for Generative AI in their Fields. *arXiv preprint arXiv:2304.01420.*

Morris, E., & Hutson, J. (2024). *Teacher Appreciation Day Study* [Data set]. Lindenwood University.

Moses, I. (1990). Teaching, research and scholarship in different disciplines. *Higher Education*, 19(3), 351–375. DOI: 10.1007/BF00133898

Murphy, B. P. (2022). Is Lensa AI Stealing from Human Art? An Expert Explains the Controversy. *Science Alert.* Retrieved: https://www-sciencealert-com.cdn.ampproject.org/c/s/www.sciencealert.com/is-lensa-ai-stealing-from-human-art-an-expert-explains-the-controversy/amp

Murphy, C., & Thomas, F. P. (2023). Generative AI in Spinal Cord Injury Research and Care: Opportunities and Challenges Ahead. *The Journal of Spinal Cord Medicine*, 46(3), 341–342. DOI: 10.1080/10790268.2023.2198926

Nabee, S. G., Mageto, J., & Pisa, N. (2020). Investigating predictors of academic plagiarism among university students. *International Journal of Learning. Teaching and Educational Research*, 19(12), 264–280.

Naddaf, Y. (2010). *Game-Independent AI Agents for Playing Atari 2600 Console Games.* University of Alberta.

Nareyek, A. (2000, October). Intelligent Agents for Computer Games. In *International Conference on Computers and Games* (pp. 414-422). Berlin, Heidelberg: Springer Berlin Heidelberg.

Nazari, N., Shabbir, M. S., & Setiawan, R. (2021). Application of Artificial Intelligence powered digital writing assistant in higher education: Randomized controlled trial. *Heliyon*, 7(5), e07014. DOI: 10.1016/j.heliyon.2021.e07014

Nerdynav. (2024). *43+ Important Generative AI Statistics (April 2024).* April 2, 2024. Retrieved March 30, 2024: https://nerdynav.com/generative-ai-statistics/

Neumann, A. (2009). *Professing to learn: Creating tenured lives and careers in the American research university.* JHU Press. DOI: 10.1353/book.3399

Ng, E., & Stanton, P. (2023). The great resignation: Managing people in a post COVID-19 pandemic world. *Personnel Review*, 52(2), 401–407. DOI: 10.1108/PR-03-2023-914

Norton-Meier, L., Hand, B., Cavagnetto, A., Akkus, R., & Gunel, M. (2009). Pedagogy, Implementation, and Professional Development for Teaching Science Literacy: How Students and Teachers Know and Learn. *Quality Research in Literacy and Science Education: International Perspectives and Gold Standards*, 169-187.

Oleksy, E. (2023). That thing ain't human: The artificiality of "human authorship" and the intelligence in expanding copyright authorship to fully-autonomous AI. *Cleveland State Law Review*, 72(1), 263.

Omar, M. S., Idrus, I. M., & Jamal, N. A. (2021). The Influence of Job Motivation on Job Satisfaction: A Case Study of Polytechnic Academic Staff. *Malaysian Journal of Social Sciences and Humanities*, 6(1), 206–213. DOI: 10.47405/mjssh.v6i1.624

Omolara, A. E., Alabdulatif, A., Abiodun, O. I., Alawida, M., Alabdulatif, A., & Arshad, H. (2022). The internet of things security: A survey encompassing unexplored areas and new insights. *Computers & Security*, 112, 102494. DOI: 10.1016/j.cose.2021.102494

Palid, O., Cashdollar, S., Deangelo, S., Chu, C., & Bates, M. (2023). Inclusion in practice: A systematic review of diversity-focused STEM programming in the United States. *International Journal of STEM Education*, 10(1), 2. DOI: 10.1186/s40594-022-00387-3

Palladino, J., & Shepard, L. A. (2023). Authentic Assessment Embedded in Project-Based Learning. *Schools of Opportunity: 10 Research-Based Models for Creating Equity*, 67.

Pan, Y. (2016). Heading toward artificial intelligence 2.0. *Engineering (Beijing)*, 2(4), 409–413. DOI: 10.1016/J.ENG.2016.04.018

Park, J. S., O'Brien, J. C., Cai, C. J., Morris, M. R., Liang, P., & Bernstein, M. S. (2023). Generative agents: Interactive simulacra of human behavior. *arXiv preprint arXiv:2304.03442* DOI: 10.1145/3586183.3606763

Park, J., Teo, T. W., Teo, A., Chang, J., Huang, J. S., & Koo, S. (2023). Integrating artificial intelligence into science lessons: Teachers' experiences and views. *International Journal of STEM Education*, 10(1), 61. DOI: 10.1186/s40594-023-00454-3

Park, S. H. (2023). Use of generative artificial intelligence, including large language models such as ChatGPT, in scientific publications: Policies of KJR and prominent authorities. *Korean Journal of Radiology*, 24(8), 715. DOI: 10.3348/kjr.2023.0643

Patel, S., Hamdan, S., & Donahue, S. (2022). Optimising telemedicine in ophthalmology during the COVID-19 pandemic. *Journal of Telemedicine and Telecare*, 28(7), 498–501. DOI: 10.1177/1357633X20949796

Patwardhan, N., Marrone, S., & Sansone, C. (2023). Transformers in the real world: A survey on nlp applications. *Information (Basel)*, 14(4), 242. DOI: 10.3390/info14040242

Pavlik, J. V. (2023). Collaborating With ChatGPT: Considering the Implications of Generative Artificial Intelligence for Journalism and Media Education. *Journalism & Mass Communication Educator*.

Perchik, J. D., Smith, A. D., Elkassem, A. A., Park, J. M., Rothenberg, S. A., Tanwar, M., Yi, P. H., Sturdivant, A., Tridandapani, S., & Sotoudeh, H. (2023). Artificial intelligence literacy: Developing a multi-institutional infrastructure for AI education. *Academic Radiology*, 30(7), 1472–1480. DOI: 10.1016/j.acra.2022.10.002

Perkin, H. (2014). History of universities. In *International Higher Education* (Vol. 1, pp. 169–204). Routledge.

Permana, A. Y., & Wening, N. (2024). The Influence of Groupthink and Bounded Rationality in Decision-Making on Public Policy. *Eduvest-Journal of Universal Studies*, 4(3), 855–870. DOI: 10.59188/eduvest.v4i3.1086

Petrilli, M. J. (2008). Wikipedia or wickedpedia? Assessing the online encyclopedia's impact on K-12 education. *Education Next*, 8(2), 87–88.

Phutane, M., Jung, C., Chen, N., & Azenkot, S. (2023, October). Speaking with My Screen Reader: Using Audio Fictions to Explore Conversational Access to Interfaces. In *Proceedings of the 25th International ACM SIGACCESS Conference on Computers and Accessibility* (pp. 1-18). DOI: 10.1145/3597638.3608404

Picard, R. W., Papert, S., Bender, W., Blumberg, B., Breazeal, C., Cavallo, D., Machover, T., Resnick, M., Roy, D., & Strohecker, C. (2004). Affective Learning—A Manifesto. *BT Technology Journal*, 22(4), 253–269. DOI: 10.1023/B:BTTJ.0000047603.37042.33

Pinzolits, R. (2024). AI in academia: An overview of selected tools and their areas of application. *MAP Education and Humanities*, 4, 37–50. DOI: 10.53880/2744-2373.2023.4.37

Platt, R. E., & Walker, L. H. (2019). Regalia remembered: Exploring the history and symbolic significance of higher education academic costume. *American Educational History Journal*, 46(1/2), 125–141.

Power, M. J. (2006). The Structure of Emotion: An Empirical Comparison of Six Models. *Cognition and Emotion*, 20(5), 694–713. DOI: 10.1080/02699930500367925

Powers, E. (2017). My news feed is filtered? Awareness of news personalization among college students. *Digital Journalism (Abingdon, England)*, 5(10), 1315–1335. DOI: 10.1080/21670811.2017.1286943

Pradhan, T. K., & Kumar, A. (2023). Plagiarism in the Research Reports of Indian Doctoral Students: Causes and a Remedial Action Plan. *Center for Educational Policy Studies Journal*, 13(3), 185–212. DOI: 10.26529/cepsj.1494

Prasad, S. G., Sharmila, V. C., & Badrinarayanan, M. K. (2023, May). Role of artificial intelligence based chat generative pre-trained transformer (chatgpt) in cyber security. In *2023 2nd International Conference on Applied Artificial Intelligence and Computing (ICAAIC)* (pp. 107-114). IEEE.

Preiss, D. D. (2022). Metacognition, Mind Wandering, and Cognitive Flexibility: Understanding Creativity. *Journal of Intelligence*, 10(3), 69. DOI: 10.3390/jintelligence10030069

Prince, M. J., Felder, R. M., & Brent, R. (2007). Does Faculty Research Improve Undergraduate Teaching? An Analysis of Existing and Potential Synergies. *Journal of Engineering Education*, 96(4), 283–294. DOI: 10.1002/j.2168-9830.2007.tb00939.x

Purdy, J. P. (2010). The changing space of research: Web 2.0 and the integration of research and writing environments. *Computers and Composition*, 27(1), 48–58. DOI: 10.1016/j.compcom.2009.12.001

Pusztahelyi, R. (2020). Emotional AI and Its Challenges in the Viewpoint of Online Marketing. *Curentul Juridic*, 81(2), 13–31.

Putra, I. E., Jazilah, N. I., Adishesa, M. S., Al Uyun, D., & Wiratraman, H. P. (2023). Denying the accusation of plagiarism: Power relations at play in dictating plagiarism as academic misconduct. *Higher Education*, 85(5), 979–997. DOI: 10.1007/s10734-022-00875-z

Rae, I. (2024, May). The effects of perceived AI use on content perceptions. In *Proceedings of the CHI Conference on Human Factors in Computing Systems* (pp. 1-14). DOI: 10.1145/3613904.3642076

Rahman, F., & Weda, S. (2019). Linguistic deviation and the rhetoric figures in Shakespeare's selected plays. *XLinguage European Scientific Language Journal*, 12(1), 37–52. DOI: 10.18355/XL.2019.12.01.03

Rahmat, N. H. (2020). Thinking about thinking in writing. *European Journal of Literature, Language and Linguistics Studies, 3*(4).

Rajaram, K. (2023). Cultural Intelligence in Teaching and Learning. In *Learning Intelligence: Innovative and Digital Transformative Learning Strategies: Cultural and Social Engineering Perspectives* (pp. 57–118). Springer Nature Singapore. DOI: 10.1007/978-981-19-9201-8_2

Randolph, J. (2019). A guide to writing the dissertation literature review. *Practical assessment, research, and evaluation, 14*(1), 13.

Rashidi, H. H., Fennell, B. D., Albahra, S., Hu, B., & Gorbett, T. (2023). The ChatGPT conundrum: Human-generated scientific manuscripts misidentified as AI creations by AI text detection tool. *Journal of Pathology Informatics*, 14, 100342. DOI: 10.1016/j.jpi.2023.100342

Ratican, J., & Hutson, J. (2023). The Six Emotional Dimension (6DE) Model: A Multidimensional Approach to Analyzing Human Emotions and Unlocking the Potential of Emotionally Intelligent Artificial Intelligence (AI) via Large Language Models (LLM). *Journal of Artificial Intelligence and Robotics*, 1(1).

Ray, P. P. (2023). ChatGPT: A Comprehensive Review on Background, Applications, Key Challenges, Bias, Ethics, Limitations and Future Scope. *Internet of Things and Cyber-Physical Systems.*

Ritchhart, R., Church, M., & Morrison, K. (2011). *Making thinking visible: How to promote engagement, understanding, and independence for all learners*. John Wiley & Sons.

Robledo, S., Grisales Aguirre, A. M., Hughes, M., & Eggers, F. (2023). "Hasta la vista, baby"–will machine learning terminate human literature reviews in entrepreneurship? *Journal of Small Business Management*, 61(3), 1314–1343. DOI: 10.1080/00472778.2021.1955125

Rodway, P., & Schepman, A. (2023). The impact of adopting AI educational technologies on projected course satisfaction in university students. *Computers and Education: Artificial Intelligence*, 5, 100150. DOI: 10.1016/j.caeai.2023.100150

Roe, J., Renandya, W. A., & Jacobs, G. M. (2023). A review of AI-powered writing tools and their implications for academic integrity in the language classroom. *Journal of English and Applied Linguistics*, 2(1), 3. DOI: 10.59588/2961-3094.1035

Rof, A., Bikfalvi, A., & Marques, P. (2022). Pandemic-accelerated digital transformation of a born digital higher education institution. *Journal of Educational Technology & Society*, 25(1), 124–141.

Romberg, T. A. (Ed.). (1992). *Mathematics assessment and evaluation: Imperatives for mathematics educators*. SUNY Press.

Ruiz-Rojas, L. I., Acosta-Vargas, P., De-Moreta-Llovet, J., & Gonzalez-Rodriguez, M. (2023). Empowering Education with Generative Artificial Intelligence Tools: Approach with an Instructional Design Matrix. *Sustainability (Basel)*, 15(15), 11524. DOI: 10.3390/su151511524

Russell, D. R. (2002). *Writing in the academic disciplines: A curricular history*. SIU Press.

Ruxton, G., & Colegrave, N. (2011). *Experimental design for the life sciences*. Oxford University Press.

Sadiq Sohail, M., & Daud, S. (2009). Knowledge Sharing in Higher Education Institutions: Perspectives from Malaysia. *Vine*, 39(2), 125–142. DOI: 10.1108/03055720910988841

Saintvilus, R. (2023). The AI gold rush: Profiting from picks and shovels. NASDAQ. November 28, 2023. Retrieved: https://www.nasdaq.com/articles/the-ai-gold-rush-profiting-from-picks-and-shovels

Saltelli, A., Ratto, M., Andres, T., Campolongo, F., Cariboni, J., Gatelli, D., & Tarantola, S. (2008). Introduction to sensitivity analysis. *Global sensitivity analysis. PRiMER: Peer-Reviewed Reports in Medical Education Research*, 1–51.

Samsonovich, A. V. (2020). Socially Emotional Brain-Inspired Cognitive Architecture Framework for Artificial Intelligence. *Cognitive Systems Research*, 60, 57–76. DOI: 10.1016/j.cogsys.2019.12.002

Santo, S. A., Engstrom, M. E., Reetz, L., Schweinle, W. E., & Reed, K. (2009). Faculty productivity barriers and supports at a school of education. *Innovative Higher Education*, 34(2), 117–129. DOI: 10.1007/s10755-009-9098-z

Sato, M., & Loewen, S. (2019). Do Teachers Care About Research? The Research–Pedagogy Dialogue. *ELT Journal*, 73(1), 1–10. DOI: 10.1093/elt/ccy048

Schiff, D. (2022). Education for AI, not AI for Education: The role of education and ethics in national AI policy strategies. *International Journal of Artificial Intelligence in Education*, 32(3), 527–563. DOI: 10.1007/s40593-021-00270-2

Schwab, K. (2017). *The Fourth Industrial Revolution*. Currency.

Selvaraj, C., Chandra, I., & Singh, S. K. (2021). Artificial Intelligence and Machine Learning Approaches for Drug Design: Challenges and Opportunities for the Pharmaceutical Industries. *Molecular Diversity*, 1–21.

Shahriar, S., & Hayawi, K. (2023). Let's Have a Chat! A Conversation with ChatGPT: Technology, Applications, and Limitations. *arXiv preprint arXiv:2302.13817.*

Shavit, Y. (Ed.). (2007). *Stratification in Higher Education: A Comparative Study.* Stanford University Press. DOI: 10.1515/9780804768146

Shehzad, W. (2011). Outlining purposes, stating the nature of the present research, and listing research questions or hypotheses in academic papers. *Journal of Technical Writing and Communication*, 41(2), 139–160. DOI: 10.2190/TW.41.2.c

Sherry, B. (2022). 3 Limits to Artificial Intelligence's Creativity (and How to Solve Them): Here's what you need to know about harnessing A.I. technology to be more creative. *Inc.* Retrieved: https://www.inc.com/ben-sherry/3-limits-to-artificial-intelligences-creativity-and-how-to-solve-them.html

Shuford, J. (2024). Deep Reinforcement Learning Unleashing the Power of AI in Decision-Making. *Journal of Artificial Intelligence General science, 1*(1).

Simmons, M. (2004). The ethics of citation: Teaching and learning scholarly values in the classroom. *College Teaching*, 52(3), 95–99.

Sinaga, P., & Feranie, S. (2017). Enhancing Critical Thinking Skills and Writing Skills through the Variation in Non-Traditional Writing Task. *International Journal of Instruction*, 10(2), 69–84. DOI: 10.12973/iji.2017.1025a

Singh, A., & Chouhan, T. (2023). Artificial Intelligence in HRM: Role of Emotional–Social Intelligence and Future Work Skill. In *The Adoption and Effect of Artificial Intelligence on Human Resources Management*, Part A (pp. 175-196). Emerald Publishing Limited.

Singh, J., Steele, K., & Singh, L. (2021). Combining the best of online and face-to-face learning: Hybrid and blended learning approach for COVID-19, post vaccine, & post-pandemic world. *Journal of Educational Technology Systems*, 50(2), 140–171. DOI: 10.1177/00472395211047865

Sohrabi, C., Mathew, G., Franchi, T., Kerwan, A., Griffin, M., Del Mundo, J. S. C., & Agha, R. (2021). Impact of the Coronavirus (COVID-19) Pandemic on Scientific Research and Implications for Clinical Academic Training–A Review. *International Journal of Surgery*, 86, 57–63. DOI: 10.1016/j.ijsu.2020.12.008

Southworth, J., Migliaccio, K., Glover, J., Reed, D., McCarty, C., Brendemuhl, J., & Thomas, A. (2023). Developing a model for AI Across the curriculum: Transforming the higher education landscape via innovation in AI literacy. *Computers and Education: Artificial Intelligence*, 4, 100127. DOI: 10.1016/j.caeai.2023.100127

Spear, K. I. (1983). Thinking and writing: A sequential curriculum for composition. *Journal of Advanced Composition*, 47–63.

Steidl, M., Felderer, M., & Ramler, R. (2023). The pipeline for the continuous development of artificial intelligence models—Current state of research and practice. *Journal of Systems and Software*, 199, 111615. DOI: 10.1016/j.jss.2023.111615

Stoesz, B. M., & Eaton, S. E. (2022). Academic integrity policies of publicly funded universities in western Canada. *Educational Policy*, 36(6), 1529–1548. DOI: 10.1177/0895904820983032

Strich, F., Mayer, A. S., & Fiedler, M. (2021). What Do I Do in a World of Artificial Intelligence? Investigating the Impact of Substitutive Decision-Making AI Systems on Employees' Professional Role Identity. *Journal of the Association for Information Systems*, 22(2), 9. DOI: 10.17705/1jais.00663

Sullivan, G. (2006). Research acts in art practice. *Studies in Art Education*, 48(1), 19–35. DOI: 10.1080/00393541.2006.11650497

Tan, S. C., & Nareyek, A. (2009). Integrating Facial, Gesture, and Posture Emotion Expression for a 3D Virtual Agent. In *Proceedings of the 14th International Conference on Computer Games: AI, Animation, Mobile, Interactive Multimedia, Educational & Serious Games* (CGames 2009 USA) (pp. 23-31).

Tang, A., Li, K. K., Kwok, K. O., Cao, L., Luong, S., & Tam, W. (2024). The importance of transparency: Declaring the use of generative artificial intelligence (AI) in academic writing. *Journal of Nursing Scholarship*, 56(2), 314–318. DOI: 10.1111/jnu.12938

Tathahira, T. (2020). Promoting students' critical thinking through online learning in higher education: Challenges and strategies. *Englisia: Journal of Language, Education, and Humanities*, 8(1), 79–92. DOI: 10.22373/ej.v8i1.6636

Tavares, O., Sin, C., Sá, C., Bugla, S., & Amaral, A. (2022). Inbreeding and Research Collaborations in Portuguese Higher Education. *Higher Education Quarterly*, 76(1), 102–115. DOI: 10.1111/hequ.12301

Taylor, J. S. (2024). Reassessing academic plagiarism. *Journal of Academic Ethics*, 22(2), 211–230. DOI: 10.1007/s10805-023-09478-4

Ter Beek, M., Wopereis, I., & Schildkamp, K. (2022). Don't Wait, Innovate! Preparing Students and Lecturers in Higher Education for the Future Labor Market. *Education Sciences*, 12(9), 620. DOI: 10.3390/educsci12090620

Terenzini, P. T., & Pascarella, E. T. (1998). Studying College Students in the 21st century: Meeting New Challenges. *Review of Higher Education*, 21(2), 151–165. DOI: 10.1353/rhe.1998.a30045

Theobald, E. J., Hill, M. J., Tran, E., Agrawal, S., Arroyo, E. N., Behling, S., Chambwe, N., Cintrón, D. L., Cooper, J. D., Dunster, G., Grummer, J. A., Hennessey, K., Hsiao, J., Iranon, N., Jones, L.II, Jordt, H., Keller, M., Lacey, M. E., Littlefield, C. E., & Freeman, S. (2020). Active learning narrows achievement gaps for underrepresented students in undergraduate science, technology, engineering, and math. *Proceedings of the National Academy of Sciences of the United States of America*, 117(12), 6476–6483. DOI: 10.1073/pnas.1916903117

Thimmanna, A. V. N. S., Naik, M. S., Radhakrishnan, S., & Sharma, A. (2024). Personalized Learning Paths: Adapting Education with AI-Driven Curriculum. *European Economic Letters*, 14(1), 31–40.

Thornhill-Miller, B., Camarda, A., Mercier, M., Burkhardt, J. M., Morisseau, T., Bourgeois-Bougrine, S., Vinchon, F., El Hayek, S., Augereau-Landais, M., Mourey, F., Feybesse, C., Sundquist, D., & Lubart, T. (2023). Creativity, Critical Thinking, Communication, and Collaboration: Assessment, Certification, and Promotion of 21st Century Skills for the Future of Work and Education. *Journal of Intelligence*, 11(3), 54. DOI: 10.3390/jintelligence11030054

Tian, S., Jin, Q., Yeganova, L., Lai, P. T., Zhu, Q., Chen, X., Yang, Y., Chen, Q., Kim, W., Comeau, D. C., Islamaj, R., Kapoor, A., Gao, X., & Lu, Z. (2024). Opportunities and challenges for ChatGPT and large language models in biomedicine and health. *Briefings in Bioinformatics*, 25(1), bbad493. DOI: 10.1093/bib/bbad493

Townes, M. (2012). The spread of TCP/IP: How the Internet became the Internet. *Millennium*, 41(1), 43–64. DOI: 10.1177/0305829812449195

Trott, C. D., Sample McMeeking, L. B., & Weinberg, A. E. (2020). Participatory Action Research Experiences for Undergraduates: Forging Critical Connections Through Community Engagement. *Studies in Higher Education*, 45(11), 2260–2273. DOI: 10.1080/03075079.2019.1602759

Turkle, S. (2011). *Alone Together: Why We Expect More from Technology and Less from Each Other*. Basic Books.

Tyson, A., & Kennedy, B. (2024). Many Americans think generative AI programs should credit the sources they rely on. *Pew Research Center.* March 26, 2024. Retrieved: https://www.pewresearch.org/short-reads/2024/03/26/many-americans-think-generative-ai-programs-should-credit-the-sources-they-rely-on/#:~:text=Adults%20with%20higher%20levels%20of%20education%20are%20more,with%20AI%20at%20least%20several%20times%20a%20week

Ulloa-Cazarez, R. L. (2020). Joseph E. Aoun: Robot-proof: higher education at the age of artificial intelligence. MIT Press.

Urhan, B. (2023). Crucial Role of Soft Skills in Challenging Times: Conceptual Analysis of Leadership Skills. In *Leadership Approaches in Global Hospitality and Tourism* (pp. 23-39). IGI Global.

Vaishya, R., Javaid, M., Khan, I. H., & Haleem, A. (2020). Artificial Intelligence (AI) applications for COVID-19 pandemic. *Diabetes & Metabolic Syndrome*, 14(4), 337–339. DOI: 10.1016/j.dsx.2020.04.012

Valentine, K. (2006). Plagiarism as literacy practice: Recognizing and rethinking ethical binaries. *College Composition and Communication*, 58(1), 89–109. DOI: 10.58680/ccc20065884

Väljataga, T., Fiedler, S. H., & Laanpere, M. (2015). Re-Thinking Digital Textbooks: Students as Co-Authors. *Advances in Web-Based Learning—ICWL 2015: 14th International Conference, Guangzhou, China, November 5-8, 2015Proceedings*, 14, 143–151.

Vaswani, A., Shazeer, N., Parmar, N., Uszkoreit, J., Jones, L., Gomez, A. N., & Polosukhin, I. (2017). Attention is all you need. *Advances in Neural Information Processing Systems*, 30.

Velliaris, D. M., & Breen, P. (2016). An institutional three-stage framework: Elevating academic writing and integrity standards of international pathway students. *Journal of International Students*, 6(2), 565–587. DOI: 10.32674/jis.v6i2.371

Vickers, B. (1993). Rhetoric. In Corns, T. N. (Ed.), *The Cambridge companion to English poetry: Donne to Marvell* (pp. 101–120). DOI: 10.1017/CCOL0521411475.005

Wagner, G., Lukyanenko, R., & Paré, G. (2022). Artificial intelligence and the conduct of literature reviews. *Journal of Information Technology*, 37(2), 209–226. DOI: 10.1177/02683962211048201

Wahle, J. P., Ruas, T., Kirstein, F., & Gipp, B. (2022). How large language models are transforming machine-paraphrased plagiarism. *arXiv preprint arXiv:2210.03568.*

Walters, W. H. (2023). The effectiveness of software designed to detect AI-generated writing: A comparison of 16 AI text detectors. *Open Information Science*, 7(1), 20220158. DOI: 10.1515/opis-2022-0158

Walton, E., Carrington, S., Saggers, B., Edwards, C., & Kimani, W. (2022). What matters in learning communities for inclusive education: A cross-case analysis. *Professional Development in Education*, 48(1), 134–148. DOI: 10.1080/19415257.2019.1689525

Wan, T., & Chen, Z. (2023). Exploring Generative AI assisted feedback writing for students' written responses to a physics conceptual question with prompt engineering and few-shot learning. *arXiv preprint arXiv:2311.06180.*

Wang, L. (2022). Exploring the relationship among teacher emotional intelligence, work engagement, teacher self-efficacy, and student academic achievement: A moderated mediation model. *Frontiers in Psychology*, 12, 810559. DOI: 10.3389/fpsyg.2021.810559

Warrier, U., John, M., & Warrier, S. (2021). Leveraging emotional intelligence competencies for sustainable development of higher education institutions in the new normal. *FIIB Business Review*, 10(1), 62–73. DOI: 10.1177/2319714521992032

Watson, D. S. (2023). On the philosophy of unsupervised learning. *Philosophy & Technology*, 36(2), 28. DOI: 10.1007/s13347-023-00635-6

Watters, C., & Lemanski, M. K. (2023). Universal skepticism of ChatGPT: A review of early literature on chat generative pre-trained transformer. *Frontiers in Big Data*, 6, 6. DOI: 10.3389/fdata.2023.1224976

Weise, M. R. (2020). *Long life learning: Preparing for jobs that don't even exist yet*. John Wiley & Sons.

Werner, M. (1980). The Hand-Held Calculator and Its Impact on Mathematics Curricula. *School Science and Mathematics*, 80(1), 29–36. DOI: 10.1111/j.1949-8594.1980.tb09556.x

Werth, E., & Williams, K. (2021). Exploring Student Perceptions as Co-Authors of Course Material. *Open Praxis*, 13(1), 53–67. DOI: 10.5944/openpraxis.13.1.1187

Werthner, H., Stanger, A., Schiaffonati, V., Knees, P., Hardman, L., & Ghezzi, C. (2023). Digital Humanism: The Time Is Now. *Computer*, 56(1), 138–142. DOI: 10.1109/MC.2022.3219528

Williams, P. (2023). AI, Analytics and a New Assessment Model for Universities. *Education Sciences*, 13(10), 1040. DOI: 10.3390/educsci13101040

Wilson, S. (2003). *Information arts: intersections of art, science, and technology*. MIT press.

Winick, M. (2018). Scholarly Enchantment. *Nineteenth-Century Literature*, 73(2), 187–226. DOI: 10.1525/ncl.2018.73.2.187

Wirtz, B. W., Weyerer, J. C., & Sturm, B. J. (2020). The dark sides of artificial intelligence: An integrated AI governance framework for public administration. *International Journal of Public Administration*, 43(9), 818–829. DOI: 10.1080/01900692.2020.1749851

Wortman, B., & Wang, J. Z. (2022). HICEM: A High-Coverage Emotion Model for Artificial Emotional Intelligence. *arXiv preprint arXiv:2206.07593.*

Wright, G. W., & Delgado, C. (2023). Generating a framework for gender and sexual diversity-inclusive STEM education. *Science Education*, 107(3), 713–740. DOI: 10.1002/sce.21786

Wu, Z., Ji, D., Yu, K., Zeng, X., Wu, D., & Shidujaman, M. (2021). AI creativity and the human-AI co-creation model. *Human-Computer Interaction. Theory, Methods and Tools: Thematic Area, HCI 2021, Held as Part of the 23rd HCI International Conference, HCII 2021, Virtual Event, July 24–29, 2021Proceedings*, 23(Part I), 171–190.

Xu, M., Niyato, D., Chen, J., Zhang, H., Kang, J., Xiong, Z., Mao, S., & Han, Z. (2023b). Generative AI-empowered simulation for autonomous driving in vehicular mixed reality metaverses. *IEEE Journal of Selected Topics in Signal Processing*, 17(5), 1064–1079. DOI: 10.1109/JSTSP.2023.3293650

Xu, W., Dainoff, M. J., Ge, L., & Gao, Z. (2023a). Transitioning to human interaction with AI systems: New challenges and opportunities for HCI professionals to enable human-centered AI. *International Journal of Human-Computer Interaction*, 39(3), 494–518. DOI: 10.1080/10447318.2022.2041900

Yang, S., & Evans, C. (2019, November). Opportunities and challenges in using AI chatbots in higher education. In *Proceedings of the 2019 3rd International Conference on Education and E-Learning* (pp. 79-83). DOI: 10.1145/3371647.3371659

Yeo, M. A. (2023). Academic integrity in the age of Artificial Intelligence (AI) authoring apps. *TESOL Journal*, 14(3), e716. DOI: 10.1002/tesj.716

Yu, H. (2023). Reflection on whether Chat GPT should be banned by academia from the perspective of education and teaching. *Frontiers in Psychology*, 14, 1181712. DOI: 10.3389/fpsyg.2023.1181712

Yu, H. (2024). The application and challenges of ChatGPT in educational transformation: New demands for teachers' roles. *Heliyon*, 10(2), e24289. DOI: 10.1016/j.heliyon.2024.e24289

Zaheer, M., Guruganesh, G., Dubey, K. A., Ainslie, J., Alberti, C., Ontanon, S., & Ahmed, A. (2020). Big bird: Transformers for longer sequences. *Advances in Neural Information Processing Systems*, 33, 17283–17297.

Zall, R., & Kangavari, M. R. (2022). Comparative Analytical Survey on Cognitive Agents with Emotional Intelligence. *Cognitive Computation*, 14(4), 1223–1246. DOI: 10.1007/s12559-022-10007-5

Zanella, A., Bui, N., Castellani, A., Vangelista, L., & Zorzi, M. (2014). Internet of things for smart cities. *IEEE Internet of Things Journal*, 1(1), 22–32. DOI: 10.1109/JIOT.2014.2306328

Zawacki-Richter, O., Marín, V. I., Bond, M., & Gouverneur, F. (2019). Systematic review of research on artificial intelligence applications in higher education–where are the educators? *International Journal of Educational Technology in Higher Education*, 16(1), 1–27. DOI: 10.1186/s41239-019-0171-0

Zeichner, K. M. (1995). Beyond the divide of teacher research and academic research. *Teachers and Teaching*, 1(2), 153–172. DOI: 10.1080/1354060950010202

Zerilli, J., Knott, A., Maclaurin, J., & Gavaghan, C. (2019). Algorithmic decision-making and the control problem. *Minds and Machines*, 29(4), 555–578. DOI: 10.1007/s11023-019-09513-7

Zhang, E., Zhu, V., Saphra, N., Kleiman, A., Edelman, B. L., Tambe, M., . . . Malach, E. (2024). Transcendence: Generative Models Can Outperform The Experts That Train Them. *arXiv preprint arXiv:2406.11741*

Zhang, K., & Aslan, A. B. (2021). AI technologies for education: Recent research & future directions. *Computers and Education: Artificial Intelligence*, 100025.

Zhang, M. (2023). AI's winning streak: Crushing the venture capital slump. *Artisana.* April 16, 2023. Retrieved: https://www.artisana.ai/articles/ais-winning-streak-crushing-the-venture-capital-slump

Zhang, H., Lee, I., Ali, S., DiPaola, D., Cheng, Y., & Breazeal, C. (2022). Integrating ethics and career futures with technical learning to promote AI literacy for middle school students: An exploratory study. *International Journal of Artificial Intelligence in Education*, 1–35.

Zhang, K., & Aslan, A. B. (2021). AI technologies for education: Recent research & future directions. *Computers and Education: Artificial Intelligence*, 2, 100025. DOI: 10.1016/j.caeai.2021.100025

Zhang, L., Carter, R. A.Jr, Qian, X., Yang, S., Rujimora, J., & Wen, S. (2022). Academia's Responses to Crisis: A Bibliometric Analysis of Literature on Online Learning in Higher Education During COVID-19. *British Journal of Educational Technology*, 53(3), 620–646. DOI: 10.1111/bjet.13191

Zhou, J., Ke, P., Qiu, X., Huang, M., & Zhang, J. (2023). ChatGPT: potential, prospects, and limitations. *Frontiers of Information Technology & Electronic Engineering*, 1-6.

About the Author

James Hutson specializes in multidisciplinary research that encompasses artificial intelligence, neurohumanities, neurodiversity, immersive realities, and the gamification of education. Earning a Bachelor of Arts in Art from the University of Tulsa, a Master of Arts in Art History from Southern Methodist University, and a Ph.D. in Art History from the University of Maryland, College Park, he later acquired additional Master's degrees in Leadership and Game Design from Lindenwood University and additional PhD in Artificial Intelligence at Capitol Technology University (2023). Over the span of his academic career since 2006, Hutson has held various pedagogical and administrative positions across five universities, including Chair of Art History, Assistant Dean of Graduate and Online Programs, and most recently, Lead XR Disruptor and Department Head of Art History and Visual Culture. Notably, his scholarly portfolio includes several books on the application of artificial intelligence in education and cultural heritage, such as Creative Convergence: The AI Renaissance in Art and Design (2024), as well as numerous articles and case studies.

Index

Symbols

A

C

D

E

L

M

P

R

S

T

U

www.ingramcontent.com/pod-product-compliance
Lightning Source LLC
LaVergne TN
LVHW081333300926
849161LV00008B/1958